Cinema in a Cathedral City

Cinema Exhibition in Durham City
and its environs 1896 - 2003

DAVID R. WILLIAMS has been an avid cinemagoer since he saw his first films at the Roxy in Leicester. During his army service in Germany, he wrote film reviews for his unit newspaper. On demobilisation, he studied to become a teacher at Borough Road College, Isleworth, was Secretary of the College Film Society and was present at the first week's showings at the South Bank National Film Theatre. He began teaching in the City of Leicester and joined the Film Society. In 1955, he began the researches into the history of cinema exhibition in Leicester that eventually emerged as the book *Cinema in Leicester 1896-1931* in 1993. He moved to Bede College, Durham University in 1964 as a Lecturer in Education, but was soon recruited into their pioneering Film and Television Department. He became Head of Department in 1974. When the University closed the Department in 1980, he returned to teaching in Special Education. His work in Film and Television continued, however, and in 2000 he was made a Fellow of the Royal Television Society for his contribution to Media Education. He has made a special study of the silent film era and is currently engaged in several research projects.

Acknowledgments

For the research facilities and primary resource materials, the author wishes to thank the staffs of **Durham City** and **Newcastle City Reference Libraries**, **Durham University Library**, **Durham County Records Office**, **British Film Institute Library**, **British Museum Newspaper Library** at Colindale, and the **Arts and Humanities Library** of Sheffield Hallam University. **Dr. Vanessa Toulmin** of the National Fairground Archive supplied valuable information and photographs connected with the Travelling Show people. **Frank Manders'** researches into County Durham cinemas and theatres were made unstintingly available, and he is to be especially thanked for sharing his encyclopædic knowledge with me. **Michael Richardson** and the many contributors to his Pictorial Histories of Durham have provided a number of illustrations. **George Nairn's** collection of local postcards and memorabilia has also contributed rarely-seen photographs. Nonagenarian **Mr. Bygate** gave me first-hand descriptions of some of the cinematograph halls he had attended as a boy and an adult, and **Mr. Middlemass** told me of his experiences as assistant projectionist at the Globe. **Ray Middleton's** photographs of the Palace have been a unique record of that theatre's final days. **Thomas H. Fox** has contributed his important remembrances and researches into the social history of Meadowfield and Langley Moor. **Robert Swainston**, for many years projectionist of the Kinema, Meadowfield, and other local halls, has also shared his experiences with me. The **Durham Heritage Centre** has been very helpful in discovering entertainment memorabilia. Over the last eight years that this research has been pursued, the support and encouragement of Rosemary Williams has been a daily delight. **Mervyn Gould** encouraged me in the completion of the manuscript and set its publication in motion through the generosity of the Mercia Cinema Society and its chairman, **Kate Taylor**.

Herbert Maxwell and his mighty Christie 2/7 organ at the Regal. Durham.
(Michael Richardson)

Cinema in a Cathedral City

Cinema Exhibition in Durham City and its environs 1896 – 2003

The Regal, Durham, under construction.
Detail from a postcard in the author's collection

DAVID R. WILLIAMS

Mercia Cinema Society

Mercia Cinema Histories
General Editor: **Kate Taylor M.A. (Oxon.)**
Series Editor: **Mervyn Gould M.A. (City)**

Set in 11 point Book Antiqua, indexed and designed by Mervyn Gould.
Printed by Q3 Digital / Litho Loughborough 01509 213456

Published by the MERCIA CINEMA SOCIETY
19 Pinder's Grove Wakefield West Yorkshire WF1 4AH
01924 372748
ISBN: 0 946406 56 1

Contents

Cover illustrations:
Front – The ex-Regal, North Road Durham. *Photograph in University Library.*
Rear – Architect's drawing of façade of Crescent Cinema Gilesgate Moor. *DCRO.*
Film poster. *Author's collection*
Centre – Palladium Cinema, Durham - auditorium. 1944 film advertisements.
Bottom – Architect's longitudinal section of the Empire, Langley Moor. *DCRO.*

Foreword — Neil Griffin

I grew up within earshot of Hartlepool's Palladium cinema in the days when it felt safe to let your children out to play in the street. As kids we'd take shelter from the wind in the deep recess of the cinema's emergency exit doors to play our childhood games against the muffled soundtrack of a WW2 battlefield, a cowpoke's shoot-out, or a 50s *film noir*: the magic seeping out to the cold pavement and into our warm imaginations.

Inside the Palladium, often and from a very early age, I was held spellbound by the allure of cinema. The feeling of excitement when the lights dimmed and my Mam, Dad, big sister and me sat in a darkened room with complete strangers to share the beautiful chemistry of sound combined with light projected through celluloid. All these years later I still get that same tingle of excitement when the lights dim. I love sharing the experience of cinematic art with people I care about and in the company of strangers.

I came to Durham University in 1977 and became a student of David Williams. I was already sold on the magic of cinema but David played a large part in confirming my instinct that it also had an immense power; that it represented and represents a major organ of our shared culture. Cinema can inform, inspire, indoctrinate, challenge, stimulate, educate and communicate, and after all, communication is power.

David's enthusiasm for cinema and the communicative power of the juxtaposed image remains infectious and resounds throughout this book. This detailed, authoritative, and affectionate chronicle of cinema in Durham is strewn with fascinating snippets of local history and highlights Durham's connection with some international stars.

The real star of the book, however, is cinema itself. I believe that public access cinema is fundamental to the cultural fabric of our city. It is a critical part of the artistic health of our community. Through the intervention of the local Council, Durham still has a foothold in the world of cinema.

See you there! Enjoy the show!

Cllr. Neil Griffin, Chairman, Durham City Arts. May 2003.

Introduction

The presentation of cinematograph films in a small northern town would seem to be unimportant in the annals of cinema history. But, Durham is no ordinary place. The presence of its Cathedral and its Bishopric gave it a certain significance. The Diocese, both locally and nationally, made numerous well publicised statements concerning public morality and social practice, and the local Free Church Councils were particularly influential in the mining communities and the strong Co-operative movements. Though the main emphasis in this history of cinema exhibition will focus upon its place in the history of social recreation and entertainment, attention will be paid to the pronouncements of the local clergy and, for the most part under their clear influence, the local judiciary. The question of the Sunday opening of cinema halls was hotly debated in the City until the 1950s whereas it had been resolved in many parts of the country decades earlier.

For this reason, the history also includes details of the development of cinematograph shows and cinema halls in some of the villages near to the city boundaries. Reports of their entertainments and their supporting advertisements were included in both the Durham Chronicle and the Durham County Advertiser from time to time. County and City Police Court and Petty Sessions were also fully reported and details of the proprietors and their occasional misdemeanours under the 1909 Cinematograph Act have provided information not available elsewhere. Although the cinema owners were generally imperilled by the tightness of regulations, the cinema history researcher is aided very much by the assiduous reporting of all infringements and licensing applications.

D. R. Williams October 2003

Chapter One   An Enthusiastic Reception

Although 1896 was the year when most areas of population in Britain experienced their first glimpse of 'animated photographs', it was, by no means, the year that the majority of people first experienced moving pictures. Optical toys and moving picture machines proliferated throughout the nineteenth century. Hand-drawn and cleverly-geared lantern slides could produce coloured animated screen shows. In the hands of talented presenters and musicians, these provided highly praised and well-patronised entertainment. The rapid improvement in photographic emulsions from 1860 onwards also enabled 'educational and uplifting' evenings of lantern slides from exotic places to be staged in Temperance and Town Halls.

The R.W. Paul Theatrograph
No.2. *N.M.P.F.T Collection*

After 1894, the appearance of peep-hole machines, such as Edison's Kinetoscope, was mostly confined to industrial cities, sea-side resorts and the travelling fair-grounds. On 26th March 1896, when an animated photograph projector appeared at the Palace Theatre in Newcastle less than a month after the unveiling of the Lumière Cinematographe in London, a report in the Newcastle Journal clearly revealed that the reporter was familiar with the Kinetoscope workings. His explanation of the way that animated photographs were taken was, he said, 'only for the uninitiated.' There had also been Cinematograph shows at the Madame Tussaud's Exhibitions in Sunderland and Newcastle during April and May 1896.[1] It is reasonable to assume, therefore, that by the time they arrived in Durham City, many local people would have already experienced their novelty.

PEOPLE'S PALACE

(LATE TUDOR'S CIRCUS).

COURT LANE, DURHAM.

Sole Manager .. · ...... G. T. CROMWELL.

MONDAY, NOVEMBER 23rd,

AND DURING WEEK.

PAUL'S ORIGINAL THEATROGRAPHE,
Direct from the Empire, Newcastle, at an
Enormous Expense.

PROFESSOR BUER'S
Miniature Circus. Comical Mule, Dogs, and
Donkey.

FRED MASON,
England's Greatest Whistling Comedian.

LYDIA DUDLEY,
Serio and Expert Top Boot Dancer.

MAJOR DEVONO,
Conjuror and Illusionist.

THE ALMO TRIO,
Three Bar Performers.

FRED ALBERTO,
English and Irish Comedian.

ARCHIE AND LEES,
The Flying Wonders.

MISS VIOLET HARRIS,
Clog, Top Boot, and Skipping Rope Dancer.

Nevertheless, the newspaper report of what appears to be the first show on Monday 23rd November at the People's Palace in Court Lane, reveals that the phenomenon still held its surprises.

"R.W. Paul's Theatrograph, after concluding a week's engagement at the Empire, Newcastle, has been affording intense amusement to crowds of people. One picture in particular, the turn out of the Newcastle Fire Brigade, has had a most enthusiastic reception, and on Tuesday was repeated amidst hearty and prolonged applause. The Gordon Highlanders leaving barracks, Grainger Street at mid-day, United Footballers at play and other local and foreign scenes are given. One very fine effect was a cave scene on the coast of Spain. The waves toss themselves into the cave and throw the spume roof high, and the scene is so realistic that the spectator might almost expect to hear the splash and the swirl of the angry waves."

◄The Gordon High-landers Leaving Barracks (NFTVA)

A Sea Cave near Lisbon. First shown in London on 22nd October 1896 *(NMPFT)*

ASSEMBLY ROOMS THEATRE,
DURHAM.

PROPRIETOR   ...   .   T. RUSHWORTH.

FOR TWO NIGHTS AND ONE MATINEE!
MONDAY AND TUESDAY, DECEMBER 7TH AND 8TH,

MOORE & BURGESS MINSTRELS.

GRAND ILLUMINATED DAY PERFORMANCE AT 2.30,
TUESDAY DECEMBER 8 (Equal to Night).

THE ANIMATED PHOTOGRAPHS,
Projected by the Marvellous "Vitagraphe," at every Performance, and the Celebrated Series of Tableaux
Vivants of "Uncle Tom's Cabin."

ADMISSION—Front Stalls (Numbered and Reserved), 3s; Second Seats (Unreserved), 2s;
Back Seats, 1s, and 6d.   Balcony, 2s and 1s.

Children and Schools Half-price to 3s and 2s Seats at Night, and 3s, 2s, and 1s Seats at Matinee.
Change of Programme each Evening.   The Celebrated "Plantation" Songs at Tuesday's Matinee.
Doors open at 2.30 and 7.30;   Commences at 3 and 8;   Carriages at 5.15 and 10.20.
Early Doors, 7 to 7.30, 3d Extra.

PLAN AND TICKETS AT RUSHWORTH'S ART GALLERY.

Anxious always to please family and out-of-town patrons, Mr. Cromwell put the Theatrograph on before nine o'clock so that they could catch the last train from nearby Elvet Station. His Saturday matinée at a special low price was designed for the benefit of parents who would like their children to see an entertainment 'that they should not miss.'

R. W. Paul's Theatrograph had been successfully exhibited at the Alhambra Theatre on the opposite side of Leicester Square from the Empire where the Lumière Cinematographe was premiered. Paul's camera and projector had also been developed from Edison's Kinetoscope, and by the time of the Durham show it was already into its third improved model.

Assembly Rooms. *Courtesy Durham Heritage Centre*

Durham's more prestigious place of entertainment, Mr. Rushworth's Assembly Rooms in the North Bailey, was the annual venue for the Moore and Burgess Minstrel Show for a two day engagement on 7th and 8th December 1896. Since June, their touring show had included a performance of Animated Photographs given by means of the Vitagraphe. The newspaper review unfortunately gives no details of the films shown.

When Paul's Theatrograph returned to the People's Palace as part of the Christmas week bill a fortnight later it once again received top billing. The newspaper reports sadly give no indication of the of the programme content. The Theatrograph was proving to be the most popular machine up and down the country with at least six places including it as a special turn in their annual pantomime.[2]

Despite the fact that there was plenty of feverish activity in the film-producing world during the 1897 Diamond Jubilee celebrations, Cinematograph shows in Durham were fairly sparse. The Assembly Rooms usually closed for the summer anyway, and the People's Palace was seeking a new owner. On September 20th, James Lovett, Timber Merchant, and previous proprietor of the Queens Theatre, Chester-le-Street and the Standard Theatre, Gateshead, reopened the People's Palace with the promise of extensive alterations and improvements. One of the first shows included Dr. Bertino's Bertinograph showing 'The best of all animated photographs' and, according to the reports, the Jubilee procession. Certainly this was in the good 'doctor's' repertoire for it had been shown in August in Liverpool. The Durham Chronicle reported only that the items shown were *A soldier's church parade at Aldershot*, a lightning cartoonist's drawing of Queen Victoria, *A Vanishing Lady*, a coloured version of Miss Loise Fuller performing her serpentine dance, and other novelties".[3] The reporter drew attention to the absence of a hissing sound which he had noticed in 'inventions of a similar nature'. Since electricity had just been installed in the theatre, it is possible that what he could no longer hear was the use of the gas cylinders needed to activate the limelight.

Alexandra, Howe and Cushing's GIGANTIC CIRCUS visited Durham on Saturday, October 2nd with 'London's Latest Scientific Craze The Cinematographe' and the claim that by its means 'Animated Photographs as exhibited at the Empire Theatre, London' would be shown. As in the case of many one-night events, both local papers failed to include a review in the following week's editions. The same anonymous fate awaited the 'cinematograph side-show' at the fifth Durham Camera Club's exhibition, in the Shakespeare Hall, North Road on 28 and 29th November. Indeed, little reporting enthusiasm is shown for most of the travelling shows, from 'top of the bill' Mellini's Cinematograph at the Palace at the end of December[4] to the appearance of the 'Biograph' amongst the Livermore Brothers' World Renowned Court Minstrels at the Assembly Rooms on February 7th 1898.

This latter presentation cannot be the Durham venue of the genuine 68mm format Biograph since the description of the films shows them to be standard 35mm gauge items; *viz.* Philip Wolff's 150 ft 3 scene, *The Death of Nelson* and Haydon & Urry's *Funeral of the actor, Mr. William Terris.*[5] The following week at the Palace Theatre Thompson & Bostock's Variety Company included the Quadrascope; 'Monstre [sic] and Exceptional Engagement from France for One Week Only, the most sensational Development of the Kinematographe.' The machine on the Monday was regarded as 'somewhat disappointing' because it had not been 'put into proper order.' It appeared to be used for showing animated photographs in reverse; unless 'back jump' is a specialised equestrian term. "It includes a very good production illustrating a back jump by mounted lancers."

From reports in the *Optical Magic Lantern Journal, and Photographic Enlarger* it is clear that the standard of presentation at travelling film shows was very varied. In June 1897, they advocated the continuation of the use of a lecturer to enhance the performance: "A cinematograph exhibition is in no sense a lecture, but whether the various scenes require an announcement, description or not, it always gives greater finish to the proceedings for one person to face the audience, rather than to speak from where the apparatus stands, besides keeping the audience in touch with what is going on."

In February 1898, the journal began a series of 'best practice' articles, which by their admonition and advice also give us an insight into some of the worst practices. Because the films exhibited were very short, and, at this time, were rarely joined together, pauses in the presentation were numerous. "During the change of film, it is better to interject an art picture either from a separate lantern or from the machine itself fitted with an attachment. It is unwise to leave the audience in darkness, neither is it desirable to give them the full glare of the light from the body of the hall or it will be difficult to see the cinematograph pictures."

The solution to the continuity problem was to buy a 'film presser', on sale at the time for 30 shillings. "The joint is made by scraping the gelatine from the surface of one film and painting the bare celluloid with an active solvent and when the treated surfaces are placed together and pressed with a proper pressing machine they will stick firmly together."

It was well into autumn before the Palace again featured 'life-size' cinematograph pictures and the Durham Flower Show and Industrial Exhibition boasted 'the Original Blue Hungarian band, and all the Latest Subjects in Animated Pictures' as part of the proceedings! Almost immediately afterwards, at the end of October, the Palace Theatre listed Lear's Eragraph as the last item on the advertised bill. "The largest living pictures ever exhibited in England. New novelties to be seen to be believed." Cinema advertising was still not far away from the barker at the fairground booth, but the Durham Chronicle reporter did think that the machine was an improvement on some that he had seen. The Eragraph was a machine marketed by Haydon & Urry, and there was a French film producer at this time called Léar, but without a description of the films shown it is impossible to conjecture their origin.[6]

The end was near for one of Durham's cinematograph venues. In December 1898, the People's Palace was refused a theatre licence by the County Bench. H. Ferens for Mr. Lovett said that considerable improvements had been made to the building. The stage had been rebuilt and re-sited; the seating had been altered so that it all faced the same way and a new exit 4ft wide had been constructed. He reported that a few weeks previously when there was a full house, Mr Lovett had timed the exit of the people as inside three minutes. He now wished to be able to change the content of his programmes and include dramatic items as well as music and dancing. He had constructed similar theatres elsewhere and had no difficulty in obtaining a licence. Workmen were still in the building making other improvements, and in his opinion it was safe.

Superintendent Burrell told a different story. It was a rotten old building, he said, and in his opinion it was totally unfit to be licensed. The alterations had been made for the worst. The steps from the gallery were narrow, and if a fire took place it would be blocked in a minute. The sanitary arrangements were also undesirable. Since the building was almost adjacent to the court the members of the bench were able to visit the site before coming to their decision. The Music and Dancing Licence was not affected at this point and was still valid until October 1899.

Almost undaunted by his rebuttal in the courts, James Lovett continued to promote popular entertainment and in February re-opened the Court Lane building as Lovett's Royal Circus. On Monday March 6th, he engaged Irving Bosco and his Great Biorama together with '15 other star turns'. The Chronicle reporter described the projection machine as "an improved invention of the cinematograph type",

LOVETT'S
ROYAL CIRCUS,
COURT LANE DURHAM.

MONDAY, March 6, 1899.

GREAT NOVELTY WEEK.

IMPORTANT ENGAGEMENT (REGARDLESS OF EXPENSE) OF
IRVING BOSCO.
GREAT BIORAMA,
With all the Latest Events
Also Engagement of the Great
FRANSFIELD FAMILY,
Lady and Gentleman Bareback Riders.
Together with other 15 Star Turns.
Day Performance Every Saturday. Guaranteed same as Evening

DURHAM SANDS RACES

and particularly praised the realistic representation of a Spanish Bullfight. This latter was probably the one marketed by the Lumière Brothers. The greatest innovation was the presentation of a special sacred entertainment on the following Sunday at which "Scenes from the Passion Play were presented with the aid of the Biorama." This series of 12 films on the Life of Christ made by Monsieur Léar would have been 550 ft long if shown altogether. Unfortunately the newspaper report gives no further detail. The following week, Lovett's Circus closed down 'until the summer months'. It was planned that it should re-open in August, but it never did.

The Sands Easter Fair was the first venue in the year for the Travelling Showmen. It has been difficult to establish when the first cinematograph booths came to Durham, but they were certainly present in 1899. "Adults and children alike have crowded in appreciative numbers into the various show booths and marvelled at the wonders of the cinematograph and special tableau".[7] The travelling shows also appeared at the 'Miners' Demonstration' in July.

But the major cinematographic event of 1899 was the first appearance in Durham of West's *Our Navy* programme of films. G. West & Son of Southsea were well-known yachting and marine photographers before the advent of the cinematograph. In 1897 the son, Alfred West, was given unprecedented access to Royal Navy activity as part of a film-and-view experiment at the Torpedo Training School. He gradually built up enough footage of naval life to take the show on tour, and to give it a permanent home at the Regent Street Polytechnic. The Durham Advertiser of 7th July 1899 gave 8 column-inches (20cms.) to its review of the programme –

> Those who would appreciate a glimpse of the varied phases of life in her Majesty's [Naval] Service should not fail to visit the Assembly Rooms this week. The whole is indicated in an immense number of animated photographs, but so interesting are the snapshots which have been taken - and the operators have had special facilities for so doing - that one is able to realise in a very full measure what a visit of inspection to the training ships and grounds themselves would tell us.

The programme was narrated by Captain F. Edwards, R.N., and

> ...the gallant officer explains with an eloquence and wit not unmingled at times with martial pride, the long series of pictures....Amongst other fine effects shown were animated photographs of the Turbinia, the fastest torpedo boat, when steaming at 35 knots an hour. Part of these were taken from the boat herself, and the spectator, imagining himself standing on the vessel looking out over the seething seas thrown up in her wake, can see the vibration caused by the tremendous speed.

The conjuror and illusionist David Devant was one of the earliest showmen in Britain to incorporate animated photos into his act. By the end of 1899 he had a prestigious touring company *and* a permanent home at the Egyptian Hall, London. His show at the Assembly Rooms, Durham in the week of December 11th 1899 attracted a large audience and uncompromising praise from the Advertiser reviewer.

> "The programme includes a very fine display of animated photographs including such stirring and up-to-date scenes as the recent embarkation of our khaki-coloured heroes on board several liners for South Africa. The pictures are amongst the best exhibited in Durham and are well worth a visit in themselves."[8]

ASSEMBLY ROOMS, THEATRE, DURHAM.

ONE NIGHT ONLY, FRIDAY, DECEMBER 21st,
MINUTES. 120 *MINUTES.*

M U S I C ,   M I R T H   A N D   M I M I C R Y .

ARTHUR JEFFERSON'S POPULAR CONCERT PARTY

Will Render their

REFINED, HIGH-CLASS, MISCELLANEOUS PROGRAMME.

Consisting of SONGS, QUARTETTES, AND INSTRUMENTALISTS.

MR NAT. GREGORY, BALLAD VOCALIST.
MISS CISSIE CLAMP, COON SONG AND DANCE ARTISTE.
MR J. W. BAKER, BASS VOCALIST.   MISS LOIS BOLKO, SOPRANO.
MR JAMES HOLTON, SOCIETY HUMOURIST.
MR WM. WOODHEAD, MUSICAL MARVEL, Performing upon Seven Instruments at one Time!

ANIMATED PICTURES, by the very Latest Machine,
"THE ROYAL RANDVOLL."
Inventor and Patentee—Mr Walter Gibbons, Hippodrome, London.

The Very Latest PICTURES, including "GENERAL BULLER'S RETURN," and the
"RETURN OF THE C.I.V.s"

Photographic Slides will be shown of various Incidents in the BOER WAR.
Snap Shots taken on the Battlefield.

DIVERS AT WORK.   TEA WITH ELLEN TERRY.   MANY HUMOROUS SUBJECTS.

Doors open at 7.30.   Commence at 8.   Prices, 6d and 1s; a few Reserved Seats at 2s.
Seats may be booked at MR RUSHWORTH'S ART GALLERY, Saddler Street.

TOWN HALL SPENNYMOOR, THURSDAY EVENING.

The first year of the new century proved to be an un-enterprising one for the travelling cinematograph shows in Durham City other than those at the fairs. With a fine Easter, over 12,000 people paid for admission on the Sands.

The only film show at the Assembly Rooms was that given in Arthur Jefferson's Popular Concert Party - a one-nighter on Friday 21st. December. According to the newspaper reports, although the presentation was good the attendance was poor. The machine used to show *General Buller's Return*, *The Galvaston Disaster*, *Divers at Work* and *Tea with Miss Ellen Terry* was advertised as the Royal Randvoll. The originator of this machine, which was aptly named for showing films of the South African War, was Walter Gibbons (later Sir) who normally used the name of the Anglo-American Bio-Tableaux when presenting his itinerant shows.

Arthur Jefferson of course was the theatre manager whose son went on to later fame as Stan Laurel. At this time there were two Arthur Jefferson Concert Parties on tour.

The death of Queen Victoria in January 1901 and the resulting royal funeral provided a great opportunity for the country's entire group of cinematograph entrepreneurs. The first opportunity that stay-at-home Dunelmians had of seeing the procession was on the return visit of West's 'Our Navy' programme to the Assembly Rooms Theatre. On the first night, however, "the non-arrival of the gas necessary for the proper manipulation of the lantern" necessitated a large crowd returning home disappointed. On the Tuesday night everything was 'in readiness' and "a first class entertainment was given to a large and thoroughly appreciative audience. After the Navy programme, film of the Highlanders entering Bloemfontein and the return of the City Imperial Volunteers to Southampton was shown." "These pictures," enthused the reporter, "were heartily applauded, in fact, so natural and realistic was everything that one could easily imagine oneself present at these stirring scenes."

Film of the funeral procession from Osborne House to the streets of London was accompanied by the playing of the Dead March in Saul and Chopin's Funeral march. More film of the Turbinia, The Viper and H.M. Battleship Jupiter completed the programme of two hours duration.

Durham Advertiser March 1st 1901

The funeral of the Queen, and King Edward VII opening Parliament, were included in the show put on by the Newcastle photographer James Dickinson in the Assembly Rooms on Monday 4th March 1901, but new elements of programming were being introduced. From the advertisement it is clear that Dickinson was not only mixing up his reality with his fantasy, but also including some fake newsreels as well. Very few battle items from the South African War were available, partly through War Department restrictions and partly because of the fluid nature of the war. So, some supposed battle scenes were re-enacted in South Africa, but the majority were fictions created in England. Two of those shown, *Winning the Victoria Cross* and *The Dispatch Bearer* were both Mitchell and Kenyon Boer war subjects from the latter half of 1900, and *Attack on a Mission Station* was one of their dramas linked to the Chinese Boxer rebellion. The origin of the 'Cinematographic' Pantomime *A Christmas Dream*, included in the same programme, is uncertain. The newspaper report describes it as a film with "dissolving tricks, spectacular tableau and Santa Claus introducing chimes, an organ and a big bell." *The Butterfly Dance* (coloured) and *Storm at Sea* were Edison Kinetoscope subjects, and the films from the Paris Exhibition of 1900 were probably Gaumont examples. Amongst the comedy films was *Dan Leno's Comic Cricketers*, a production of Birt Acre's Northern Photographic Works directed by Arthur Melbourne-Cooper and all of 100 feet long!! The major innovation in Dickinson's show was his Phono-Cinematograph. The Durham Chronicle reported:

> The results obtained by combining a sound reproducing machine with the cinematograph are marvellous, and not only do the audience see the picture's moving figures, but they hear them talk, sing and cheer.

Examples of a Phono-Cinematograph had been shown at the Paris Exhibition and this may be the origin of Dickinson's items. The kind of presentation was establishing a growing trend in the concept of cinema-going; a film programme could be sufficiently interesting and varied to stand alone without supporting live acts. The only addition to the 'cleverly manipulated lantern' was the piano and singing accompaniment of Madame Corrigall.

The publicity for the return visit of this show on 9th December 1901 further emphasised the sound elements of the show; with

'THE WORLD'S EVENTS illustrated with SCENE, SOUND and GESTURE Perfectly Synchronised. SEE AND HEAR. ASTONISHING EFFECTS.' The Durham Advertiser reported that "the pictures are a splendid collection; the introduction of accompanying sounds to the various events depicted gives them a realistic effect." The sound effects are most likely to have been achieved through the efforts of a behind-the screen group of enthusiastic percussionists, as in the old lantern slide shows.

The enterprising Mr. Dickinson had also been out and about in Durham taking some local material. He filmed the students leaving a lecture room on Palace Green. The presence of undergraduates in the audience seems to be confirmed by the fact that the appearance of Canon Farrar was greeted with 'hearty cheers' and that the audience called for, and were rewarded with, a re-run of the film!

Another innovation was accompaniment by the Olympian Orchestra conducted by Oswald Tate. One of the publicised films boasted *The Duke and Duchess of York Return - London's Welcome* (you hear the crowd cheer). The report also noted "one of the best pictures, *Ora Pro Nobis* a pathetic item which touches a responsive chord in the breasts of the audience." In this film, additionally titled *The Poor Orphan's Prayer,* an orphan dies in the snow and angels bear his spirit up to heaven. It was made by Walter Booth for R.W. Paul's Film Company as one of a series of three song films. The soloist in Durham was once again Madame Corrigal. Song Slides had long been a staple diet of Palaces of Variety, their colourful illustrations often containing the words for expected audience participation. *Ora Pro Nobis* was obviously a favourite since it was re-made as a synchronised song film by Warwick Cinephone Films in 1909.

Toilers of the Deep, the longest single film shown in Durham up to this time, was concerned with the Newfoundland fishing industry. Its 1,050 ft length would have taken about 25 minutes to project. It was made up from 22 separate scenes shown as the report says, "without a break." A spool capacity of this size was rare on projectors of the time.

February 1902 looked to be an auspicious occasion for the future of entertainment in Durham. There had been talk in the town that a new theatre for Durham was being planned. On 14th

- ELEVATION TO CLAYPATH -

February the Durham Chronicle published a drawing of the proposed building *(see left)*. It was to be erected on the corner of Claypath and Providence Row, on the site now occupied by the old Post Office building and the housing development, Claypath Court.

The proposal was dependent upon there being sufficient capital raised. The designers were Messrs. William & T. R. Milburn of Sunderland, and it was expected to hold an audience of between 1,200 and 1,500. Gerald Spencer, the proprietor of the transportable theatre that regularly presented a series of plays on the Sands, was one of the main promoters. In March the City Council approved the application for the theatre to be built despite strong opposition from the adjoining Congregational Church. Unfortunately, the flotation of the Durham and District Theatres Company failed to attract sufficient investment and the 'Coronation Theatre' plan was abandoned.

On 7th February, the New Drill Hall in Gilesgate was opened with a 'subscription ball inaugurated and carried out by the 4th Volunteer battalion of the Durham Light Infantry'. This large hall, which on its first night accommodated 400 people, was lit by electricity and had an efficient radiator heating system. It was quickly in use for band and

The Drill Hall, Gilesgate

orchestral concerts and on Whit Monday, May 19th, it was the venue for the Poole's 'Royal Myriorama'. This travelling show was of large painted canvases illuminated from the front and the rear in a form similar to our contemporary 'son et lumière', and also included filmed items of the Boer War. "There is no doubt," declared the Chronicle reporter "that by this means, every Englishman is brought to sympathise with Tommy Atkins in the many hardships and privations he has had to suffer."

First Visit of the BIG SHOW,
THE MONARCH OF ALL SIMILAR EXHIBITIONS.

NEW DRILL HALL, DURHAM.

One Week Only—Commencing Whit-Monday, May 19.

Nightly at 8; Doors open at 7·30.
Grand Matinee on SATURDAY at 2.—Doors open at 1·30.
Early Doors (to avoid the crush and with choice of Seats), open at 2·15 and 7·15, 3d extra to all parts.
Popular Prices—2s, 1s 6d, 1s, and 6d.
Children Half-price, except to Back Seats.
Reserved Tickets and Plan at the usual place.

THE " CHAS. W."
POOLE'S ROYAL MYRIORAMA.
A Bit of the Best of Everything, including Magnificent Series of Historical Tableaux, representing the Great Decisive Battle of WATERLOO! The Entire Battle, from Start to Finish.
Also Faithful Series of Scenes, showing all Events connected with
THE BOER WAR.
Everything up to Date.
THE CHINESE CRISIS.
Poole's Mammoth Amusement Consolidation.
13   STAR TURNS.   13
Poole's Famous Orchestra of Solo Performers.
Musical Director—Mr H. Walton.
DON'T FORGET OPENING DATE—
WHIT-MONDAY.

In the earlier Sands Easter Fair, both the Manders' and the Halliday Cinematograph Booths were present. Reports said that they did only 'moderate business'. Some minor vandalism had caused part of Mr. Halliday's booth to be damaged by fire, but it did not interrupt his performances and the newspaper report gave him some valuable publicity.

The Story of Joan of Arc is told in his show in a series of cinematograph illustrations of an amazingly ambitious nature. The humble shepherdess was presented in all her meekness following the peaceful vocation in life to which fate and her parents had called her. The angel St. Michael was seen to present himself; her appointment to command the French troops is depicted; her triumphal entry after victory; her indictment; trial by torture and death at the stake were all rolled out before the eyes of the expectant public, and one would have expected to find this last great scene the termination of the story. But the cinematograph is a wonderful creation, and the grand finale was something more elaborate still, no less than the ascension of Joan of Arc, and her passing to a place amongst the elect; truly the height of imagery. What more could be expected for 2d?[9]

The coronation of King Edward VIIth and its associated pageants and processions on 15th August 1902 marked another milestone in the popularity of the cinematograph. Film producers gathered a host of cameras and operators together and vied for prime positions on the routes. There was no doubt that there would be a general clamour to view their resulting films. The opportunity arose in Durham when New Century Pictures paid their first visit to the city at the Drill Hall on Friday 5th September after a successful five-week stay at the Victoria Hall, Sunderland. The posters announced "The complete reproduction of the ROYAL CORONATION; procession to Westminster, the Bishop and the clergy Bearing the regalia, Scenes in the Abbey, etc." This film was, in fact, a mixture of newsreel and theatrical presentation since cameras were not permitted to be in the Abbey, and, in any case, there may not have been sufficient light for the filming. The staged interiors were produced by the French pioneer, Georges Méliès with quite convincing look-alikes but somewhat cramped surroundings. Though the Chronicle reporter is enthusiastic about the Coronation pictures, he is just as enthusiastic over the film of the return of Lord Kitchener from the Boer War.[10]

The New Century Animated Picture Company was the enterprise of Walter Jeffs of Birmingham and Sydney Carter of Bradford. Jeffs had established his fairly permanent cinematograph shows at the Curzon Hall in Birmingham after travelling with several showmen as projectionist. He had seen the opportunity of expanding his business and making a much more economical use of his films by combining with Carter to establish travelling shows consisting almost exclusively of film items. Moreover, the company's innovative policy of sending a cameraman in advance to the places where shows were to take place provided special local reasons for people to patronise his performances. In the Durham area, the cameraman captured pictures of the inspection of the Sunderland Police and Fire Brigade by the former chief constable of the county,

THE
NEW DRILL HALL,
DURHAM.
Last Three Nights!
Last Three Nights!
Last Three Nights!
THE NEW CENTURY
ANIMATED PICTURES.
Under the Management of Mr H. G. Carter.
Unprecedented Success.
The Popular Verdict — "Nothing like the New Century Pictures ever before been seen in Durham."
THE DURHAM
CORONATION FESTIVITIES.
The Children's Procession to Hollow Drift.
THE GREAT BRAMHAM MOOR FOX HUNT,
Specially taken by permission of Captain Lane-Fox, M.F.H.
A TRIP
ACROSS THE ATLANTIC,
Magnificent New Series Depicting
A HOLIDAY IN SWITZERLAND.
The Devil's Bridge. Ascent of Jungfrau,
Tobogganing at Grindelwald,
Picturesque Waterfalls and Rugged Mountain Scenery.
Last three nights of the
GREAT MOTOR CAR SMASH,
Last three nights of
THE WRESTLERS,
LAST THREE NIGHTS!
LAST THREE NIGHTS!
LAST THREE NIGHTS!
To-night and every Evening at 8.
Doors open at 7.30; Early Doors (3d extra) at 7.
Price of admission, 2s, 1s, and 4d.
Children, Half-price.
Seats booked at Messrs Procter's and Co., Stationer, &c., Market Place.

Lieutenant Colonel Eden, and the procession of the school children from Durham Market Place to Hollow Drift for the coronation festivities, which had only taken place on September 3rd. This programme of films was shot by Mitchell & Kenyon for the New Century Company.

Some of the footage of The Sunderland Police Parade and the children's procession has survived in the Peter Worden Collection now preserved at the National Film and Television Archive. The huge procession was filmed with a telescopic lens from the pavement in front of Elvet Station by one of the Mitchell & Kenyon cameramen. The cameraman had not quite mastered the restricted view of the new lens and so most of the participants are only seen from the shoulder upwards. The surviving negative is in four reels of about 120 ft. each.

At the weekend, the cameramen also captured film of the congregation leaving the Sunday morning service at the Cathedral.

The Durham Chronicle reporter gave a particularly detailed description of the content of the local films –

> In the first picture, which contained 100 ft of film, Dr. Armes was most conspicuous standing on the platform in front of the Londonderry monument, and the conducting and singing of Mr. B. Scott-Ellis's Coronation Ode, whilst the Mayor of Durham (Councillor R. T. Herring) could be seen ascending the platform in order to address the children. In the procession to Hollow Drift, many local ladies and gentlemen were easily recognised. Taken all round, it was a splendid reproduction and it has nightly been received with applause. Altogether the film is 500 feet in length and occupies about a quarter of an hour to reproduce. Fifteen pictures were taken in every foot of film and they were thrown onto the screen at about one foot per second.

It would appear, from the timing given, that either the projectionist put each of the five reels on separately, or under-cranked a spliced-together series to lengthen the item.

In another part of the programme was *Trip Across The Atlantic* taken on board the Norddeutsche-Lloyd Steam Ship 'Kronprinz Wilhelm' from Southampton to New York by Charles Urban. The film itself, unfortunately, has not survived but a cue sheet for its presentation has, said to have been written for Sidney Carter by Walter Jeffs: [11]

Pictures	Music	Effects.
Panorama of Southampton	Life on Ocean wave	Steam Whistle
Leaving Port	Anchors are weighed	
Down Channel		
Warships and Torpedo Boats	Hearts of Oak	Foam effect
View of the KronPrinz Wilhelm	Tacet	Foam Effect
On Board	-	
Fine weather	Hornpipe	Lecturer's Note:
Captain on the bridge		The captain has got his sea Legs on!
Man Overboard	Cries : Man Overboard Man the boats	
Song	**The Little Hero (Vocalist)**	
Rough Weather	Storm Movement	Sand paper, rainbox and muffled drum roll for waves
Statue of Liberty (slide) breaking over bow		
New York Harbour	Yankee Doodle or Sousa March Liberty Bell.	

Other films were - *The Great Bramham Moor Fox Hunt Meet, Ora Pro Nobis* sung by Miss Jenny Whitehead and, in the familiar words of early cinema entrepreneurs, '1,000 New, Humorous, Topical and Sensational Pictures'. With three admission prices of two shillings, one shilling, and sixpence (and half-price for children), this was no 'penny gaff'. In the second week of its presentation there was an even greater attendance and on two evenings people had to be turned away. The local film was shown again to loud applause, but the Westminster Abbey coronation film was replaced by another travel film *A Holiday in Switzerland, The Great Motor Car Smash* and *The Wrestlers*. The Chronicle confirms a detail, not often reported on, that a narrator, in this case G. Travers, was employed to "describe the pictures presented to the audience in a lucid and comprehensive manner." The newspaper report also predicted that a return visit was being planned, and this was fulfilled on the week of December 1st. Although it was advertised as an entire change of programme, the Hollow Drift Procession was evidently central to the continued popularity of the show.

ST. CATHERINE'S HOME, ALLERGATE
DURHAM.

MR DUNCANSON
BEGS to ANNOUNCE a POPULAR and HUMOROUS

C O N C E R T ,
On behalf of the FUNDS of the above INSTITUTION to be given in the

TOWN HALL, DURHAM,
On MONDAY, 30TH MARCH, 1903.

WHEN HE WILL BE ASSISTED BY
THE MUSICAL BENTLEYS,
In their very Entertaining and Amusing Musical Melange.

MADAME MIMI BEERS,
The Great Northern Contralto,

THE ROYAL BENOGRAPH,
With The Latest Pictures of the Delhi Durbar and a Fine Collection of
HUMOROUS AND TRICK PICTURES.

THE LIVING LILIPUTIANS
GEORGE W. NICHOLSON,
The Great Yorkshire Humorist,

Accompanist, MRS. DUNCANSON.

Doors open at 7·30; Concert at 8 o'clock.

Tickets:—2s (Reserved) and 1s, to be had at Mr HILLER'S, Music Warehouse, Sadler Street.

TOWN HALL, DURHAM.

TWO NIGHTS ONLY.

WEDNESDAY and THURSDAY,
MARCH 25th and 26th,

Reserved Seats, 2s; Front Seats, 1s 6d; Second Seats, 1s; Back, 6d.
Doors open at 7·30; commence at 8.
Early doors at 7.

R. SILVESTER'S HIGH-CLASS
AND
REFINED VARIETY COMPANY
AND
ANIMATED PICTURES·
16   STAR ARTISTES.   16

Special Engagement of the Singing Collier, Mr R. SHARP, of Pelton Fell.

Just added, the Beautiful Coloured Pictures,
THE SIGN OF THE CROSS.

Georges Méliès' film *A Trip to The Moon* was advertised as "The season's sensation" and described by the newspaper as "an imaginary reproduction in 30 scenes". Another film, *A Soldier's Return* (185 ft), was from the studio of the Brighton pioneer James Williamson, and *How To Stop a Motor Car* (100 ft) from the inventive mind of Cecil Hepworth. The first version of *East Lynn* made for the distributors Harrison and Sons of London was only 500 feet long, so its five scenes hardly covered the bare bones of the plot.

Pauline Jowett was the vocalist and the Durham City Band played selections during the evening under their leader Mr. Coltman.[12]

(right) **Durham Advertiser 12th September 1902**

Few entertainments seemed to be able to survive without some recourse to a cinematographic interlude. Mark Moore's Empire Choir and Scenorama boasted '18 artistes, Pretty Songs, Pretty Dances Pretty Dresses and Animated photos; Majestic, Realistic. Artistic and Comic.' The Chronicle was praising in its review and pointed out that the nightly programme change meant Dunelmians could visit the Hall "with no fear of the entertainment being monotonous."

Some of the animated pictures seemed to be related to the Empire theme of the choir. 'Over 3,000 scenes depicting excursions in Britain's Colonial Empire and other lands are shown.'[13]

On March 25th and 26th 1903 the Town Hall was the venue for 'R. Silvester's High-Class and Refined Variety Company and Animated Pictures'. Included amongst its '16 Star artistes' was Mr. R. Sharp, the singing miner from Pelton Fell. The films included a coloured version of Mr. Wilson Barrett's play *The Sign of the Cross.* This particular film was made by the Welsh showman, turned successful film producer, William Haggar. The 700ft. production starred Haggar's own son as Marcus Superbus.

The Town Hall also provided accommodation for a charity concert in aid of St. Catherine's Home, Allergate, on March 30th.[14] The main artists were the Musical Bentleys, a troupe who showed their animated films under the name of 'The Royal Benograph'. The programme included scenes of the Delhi Durbar.

Hot on the heels of these two shows, New Century Pictures returned to the Drill Hall on Monday April 6th 1903 for a two week engagement *The Imperial Durbar at Delhi* was one of its key films with a return visit of Méliès' *Trip to The Moon,* and *Ora Pro Nobis,* locally taken film of the *Return of the Faithful Durhams (The 1st Volunteer Battalion)* and "hundreds of new humorous pictures never before exhibited" completed the programme. There was support from Victor Ritter, the original grotesque comedian in his turns 'Wait a Minit' and 'Less Quietness, Please', and Miss Pauline Jowett who sang 'Killarney'. The manager H. G. Carter had proposed to the City authorities that he might put on a special sacred concert and cinematograph show on the Good Friday, but permission had been refused. The New Century cameraman it seems then took himself on a tour of the city and obtained some splendid views of the river banks and the sports activities on the Sands. These films were then projected on the Monday evening. "Many well-known faces were recognisable amongst the most prominent being Dr. Deighton. Another novel series of pictures is a number of scenes in London taken at night by the aid of a policeman's bull's eye."

According to the newspaper reports, there were full houses each night, and at the request of a large number of patrons the

Hollow Drift children's procession was once again projected. The 'Bramham Park Foxhunt Meet', and a film also previously shown depicting 'A Miner's Life', formed part of the programme, too. As part of the second week's programme change a coloured presentation of the story of *The Prodigal Son* shared billing with a lengthy travelogue of the railway journey from Montreal to Vancouver.[15]

At the end of March a number of cases of smallpox had been reported in Durham and rumours had been circulating that there had been a smallpox outbreak among the travelling people constituting the Sands Easter Fair. Poor attendances followed the rumours, though it later transpired that there had been no such outbreak.

Co-incidental with the New Century Pictures visit at the Drill Hall, Mr. Rushworth's Assembly Rooms Theatre was the venue for Edison and Barnum's Electric Animated Pictures. The show displayed had nothing to do with Thomas Alva Edison or the Barnum of Barnum and Bailey, but a great deal to with a certain Arthur Duncan Thomas. He had had a travelling cinematograph

ASSEMBLY ROOMS THEATRE,

DURHAM.

PROPRIETOR ... ... T. RUSHWORTH.

EASTER MONDAY, APRIL 13, 1903, AND FIVE FOLLOWING NIGHTS.

Afternoon Performance, Saturday, April 18, at 2-30. Children will be
Admitted at 2d, 3d, and 6d.

EDISON and BARNUM'S

ELECTRIC ANIMATED PICTURES.

AN ENTIRELY NEW PROGRAMME. EDISON'S GLORIOUS ANIMATED

PANTOMIME, "Little Red Riding Hood"

The Great DELHI DURBAR.

Edison's Grand Concert Company of Star Artistes.

Doors Open at 7:15; Commence at 7:45 p.m. prompt.
Admission—Stalls, 3s; Second Seats, 2s; Back Seats, 1s and 6d; Balcony, 2s and 1s.
Seats can now be Booked at MR. RUSHWORTH'S ART GALLERY, Saddler Street.
Early Door (6:45), 3d Extra to all Parts.
THE ORGAN AND PIANO IN USE IS A STORY AND CLARK, SUPPLIED BY
W. H. ARMSTRONG, NORTH ROAD, DURHAM—SOLE AGENT.

show since 1898, and he was described by his contemporaries as the most colourful showman who ever lived. In order to gain recognition, he changed his advertising name to Edison-Thomas, and later to Thomas-Edison. Although some of his advertisements included the information that he was "The pioneer of Animated Pictures", he did not correct those who thought this must mean he was their inventor.

This Devon man thought big. He had large numbers of shows on the road in circuits ranging from the Midlands to the North-west, the North-east and the Borders. Walter Jeffs had once been in his employment, and had learned his trade therein. He knew how to attract the crowds with special Boer War Nights, St. Patrick's Nights, and Scottish Nights. His current attachment to the name Barnum only emphasised his high profile 'barking'.[16]

The reviewer in the Durham Advertiser of 10th April had taken the occasion to write a thoughtful if somewhat derivative account of the current state of the cinematographic art –

> These pictures projecting on to the screen in their moving reality, scenes from actual life, have never lost their novelty or attractiveness because they are being constantly kept up-to-date. The Thomas Edison Company, which as stated, has some four and twenty machines in different parts of the country touring the land from end to end, keeps 28 operators continually travelling all round the world, registering new scenes for present instruction and for future preservation. One is tempted to think the future generations will have the advantage in this study of history over the present. The biograph will reproduce for them the actual scenes as they occurred, and the phonograph will tell them the speeches of the great men of today in the very words as they have been spoken. The schoolboy of the year 2,000 will live in a paradise compared with the urchin of today. The young student of the present has often been heard to pity the schoolboy of the future because of the extended history he will have to memorise. But, there are always compensations.

The Durham Chronicle reporter by using *exactly* the same opening sentence as the above confirms the existence of a press hand-out, and his second sentence surely adds to this: - "Animated pictures are not quite new, although the method of taking and displaying them have been so improved by Mr. Edison that they have burst upon the people with all the freshness of a new invention." [17]

It was stated in the publicity that the programme would be changed each evening, though it seems certain the two advertised films *The Great Delhi Durbar* and *Little Red Riding Hood* would be shown each night. One of the additional films can be identified as James Williamson's *Fire* - "One of the most realistic scenes was the turn-out of the Fire Brigade at Hove. The alarm, the saddling, the mad rush through the streets, the burning building, the gallant rescue are all flashed before the eye with startling vividness, and when this scene was wiped out a prolonged hand-clapping testified to the pleasure and delight it had created."[18]

On 14th September 1903 at the Drill Hall, Leon Vint's *Globe* Choir and Scenorama seemed to be going one better than Moore's *Empire* Choir that had appeared in February, although the format was the same; songs and scenery. The addition of Madame Vint, Leon's wife, as a clairvoyant answering questions about missing friends and stolen goods, provided a diversion. The machine used for the projection of the films was declared to be a Thomas Edison Biograph; another piece of showmanship since the Biograph projector used a 68mm film and had nothing to do with Edison. The Scenorama was, in fact, achieved by the use of coloured photographic slides. The film show had, as its main attraction, actuality film of the Gordon-Bennett motor race in Dublin.

The New Century Excursions and Amusements Co. were at the Assembly Rooms Theatre for two weeks beginning 21st December 1903. The style of their advertising indicates that they were not connected with the New Century Animated Pictures Company that now had a regular venue in Durham. Despite the fact that this was the festive and holiday season, attendances were poor. Their major film was a travelogue on a trip to Norway painstakingly described by the Advertiser reviewer. Also in the programme were some milestones of British films. *Attack on the Mail* as described by the report is clearly *Robbery of the Mail Coach* (375ft) made by Frank Mottershaw's Sheffield Films Company in 1903. *Mary Jane's Mishap* (250ft) was a cautionary comedy made in George Albert Smith's studio in Brighton. *A Desperate Poaching Affray* (220ft.) was made by William Haggar. The film advertised as *When Jack Comes Home* must surely have been James Williamson's seven-scene drama *Wait Till Jack Comes Home* (430ft). [19]

Mary-Jane's Mis-hap *(Courtesy NFVC.)*

Another of the films included was a coloured version of Buffalo Bill's Parade, obviously taken during his nation-wide tour. The arrival of this show in Durham on 20th July 1904 received sensational advertising and newspaper coverage. Although the advertisements gave the venue as the Sands, the reports described the place as 'the engine field adjoining Elvet Colliery.' This was transformed into the Wild West for an afternoon and an evening performance. Despite the fact that ticket prices ranged from one shilling to four shillings alongside the arena, and 5 shillings and 7 shillings and sixpence in the boxes, no less than 26,000 people paid for admission.

The sight of North American Indians in full war-paint visiting the cathedral and the castle on Wednesday morning was captured in still photographs by Mrs. Gee, but there are no reports of anyone taking cinematograph pictures.[20]

At the end of August, the Anglo-American Animated Photo Company visited the Drill Hall, Durham, for the first time with a supporting concert party and band. This was a travelling show run by Walter (later Sir Walter) Gibbons. Gibbons had launched his Anglo-American Bio-Tableaux Company in 1898, and in 1903 had acquired the cinematograph interests of A. D. Thomas, the Thomas - Edison described above. Included in the programme was a film carefully advertised as 'A vivid *representation* of The Russo - Japanese War.' It was, in fact, a 250 ft. 'fake-newsreel' made by Mottershaw's of Sheffield, and

NEW DRILL HALL, DURHAM.
_____

MONDAY, AUGUST 29th, For Six Nights.
GRAND ATTRACTION OF THE
ANGLO-AMERICAN ANIMATED PHOTO COMPANY.
_____

WAR IN THE FAR EAST,
VIVID REPRESENTATION OF THE
RUSSO-JAPANESE WAR
AND
1,000. NEW PICTURES. 1,000.
Supported by GRAND CONCERT PARTY and EXCELLENT BAND.
_____

PRICES—2/-, 1/-, 6d. AND 3d (LIMITED).
Matinee on SATURDAY at 3, Children Half-Price.

illustrating a supposed attack upon a column of Japanese soldiers by a party of Cossacks.[21]

Other films were listed as *The Ascent of Mount Blanc* and *The Great Fire at Lloyd's Bank*. Unfortunately there is no report of the show in the Advertiser, and the Chronicle does little more than repeat the wording of the advertisement.[22]

The popular return of the New Century Animated Pictures on Monday 7th November was under the new management of F. D. Sunderland and in the new venue of the Assembly Rooms. Both newspapers included full reports and from the descriptions it is possible to piece together the details of part of the programme presented. Of topical import were the pictures of the Hull Trawlers 'Mino' and 'Moulmien' which had been fired on by elements of the Russian Baltic Fleet in the North Sea. "Pictures of the survivors, the widows and children, the skipper of the sunken trawler 'The Crane' and the funeral procession are shown." Items from the Russo-Japanese conflict were also included, but it is not clear whether these were actuality items or faked incidents. A documentary on steel-making and a coloured travelogue about Venice completed the factual content of the programme.

The Buffalo Bill visit must have inspired the presentation of "the extremely fascinating story of Cowboys and Indians. The punishment of an Indian Scout, his pantomimic threats of revenge, the departure of the stagecoach with the Cowboy's wife and child, the attack and capture of the coach by the Indian and his friends, the despatch home of a messenger dog by a wounded traveller, the hot pursuit by cowboys, and finally the rescue of the captives after a great deal of revolver shooting, form a vivid and dramatic story."

The Train Robbery - a long and realistic tale in moving pictures, 'which elicited enthusiastic applause' would seem to be W. S. Porter's *The Great Train Robbery*.[23] Ranked in film history as one of the key films in the development of film narrative, it is interesting to note that here it receives only scant mention. *A Tragedy in Mid-air* concerned the voyage of a balloon that eventually takes fire and falls through space, the two occupants being rescued from the sea. The story of the Stowaway as told in another series, is intensely pathetic, and the same may be said of *Driven from Home*. The former was a 550 ft. nine scene drama from James Williamson of a young stowaway who returns home to find his drunken mother reformed, and the latter was

EDISCOPE AND BARNUM'S

10,000 Latest Master Pieces. War Pictures. The Baltic Fleet Outrage.

500 New Comic and Magic Subjects, supported by the greatest Variety Co. ever seen in Durham.

W. A. KAY, America's Greatest Miniature Vaudeville Entertainer, from all the principal Halls and Theatres.

CLOWN OHMY, with his clever performing Dog Toby.

LE BRUN AND MDLLE IRENE, Continental Double Jugglers.

WILL IVOR, The Renowned American High Stilt Performer.

LODER LYONS, Royal Ventriloquist.

3 FUNNYOSSITIES, 3 Sketch Artistes.

MUSICAL CORLLETTIES

MONS. EDGAR, in his Marvellous Musical Trapeze Act, from the London Hippodrome.

WALTON BEEL, Mimic.

Singing Lancashire Mill hand, MISS JESSIE HARPER.

THE GREATEST NOVELTY EVER PRODUCED IN DURHAM

A "Snap-Shot" Competition. £10 IN PRIZES.

Our Artist will be snapping in the City All during this week: the Pictures will be exhibited on the screen each evening, and all persons in the Hall

Whose pictures are shown receive 5/- each.

You may be the one.

Popular Prices, 2s, 1s, and 6d. Doors open 7 o'clock, begin 7-30.

Day Performance for School Children, Saturday, 2.30. Children admitted at 2d, 3d, and 4d.

Durham Advertiser, December 30th 1904

a 390ft seven-scene film by Mitchell & Kenyon described in the catalogue as 'A disowned girl's husband dies in poverty and her father repents and saves her from eviction. A pathetic drama.' *The Clown's Telegram* was also a James Williamson film about a clown who goes on with his performance despite hearing of the death of his daughter. "Uproarious laughter testified to the humour of Mr. and Mrs. Brown and family *Off for a Holiday*." This 375ft film was the first to be released by the newly formed British company Clarendon, and was made in their Limes Road Studio in Croydon. Though there were other items not described in the reviews, it can be construed that most of the programme was of a 'home - grown' nature. British studios were thriving at this time, and through various agencies they were supplying large numbers of copies of some of their films to the United States.

The changing prosperity of differing styles of visual entertainment can be judged by the fact that on 10th November only 30 people attended an illustrated talk at the Town Hall on the subject of 'The Kodak in Peace and War', whereas in the same week the Drill Hall's new impresario, Mr. Duncanson, promised musical concerts and cinematograph entertainments as part of his planned events. On 12th November he supplied both with two concerts by the world champion Hebburn-on-Tyne Colliery Prize Silver Band and as an interval entertainment 'Animated Pictures of the Russo-Japanese War'. On 2nd January 1905 films were the main attraction, though by no means the whole programme, when Ediscope and Barnum's Electric Pictures were engaged. A. D. Thomas had ceased to be involved in this enterprise, but with a slight word change the new owners still managed to give the impression that they were linked to the American Edison Company. The crowd-puller on this occasion was a 'snap-shot' competition. A photographer had been in Durham the previous week and had taken pictures of people in the town centre. If anyone attending the show recognised themselves, they would each receive five shillings. The admission prices were two shilling, one shilling, and sixpence, so it was possible for profit to be made! The Chronicle's report on the show said that nobody had publicly made a claim, although some people were recognised by the audience. "One lady recognised herself, but could not nerve herself to the ordeal of going on the stage to collect the award."[24] The newsreel items on the Baltic Fleet outrage did not seem to be very up-to-date, but there was something of an innovation in having a children's film matinée on the Saturday at which the previously seen Edison film *Little Red Riding Hood* was shown and a new one, Méliès' *Robinson Crusoe.*

The Cinematograph Booths at the Sands Fair in April and the Miners' Demonstration in July appear to have been the only opportunities to see films in Durham during the rest of the year.

In January 1906 the advertisement in the Durham Advertiser promised

> A 20th Century Programme of Up-to Date Comic Pictures, Football Pictures, Pantomime Pictures, Circus Pictures, War Pictures, Dramatic Pictures and Pictures from all parts of the World.

The Chronicle reported that the third visit of the New Century Picture Company was about to take place, and, clearly quoting from their press release, gave glowing details of the joys in store:

> "The reputation of this company is known throughout Great Britain and Ireland and they have visited all the large towns including Bristol, Birmingham, Newcastle, Edinburgh, Bradford, etc. At many places, they have had crowded audiences and have had successful runs of twenty weeks duration. They have received favourable notices in the press and parents and guardians need have no scruples about taking their children to see an entertainment which is healthy in tone, as well as entertaining and instructive. The films number over 10,000 and include scenes depicting The Life of Napoleon with his final overthrow at Waterloo and his death on St. Helena; The Return of the Prodigal Son, a boar hunt, and these are supplemented by war, dramatic and comic pictures."[25]

The review in the next week's columns only added *The Turn out of the Fire Brigade* and *Man the Lifeboat* to the detail of the programme.

A six-day visit from the Royal Canadian Company's Animated Pictures began on May 2nd 1906. Reports of 'packed houses' testify to the success of the advertising and the quality of the programme. The show had apparently been seen by the King and Queen - "*How Father Spent his Holidays,* the Picture that made the King laugh" and "*The Brown Hat* the picture that made the Queen laugh".

Items concerned with the Russo-Japanese War still occupied the actuality sections with *Admiral Togo's Japanese Sailors on the Tyne* and *The Heroes of Port Arthur,* along with *The Eruption of Mount Vesuvius, The Prince of Wales' Tour through India* and *The King*

TO-NIGHT AT 8.

THE TALK OF DURHAM.

ASSEMBLY ROOMS, DURHAM

FOR SIX-DAYS.

Commencing WEDNESDAY, MAY 2, 1906

The ROYAL CANADIAN Co.'s

ANIMATED

PICTURES

AS EXHIBITED BEFORE

THE KING AND QUEEN

(By Royal Command).

Depicting the World We Live In.

THE PRINCE OF WALES'

TOUR THROUGH INDIA.

The Eruption of Vesuvius,

The Burning Mountain!

HOW FATHER SPENT HIS HOLIDAYS!

The Picture that made the King Laugh.

King Edward VII. Laying the Foundation-

Stone of the Liverpool New Cathedral.

600 ADMIRAL TOGO'S 600
     JAPANESE SAILORS.

The Brown Hat!

The Picture that made the Queen laugh.

THE HEROES OF PORT ARTHUR.

A Mystery of the Sea!

Foil of Seafaring Romance.

Great Football Match—

Sunderland v Aston Villa.

The World's Latest Events in Animated

Photography.

REMEMBER—GRAND

SACRED PERFORMANCE,

On SUNDAY FIRST, at 8 P.M.

SPECIAL AND APPROPRIATE PROGRAMME.

COME EARLY.

N.B.—The last Usual Performance will be given on
MONDAY, May 7th.

FIRST TIME IN DURHAM.

Doors open 7·30.   Commence at 8,

Popular prices—3d, 2s, 1s, 6d, and 3d.

Nota—Reserved Seats, 3s and 2s, booked at Rush-
worths.

GRAND CHILDREN'S MATINEE

On SATURDAY, AT 3.

Prices—2d, 3d, 6d.· Adults Half the Usual Price.

Durham Chronicle May 4th '06

Laying the Foundation Stone of Liverpool Cathedral. Football enthusiasts could thrill to scenes from the match between Sunderland and Aston Villa. There is unfortunately no report on the composition of the Children's Matinée on the Saturday or the Sacred Performance on the Sunday.

A new series of films entitled *Christ Among Men* was shown as part of a 'Grand Holiday Attraction' given by the U.S.A. and Greater Britain's Animated Picture Company at the Assembly Rooms for the week beginning August 6th 1906. Produced by the French Gaumont Company the total length of all the episodes spliced together was advertised in the Optical Lantern and Kinematograph Journal at 2,150 ft.[26] If, as the Advertiser report suggests, all the episodes were shown, this would have taken about 40 minutes. The Durham Chronicle of 3rd August reported that the clergy had spoken highly of the film series, after its eleven-week presentation at the Olympia, Newcastle.

Also included in the programme was a newsreel of the King and Queen's visit to Newcastle, and the Royal Wedding at Madrid. One of the comedy films was Clarendon's *When Father Got a Holiday* relating the mishaps on a family cycling trip. This had been seen in May under the title *How Father Spent His Holiday*. It wasn't uncommon for showmen's films to appear under several titles.

The Chronicle reporter found the relaxation of watching films particularly pleasing during the summer days.

"The weather is certainly too warm to sit and listen to a heavy dramatic play, and even a comedy is somewhat apt to pall before the final curtain comes down. This can hardly be said to apply, however, when interesting and instructional animated pictures are provided as the means of entertainment, for the brain has no need to attempt to solve intricate plots, and singing may-hap of doubtful quality does not jar the ear. One has only to loll in one's seat, and watch the ever changing panorama which is constantly passing with refreshing variety before the eyes." [27]

* * * * * * *

Manders' Fairground Cinematograph Booth at Hull fair in 1904.
This show was a regular at the Durham Sands Easter Fair.
By courtesy of the National Fairground Archive.

Chapter Two   Finding a Home 1907 - 1914

Already in many parts of the country, buildings were being converted as permanent showplaces for films. Film rental was gradually overtaking film purchase as the means of providing a programme and it was possible to make complete changes of programme at reasonable rates. But the travelling cinema was still very popular in rural and suburban areas, and a number of travelling showmen visited Durham in the first few months of 1907. The first show of the year at the Drill Hall was the return of Poole's 'Myriorama' with its large illuminated canvases, live entertainment and the cinematograph films.[1] "The performance on this visit is entirely new," said the Advertiser reporter. "Many startling features have been introduced. The trip described by the proprietors as a journey from hemisphere to hemisphere shows us the world's most interesting sights made manifest by picture and lecture, the most notable of the subjects being a magnificent view of the ancient city of Newcastle. The animated pictures are projected by the new Poole process and include some capital subjects." The appearance of 'the New Poole Process' was typical of a showman's desire to inject novelty into standard entertainment. It is possible that the Pooles had simply acquired a new projector. Included in the actuality films was news footage of the 'Recent wreck of the Berlin off the Hook of Holland.' This maritime disaster, in which 120 passengers died, had some local interest, since one of the victims was Charles Brockett of Hartlepool. In a fierce gale on 21st February 1907, the Great Eastern Railway Company's Harwich-Hook ferry was swept across the mole. The bows broke off and sank. Only 10 passengers and 5 crew were saved.[2]

The Assembly Rooms hosted a further visit of the Ediscope & Barnum's Electric Animated Pictures in March. This confusingly named show was obviously attempting to catch the eye of the gullible public with its combination of Ediscope, suggesting Thomas Edison, and Barnum suggesting the Barnum and Bailey Circus. Actually, the proprietors were the American Photo

Company. They were booked in for two weeks, and the opening programme was reported as containing 'the latest comic, pantomime, football, circus, war and dramatic pictures' and a series of pictures which were declared to 'illustrate the history of our times.' The films were included in a 'selected company of artists'.[3] Full houses were reported in the Advertiser and multiple visits were encouraged by the fact that there was an entire change of the films every second night.[4]

There was no report of any cinematograph showmen at the Easter Fair or the Miners' Demonstration but it is certain that these would have been present. The tented travelling shows were not just touring for the Summer Festivities. Manders' Electric Coliseum is reported as playing to crowded houses during the Christmas Holidays at Gateshead's Quarry Ground.[5]

1908

The first reported show of 1908 was also at the Drill Hall in March. It had the grand title of 'Prince Edward's Pictures' but its royal provenance could only be attributed to the name of the proprietor, Sydney Prince. A large audience was attracted to its opening performance on Wednesday night, when they were entertained by '40 miles of animated pictures'. It was not unusual for showmen to express the size of their programme in length of footage. Since film passed through the projector at about one foot per second, Mr Prince's film selection would have lasted about an hour, with reel changes. The main attraction appears to have been 'human talking pictures'. The Advertiser report suggests that the introduction of dialogue from behind the screen added a touch of realism that was far in advance of the gramophone. The dramatic film included in the programme was a sixteen-scene version of *Ben Hur*. The dramatisation of the novel by General Lew Wallace had been a crowd-puller in a New York theatre in 1899, the chariot race being performed on the stage by a tread-wheel device.[6] This first film version was made in the USA for the Kalem Company by the Irishman Sydney Olcott. He took the opportunity of filming a chariot race taking place on a local race track, added a few studio scenes and released it. It was only one reel in length and would have lasted about 15 minutes.[7] As usual, the film programme was accompanied by a musical entertainment, this time by the 'Prince Edward Choristers'. The show was presented for four nights and a special matinée was given on the Saturday afternoon.[8]

The Assembly Rooms as a venue was praised by a correspondent to the Advertiser in April. "We have a nice little comfortable well-equipped theatre (the Assembly Rooms). The proprietor only runs it in the season and then for only three nights in the week. He gets the most excellent companies and the best class of plays. What is the result? Well, very rarely do the visits pay either the company or the proprietor. But I am told that the latter and his son like it, and I have heard them say it is always something for them to do and to think about. It makes work for his men and causes money to be spent in the town." The writer does not make mention of the cinematograph shows, but the letter does indicate that concerts at the Drill Hall were less well attended than those at the Assembly rooms.[9]

A postcard showing Cottrell's Coliseum Cinematograph Show.
Author's Collection

The Advertiser reported that at the Easter Fair 'most in evidence were the Cinematograph Shows'. Attending this year were John Cottrell's New Coliseum; Manders' Yankee Show and Singing and Talking Pictures; Mrs. Paine's Bioscope Theatre, and

Henry Testo's Exhibition of Moving Images. Despite the 'boisterous weather', the shows were well attended.[10]

Not everyone was content with the financial state of the travelling shows, however. Mrs. Crow of Middlesborough advertised her Cinematograph Show for sale in January 1908, which gives us an idea of what made up a particular show -

> Shuttered Booth 28 ft by 30 ft; 2 Walk-ups, Bonnie Front, Black Tilt Organ with drums and two barrells [Sic!], New Walturdaw Bioscope, with Arc and gas lamp, about 6,000ft of film with spools; all ready for taking money. Can be seen built by applying day before coming. Mrs. Crow, Snowdon Road, Middlesborough.[11]

Rumblings of what the future might hold for the travelling showman were being published in the Trade journals. A. C. Bromhead of the British branch of the Gaumont Company reviewed the situation in May 1908. He described how the penny booths had given way to the travelling cinematograph shows, and how many of the 'present prosperous showmen of the Cinematograph, travelling with their portable theatres, huge and costly organs, traction engines and immense illuminated fronts' were earning a much more modest profit from such establishments than previously. A change was in sight, and he described how travelling showmen had practically ceased to exist in America. That trade was now mostly represented by lecturers who employed the cinematograph to illustrate their travels. They occasionally included a few comic films 'to relieve the monotony'.

"In America, the 'Nickelodeon' will be the future of the Cinematograph - the 'Bijou Theatre' situated on a main street," he declared. "The Nickelodeon proprietor hires films rather than buys them and thus he has a far greater variety of films at his disposal for less outlay. He also becomes well-known to his clientele." He went on to predict that new proposed legislation "will put Cinematograph entertainment on a proper footing."[12] It is significant that shortly after the appearance of this article the Gaumont Company announced the setting up of a Film Hire Service.[13]

The usual Cinematograph Shows were contracted to appear at the Miners' Demonstration in July, but there were no other advertised film performances until September when the Oxford Animated Picture Co. spent a fortnight at the Drill Hall.[14] The programme included scenes from the famous Olympic Marathon in which Dorando was assisted to the finish line, and also scenes of the 1908 Dieppe Motor Race. Another advertised film was *Harry Lauder in A Hurry,* an Alf Collins comedy made by the Gaumont Company and released in July 1908.

They played a Saturday Matinée with children's price at 2d, 3d, and 6d; evening adult prices were 3d, 4d, and 6d in the body of the hall, rear seats could be reserved at 1/-. There was an entire change of programme for the second week but no details. The newspaper advert tantalisingly says 'For full Programme see playbill'. Oh that we could!

▲ A postcard of a scene from the Pathé film *The Life of Christ* shown in the London Animated Picture Company's show. *Author's collection*
▼ The Oxford Animated Picture Company.

THE OXFORD ANIMATED PICTURE COMPANY.

DRILL HALL, GILESGATE, DURHAM.

MONDAY, SEPTEMBER 14th, AND DURING THE WEEK,
EVERY NIGHT AT EIGHT.

A PROGRAMME SECOND TO NONE!

OWING TO HUGE SUCCESS.

The Management have decided to **STAY ONE WEEK LONGER,** with an

ENTIRE AND UP-TO-DATE CHANGE OF PROGRAMME,

And a Continuation of Serio & Comic Up-to-Date Pictures the whole Evening

FOR FULL PROGRAMME SEE PLAY BILL.

Two months later another geographically named company, the London Animated Picture Company, occupied the same venue. One of its main films was *The Life of Christ*.[15] The scenes are described as the Birth of Christ, five Tableaux; the Childhood of Christ eight Tableaux; the Public Life of Christ, nine tableaux, the Passion and Death of Christ fifteen Tableaux; the Resurrection and Ascension, three Tableaux. This was probably the Pathé *Life and Passion of Jesus Christ* made in 1907.

Also present on the programme, and advertised as such, was a 'Unique Picture series of FAUST with Scenery, Dresses and Decorations by G. Melies, Paris'. This film was first released in 1903, but it is a timeless story and no doubt the Méliès Company re-released it many times.

The Christmas Show at the Drill Hall was well-praised by the local reporter –

> The Pick of the Pack. Animated Pictures under the direction of Mr. Wallace Davidson open here on Monday Night. The principal feature will be a gorgeously coloured and superbly acted Pantomime entitled *The Sleeping Beauty* in which 200 artistes and auxiliaries take part. Dramatic subjects are represented by *The Scar* - a vision of Death, and a beautiful pathetic story *Blind*. Some screamingly funny films are *An Energetic Woman, New-laid Eggs* and *The Wonderful Fertilizer*. One of the beauties of France, *The Fountains of Versailles* will form another attraction.

The advertisement in its attempt to appeal to the widest audience declares that the pictures are 'Dramatic, Pathetic, Comic, Educative, Instructive and Entertaining'. The report goes on to say that the projector used did not suffer from 'the fluttering which is so irritating', and that 'the pictures are certainly the finest which have been shown in the city'. The show was under the management of Mr. Wallace Davidson with the assistance of Mr. Francis McDermott. One of the comedy films was *Archie Goes Shopping with the Girls*, a 100 metre British film made by the Warwick Company and released in September 1908. Both *The Scar* (La Cicatrice) and *The Sleeping Beauty* (La Belle au Bois Dormant) were Pathé films coloured by means of their ingenious stencil process.[16]

A picture postcard with a scene from *La Belle au Bois Dormant.*
One of series of ten. *Author's Collection*

1909

The Church Mission Society used the Town Hall for an illustrated lecture on 11th March 1909. "Animated Photographs of Uganda shown by means of the Church Mission Society's Famous Cinematograph", declared the advertisement in a hark-back to the kind of publicity used almost a decade before. The film was reported to show life and work in Uganda, travel by canoe and railway train, the young King of Uganda playing in a football match, and the way an African behaves when he has just had a tooth extracted. The film was to be described by the Revd. J. E. M. Harrington and would be accompanied by 'appropriate music'. The event was important enough to be chaired by the Mayor.[17]

Cinematograph Act

One of the hazards of cinematograph performance, and the reason for the passing of the 1909 Cinematograph Act, was the flammable nature of cellulose nitrate film. No mishaps had been reported in Durham itself, but there were a number in the county. In March 1909, the performance of the New Edison Picture Company at the Central Hall, Darlington was interrupted by a fire in the projection box.[18] These wooden transportable projection booths had been in common use for a number of years before they were demanded by the Cinematograph Act. They were usually lined with asbestos and had iron shutters to protect the audience in case of fire.

On this occasion, the box was placed under the edge of the gallery near the main entrance.

"The first performance commenced at seven o'clock and the third picture was in the process of being run through the machine when the fire occurred. The film was a new one and Mr. Branford, the manager who was standing in the centre of the hall, said, "It did not fit into place properly." *(This was often a problem with new or "green" film stock even into modern times.)* The film broke and caught fire. The operator hearing a shout of 'Fire' glanced up and stepped hurriedly aside, closing the door. In that instant the film blazed up in a sheet of flame.

"Immediately, there was a scene of great disorder. Women and children screamed and, shouting, rushed toward the door. Several efforts were made by attendants to pacify their fears, but the sight of the operator's box blazing fiercely horrified them, and overturning chairs and seats, they scrambled wildly towards the staircase.

Fortunately, Police Inspector Thompson was standing just inside the hall at the top of the main staircase and, assisted by a gentleman from a neighbouring village who was also standing near, he succeeded to some extent in checking the rush to the staircase. At one time it was feared there would be serious loss of life. Many people in their eagerness to get out of the hall tumbled down the stairs and sustained bruises. The steps are not steep, and there is a good strong balustrade all the way down.

Fortunately, no-one was hurt. As soon as the fire broke out, the staff rushed with buckets of water and threw them on the burning box. The Darlington Fire Brigade were informed of what was happening by telephone and in 3 or 4 minutes Captain Uttley and some men were on the scene with the steam fire engine.

They succeeded by means of buckets of water to extinguish the flames but by that time the kinematograph machine was completely wrecked. The operator's box, a smouldering heap of wood, was dragged down the steps into the street.

The machine, films and wooden box in which they were enclosed were totally destroyed, and the damage was estimated at £150."[19]

The highlighted building is the wool warehouse that was converted into the Palace Theatre. A detail from a postcard of 1908. *Author's collection.*

The Cinematograph Act of 1909, which actually did not come into operation until 1st January, 1910, was a statutory tidying up of many safety precaution bye-laws that already existed in most conurbations. It was applauded by most of the showmen, though, as we shall see later, some of its vagaries permitted local authority control over what could be projected rather than the mere technology of projection. All buildings in which cinematograph shows were to take place needed long-term or short-term licences granted only after inspection by the local fire brigade. In most places, the granting of licences was placed in the hands of the licensing magistrates, and the renewal inspections were carried out by police superintendents. Travelling showmen could obtain licences by applying in advance to the police authority, and submitting their projection boxes for inspection.

Theatres were already subject to licensing both for performance and music. On 5th August 1909, a theatre licence was granted by Durham magistrates to Thomas Rawes. The next day the

Advertiser gave full detail of Durham's New Music Hall, though unfortunately without any drawings or diagrams.

"Durham's New Music Hall is now nearing completion, and everything is being prepared for Monday's opening ceremony. It hardly seems credible that such a transformation could have taken place in the disused wool warehouse during so brief a period so as to produce a cosy, up-to-date music hall. On the ground floor are the pit and pit stalls with a seating capacity of 400, and that of the centre circle and the side circle above will accommodate 300, or 700 in all. The centre circle is furnished with tip-up seats whilst independent of the seating accommodation there is a promenade for those who care to stroll about. The pit stalls and the pit are also made as comfortable as possible. The floor has a slope, so that there will be little for those at the back to complain of with respect of a full view of the stage. Everyone will be able to see and hear excellently no matter where they sit. A large stage has been prepared with all the necessary equipments. It has a proscenium opening of 22 feet, and the stage itself is 40 feet wide from wall to wall with a depth of 25 ft. and a height of 32 ft. It will be capable of holding some of the largest scenery and companies upon the road. Splendid new scenery is the next acquisition. It has been specially painted by Mr. W. B. Robinson of London. The stage manager is Mr. Fred Watson. The scenery at present available consists of a palace scene, a wood set, interior of a palace, and street scenes, The North Road, Durham etc.

Shortly, there will be a fireproof advertisement curtain. At the back of the stage are the artistes' dressing rooms all of which have been fitted up as neat as possible. The electric light has been installed, with gas as a reserve light. Around the sides of the circle are displayed some artistic plaster work. The transformation reflects great credit on the architect Mr. H. T. Gradon, Durham and the contractor, Mr. P. Strangeways of Newcastle, under whose joint supervision the work has been carried to such a successful venture at a cost, we understand, of probably £1,000. The artists will be accompanied by a first class orchestra consisting of eight performers under the direction of Mr. C.V. Burton of North Shields. The prices of the various seats are to be: Centre circle, 1s., side circle 9d., pit stalls, 6d., and pit 4d., and the performances are to be worked on the twice nightly system at seven and nine. It is the intention of the owner Mr. T. C. Rawes, proprietor also of the Victoria Theatre, Stanley, to get the very best talent possible according to the run of the place. Everything in the way of public safety in case of fire has been well taken into consideration by the proprietor, and apart from the fireproof curtain, there are five fire exits in the building, whilst fire extinguisher appliances will also be placed for immediate use. A talented body of artists are billed for the opening week, and it only remains now for Durham and district pleasure seekers to give the new undertaking a rattling good send-off."[20]

The newspaper report of the actual opening of the Palace is full of fascinating detail -

"This new venture and acquisition to the city of Durham opened its doors for the first time to the public on Monday evening and truly its debut was a most successful one indeed. There was a capital audience at the first house, the programme being set a-rolling by the singing of the National Anthem by Madame Louie Gilbert, the audience enthusiastically joining in. Mr. Harry Metcalfe, sole manager for Mr. Rawes, then made his appearance on stage, and after applause had subsided he first thanked all present at the first house performance for their kind patronage on behalf of Mr. Rawes, the proprietor, who had had the courage, nerve and grit in him to try single-handed in giving them a place of entertainment which had been required in that town he should say for a number of years. Some years ago, explained Mr. Metcalfe, he had visited Durham with Tudor's Circus as manager, but they certainly never had a place like that before in the town."

THE PALACE, DURHAM

PROPRIETOR .. .. MR T. C. RAWES.
LIGHTED BY ELECTRICITY.

MONDAY, 9th AUGUST, 1909, and During the Week.] /7 TWICE NIGHTLY 9.
A REMARKABLE AGGREGATION OF TALENT.

Special Engagement of HIMSELF— CLIFF RYLAND, The Popular London Comedian, with Droll Songs and Sayings,

ETHEL DONNA, Chic Comedienne and Dancer.

Important Engagement of MASSONA, the Great Comedy Juggler.

Expensive Engagement of JACK NORTH, the New Comedian.

THREE ROYAL TEMPLES,
Operatic Vocalists, including Madame Louie Gilbert, the Celebrated Soprano.

THE CATHEDOSCOPE, with the Latest Up-to-Date Living Pictures.

Starring Engagement of THE THREE HODGINIS,
The Continental Aerial Gymnastic Wonders, in their Sensational Display on the Revolving Ladder.

PRICES:-CENTRE CIRCLE, 1/-; SIDE CIRCLE, 9d; PIT STALLS, 6d; PIT 4d.
7 AND 9 TWICE NIGHTLY 7 AND 9.

Doors Open 6.30 and 8.45. Performance finishes First House 8.44.
Performance finishes Second House 10.40

Pass-Out Checks not transferable. N.B.—Infants in Arms admitted only on the understanding that they will be removed when crying. The Management reserve the right to refuse admission to any person or persons whose presence they may deem undesirable or objectionable.

The first newspaper advertisement for the Palace Theatre, Durham
6 August 1909

The report goes on to itemise the artists and the songs ...."Ethel Donna with the song 'Make Hay While the Sun Shines'; Massona, a comedy juggler; and Jack North, comedian." Then, possibly as a prelude to the interval 'a very funny but wonderfully clear film was shown on the Cathedoscope, entitled *William's Suicide'*. After the interval, there was 'a clever turn by The Three Hodginis, aerial gymnasts; excellent singing by The Three Royal Temples, operatic vocalists, including Madame Louie Gilbert; the London comedian Cliff Ryland, and the last item on the programme was the Cathedoscope with a very fine picture *Nick Carter, Detective*.[21]

The casual nature of the aptly-named Cathedoscope can be judged by the fact that the film section of the programme was often billed as 'time permitting'.[22] It is also clear from its position on the bill, that it was being used as a 'chaser' enabling patrons to get to the bar at the interval and to begin leaving at the end of the show. There was a compensation for the youngsters of the town, however, since the management decided to hold Picture Matinées beginning on Saturday 28th August at 2 p.m. Prices were 1d, 2d, and 3d for children and 2d, 4d, and 6d for accompanying adults. It is interesting that children-in-arms were be admitted on the understanding that they would be removed when crying. This was in marked contrast to the Assembly Rooms matinées where children-in-arms were definitely not admitted.

Film shows continued at the Assembly Rooms and in October, Joshua Dyson's Gypsy Choir and Diorama paid a visit. The 'ever pleasing animated pictures' were presented, it was stated, 'without wait or interval.' This either implied that the films were reeled together onto a larger spool, or that two projectors were used. A newsreel of the aviation week at Blackpool is the only part of the film programme described.[23]

The Palace programme each week advertised the name of two films. One or both would be played at the theatre depending upon the running time of the rest of the bill. For the week of 29th Nov. the choice was to be *An Indian Runner's Romance* (a 1908 American Biograph directed by D. W. Griffith) and *A Glass of Goat's Milk* (a British Clarendon film directed by Percy Stow and released in September 1909).

There was further news of possible theatre activity in the city with the announcement that the Hippodrome was to be built on the corner of Claypath and Providence Row. At Durham city police court on Monday 21st November, the magistrates granted sanction for a future licence to the Hippodrome Ltd. when building was completed. There were objections from the Congregational Church on the ground that its schoolrooms, which were in use on most evenings, would be affected by noise from the theatre.

ASSEMBLY ROOMS THEATRE,
DURHAM.

PROPRIETOR   ...   .   T. RUSHWORTH.

NAT. TELEPHONE No. 0195.

FOR SIX NIGHTS AND MATINEE SATURDAY.
OPENING MONDAY NEXT, NOVEMBER 1st, 1909.
JOSHUA DYSON'S GIPSY CHOIR AND DIORAMAS.
DYSON'S, THE ORIGINAL.
DYSON'S, THE PREMIER MUSICAL AND PICTORIAL ENTERTAINMENTS EXTANT.
ESTABLISHED 1855. CONTINUOUS SINCE.
Coming Direct from The Great Town Hall, Newcastle, after a Most Successful Season; Victoria Hall, Sunderland; Town Hall, West Hartlepool.
PICTORIAL TOURS NIGHTLY.
MONDAY, November 1st -PICTURESQUE WALES. TUESDAY—AMERICA. WEDNESDAY—BONNIE SCOTLAND. THURSDAY—A TRIP TO PARIS. FRIDAY—THE GREAT FRANCO-BRITISH EXHIBITION. SPECIAL MATINEE SATURDAY at 3—AUSTRALIA. SATURDAY, Last Entertainment, 7-45—A TRIP TO LONDON.
20 TALENTED ARTISTES NIGHTLY 20. Also ANIMATED PICTURES
Dyson's POPULAR PRICES—4/6, 1/-, 6d. and 3d. Schools and Children Half-price to all except 3d.
Booking Office at Hill & Co's, Music Warehouse, Saddler Street.   No Early Door Prices.
NEW PROGRAMME AT EVERY PERFORMANCE.
THE IDEAL FAMILY ENTERTAINMENT.   ONE WEEK, OPENING MONDAY.

Durham County Advertiser. 29th October 1909

They argued that since there was now a Music Hall in the city, no new theatre was needed. They also thought that the enterprise of owners of the Palace would be threatened by the arrival of another theatre. The theatre proposal was for a building accommodating about 1,400 people. It was expected to cost £10,000 to build and would be the third theatre of the company that already had houses in Darlington and Middlesborough. H. E. Ferens, on behalf of the company, said that it would bring improvement to an area of Durham that was becoming dilapidated. It would draw people to that area again and considerably increase the rateable value of the neighbourhood. He was of the opinion that the theatre would be far enough away from the schoolroom not to cause disturbance, and that every effort would be made to ensure this. The magistrates, in approving the request, said that it must be understood that they could not bind any future magistrates to their current opinion.[24]

Another form of entertainment appeared in the city, during Christmas week. Roller-skating was becoming a nation-wide craze. A rink had recently been opened in Spennymoor, and now the Olympia Rink was opened on a site in Walkergate from a working capital of £3,500.[25]

1910

The first visitor of the New Year was Randall Williams' Cinematograph Show, which set up the frontage and tents in the Market Place. The newspaper report clearly indicated that this was a regular venue for his show, though no previous description has yet been found. Obviously keen to court the favours of the town and its councillors, Richard Monte (professional name - Randall Williams) donated the first night takings of 'this high class cinematograph show' to the Durham County Hospital's General Fund.

Randall Williams' Cinematograph Show at Wingate, Co. Durham in 1909.
Durham County Records Office.

There were three performances during the evening under the patronage of the Mayor and Corporation. The report read "Despite counter attractions, good business was done, and although the returns are not yet to hand, we understand the benefit will result in the coffers of the excellent institution at the head of North Road being substantially increased." On Thursday night another benefit was given for the Samaritan Nurses Society and it was understood that the third benefit night would be in aid of the Lift Fund of Durham County Hospital.[26]

The travelling shows were struck their first blow in this district with the re-opening of the Assembly Rooms, Clarence Villas, Coxhoe as a permanent site for cinematograph entertainment. The hall had been built in 1893. Now, under the management of J. Coleridge and with his wife Lena ('Gold Medallist, late of a London Orchestra') as the musical accompaniment, there was to be a whole evening's presentation of films. At various intervals, there was to be live entertainment by well-known local comedians Messrs Barnes and Sons and illustrated slide songs by Miss Maude Coates. The Advertiser reported that

> A very welcome attraction is being offered to the inhabitants of Coxhoe and district by the opening under entirely new management of the Royal Picture Company of the Assembly Hall, Coxhoe, where a varied and attractive programme will be given each night. The hall is warmed and lighted by Wells' Patent Lamps and the management are determined that everything possible will be done for the comfort of their patrons to whom they promise a first class programme.

Reserved seats cost 1/-, Chairs were 6d, Back seats 3d. Each Wednesday night would be reserved for dancing with pictures in the intervals.[27] The film programme was announced as containing the following films - *The Little Father* (not identified), *Father's Baby Boy* - Clarendon 460ft trick film, *Airship Destroyer* futuristic Urban 685ft drama, *A Tantalising Young Lady* - a 545ft Pathé comedy film starring Max Linder, *Nick Carter - Detective,* Éclair 695ft, *Saved by Carlo* - Cricks & Martin 510ft, *Race for Monkey* - Itala 425ft, *Paper Hanging by Novice* (not identified), *Young Redskins* - Cricks & Martin 415ft comedy.

On their second week of operation, the lessees also announced that they would present Sunday shows and donate the profits to charity.[28] One of the anomalies immediately apparent in the passing of the 1909 Cinematograph Act was that the licensing authorities had the power to determine the opening and closing times of cinemas. It quickly became apparent that the Act was as much concerned with control as it was with safety. Most cinematograph licences were granted for six days of the week, and where Sunday opening was permitted the films were to be of a sacred nature and the profits were to be donated to good causes. First reports of the Sunday concerts at Coxhoe indicated that they were well attended.[29]

ASSEMBLY HALL, COXHOE.

MANAGING DIRECTOR .. .. MR J. COLERIDGE.

GREAT SUCCESS, ENTHUSIASTIC AUDIENCES. EVERY COMFORT. POPULAR PRICES.
Respectability Guaranteed. Change of Programme Weekly. Up-to-Date Management.
Safety Assured. NEWEST PICTURES Direct from London. Newly Seated. Wells' Patent Lamps
OUR MOTTO—THE BEST FOR THE PEOPLE.
PICTURES ENTICING, THRILLING, AND HUMOROUS. GRAND VARIETY ENTERTAINMENT.
Next Week's Programme, Commencing Monday, Feb. 14th.
MISS MAUDE COATES, Illustrated Songs, Hand Painted Slides.
BY REQUEST, MESSRS. BARNES and SONS, well-known Local Comedians.
LATEST PICTURES—The Little Father; Father's Baby Boy; Airship Destroyer; A
Tantalising Young Lady; Nick Carter, Detective; Saved by Carlo;
Race for Monkey; Paper Hanging by Novice; Young Redskins, &c.
PIANIST, MADAME LENA COLERIDGE, Gold Medalist, late of London Orchestra.
OVERTURE .. MADAME COLERIDGE .. "ZAMPA."
WEDNESDAY NIGHTS RESERVED FOR DANCING AND PICTURE INTERVALS.
POPULAR PRICES. OPEN 7 P.M. COMMENCE 7-45 P.M.

Durham Chronicle, February 11th, 1910

The Coxhoe Assembly Rooms must have initially presented some problems with screen visibility, and the management announced that they had submitted plans to provide raking from the stage to the back of the hall. In March, the Royal Picture Company under the management of Mr Coleridge also advertised that they ran a Picture Show at Coundon. The programme was probably run in conjunction with Coxhoe. The dance night there was changed to Thursdays.

Chester-le-Street was also ahead of Durham city in getting a permanent cinematograph show. In February, a new picture theatre to be called the Hippodrome was announced for the Market Place, which would have accommodation for 750 people. John Stoker, jnr. is described as the proprietor, and the responsible manager J. Harris, his assistant.[30] The entertainer and narrator was to be Leon Gould. The showmen knew him, as one of the most popular cinematograph lecturers - he had held positions with Edison Thomas Cinematograph Shows, President Kemp's Fairground Shows, and also those of Ralph & Pedley.[31] It is easy for us to forget that most of the early film shows had someone on the staff to introduce the films whilst the projectionist threaded-up, and to narrate the plot in case the audience were unable to interpret the images or to read the inter-scene titles. As films developed a more cohesive narrative style, the role of the narrator became less important and gradually disappeared. As the narrator's role faded, the musical accompaniment took on a greater importance.

Promotional competitions and events were very much part of the new picture houses. Advertisements were at pains to point out the respectability of the cinemas and to counter the view that the darkness was a cover for immorality. No doubt to emphasise this point, in March, the Assembly Rooms Coxhoe staged a Ladies Week with special features in the programme. There was no implication that men were not permitted to be there. *The Great Unknown* was a picture shown as a competition for ladies. Mr Coleridge offered a prize of 10s for the lady who solved the correct title of the picture.[32]

There was no mention in the newspapers of cinematograph shows at the Easter Fair or the Miners' Gala, in the local press or the Showman's magazine. It must be assumed that the regulars were present, since they are listed in the reports of other local fairs.

The films at the Palace were not always dramas or comedies. When there was a significant event, the proprietors usually managed to obtain a current newsreel. In the week that King Edward VII died they showed the cup final between Newcastle United and Barnsley played at Everton football ground.[33] The following week scenes of the funeral were shown with the audience standing in silence.[34] In July, the Palace proprietors, after almost a year's operation, proposed to make a number of improvements to the auditorium, and the theatre was closed for the whole of July to enable these to take place -

"One of the chief improvements is to be made in respect to the proscenium opening, the present design of which is to be rejected for one of absolute splendour. At each of the sides are to be erected two massive marble columns bearing Corinthian Capitals, whilst the remainder of the proscenium under attention will be the charming Fabric plaster designs. Adjoining the above mentioned proposed columns are to be two elegantly fitted up boxes to hold eight people-another long felt want remedied. At present the walls and windows have always been a set back in the way of Mr. Rawes risky undertaking, but it is now proposed to transform all such nude structural work into artistic plaster work. Besides other improvements to be effected, much too numerous to mention, is the repainting of scenery, and we are informed that nothing in the way of expense will be spared in considering the patron's comfort. With such alterations accomplished the Durham Hall will be regarded as one of the smartest, prettiest and cosiest of its kind in the North of England. The work has been entrusted to Messrs Rule and Hatfield of Sunderland, and it is estimated to cost something like £300. The hall will be re-opened on August Bank Holiday."[35]

Just as the Palace's grand re-opening took place, the Assembly Rooms in the Bailey were preparing to switch to full-time cinematograph shows for a season. Wells' Animated Pictures, or as

ASSEMBLY ROOMS THEATRE
DURHAM.

DON'T MISS SEEING
WELLS' ANIMATED PICTURES

Saturday, August 13th.

Performances, 3, 7, and 9; Following Weeks, 7 and 9.

POPULAR PRICES :

Stalls, 1s ; Second Seats, 6d ; Back, 3d ; Balcony, 1s and 6d.

Doors Open 2-30, 6-30, and 8-40.

The PIANO in use is Supplied by HILLER and SON, 71, Saddler Street, Durham. Agents for BECHSTEIN and all leading Pianos.

they were more fully known, Wells' Life Motion Pictures began showing their programmes on Saturday 13th August at 3 p.m., 7 p.m. and 9 p.m. Although the report suggests that the proprietors of the show are 'well-known', their origins have proved elusive.

The admission prices reflected the then current cinema dilemma as to which order of seats gave the audience most advantage. The principle seemed to be that of the live theatre with those closest to the stage paying more than those furthest away. Thus Stalls seats were 1s. Second seats were 6d and Back seats were 3d. Balcony seats had two prices at 1s and at 6d, though there was no indication concerning the relative position of these.[36]

The conversion of the hall to a picture theatre had required alterations both for regulatory reasons and for comfort factors. Fortunately, the Durham County Advertiser re-ported the changes in great detail.

> "The interior presents a very attractive appearance, and looks quite warm and cosy with its buff-coloured ceiling and walls and smart crimson dado. A striking feature of the interior decorations are the Renaissance embellishments which adorn the panelled walls. These ornamentations which are both chaste and effective are emblematic of music and art, and appropriately enough include the city coat of arms. Their beauty is further enhanced by handsome floral festoons, which with the rest of the renaissance work are pricked out in white and stand out in bold and striking relief on the buff groundwork of the walls. This particular work has been entrusted to the celebrated firm of London artists, Messrs. Gaze and Co., a firm well known in the realm of theatrical decoration. A new plush stage curtain of green and gold lends an added warmth and colour to the interior decorations, and we believe that we are correct in saying that Mr. Rushworth has new seating in preparation. Visitors to the Assembly Rooms this week are loud in their praise of the decorations, and it is to be hoped they will show their appreciation in a practical manner by rallying round Mr Rushworth and giving him bumper houses throughout the coming season. The exterior of the building has been treated with buff-colouring and the glass entrance doors glisten with the attentions of the painter and decorator"[37]

The first week's film fare is also fully described -

> "The programme includes the great gunboat picture *Lt. Rose, R.N.* showing the pluck of an English Officer; *Borrowed Clothes* is descriptive of how an artist goes to a dinner in another man's clothes; *The Vintage Season* is another magnificent coloured spool, well worth seeing; *The Skating Carnival* caused roars of laughter; whilst *The Cloister's Touch* shows one what poor slaves had to undergo in olden times. In *A Sticky Proposition* two children are showing what fun they are having at the expense of their father. *The Girl and The Judge* is a picture with plenty of excitement in it. *Calino Amongst The Cannibals* causes laughter from start to finish."[38]

The manager was C. H. Ford and the orchestra was under the direction of J. W. Pinchen. At various intervals, musical diversions on a number of musical instruments were provided by Miss Cissy

Clamp.[39] There were two houses nightly and a full programme matinée on Saturday afternoon.

In the description of the second week's programme the reviewer, no doubt using the theatre publicity for his guide, declared on the quality of the projection. "The pictures are steady and clear with an almost entire absence of that flickering which is often met with, to the detriment of many an otherwise good exhibition. The programme should be seen by all lovers of cinematograph displays, and these pictures quite justify the claim of being the largest and best ever shown in Durham." He was also able to assure potential audiences that the weekly change of programme meant that they had "no fear of seeing the same film twice."

Once again, the proprietors looking to client approval for their activities donated the Tuesday evening takings equally between the Durham Lying-in Charity and the County Hospital. "There were not such large houses as one would like to have seen, although we understand a fairly substantial sum was handed over for the benefit of each of the above named objects." [40]

Actualities of boxing films had been eagerly sought after by exhibitors since the earliest days of cinematograph, so it is not surprising to find that the Jack Johnson v. Tommy Burns World Heavyweight championship fight was captured on celluloid. But it *is* surprising that it was billed as the main film in the week of 12th September at the Assembly Rooms 18 months after the actual fight had taken place on 28th December 1908, in Sydney. It received much notoriety because it was the first time that a black American had held the title - such a ferocious fight that, towards the end of the fourteenth round, the police had to step into the ring to stop Canadian Tommy Burns from receiving any more injuries. 'The film clearly represents the great fight in every detail,' said the Advertiser reporter.[41]

The Wells' involvement in the Assembly Rooms was only the prelude for a Rushworth take-over. From 19th September, the adverts read 'Life Motion Electric Pictures, Proprietor T. Rushworth'.[42] There was no change in pricing but by the end of the month, it was decided to make the weekly change of programme on Thursday. The newspaper proposed that its readers should give him the support they had given to the previous enterprise.

The up-to-dateness of the Assembly Room programme can be illustrated by the advertising of 25th November. Films in the Clarendon Co's *Lieutenant Rose* series had appeared regularly. *Lieutenant Rose and The Chinese Pirates* that week had only been released at the end of October. The reviewer gives the whole plot away!! "Lieutenant Rose and some ladies are captured by Chinese Pirates, their timely rescue following the Lieutenant's dog swimming from the prisoners to the ship. This splendid picture shows the subsequent blowing-up of the pirate's stronghold by the ship's big guns." The other highlighted films were *The Girl from Arizona* "a fine thrilling Western drama, *The Little Mother at the Baby Show* a film full of pathos, whilst the comedy was provided by *Seven Days*, *The Two Julians*, and *Two Bears*.[43]

ASSEMBLY ROOMS

THEATRE, DURHAM.

PROPRIETOR......................T. RUSHWORTH.

LIFE MOTION
ELECTRIC PICTURES.

COMMENCING

MONDAY, SEPT. 19. Every

7. EVENING 9.

POPULAR PRICES: 3d, 6d, 1s.

The Piano in use is supplied by Miller and Son, 71, Saddler Street, Durham. Agents for Bechstein and all leading Pianos.

Mr. Rushworth Takes Over. *Durham Chronicle, 16th Sept 1910*

A mysterious entry had appeared in the trade magazine *The Bioscope* for 18th August 1910: "T. F. McDonald one of the pioneers of pictures in the North and Ralph Allan have secured a valuable site in the centre of Durham where they intend to build a first class picture theatre capable of seating 2,000 people. Plans have been prepared and, pending approval of the local authority, building will proceed at once." There is no local newspaper reference, and no extant planning application in the Records Office, but an illustration appeared in the Newcastle Illustrated Chronicle of 17th August 1910. Frank Manders, the Newcastle cinema historian, confirms that the partners referred to had opened Tyneside cinemas at this time.

The proposed building in Claypath Durham *from* Newcastle Illustrated Chronicle *17th August 1910*

Picture houses were proliferating throughout the county. In Spennymoor, Gowland's Arcadia Electric Palace had opened on Monday, 1st August to a packed audience.[44] The Tivoli in the same town had also recently opened. Mr. Sleep, the proprietor, advertised his shows as 'Sleep's Splendid Scenic and Side Splitting Specialities', and his wit and enterprise drew large audiences.[45]

In the same week that the Durham City Assembly Room changes were announced, magistrates granted a cinematograph licence to J. Gibb for the Olympia, Church Street, Murton. A previous inspection had found the exits to be inadequate, but Superintendent Best now stated that these were now within the regulations. The licence permitted the presentation of films and variety acts.[46]

The Shakespeare Hall, North Road was the venue for a 'cinematograph entertainment, Living Canada' in October.[47] The ticket prices of 1s, 6d and 3d seem rather steep for an educational presentation, but there was a children's special show at 5 p.m. for 1d. The hall was not normally licensed for such shows and the organisers would have needed to give notice to the Chief Constable if the machine was using flammable stock. A number of 17.5 mm. sub-standard film gauges on non-inflammable stock had existed for several years but they were very rare. Non-flam 35mm. stock, which had been available for many years, was largely shunned by the film industry. It is more than likely, therefore, that the lecturer, A. Ward, a Fellow of the Royal Geographical Society, would be using a portable 35mm. projector, and that the hall would have applied for a casual licence. The presence of John Wilson, M.P. at the show must have given in it a high profile. It is unfortunate that none of the applications for casual cinematograph licences, and for travelling showmen's permits, appear to have survived.

At the end of October, Mr. Rushworth demonstrated that he hadn't completely abandoned live theatre at the Assembly rooms. For three days, Wilson Barrett's play *The Sign of the Cross* was presented by a 'specially selected London Company'. Prices of admission were almost double those for the film performances, though after nine o'clock tickets were half-price!! [48]

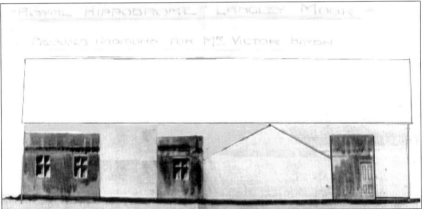

The only surviving plan for the Royal Hippodrome, Langley Moor submitted in 1912 when additional exits were constructed. *(Plan 001733 30 August 12 DCRO.)*

The Durham Chronicle announced the opening of the Royal Hippodrome Electric Theatre, Langley Moor on the previous Monday 11th November 1910. The wooden building was 86 feet by 40 feet. Its corrugated iron roof must have provided some additional sound effects on rainy evenings! It was provided with tip-up seats and a raked floor, and for the comfort of patrons was heated with electric radiators. A 12½h.p. Crossley gas engine provided the DC current for the projector. The proprietor, Stanley Johnson of Whitley Bay, spent approximately £1000 on the construction and handed the operation of the enterprise over to licensees T. Scott and W.H. Barnard. The report also went on to say that the projector operator was J. Bell and that on the opening night there was a six-piece orchestra. The seating capacity was indicated as 800, but in later licensing applications, after the alteration of the stage, this had been reduced to 455.

1911

The seasonal appearance of Randall Williams' Cinematograph Show in the Market place ended in recrimination. At the time of his arrival, he had already had some opposition voiced to his presence. The December application for his May visit, presented by his agent Mr Hoadley, had only been granted conditionally. He was requested to regulate the smoke from his chimneys, and warned that should the Coronation of George V take place at that time the permission would be withdrawn.

Randall Williams' Cinematograph Show circa 1911. Note the traction engine on the right of the picture. *National Fairground Archive.*

Randall Williams' road locomotives at Bishop Auckland in 1909.
National Fairground Archive.

It would seem that his show was in the market place at the time of King Edward VII's death and that this seriously obstructed the general public's view of the Proclamation. In February, he was still there, to the consternation of the residents. They presented a memorial to the city council and asked for some action. At a city council meeting, Cllr Caldcleugh said that the memorial, which was presented by a very large population of rate-payers and residents in the city, was couched in such courteous, and reasonable terms, that the committee recommended that the proprietor of the show be asked to terminate his visit.

The following full text of the memorial is extremely interesting because it gives the dimensions of the Randall Williams Cinematograph Booth:

"Gentlemen, We the undersigned residents and occupiers of premises in the Market Place desire to strongly protest against the action of the Durham City Council in allowing the market place to be used as a stand for shows for an extended period. We are certainly of the opinion that no one should be allowed to remain for more than a fortnight at any one time and that there be considerable intervals between such lettings in order that so confined an area should be constantly blocked as often now happens.

At the present time there is standing in the Market Place a show 32 yards by 16 yards, two large dwelling vans, two huge road locomotives and a kitchen erection, and these quite apart from the noise of the organ and the emitting of volumes of smoke from the chimney constitute an objectionable nuisance. and an eyesore. We understand that the show has permission to remain for a period of three months from the time of entering which is wholly unnecessary as the city provides ample amusement of all kinds to the general public They felt that whilst Mr. Williams and his show were at any time welcome, he had this time spent too long a period to be pleasant to those who lived in the market place. There had been a considerable amount of dissatisfaction expressed for some weeks past and it had terminated in the memorial"

Other councillors agreed with the sentiment. The Chairman said that he has spoken with Mr. Williams on the previous night and he (Mr. Williams) had said that on account of the bad weather, he was unable to leave. He was not staying out of spite but because it was difficult for horses to travel. He assured the Chairman that he would leave for Bishop Auckland at the first opportunity. Alderman Pattison suggested that a small committee should be appointed to meet whenever shows were going to make an application. He moved that the committee should consist of The Mayor, Alderman Ferens, Alderman Proctor, Councillor Caldcleugh and Councillor Dickinson.[49]

The residents of Willington had a new picture palace, the Empire, on 2nd February, 1911. News of the conversion of the original hall had been signalled in the previous September and the original plan was for an opening date of October 24th.[50] For the first night, the 'commodious hall' was packed to its 1000 capacity. It was fitted out with the latest tip-up seats and supplied with electricity from a dynamo supplied by Holmes & Co. of Newcastle, and driven by an 18 horsepower gas engine. Gaslights were also fitted in case of emergency. The pictures were projected by means of a Butcher & Sons No.2 Empire cinematograph. With a 70ft throw, this gave an 18ft wide picture at the screen. The hall was also fitted out with a stage for variety turns and in the opening week Messrs. J. W. Sutherland and Gornall Fox provided the musical entertainment. The film programme was to be changed every Thursday.[51] Despite these opening accolades, the cinema did not advertise its programmes in the newspaper.

Another cinema in the neighbourhood was doing good business. So great was the throng at Cottrell's Thornley Picture Palace at the bottom end of Hartlepool Lane on Saturday 4th

February 1911, that over 200 people were unable to gain admission. The actual programme was not itemised, but the local reporter described it as 'above the ordinary quality'.[52]

Wheatley Hill was also in the news with the announcement that the new Miners' Hall was about to be fitted out with cinematograph equipment.[53] The imminent opening may have prompted the Revd. P. T. Casey, curate in charge at Wheatley Hill parish church, to ask his parishioners not to attend any Sunday openings of picture shows. He said that it was a bad way of ending up their Sunday. "God is not in the picture shows. It is all very well for people to say this and that and the other about the pictures being sacred, and so on, but I am confident that they served no good purpose by being shown on Sunday."[54]

Alfred West was still trying to keep his travelling exhibition of 'Our Navy' films going despite the growth of picture halls. At least, now he and his son didn't need to carry their own projection box. Their appearance for one week at the Assembly Rooms in February prompted the Advertiser columnist to declare - "Teaching Patriotism by pictures. That briefly is the main object at which Mr. Alfred West, F.R.G.S. appears to aim in a truly remarkable entertainment which he is billed to give at the Assembly Rooms for the whole of next week." He also added that the orchestra under the direction of Julian Fredericks played descriptive music.[55] His 'popular' prices at 2s, 1s, 6d and 3d (limited) were an increase on the normal Assembly Rooms cinema prices, but even so, it was reported that at some houses numbers of people had to be turned away.

The Langley Park Hippodrome, Langley Street, which had been on a mixture of live acts and film, switched to cinema at its re-opening on Monday 20th March, 1911. The building is described as being 75ft x 40ft with a stage frontage of 30ft. Its construction, consisting of corrugated iron with an internal lining of wood, sounds particularly flimsy. The proprietors are listed as Messrs Dixon & Winter, and their enterprise, at least on the opening night, was met with a full house.[56]

The Medical Officer for the Rural District of Chester-le-Street, Dr. Taylor, in one of his reports, had come to the conclusion that with every village now seeming to possess a picture hall, theatre or dance club, there was an endeavour to lessen conception. It was much easier to attend these places of amusement he thought untrammelled with infants, he observed, and those keen for amusement and holiday-making were not keen upon children!![57]

Langley Park New Hippodrome. *Illustrated Chronicle (Newcastle) 2nd April 1911*

The Palace Theatre was progressively increasing the number of films that it included on its bill, though its compliance with the Cinematograph Act had been questioned when it applied for renewal in February. Head Constable Kerslake indicated that corridors and passageways were allowed to be crowded at times. As a condition of the renewal Mr. Rawes promised to keep them clear.[58] In March it was reported that moving pictures were becoming very popular, and that they were interspersed with smart and enjoyable turns. Four films were listed for the first week in April, *Philamon and Bancis* (historical drama) *Jones' Nightmare* (a comedy by Acme Films (GB) 435 ft with Fred Rains), *Suspicion* and *Great Call* (dramas).[59]

The popularity of films is again indicated by the fact that W. Wilson, the Monte Brothers (Randall Williams) and Mrs. Paine, all had their cinematograph booths at the Durham Easter Fair in April.[60]

By May, advertisements for Cottrell's Perfect Pictures and Smart Varieties appeared.[61] The week before, his enterprise at the Thornley Palace was terminated when the wooden building was demolished to make way for a brick and stone structure.[62] The Advertiser reported,

"Mr. Cottrell, well known caterer of amusements in and around Durham, has taken on the management of the Palace for an indefinite period and commenced the first show on Monday evening, which we are sure will do him infinite credit. He is exhibiting a really magnificent set of pictures whilst varied turns are given by several equally accomplished artists."[63]

The cinematograph licence was transferred to his name on 8th June, 1911.[64]

The policeman who had been in charge of the supervision of the Cinematograph Act in the city and county for the past eighteen months, Superintendent W. W. Dunn, was selected to be the Head Constable of Durham. He was himself the son of a local police superintendent and had been educated at Durham School.[65]

In the week of Superintendent Dunn's promotion, his successor must have been gained some satisfaction from the results of a fire at the Tivoli Picture House in Spennymoor. On Thursday night 25th May during the first performance, the film stuck in the gate and immediately ignited. The fire was confined to the operator's box, and though most of the film was burned, the operating machine was practically undamaged. The alarm was raised and the packed audience was safely evacuated from the building in one-and-a-half minutes. The fire brigade was quickly on the scene but was not required. There was a cautionary note to the report that the noise of the fire alarm had brought crowds of people into the street causing some delay to the arrival of the fire crew. The manager at this time was Alfred Burrows, the projectionist was J. Bullock and the pianist was J. Irving.[66]

The Palace film programme continued to please the Advertiser

THE PALACE, DURHAM

MONDAY, MAY 15th, 1911, AND DURING THE WEEK.

COTTRELL'S PERFECT PICTURES AND SMART VARIETIES.

7.   EVERY EVENING   9.

PICTURE MATINEE EVERY SATURDAY AT 3.

Conspiracy, in the reign of Henry VIII.

Starring Engagement of **VIRTO and VENITA**, in a Refined Musical Act.

Pleasing Appearance of **JESSIE WILTON**, Character Comedian.

Special Engagement of **VICTOR and LOUIS**, Comedians, in

"**The Golfer and the Caddie.**"

ENTIRE CHANGE OF PICTURES ON THURSDAY, INCLUDING

The Spy, Sensational Dramatic Picture of Military Life in Warfare.

―――――

Popular Prices   -   -.   -   3d, 4d, 6d, 9d, and 1s Each.

reporter and it even prompted him to talk of 'high-class' entertainment.

This may have been prompted by the fact that a film version of Marie Correlli's novel *Thelma* was included. This 1000ft production made in June 1910 by the American Thanhouser Company starred Alphonse Ethier as Viking Olaf and Anne Rosamond as Thelma. Though almost completely ignored by modern literary critics, Marie Corelli (Mary Mackay) still has a following amongst science fiction aficionados. At the time of the film's release, her novels were known for sublimated sex, fervent religiosity and far-fetched fantasy.[67]

The Assembly Rooms now had positive competition and they came up with a Whitsunday Holiday Special. Despite the fact that there was a spell of almost tropical weather, there were nearly full houses each night according to the Advertiser report. The main film was called *The Train Wreckers*, the story of how a brave signalman saved an express from a band of train robbers. The Thursday films contained a screen version of *The Lyons Mail*, a play that had featured the Assembly rooms stage on several occasions in the recent past. Re-named *The Courier of Lyons* it starred the noted French actor Monsieur Rivet in the dual role of Lesurquay and Dubois. Made by Pathé, its 30 scenes were filmed on the actual sites of the hundred year-old crime. It had a running time of 45 minutes, and the reviewer thought that this film alone was worth the admission price. Indeed he reckoned that the arrival of the longer adaptations of novels was a new departure for the cinema. In the following week, the Vitagraph three-reel version of Dicken's *A Tale of Two Cities* starring Maurice Costello, Norma Talmadge and Florence Turner, would be the attraction.[68]

But, of course there was nothing like newsreel photographs of the Coronation of King George V to really have the town talking –

"The biggest attraction which Mr. Rushworth has as yet secured for his Assembly Rooms patrons is the Coronation procession in London and the Coronation naval review at Spithead, which are being shown this week. The London pictures have been included in the programme since last Friday and large houses have applauded what is undoubtedly the finest film ever seen in Durham. The picture was again shown on Monday, Tuesday and Wednesday, when there was added to the bill of fare a set of pictures depicting the naval review at Spithead. As the King and Queen pass through the streets of London in their State coach drawn by the famous eight cream horses, the enthusiasm of the crowd could not be restrained, and loud cheers rang through the packed hall from end to end. As their majesties smiled left and right to the cheering London crowds the Assembly Rooms audience caught the infection and rising to their feet greeted them with a hearty rendering of God Save The King. The various nobilities in the Royal procession were easily noticeable, "Bobs" receiving a hearty round of cheers as the Field Marshals in their glorious uniforms rode across the screen. From the London procession, with its unparalleled scenes of splendour, the audience were spirited away to Spithead to the wonders of Britain's mighty Armada. Every important feature of the Royal progress through the mighty aggregation of warships was faithfully filmed, and cheered to the echo by a delighted and enthusiastic audience. This picture will be shown all the week in both houses. On Thursday, there was the usual change of programme, and in addition to the Naval Review a dramatic photo play entitled *The Strike At The Mine* was billed. It is a splendid picture, and one which is sure to please. Other films are: *Toddles the Scout*, (comic), *Champion Wrestlers of Japan* (a fine sporting subject), and *Thwarted Vengeance* (A sensational Essanay Western dramatic). It should be made clear that despite the enormous cost in securing the Coronation pictures there is no extra charge for admission, the prices standing as usual - 3d., 6d, and 1s."[69]

In July, as usual the Assembly Rooms closed for two weeks renovation and cleaning and re-opened on August Bank Holiday

Monday with what was described, again, as a as a Special Holiday Programme. Their new advertising slogan was 'THE HALL MARK OF PICTUREDOM'. The film programme included *The Still Alarm* 'The greatest fire scenes ever filmed' 995ft, *The Shelling of the San Marcus* - destruction of an old Battleship 482ft, *A Child of the Wild*, a Bison western drama 955 ft, *Alkali Ike's Auto*, an Essanay Comedy Western 1000 ft, and *How Bella Was Won*, an Edison dramatisation of Charles Dickens' *Our Mutual Friend* 1000ft. The listed films alone account for over one hour's running time.[70]

The Palace programme that same week featured the titles of twelve films and three musical acts. The length and variety of the programme can be judged from this almost complete listing.[71] -

EVER THE ACCUSER,	Reliance	Drama	965 ft
THE STILL ALARM,	Selig	Drama	995 ft
A DREAM WITH A LESSON	(not known)		
THE BRAGGER,	Pathé	Comedy	660 ft
TWIN ROSES*	Hepworth	Comedy	550 ft
THE WRITING ON THE BLOTTER	(not known)		
CAPTAIN BARNACLE'S COURTSHIP	Vitagraph	Comedy	965 ft
TRYING TO GROW,	(not known)		
LOST AND WON,	Selig	Drama	1000ft
THE SAVAGE	Nestor	Comedy	560 ft.

If the two unknown films made up one reel between them (1000ft), then the programme length would have been 6,595 feet or almost 1 hour and 50 minutes running time. With the addition of the live acts this would adequately have filled the two and half hour programme. Most of the films had a July release date, and all but one were foreign.

The full and meticulous reporting of the programmes at both venues is testament to the wide patron interest, and the intensity of the advertising is an indication of the desire for the popularity to continue. Each week patrons are urged to arrive early at the Assembly rooms to avoid disappointment. The local reviewer endorses quality - "The ever-growing popularity of Mr. Rushworth's Theatre continues. Good wine needs no bush and certainly the Assembly Rooms Pictures require no recommendation at our hands"[72] The Palace advertisements seek a certain intimacy with their audience by calling all their films 'Our Animated Playlets' and the live interludes as 'Our Artists'.[73]

When picture halls were first opened, they tended to be the enterprise of single entrepreneurs. Some of these obtained group protection by continuing their previous affiliation to the Showman's Guild. With the rapid growth of the exhibition side of cinema, the proprietors in this area had formed themselves into the Northumberland and Durham Picture Hall Managers Association. In July, this group decided to affiliate to the national body, the Cinematograph Exhibitors Association, which had been formed in 1908 as a 'defensive and a promotional organisation'.

The Durham County Advertiser of 22nd September gave space for a full report on the re-opening of the Pavilion, Esh Winning-

"Partly rebuilt, and wholly re-modelled, the theatre at Esh Winning - henceforth to be known as the Pavilion presents an attractive exterior and an interior which for comfort and embellishment is quite equal to any similar building in city or district. Mr. G. T. Storey, of Cornsay, merits congratulation in providing Waterhouses and District with such an elegantly equipped building, and the entertainment and the enterprise this gentleman has shown will doubtless be fully appreciated, providing, as it does, a long felt want in the neighbourhood. The general scheme of decoration was greatly admired on Monday evening. The proprietor and Mr. Hogg, the manager, had issued invitations to representative bodies of the district and influential gentlemen. These were provided with accommodation in the circle. Other patrons crowded the remaining portions of the building, and when Mr. M. Curry, manager of Messrs Ferens and Love's Cornsay Colliery, declared the building opening, the scene was one of immense enthusiasm." "The accommodation was estimated at 800, and whilst he hoped every care would be exercised by Mr. Storey to guard against danger, he, the speaker, was informed that under such contingency the building could be emptied in two minutes. He had great pleasure in declaring the building open for entertainment, accompanied with his best wishes for its success. Mr. Storey responded and thanked Mr. Curry for opening the Pavilion, and for the crowded patronage that was associated with the ceremony. They would do their best to give comfort and enjoyment (cheers). After the singing of "God Save The King", the programme was proceeded with. Each picture was enthusiastically received and the films reflected on the screen were exceptionally clear, especially when it is considered that everything was new. Miss Nora Chrena, a mezzo soprano, sang in an accomplished and pleasing manner. Amongst the pictures on show this week were:- *Big Hearted Jim; The*

Standard, Unexpected Review, a fine military comic; *Manning's Ghost,* a fine travel picture, and &c.

PAVILION WATERHOUSES, ESH WINNING

PROPRIETOR .. .. .. G. T. STOREY. | MANAGER .. .. W. HO

THE HOUSE OF LATEST PICTURES AND FINEST VARIETY AT POPULAR PRICES

MONDAYS AND SATURDAYS, TWICE NIGHTLY, 6-45 AND 8-45.
TUESDAY, WEDNESDAY, THURSDAY, AND FRIDAY, ONE HOUSE NIGHTLY,
Commencing 7.30.
The Hall is distinctly the Most Up-to-Date in the County, being Brilliantly Illuminated and
Decorated, Comfortable and Warm.

The newspaper advertisement for the opening contained a somewhat indistinct photographic block of the building. For clarity, this has been combined with a slightly later photograph of the building. *From the George Nairn Collection 1912*

The first announcements for the New Electric Theatre, on Commercial Street, Coxhoe appeared in the Durham County Advertiser on 29th December, 1911, but the report in the next week's edition would seem to indicate that it had been open for some time before this. "Two full houses expressed their hearty approval on Monday night and again on Tuesday. The popularity of the theatre increases each week".[74] The purpose built hall had accommodation for 400 people and its proprietor and manager,

Gordon Gray, must have been well pleased with its initial popularity and the publicity afforded it.

NEW ELECTRIC THEATRE, COXHOE.

PROPRIETOR   ..   ..   GORDON GRAY.

SPECIAL ATTRACTIONS NEXT WEEK.

ZIGOMAR. THE GREATEST PICTURE EVER SHOWN, 3,000 FEET FILM.

AMOR AND ROMA, in their Refined Vocal Scene.

GREAT SELECTION OF COMIC AND DRAMATIC PICTURES

SIXPENNY SEATS CAN BE BOOKED IN ADVANCE—THREEPENCE EXTRA.

Time and Prices as usual.

Durham County Advertiser January 6th, 1912

The programme was changed twice weekly, and commonly was made up of a collection of short comedies and dramas probably occupying about 80 minutes projection time - *The Capture of Fort Ticondenago, The Cattle Rustler's End* – Western Drama; *The Backwoodsman's Suspicion* Western Drama; *The Half-Breed's Sacrifice* Indian Drama; *Bertie's Reformation* Comedy; *Betty Becomes a Maid* Comedy; *Wealthy Brother John* Comedy (Hepworth 650 ft) and *By Aid of a Lariat* Comedy.

There were also items by the Acmes, a musical group that the reviewer thought was 'sufficient entertainment in itself'. There was an orchestra, but there is no indication of its duties. The cinematograph licence included opening for a special children's matinée on Saturday afternoon and Sunday evening performance of 'suitable pictures'. Its sixpenny seats could be booked in advance for an additional three-pence. The second week of advertising announced the showing of a 3,000ft film *Zigomar*. This would have taken just under an hour to project.

The hall was closed for a short time in April of 1912 for improvements to be made in the seating. At this time *two* evening performances were inaugurated.

Cottrell's Pictures at the Palace Theatre in Durham put on a special New Year's Day treat for local children. Invited youngsters filled the hall, and it was reported that the door-keepers let in other poor children 'out of sympathy'. Altogether 650 children were catered for with 'delicacies consisting of coffee, buns and oranges followed by a splendid programme of pictures'.[75]

In the second week of January, the Assembly Rooms showed *"The Great Mine Disaster - A Tale of a Miner's Love and Heroism."* Since the subject matter was of significant local interest, the reviewer quoted liberally from the publicity brochure –

> "This is a most realistic subject, bold in conception, perfect in detail and vigorous in action. Add the romance, danger and heroism so connected with a miner's life and the result is a combination of dramatic force and human interest, which is certain of success. The wonderfully realistic manner in which the setting of this drama has been got up, and the impressive scale of the staging, justify us in proclaiming it to be one of the boldest and most successful pieces of its kind ever produced."

The newspaper advertisement for the film indicated that it was 2,420 ft in length.[76] The Assembly Rooms certainly seemed to be capturing the quality programmes at this time. The beautifully stencilled Pathécolor films were a regular feature. A Three Musketeers film, *The Queen's Necklace*, was played in January, and the same company's *Romeo and Juliet* (2,500ft) filled the main slot in February. In May, there was a rare treat with Sarah Bernhardt's *La Dame aux Camélias*. This 2,319 ft film had been playing to crowded houses in London, and such was the expected demand for it in Durham that it was possible, unusually, to book your seat at the Assembly Rooms.[77]

In February, the Advertiser had reported that despite the excellence of the programmes at the Palace patronage had diminished.[78] It was not surprising then, that, when Cottrell's contract with the proprietors expired in June, he did not renew it. His departure was announced with some regret by the Advertiser. Both houses on June 13th were be set aside as a benefit night for the manager, George Haines. He was taking up a similar post in Barnsley.[79]

Mr. Rawes was taking over the management again and he supervised a major cleaning and re-decoration programme. "So much so," said the report, that "on Bank Holiday evening, patrons will be charmed with the pretty, cosy interior. Mr. Rawes has again spared no pains in adding comfort to this popular place of amusement." The bill of fare once again included more live items than films. The orchestra was to be under the direction of T. H. Hodgson and the pictures were to be described by J. O. Ormiston.[80]

A Film Describer on a postcard posted in Cleethorpes in 1909. *Author's collection.*

Cinema lecturers, or picture describers, are rarely mentioned in cinema histories, and yet they were an important appendage to the shows. Though increasing literacy in the general public decreased the need for their services, film narrators brought distinctive styles to their task, and some became nationally famous for their apposite and witty commentaries. A number of booklet guides to good narration were advertised in the trade journals and some films were rented with a printed synopsis to assist relevant story-telling.[81]

In the same week that the Palace re-opened, the Assembly Rooms now announced itself as *The Ideal Picture Playhouse; The Hall Mark of Picturedom.* Its twice-nightly programmes would commence at 7 p.m. and 9 p.m. and there would be a complete change of programme on Thursday. The first three days of the week were largely devoted to a programme of shortish subjects, whilst the latter part was mostly reserved for multiple reel films. Topical events were still considered to be crowd-pullers -

"The picture *Army Airmen* shows the War Office test of flying machines on Salisbury Plain which will prove as interesting to the Assembly Rooms audiences as they did to the Members of Parliament before whom the actual tests were made. Another interesting picture is that recording Mr. McClean's record waterplane flight on the Thames from Eastchurch to Westminster. This is a fascinating film and Dunelmians are afforded an equal opportunity of witnessing the latest development in flying as the vast crowds who on Saturday lined the banks of the Thames. Another picture dealing with a subject that has been prominently brought before the public is that entitled *The Boy Scouts' Funeral* which shows the last sad ceremony at Walworth following the drowning disaster off the Isle of Sheppey. Other pictures of the series are *Railway Disaster* which pictures the terrible collision in the Lozanne [sic !] Tunnel near Lyons and *Italy's Fighting Men*.[82]

The Hippodrome, Thornley.

A contemporary postcard of the new Picture Hall. *Author's Collection*

The Hippodrome at Thornley opened on Monday 23rd of September. The proprietor was Thomas Thompson of Middlesborough, who already had a chain of 15 more halls and stated that he intended to run the cinema 'on the boldest of town lines'. There would be a programme of films and two 'turns'. The building itself had accommodation for 1000 people; 400 in the pit

(3d), 400 in the stalls (4d), and 200 in the overhead gallery (6d). The Advertiser reported- "The seats are arranged in the latest picture hall idea, the pit in front, the stalls behind and the circle above furthest away from the screen, so that no flicker of the pictures is observable."

The chairs and the benches were all of the cushioned pick-up type. There was a rake on the floor of 5ft from back to front, so that there was no interruption of view. In many picture halls, the noise from the motors generating the D.C. current for the projector arc lamps gave rise to complaints. The Hippodrome designers had attempted to reduce this by placing them under the stage. There were two dressing rooms for male artists and two for ladies. An electric fan in the roof was intended to ensure a clear atmosphere, and the heating was supplied by the National Radiator Company.[83]

The so-called 'Sunday First' programmes at the Electric Theatre, Coxhoe were exceedingly popular. Though the subject matter was supposed to reflect the sacred nature of the day, the programme for Sunday 29th September was headed by the film *Blazing The Trail*. Perhaps there may have been objection to this programming, since the film for 17th November was announced as *The Judgement of Solomon*, a recently released 1300ft Pathé film.

More picture hall activity in the Durham area led to the Grand Opening night of the Empire, Ushaw Moor on 18th November 1912. The design of the building was by Fred W. Storey, son of the managing director, G. T. Storey of Cornsay Colliery. The newspaper report of the building is worthy of quotation in full: [84]

"It is a brick building of noble structure, ideally situated and its interior comfortable, luxurious and charming. The facade of stone has a striking appearance. Over the entrance doors is the name of the building in stained glass. The entrance hall is of beautiful design, and erected to deal rapidly and easily with the crowd, no matter how large.

Over the box-office is the manager's section. From there by aid of windows, the stage or entrance can be viewed. The hall is lofty and its roof affords much pleasure to the artistic eye, having many exquisite paintings. The walls are distempered and on either side are panel paintings of old Durham - one of the Cathedral and boat-house and the other of Framwellgate Bridge. It is heated by steam radiators. There is seating accommodation for 800 to 900 people and all can view the performance with comfort. From the proscenium, the floor is gradually sloped. The lesser-priced seats are on the ground floor and have leather upholstery. The circle contains nine tiers of tip-up plush chairs. On either side of the circle are boxes chastely decorated and a study in comfort.

A Photograph of the altered frontage of the Empire Cinema Building in 1997

EMPIRE, USHAW MOOR.

PROPRIETOR ..   .. O. T. STORY. | BUSINESS MANAGER ..   .. W. HOGG.
                ACTING MANAGER ..   .. H. McDONALD.

USHAW MOOR'S LUXURIOUS PICTURE PLAYHOUSE.
PLEASING PROGRAMMES AT POPULAR PRICES
LIFE MOTION PICTURES AND FINEST VARIETY.
GRAND OPENING NIGHT, MONDAY, NOVEMBER 18th, 1912.
TWICE NIGHTLY, 6-45 and 8-45.
DAN MAXFORD'S THREE CASINOS—Kitty, Frank, and Reg.
One of the Neatest Acts in Vaudeville. They just begin where others leave off. A Real Treat.
Don't Miss Them.

GREAT LAURIE Britain's Foremost Ventriloquial Artiste, presenting his Wonderful and Extraordinary Act, introducing his own exclusive novelties. Great Laurie walks amongst you.

The opening advertisement - Durham Chronicle November 15th, 1912

A large fire-proof operating room is placed at the rear of the circle, where up-to-date pictures will be projected by an electrically driven Nucentric Kalem [sic] machine.[85]

Much care has been exercised in the design of the proscenium. In the flood of the light, this portion of the building largely contributed to the general charm of the interior. On the right is the musician's room and on the left a room from which the whole of the electric lighting can be worked. Under the direction of Mr. G.T. Lewis, Station Road, Ushaw Moor the electrical equipment has been installed. The scheme of lighting is quite new. The centre of the building is wired from the top thus dispensing with side lights and relying solely on ceiling lighting.

OPENING OF THE BUILDING

There was a huge crowd to witness the opening of the building which took place on Monday evening. Mr. M. Curry, J.P. manager of Messrs Ferens and Love's Cornsay Colliery, performed the ceremony. He said he could not understand why he was so much in request. He could only account for it by having taken part in the opening of the Esh Winning Pavilion. That had been such a huge success that the proprietors thought similar good fortune would attend the Ushaw Moor Empire. He certainly desired the Empire to be a success, and this had caused him to respond to Mr. Storey and his partner's wishes. The building was very beautiful and quite exceeded expectation. It was second to none in the neighbourhood. It had his best wishes for success, and if that night's house could be any guide it was a success already. The building had been erected under the supervision of a very great friend of his. Mr. Storey, to whom he referred, was a very painstaking man. All they saw that night was simply perfect. The accommodation was such as to meet the needs of the district and the exits in case of fire met the requirements under the Act. It was a building erected for amusement, and he hoped no one would have any cause to regret spending a few hours under its roof. (Cheers) Mr. Cecil Lyddon, musical director responded on behalf of the proprietors, and expressed pleasure at Mr. Curry's kind words. He thought that the sporting and pleasure seeking instinct was very great in the North, and, therefore, did not think there was any doubt of their support. Subsequently, Mr. R. McDonald, acting manager, announced that Mr. Lyddon and party would open the programme with a march, specially composed by the musical director for the occasion of the opening of the building.

Dan Maxford's three Casinos headed the variety poster, their dances were especially clever and received rounds of applause. The bright and catchy choruses are likely to be heard later. Great Laurie had a wonderful ventriloquial [sic] performance. Associated with his act was much novelty and humour. As an entertainer, he is quite in the forefront. *Dr. Gar El Hama* was the star picture. Being a Nordisk film it quite maintained the high reputation of these producers. It dealt with the running to earth of a poisoner. *Eyes That See Not* was a tale of a long strike in which want and poverty overcame the stubbornness of the owner of the mill. *Target Practice of the Atlantic Navy, U.S.A.* was a very interesting film. Two amusing films concluded the entertainment which passed off without a hitch. Mr. Alan Wardle deserves a word of praise for the success attending the picture operation and Messrs W. Hogg and R. McDonald for the splendid arrangements at this new Ushaw Moor enterprise."

The Empire had twice nightly performances on Saturday at 6.45p.m. and 8.45 p.m. In the week, there was only one performance at 7.30 p.m.[86] Sunday opening with specially selected films began on 15th December 1912 commencing at 8 p.m.[87]

The regulations for Sunday opening were spelled out at the Durham Petty Sessions in February 1913.[88]

1. The hall must not be opened before 7.45 p.m. and must be closed at 10 p.m.

2. The manager shall submit to the Superintendent of Police for his approval before 10 o'clock on Friday in each week the programme of pictures to be shown on the following Sunday, and no deviation from the programme will be permitted.

3. Pictures of a sectarian or comic character must not be shown, and there must be no sectarian or comic singing of any kind.

4. The usual charges for admission to the various seats must be made and there must be no collection.

5. No persons shall be employed in or about the hall on Sunday against their will. The management must give an undertaking that the engagement of employees will be for weekdays only, and that refusal by any person to working on a Sunday will in no way affect his or her employment on week days.

6.The manager shall do his best to maintain good order and decent behaviour in the hall during the hours of public performance.

7. Police officers in uniform or plain clothes shall be admitted to the building at all times during public performances.

Sunday opening was only permitted in some Durham county cinemas. Licences granted for the City and for the Lanchester Divisions did not permit Sunday Opening

The question of what constituted a sacred picture was debated both in the local council meetings and in magistrates courts. In January 1911, at Royton police court in Lancashire, the manager of a picture hall in Shaw was summoned for breach of the

Cinematograph Act. A police sergeant had visited the hall on a Sunday night and asked the manager to point out which parts of the programme were sacred. When the manager could not identify any section, he was told he would be reported. In his defence, the manager through his solicitor said that even though the pictures could not be described as sacred they did have a moral purpose. He offered the information that he only knew of three absolutely sacred pictures that were available for hire. It was for the magistrates to decide if a picture was sacred or not. It might be sacred or semi-sacred even if it was not a Biblical picture. The magistrates accepted the manager's promise not to show anything but sacred pictures in future under threat of a £20 if he appeared again on the same charge.[89]

Morality and the Cinema was very much a topic of discussion amongst regulatory bodies during 1913. The British Board of Film Censors had begun its work on January 1st. Its first president, the ageing G. A. Redford, a former bank manager, had been part of the Lord Chamberlain's Office as an Examiner of plays since 1895. It seemed logical that there should be a discerned continuity between the censorship of drama and the censorship of films. The Board was set up by the Film Industry itself and was financed by a sliding scale of fees paid for each film reviewed. An article in *The World's Fair* described some aspects of Mr. Redford's own views on film content. He indicated his aversion to such subjects as - "mixed bathing pictures; "faked" pictures of disorder; dog fights; scenes of unnecessary cruelty; undignified treatment (by picture) of high officials; and lachryimous [sic] funeral scenes." [90] In its first year of operation, 7,488 films were submitted for examination. 6,861 were given a Universal certificate, 627 per classed as "A" certificate films, and exception was taken to 166. After editing and resubmission only 22 of these were rejected entirely.[91] Despite the introduction of this certification principle, there is no indication of it on any of the Durham cinema advertisements during this period. It would seem that the regulations only required notification on the picture hall premises.

Durham itself was still without a purpose-built picture hall, but the situation was about to change. The Durham County Advertiser described how plans for two theatres in Claypath had not been pursued, and schemes for two picture halls in North Road had recently been submitted. One of these for the Durham Cinema Company had been approved and the building was taking shape on the site of Messrs Kell's joinery workshop.[92]

In obvious anticipation of the competition, the Assembly Rooms Theatre was re-furnished by Mr. Rushworth to the obvious satisfaction of the Advertiser reporter –

"Following the re-seating and alterations just completed, the Durham Assembly Rooms now easily ranks as one of the best equipped picturedromes in the North. The entire hall, both upstairs and down, has been re-seated, and arrangement has been made by which the better class seats are now at the back, and the cheaper seats at the front. This obtains at all up-to-date pictures halls, and the wisdom of such arrangements is obvious to all who have sat too near to the screen. To obviate any discomfort to front seaters, Mr. Rushworth has taken the screen back several feet., and thus flickering is reduced to a minimum. The seats are all of the latest tip-up variety, whilst those in the balcony are pneumatic and present the acme of comfort. The floor downstairs has been raised towards the back, and the slope now affords a capital view of the screen from all parts of the building. Patrons are delighted with the alterations and Mr. Rushworth's solicitude for their comfort and convenience is having its reward with bumper houses."[93]

The big attraction the week after it's re-opening was *The Fighting Parson*, a 3,000ft drama from the Barker Film Company and their Ealing Green Studio. The story, based upon fact, concerned a disowned heir taking the blame for his brother's illegitimate child, joining the church and fighting the local slum bully.[94] Though given very little prominence in British film histories, the Advertiser reviewer, clearly quoting from a publicity hand-out, went overboard in its praise -

"Judging by the spontaneous, enthusiastic, and hearty tokens of appreciation laudably expressed by Press and public, "The Fighting Parson" reasonably stands for the most notable achievement in the variety world in recent years. It has been unanimously acknowledged to be a drama, tinted with humour, wit and tender pathos, and like most things wherein merit alone aims, the story is founded upon actual facts and incidents. Laughter, tears, excitement and cheers. All these expressions of human interest find favour as the meaning of its various realistic scenes make themselves manifest. It is of interest to know that many prominent members of the clergy have from time to time witnessed the performances, and have been quick to recognises the immense possibilities of the play - morally and intellectually. Indeed, it is from this source that has prompted Mr. Gray to produce the play upon the film. This has entailed considerable expense, and no less than 250 people have been engaged in the production. Notwithstanding the great expense, Mr. Rushworth has been put to in securing this film, we understand there is no increase in prices of admission". [95]

The Assembly Rooms also sought to increase its clientele by filming and screening local events. A football match between the Durham Taverners and the Police at the Hollow Drift Ground was filmed on the Wednesday afternoon April 9th and the next evening. On April 26th, Mr. Rushworth was given permission by the university authorities to film the procession during the installation of the Duke of Northumberland as Chancellor of the University.[96] When the film was shown on Monday May 5th, its content was described -

"Chief interest in the programme at the Assembly Rooms Theatre this week centres in the picture of scenes in connection with the installation of the Duke of Northumberland as Chancellor of Durham University last Saturday. A large audience assembled to witness the reproduction and many to see if they could discern themselves among the multitude of people. Mr. Rushworth is nothing if not enterprising and his latest success is worthy of the highest praise. The distinguished men of State and Church, of science and of letters are seen assembling in the quadrangle, and later leaving the castle entrance on their way to the cathedral service. Another glimpse of them is obtained when accompanied by members of the Officer Training Corps they are seen entering the grounds of Hatfield Hall. Gownsmen are very prominent upon the screen."

When the Globe Theatre did announce its opening for Monday 5th May, 1913, the event was described in detail by both the local papers.[97] We learn that the building was designed by Messrs Shewbrooks, Kell & Wylie of Newcastle-on-Tyne, and constructed by Messrs Jasper Kell & Sons. The electrical equipment was supplied by the British Westinghouse Company of Manchester and fitted by Messrs Carr & Co. of Newcastle. The interior decoration was by the local firm of Hopper & Sons, "the effects produced being of a most pleasing description, the scheme being reminiscent of the early Georgian period." The furniture was supplied by Messrs Harkers Ltd. [sic!] of Sunderland.[98] The uniforms worn by the attendants were supplied by J. M. Lynch of Durham.

The building was 70 feet in length and 25 feet in width, with a gallery at the rear. The Chronicle suggested that its dimensions were 'rather bijou in size'. There was accommodation for about 500 spectators. There were tip-up seats in all parts of the house. In the gallery, the seats were divided into threes "to prevent the inconvenient 'wedging', which is so frequently noticeable in places of amusement." The exits were sufficiently numerous and wide to enable the hall to be cleared rapidly in the event of any mishaps.

The opening performance was attended by the Mayor and Mayoress of Durham in front of 'a large and delighted company':

"The projected image was clear and steady and the film programme entertaining and enjoyable. Mr. Jasper Kell offered a few words of welcome on behalf of the management. The management, he said, had delegated to him the duty of thanking those present for their patronage. He hoped the building and equipping of the hall would provide the public with a comfortable place of entertainment and would meet with their approval. The programme which would be submitted that evening had been carefully selected and procured at a large expense. The management were particularly gratified for the attendance of the Mayor and Mayoress, and he therefore called upon him to perform the duty of declaring the building open.[99]

THE GLOBE CINEMA HALL,
NORTH ROAD, DURHAM.

SUBJECT TO THE GRANTING OF LICENCE, THE MANAGEMENT HAVE PLEASURE IN ANNOUNCING

The Opening OF THE ABOVE HALL ON **Monday, 5th May,**

With an Expensive and Up-to-Date Show of the **Latest Films** by Reputed and Well-known Makers,

Commencing 6·45 p m.   Doors Open 6·15 p.m,

UNDER THE PATRONAGE OF

THE MAYOR AND MAYORESS OF DURHAM.

Second Performance, 9 o'clock.

ADMISSION - - - - - **3d, 6d, 1/-.**

The opening advert. Normal times of perform-ance were 7 o'clock and 9'oclock. Durham County Advertiser *May 2nd 1913*

The entrance of the Globe Cinema can be seen at the left of this 1914 postcard. The auditorium was reached by a covered corridor. *Author's Collection*

The Mayor, (Councillor R. McLean) said that in recent times picture halls had become a tremendous craze in the country, and one could not help but marvel at their remarkable success. It was evidence of the fact of the great and growing demand for entertainments of that kind, and, without doubt, they served a useful purpose. In Durham City with its large surrounding population, there was no doubt room for another picture hall, and he trusted the promoters of the Globe would reap the reward they deserved for their enterprise. He understood it was their intention to secure the very best pictures obtainable. He was glad that a conspicuous feature of the picture hall was to be the week's record, whereby people at home could follow very closely the events that were happening in various parts of the country. His Worship concluded amid loud applause, by formally declaring the new picture hall open. Other guests at the opening were Alderman Herring, Alderman Brownless, Alderman Proctor, Councillor Lumsden, and The Head Constable.

The first film thrown onto the screen showed the building of the great water aqueduct at Los Angeles. This was followed by a film of a journey from Harben to Yokohama. The main film was *The New Magdalene*, 'a fine dramatic subject'. It was accompanied by two comic films, *What Katie Did* and *Taking Care of Baby*, and *The Fugitive* a Western picture describing an exciting man-hunt. A coloured photographic slide of the Mayor and Mayoress was also projected. A long queue was waiting outside for the second house.

The change of programme on Thursday included *A Human Target*, depicting a gypsy girl's hairbreadth escape from death, and how she is saved by her lover's marvellous skill under trying circumstances: *A New Cure for Divorce*, a Thanhouser honeymoon comedy 'introducing a novel and hilarious situation'; and *The Transgression of Manuel* an exciting Western drama. The Saturday matinee would begin at 2.30 p.m. with prices for children at 2d, 3d, and 6d and normal prices for adults.

The Durham County Advertiser of 20th June 1913 promised, in describing the programme at the Assembly Rooms, and almost in the words of the music hall interlocutor, 'the pleasures of pictorial perfection'. The Assembly Rooms, themselves, spoke of their offerings as 'The Picture Pastime to Perfection'. Whilst describing their current programme as *The House of Mystery* in two parts, *The Cycling Policeman*, *The Little Tease* and *The Latest Animated News*, they also had space to advise that next week they would be showing *East Lynne*, and George Grossmith and Phyllis Dare dancing to the Tango, with special music.[100]

The Globe also gave prominence to *The Little Tease*, a modest 1½ reel film, directed by D.W. Griffith and released in America in April 1913. Their publicity also promised 'the finest Comic and Dramatic Films available'. It seems that they were trying to match the hyperbole of the exclusive showing of the Italian epic *Quo Vadis* at the Palace; 'Beauty, Fascination, Magnificence and Power'.[101]

The Pavilion Waterhouses had 'Up-to-date Pictures and Finest Variety at Popular Prices', and the Empire, Ushaw Moor in their 'Luxurious Picture House' had 'Pleasing Programmes at Popular Prices' and a challenge to enter the grand rope climbing competition!!

Cinema rivalry was certainly heating up and newspaper reports were allies in the enterprise –

"This week the variety artiste is conspicuous by his absence from the bill at the Palace, and the sole attraction is "Quo Vadis," which has been described as the monarch of spectacular plays. It was a bold experiment on the part of Mr. Rawes to dispense with the varieties and confine the entertainment to a play depicted on the screen and lasting nearly two hours. The success which has attended the innovation proves, if proof were necessary, that the proprietor knows the business of catering for the public taste thoroughly. Up to the time of writing the audiences have been large and the bookings for the remainder of the week are highly satisfactory. Newcastle gave "Quo Vadis" a big reception and Durham has followed suit. Words fail to convey the beauty, the fascination, magnificence and power of the production, and its claim to be considered a masterpiece in the world of picturedom is well founded. These who have seen the play "The Sign of The Cross" should not miss "Whither Goest Thou?" There is a similarity between the plays, and in each case the teaching is good. In fact "Quo Vadis" is calculated to have more effect on the spiritual side of life than many sermons which are delivered from pulpits." The latter part of the review clearly reveals that there was only one projector in the Palace box. "There are six scenes with a very short interval between them, and the whole time, the audience is spellbound. The spectacle is an impressive one, and we would advise our readers to avail themselves of the opportunity of seeing this remarkable picture-play. Vivid scenes are the burning of Rome, and the sacrifice of the Christians. The attention of the spectator is riveted from start to finish.[102]

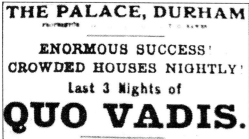

Durham County Advertiser June 20th
1913

The moral tone of *Quo Vadis* was somewhat invalidated by the reviewer's emphasis on two of the more violent episodes in the film. A report of the county education committee in July seemed to condemn the atmosphere in the cinema. A correction to this report was made by T. W. Powell in the letter a week later.[103] He indicated that he was referring to the possible breakdown of hygienic conditions in entertainment houses, and he was at pains to point out that he was not referring to any particular establishment in the locality.

Bank Holiday Week in Durham was replete with entertainment possibilities. On the Sands, Jones' Portable Theatre, which had been touring the towns and villages of England since 1882, played to crowded houses with Mrs. Henry Woods' *East Lynne*, despite its recent celluloid exposure, and the expected arrival of another film version on 15th August. The Assembly Rooms had a two-reel version of *Dr. Jekyll and Mr. Hyde*. The Globe had *1812* with a promised rendition of the overture by the Globe Orchestra. The Palace had four short films interleaved with a strong bill headed by Marie Santoi's musical comedy *A Night in Japan*. The Hippodrome, Langley Moor re-opened after a closure of several weeks with a mixture of 'Star Pictures and Artists'. The Pavilion Waterhouses, with its ceiling fans claiming to make it 'the coolest place to be on a hot night', was featuring South Shields-born boy comedian and future British film comedian, Albert Burdon. The Empire, Ushaw Moor had been re-decorated, and ceiling lights had been fixed in the auditorium. The entrance, too, had been enhanced with artwork by the manager R. McDonald.[104]

A 1912 edition of Pictures Magazine, which began publication in 1910.
Author's collection.

In Chester-le-Street at the licensing magistrates' court, Mr. Turnbull on behalf of the various picture halls in the district was seeking permission for the halls to open on Sundays. The Chester-le Street urban district council on 17th July had passed a resolution approving Sunday opening as being beneficial to the district, and they urged the magistrates to give the matter favourable consideration. Houghton-le-Spring colliery officials said that they got a better percentage of men attending on Monday mornings when the picture halls were open on a Sunday evening. He had a petition in favour with 6,000 signatures, and he did not know any opposition except from some of the religious bodies, and he was informed that at the Durham Road Central Primitive Methodist Church a resolution was passed in favour. He very much questioned whether the opposition was in the true interests of religion because if all the Churches and Chapels were filled there would still be a surplus of population who had to go somewhere else. These performances did not clash with attendances at churches since they would not commence till 8.15 p.m. There would be no turns of any sort and the pictures would be of a sacred and historical character. Councillors and representatives of the management of Grange Villa, South Pelaw and Pelton Collieries attended the hearing and spoke in favour of Sunday opening. The Revd. A. B. de Moleyns said he was in favour of the halls being open on Sunday nights after church services subject to certain restrictions concerning the content of the programmes. The police representatives appeared to be at odds. Inspector Barlow spoke in favour, but Superintendent Gargate thought they certainly should not be open between May and September. The Methodists too seemed to differ since the Durham Road Primitive Methodist and the Central Wesley were both objectors along with the Wesley Guild, Congregational Church, the Pelton Church, the U. M. F. Church Pelton Fell, and the Free Church Council Pelton Fell. The magistrates decided to grant the application under the conditions previously accepted by Durham County Council for such eventualities.[105]

A fortnight later, however, the situation was reversed. On August 13th, the chairman of the Chester-le-Street Bench, N. H. Martin, said that personally he was disappointed that the restriction had been removed. "He himself had not frequented picture halls, but he had seen one religious picture treated from a showman's point of view. And it was a travesty of a religious subject and not calculated to raise the morals of the public. The programmes that had been submitted for exhibition on Sunday in his view were not suitable for showing. The other magistrates then examined the titles of the submitted programmes and came to the same conclusion."[106]

When the Assembly Rooms was showing Barker's five act film *East Lynne* in the week of August 18th and advertising its star actress, Blanche Forsythe, as 'the greatest English Emotional Actress', the Globe countered with the information that Miss Anna Nielsen 'The Celebrated English Emotional Actress' could be seen in the film *Spanish Blood*. How many of the audience would have known that Miss Nielsen was Danish and that the film *Der Tod in Savilla* (Death in Saville) had been made in Germany?

It is possible that some would be more knowledgeable than the Globe expected. The first film fan magazines were beginning to appear and the first card set featuring film stars was already loaded into the packets of Major Drapkin Cigarettes.

Film stars in the 96-cigarette card set of Cinematograph Actors issued in 1913 by the Major Drapkin Tobacco Company. *Author's collection.*

A technical innovation new to Durham was launched at the Palace in the week of August 25th. Hand-coloured and stencil-coloured film had been common since the early years of the century, but Kinemacolor was one of the first of the natural colour processes. Though there seems little natural about film taken via rotating red and green filters at 32 frames per second, and then projected on to the screen by a similar mechanism. The natural part was that it was the action of the light itself that produced the tonal variations rather than the action of a paintbrush or a toning agent. The machine had first been demonstrated as long ago as 1908, but its first commercial showings didn't take place until April 1911 at the Scala Theatre London. Its most prestigious achievement was the filming of the Coronation of George V in June 1911 and the Delhi Durbar in 1912.[107] Since the process required a special projector and operator, the Kinemacolor Company only negotiated the exhibition of their products to one picture hall in each location. The Palace devoted a whole week and its entire programme to the presentation, and for several weeks afterwards some Kinemacolor films were shown as one part of the programme.[108]

Montage of Kinemacolor advertisement and souvenir programmes.
Durham Chronicle August 22nd 1913

The Advertiser gave the show a considerable amount of pre-publicity - "Kinemacolor spells the last word in coloured photography and is the only process in existence which reproduces actual scenes in living vivid colours. Every tint and tone from fore-ground to horizon is reproduced - the green of verdure, the colours

of rocks, the blue of the sea, the purples and greys of distant hills".
Of course, the complete spectrum was not possible from a two-
colour filter system, but this did not prevent the impact of the
system from registering its audience.

The main feature of the programme was the presentation of the
Durbar before King George V and Queen Mary. When shown in
London, each of its two parts lasted three hours. In Durham only a
portion of the journey to India and the pageant of the procession in
Delhi was shown. Other factual films shown were a travelogue on
the Panama Canal, scenes of a Spanish Bullfight, life in Lapland,
the Carnival in Nice, and views of an Italian Lake. Two fiction
films, *A Girl Worth Having* and *Mumps*, were also included.

The Hippodrome, Langley Moor applied for a dramatic licence
so that it could be the venue for plays, and temporarily suspended
its mixture of variety turns and films. In the week of 26th
September it presented Harvey and Stanton's London Sketch
Company in *The Coiner's Crib*.[109] The advertising tag 'A Play of The
People – For The People' appeared to pay off, for the newspaper
reports over the next few months reveal well-patronised houses.

Dramatic presentations on the screen were also attracting much
attention. In the week of 15th Sept, the Assembly Rooms had a film
version of a famous production of *The Miracle.* Though the cast of
the film was almost identical to the 1912 London production, the
film was, in fact, made and directed by Max Reinhardt in
Germany. The presentation had a musical score by Professor
Englebert Humperdink and vocal effects, and it was described in
the advertisements as 'a lyriscope play in colours'. Such was the
expected attendance that the Assembly Rooms introduced booking
for all seats.[110]

The Sunday opening of picture halls was the main topic of a
meeting of the Durham Free Church Council in the schoolrooms in
Crossgate. The main speaker, the Revd. H. Fletcher, was reporting
on his attendance at a conference in Swanwick. The message from
this conference was that there should be unity on the question of
the desecration of Sundays. The chairman, the Revd. J. Hooley of
the Bethel Chapel, seemed to be alone in his contention that they
ought to begin agitation for the closing of picture halls altogether.
One speaker suggested that if picture halls were open that the

magistrates should exercise their rights in supervising the content of the programmes. Mr. Clifford of Sacriston Primitive Methodists said that in his area there was no such supervision. J. Adair, jnr. said that in his district, two miles away, two cinemas opened on Sundays but there was no effect upon congregations as the opening was after service. The chairman said it was a deplorable state of affairs that members of any churches should go to the picture halls on a Sunday night. When questioned about his opposition, by Mr. Adair, he said that it was a desecration of the Lord's Day, and that if a man went to the pictures on a Sunday he was not as good as he would have been if he had stayed away. Mr. Adair held the opinion that men went with their families to the picture halls whereas they might have been in pubs and clubs on their own. Of the two evils he thought that they had chosen the lesser one. George Peart repeated the notion that colliery owners had reported less absenteeism in areas with Sunday shows. The debate ended with Mr. Clifford of the Primitive Methodists stating that they had not got to the point of Sunday opening in Durham city, and that, with the Church of England being opposed to it as well, there was little likelihood of it being permitted.[111]

Ironically, the Globe was showing 'The Great Morality Play' - *Satan* for the whole of the week. The Chronicle's evocation of the film countered the arguments of some members of the Free Church Council. "When animated pictures first made their appearance some years ago, the prophecy was then advanced that some day they would be turned to account in the matter of influencing the public for good. Judging by the class of pictures displayed on the screen at the Globe this week, it would appear that the day has arrived for nothing but real good can result from the exhibition of the admirable subject of *Satan*."[112] The reviewer's description reveals its content. "The story of evil through the ages. Part One Adam and Eve, Cain and Abel, The Tower of Babel, Christ entering Jerusalem,...Pilate washing his hands. But the sensitive will find no scenes of the scourging or the crucifixion of Christ. There is the conquest of evil beneath the star of the Sepulchre. Part Two Satan in Medieval Times. Part Three portrays the evil of drink Part Four shows evil today with the influence of Satan on two lovers Joe and Mary. Not a dull moment from start to finish."[113]

The Assembly Rooms as a part of their programme were showing *What Happened To Mary*. This series of Edison films starring Mary Fuller is often referred to as the first serial film, though each had a self-contained story. The Advertiser reviewer was impressed by the film: "One becomes more interested and excited every minute, and feels a genuine pang of regret as the picture fades from the screen."[114]

Though there had been no previous indication that the Central Co-operative Hall, Meadowfield had been used for cinematograph performances, a report of its re-opening on Monday 29th September 1913 revealed that the operator's box had been fireproofed and the hall redesigned to comply with the number of exits required by the Cinematograph Act. The hall itself had been built by the Co-operative Society in 1902, and for many years it was acclaimed as being the finest dance hall in the area. Locally, it was only ever referred to as 'The Hall'.

The Central Co-operative Hall, Meadowfield: Brandon & Byshottles Co-operative Building. The cinema entrance was by the advertising board to the left of the picture, and the hall was on the first floor.
From a postcard in Durham City Library Collection.

The cinematograph arc-lamp had to provide sufficient light to project the image on to the screen, 100ft away. Extensive alterations also included a new side entrance, a gangway leading to the dressing room, and an increase in the size of the stage. The first-floor entrance to the auditorium was completely altered to give the floor an adequate rake and an up-to-date pay box was added. J. Craven of Newcastle-on-Tyne carried out the work at a cost of £700.

There was a good attendance for the re-opening by Mr. Eddy, president of the Brandon & Byshottles Co-operative Society. The programme was normally a mixture of live acts and films.[115]

The Palace Theatre, Wheatley Hill was opened on 20th October with James Porter as manager. The newspaper reported a packed house, but gave no indication of the programme content. The proprietor is listed as George Alfred Harker of Jesmond.[116] The Co-operative Hall at Sherburn Hill had also opened as a cinema at about this time with Andrew Kerr Mack as its manager. In 1915, he became manager at the Palace. [117]

More literary drama filled the bill at the Assembly Rooms in the 13th October week. Pathé's 2½ hour (11,000ft) version of *Les Misérables* could only be shown with one house nightly, the only supporting item being episode 4 of *What Happened To Mary*. On the Wednesday afternoon, scholars from Durham School were given a 'very enjoyable' private view.[118]

The Durham Chronicle reviewer, no doubt prompted by the publicity brochure, took a slightly different stance for *Cleopatra* being shown at the Globe on 3rd November. "This moving picture does not purport to be realistic," he declared, "it is a romantic idealisation of the Queen of Egypt and must be considered as such. The treatment is designed to attract and interest through its beauty of thought, pictorial arrangement and dramatic nature, and its profound respect for those qualities in womanhood which are little understood by man and to which sympathy is rarely extended by a prudish world. Above all the object has been to record in pictures a story of this wonderful woman which should not jar nor injure the tenderest susceptibilities."[119] Despite his caution, 'a large and enthusiastic audience' flocked to the cinema to view this 6,000ft film and to 'participate in the delights of the story of one of the most remarkable figures in history.' Cleopatra was played by Helen Gardner, one of Vitagraph's most valued stars. [120]

The international nature of the silent cinema is signalled by the fact that neither the reviewers nor the advertisements stress a film's country of origin. Thus the French film *Fantomas*, the German films of Henny Porten and the Danish films of Asta Nielsen are not distinguished from those of American origin. A touch of nationalism creeps in when in British films are commonly identified as such.

A novel magazine tie-in provided the audience at the Assembly Rooms with a challenge. The advertisement declared *See The Tit-bits Great Nameless film* but the Advertiser reporter was more coy about the origin. "The green cover of a popular weekly

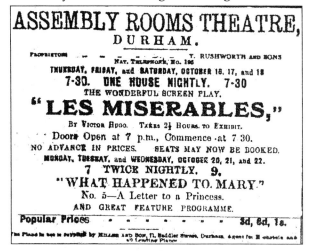

publication was much in evidence at the Assembly Rooms on Monday evening. This publication offers £100 for the best title to a serial story, a picture of which was shown on Monday and created considerable interest. Nobody would be more delighted than Messrs. Rushworth if one of the numerous patrons was successful, but admittedly the task is by no means an easy one. An original title of not more than five words is what is required. The story was exciting and the pictures remarkably clear, so clever was the production and yet the majority of the audience found it impossible to unhesitatingly name a suitable title."[121]

The Chronicle offered the information that "The principal characters are a Spanish spy and his wife, a Cuban insurrecto and a Cuban woman. The story itself is very exciting and should prove a great attraction." Patrons were informed that it was only being shown on the first three days of the week.[122] In the Northern area, besides its Durham venue, the film was being shown at the Assembly Rooms, Darlington on 12th December, the Royal Electric Palace, Dipton on 30th December, the Theatre Royal, Blyth on 5th January, the Empire, West Hartlepool on 12th, the Royal Hippodrome, Langley Moor on 16th, and the Palace, Gateshead on 19th January. Details of the competition rules, a fairly detailed plot synopsis and entry form appeared in the 1st November and subsequent editions of Tit-bits.

In February 1914, the winner was named as painter and decorator, Henry Smith of 11, Polar Place, Tredegar, Monmouthshire. His winning title was *Behind the Clouds of Battle*. He had sent in twelve suggestions. Both he and the Queen's Cinema, Tredegar received £100.[123] The film, 2,700ft long, had been made by the 101 Bison company and was distributed in this country by Ruffles Exclusives.[124]

Winter weather hampered the opening of a cinema at Tudhoe. Severe gales caused a great deal of damage in the Spennymoor area and at Tudhoe Colliery the wooden structure of an almost completed cinema was totally wrecked. The proprietor, Percy V. Morton, had intended to open it in time for Christmas, It was eventually rebuilt and opened as the Electric Picture Palace in 1914.[125]

A summons before the Durham District Magistrates in December, 1913, is an interesting revelation of the popularity of Sunday Cinema attendance. Ernest M. Tweddle of West Hartlepool, the licensee of the Shotton Colliery Picture Hall, was charged with contravening the Cinematograph Act by allowing the gangways of the hall to be obstructed. On Sunday night 16th November, Sergeant Clark said that he had visited the hall and found it over-crowded. In the right-hand side gangway there were eleven persons and two attendants standing and in the left hand gangway there were seventeen persons and a lady sitting in a chair. The manager agreed that the hall was too full, adding that people came in whilst he was up in the operating box. Joseph Smith, for the defendant, said that the chief object of the Act was to keep the exits clear, and on the night in question there were eight persons in the hall over its capacity. Women who took their babies to the picture hall often left their seats and stood in the gangways to pacify the infants when they became restless, and men went there when they wanted to smoke. The exits, he understood, had been kept perfectly clear. The manager of the hall said that there was seating accommodation for 460 and on the night there were 468 persons present including 51 children. At some period of the performance the bulk of the people in the gangways had been seated. The magistrates found against the defendant and fined him 20s with costs.[126]

The Shotton Picture Hall had had something of a chequered history. The manager and proprietor Fred Robert Hodges had opened it on Front Street in February 1911 as the Electric Empire. On 6th February 1913, when the licence was due for renewal, Superintendent Thompson objected on the grounds that not all the exits had panic bolts fitted, and that the hall was not in a safe condition. Mr. Hodges said that all the *exit* doors had got panic bolts. The one that hadn't was an ingress door. Plans had been passed for alterations to be made. Supt. Thompson said that the hall was in a filthy state, and the magistrates decided not to renew the licence until things were put in order.[127] On 8th March 1913 the cinematograph licence for the hall was transferred to J. S. Nicholson. The police superintendent reported that everything in the hall was now in order.[128]

Activities in other county cinemas and theatres were reported in the Durham Chronicle of 31st October and in the showman's magazine 'World's Fair' of 1st November. The New Princess Theatre at Seaham harbour opened with accommodation for 1000 people in its spacious pit, four boxes and circle. The manager appointed had previously been manager at the Wingate Empire Theatre. The Miner's Hall at Annfield Plain was entirely destroyed by fire in the early hours of 28th October, although the caretaker's house was saved. The damage, estimated at £9,000, was covered by insurance, but no explanation of the cause of the fire was given.

The presentation of films featuring local events still held the utmost attraction. The 5th December Durham Chronicle reported two crowded houses at the Assembly Rooms on the Monday of the previous week. "The film that attracted most attention was undoubtedly the visit of the Queen to the aged miners' homes of Ushaw Moor, Middlestone Moor, and Shincliffe. The pictures were remarkably distinct and several people were recognisable. Ever since its production, the film has proved a most gratifying attraction, and the enterprise in securing it has had a well-merited reward."

An amusing but revealing instance of the social effects of cinema attendance surfaced in the Durham city magistrates court in January, 1914. John Ord, a mason of Bowburn, was summoned by his wife for desertion. The court heard that when Mr. Ord returned from a football match at Newcastle somewhat under the influence of drink, he found the fire out and no supper ready. His wife, Martha, was out of the house at the picture hall. When she returned with her sister, he threatened them both and she left the house saying she would not come back. The magistrate dismissed the case saying that if the woman would not go to the pictures so often, and he not go to too may football matches, they might be happy!![129]

The police supervision of Sunday cinema shows was discussed in the Durham county magistrates court in February. Superintendent Waller said that according to the regulations the programme content had to be delivered to his office by 10 a.m. on Friday but this gave him little time to consider them. In some instances programmes that were submitted were not adhered to. He was having to spend a good deal of time and trouble on this business when he had other duties to perform. The magistrates granted the licences for another month and hoped that managers would correctly observe the regulations.[130]

The Seventh Day, a British film made by the Regent Film Company and released in February 1914, had a plot very relevant to the Sunday Opening debate. The hero of the film meets with an accident because his favourite picture house was closed on Sundays. One report gives the location of this story as Northumberland, and the trade of the young man as a steel-worker.[131]

The Assembly Rooms included some special presentation in the early part of the year. The Italian Ambrosio production of *The Last Days of Pompeii* was shown for six nights. Patrons could book their seats for "this beautiful and spectacular film, introducing 15 lions, 50 horses, 5 boats and thousands of individuals. It is wonderfully impressive. The production is perfect in every detail and the great scenes of the eruption of the volcano must be seen to be believed.[132]

A week later a documentary film dealing with the work of sanatoria was shown. Film taken at the Home Office Sanatorium in Benenden, Kent, showed the progress of the movement for the prevention of tuberculosis. The showing appears to have been sponsored by the Durham County Insurance Committee. A special matinee was given on the Wednesday afternoon in aid of St. Catherine's Home, Durham at 3p.m. with a Ladies Orchestra conducted by Bernard Hahn.[133]

On Monday, 9th March the main film at the Assembly Rooms was *The Old Wood Carver*. This was the first film produced at his Bushey Studios by the artist Sir Hubert von Herkomer. Set in 14th-century England the drama is said to 'give a picture of the home life and surroundings of the craftsmen of the middle ages.' The wood carver was played by Sir Hubert himself, and the film was directed by his son Siegfried. After making only four films Sir Hubert died and production ceased. The Durham County Advertiser reporter says that the film has added interest because Durham Town Hall's art collection boasted a good example of the artist's work. The painting of Baron Hershell is still maintained in the Town Hall.[134]

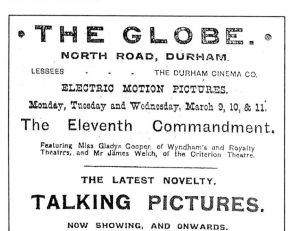

THE GLOBE.

NORTH ROAD, DURHAM.

LESSEES   -   -   -   THE DURHAM CINEMA CO.

ELECTRIC MOTION PICTURES.

Monday, Tuesday and Wednesday, March 9, 10, & 11.

The   Eleventh   Commandment.

Featuring Miss Gladys Cooper, of Wyndham's and Royalty Theatres, and Mr James Welch, of the Criterion Theatre.

THE LATEST NOVELTY.

TALKING PICTURES.

NOW SHOWING, AND ONWARDS.

At the Globe Cinema, the novelty of Talking Pictures formed part of the programme for several weeks from 2nd March 1914. The titles in the first show were *Away Back Home* 'a darky minstrel song', and *The Ragtime Violin*.[135] "Both," said the report, "were capital talking pictures and the effect produced was very realistic." On the opening night there was a full house and there were 'bumper houses' on the Tuesday and Wednesday. A week later, the singing picture *The Land I Dunno Where* received rounds of applause at its completion.[136]

The device used to synchronise the gramophone recordings with the films was the Vivaphone, from the Hepworth Manufacturing Company. The synchroniser had a vertical pointer, the position of which was set by two electromagnets at each side. One was fed with impulses from a contact breaker on the gramophone side, and the other with pulses from a contact breaker fitted to the projector drive-shaft. The projectionist needed to turn his projector handle so that the needle remained vertical. The device was simple and effective and could be fitted to any projector at a cost of five guineas. Each film was made by artists miming to a pre-recorded disc. This allowed them to move about the scene without restriction; a technique not yet possible with contemporary microphone devices.[137]

Adverse criticism of the effects of cinema attendance was still evident. A coroner's inquest in Durham heard that a Darlington schoolboy had travelled to Durham and put himself under a train by the Redhills cemetery. His father said that it was his son's habit to attend pictures halls. The pictures seemed to very much impress him, and he could always vividly recount and recall what he had seen. The Coroner suggested that some of the pictures might not have been of a very instructive nature, and the father said that his son had told him he had seen men knocked down by trains. The Coroner, clearly not a frequenter of cinemas, further reflected that "one of the evils of the picture halls was that there was a good deal of revolver firing on show and sometimes they showed the ways of clever burglaries and that sort of thing." In his summing up, however, he was less harsh and suggested that since there were no picture hall proprietors present, it would not be right to say hard things in respect of them.[138]

Another court case in Durham provided interesting information concerning the financing of cinemas. The projectionist of the Empire Electric Theatre, Wingate was accused of stealing the takings for Friday, Saturday and Sunday night, less the money paid out to the artists. The amount was £31 15s 2d. It was stated that the man's weekly wage was £2 plus 5% of the takings. He was found guilty of the theft, but not guilty of another charge that he attempted to set fire to the theatre to conceal his crime.[139] The sum quoted probably represents the takings for five houses, two each on Friday and Saturday and one on Sunday. If the average ticket price could be seen as 4d (6d for adults and 3d for children) and assuming that the overall takings would have been in the region of £36, then it is possible to suggest that the audience on each night would have exceeded 400 people. In 1912, the seating capacity of the Empire was 600.

The Palace increased its publicity and its film content for one week in March with the exclusive showing of the Barker's film *In the Hands of The London Crooks*. "The Programme of the Season," declared the advertisement. "Sport, Drama Villainy and treachery in 4 sensational reels." The term 'Exclusive' was appearing more and more in trade negotiations. Cinemas and circuits could take up certain attractive titles exclusively in their area, and these did not appear on the open market until the exclusive period was over. Interestingly, this particular film had been released in December 1913, and thus enjoyed four months of 'exclusive' exposure in other places before arriving in Durham. Made at Barker's Ealing studios it starred Thomas MacDonald, Blanche Forsythe, Fred Paul, Roy Travers, Dora de Winton and J. Hastings Batson. Its story concerned the life of a disowned gambler who became a military hero in Afghanistan, and returned to win at Goodwood.[140]

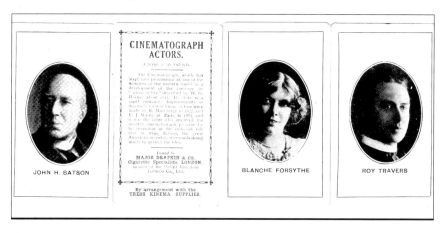

Some of the actors of *In the Hands of the London Crooks* in the 1913 cigarette card set from Major Drapkin.

A number of cinemas attempted to overcome the opposition to Sunday opening and, by the same token, exemption from the Cinematograph Act regulations by securing non-inflammable films for showing on that day. But, there was a shortage of titles on this kind of stock, and it was not unknown for managers to slip the odd flammable film in with the safety stock. The Spennymoor Town Hall Co. Ltd. was prosecuted for this offence. On 1st March, Superintendent Brock had visited the Town Hall and saw some films exhibited. At the close of the programme he examined the films and found two of them were inflammable and three of them were non-inflammable. The defendants admitted showing the films but said they were not aware that they were incorrectly labelled until the inspector tested them. At his point, the inspector tested some film stock in court to show the difference between the films. It is quite clear that the manager was trying to hide his guilt, for when questioned about the length of time a flammable film could be in front of the lantern before it ignited, he said a minute or half a minute. The inspector said that ignition would take place in four seconds or less. The magistrates found against the proprietors but amazingly, accepted the manager Mr Hills' ignorance of the conditions and dismissed the case with costs of 6s 6d, hoping that the defendants would take more care in future.[141]

The change in cinema programming moved the Chronicle reviewer to say that at the Globe "the major portion of the performance is generally occupied by what is known as the important picture of the evening."[142] Occasionally a special element shifted the emphasis. In June, a cameraman employed by the Assembly Rooms took scenes of the student 'rag' procession as it meandered through the town. Though the procession did not finish until after 4 p.m., the film was processed and ready for projection in time for the evening performance at 7 p.m. "It was accorded a magnificent reception; various people were easily recognised and the film was a splendid success."[143]

The pleasures of the hot 1914 summer were observed to have affected audiences. Referring to the Royal Hippodrome, Langley Moor programme, the Chronicle reporter said, "Many managers of music halls have had to record a decrease in takings chiefly arising from the fact that patrons have preferred outdoor to indoor entertainment. This is not to be wondered at, but at the same time, the up-to-date manager has to take the rough with the smooth. There are some outstanding turns this week. The pictures are good, too." But, at the Globe, "the intense heat of Monday did not prevent a large audience from attending to witness a series of pictures which will rank amongst the best display ever seen here. Another edition of *Fantomas* has created interest. When the film was announced the audience was agog with expectation.[144]

No fairground cinematograph booths for the Miners' Demonstration were listed in the *Worlds' Fair* for 1914, but the Assembly Rooms clearly recognised a possible audience on the day and put on a special Gala Day show at 11 a.m. The Globe in the same week was showing a British drama to packed houses. The film version of Walter Howard's Lyceum success *The Midnight Wedding* was made by British and Colonial. It was directed by *and* starred Ernest Batley. It had only been released in April 1914.[145]

Durham Chronicle August 14th, 1914

In the week that saw the declaration of war the Globe was showing a production of *Dante's Inferno*. "There were exceptionally large audiences and on Monday evening the hall was filled to capacity. All the important features of the great work are exhibited.

It can be regarded as a remarkable triumph in the animated picture world that so extraordinary a book has been cleverly and richly produced for the masses of people."[146] "Many months have been spent on the endeavour to produce the picture and within the work there have been assistant painters, sculptors, musicians, scholars, poets, and authors."[147] The report went on to say that by seeing the film patrons would save themselves many hours of reading.

A serious contravention of the Cinematograph Act was perpetrated in Coxhoe between 8th and 17th August. The case came before the county police court on 2nd September when Leland Jones was charged with allowing his premises to be used for a cinematograph exhibition without obtaining a licence. He pleaded guilty. Jones was the proprietor of a travelling theatre, which often visited Durham City. It seems that he occasionally took out a licence for cinematograph shows since they were more profitable than his live theatre business. Deputy Chief Constable Waller said that Jones had visited the Coxhoe and Quarrington Hill district with his theatre and had notified him of the intention to apply for a licence for the theatre. Before that application could be attended to, the theatre had removed from Quarrington Hill to Coxhoe, and another man named Evans had taken it over. He obtained a licence for his theatre for 26th August, but because of the removal of the theatre, there was no licence for Quarrington Hill. Mr. Jones then got hold of an old school and converted it into a cinematograph hall. He didn't inform the police of the change, but when some of the films caught fire it became known to the police. Mr. Waller said that he understood the defendant was in "very straitened circumstances' and the magistrates only imposed a fine of 20 shillings plus costs.[148]

The war's influence on programmes was soon apparent. One of the major turns at the Palace was expected to be 'the Moxon trio of jugglers, dancers and foot equilibrists.' But they were German, and an announcement on the screen indicated they had been detained and consequently were unable to fulfil their engagement. "The announcement caused disappointment, mingled with expressions of sentiments which were not exactly flattering to the German Emperor." The Assembly Rooms were reported as showing a 'lengthy film' of Army manoeuvres. "An imitation invasion of England illustrated the thoroughness with which the British soldier enters into the preparation for war." Each war picture was greeted with enthusiastic applause. The Globe had a special short film entitled *Britain's Might*, "A series of most interesting illustrations of Britain's first line of defence."[149]

The Sherburn Hill Show was a victim of the war situation. A meeting of the committee in August had decided on cancellation, but a later meeting reversed this. Unfortunately, the notice was too short for Mr. Morley to bring his roundabouts from Cleveland. In the evening, however, Mrs. Paine's cinematograph show was present and 'a little brightness was shed on the field, but everyone felt that something was lacking.'[150]

FROM SUNDAY 8th to SUNDAY 15th NOVEMBER Inclusive

THE CREATION.

Admission Free.   Sundays 3 and 8·15 ; week-days 3 and 8.

INTERNATIONAL BIBLE STUDENTS' ASSOCIATION.

Photo Drama of Creation

World's Greaestt Biblical Film. Explained by Powerful Gramophone.

EXHIBITED FREE
In the Globe Cinema, Durham,

In four Parts, Commencing Sunday, Nov. 8th, 8·15 p.m.

PART 1.—NOV. 8-9.   PART 2.—NOV. 10-11.   PART 3.—NOV. 12-13.
PART 4.—NOV. 14,   GRAND FINALE—NOV, 15.
Week-days at 3 and 8 p.m,   Sundays at 3 and 8·15. p.m.

ALL SEATS FREE.   NO COLLECTION.

Durham Chronicle 6th November

There was a novel presentation at the Globe from Sunday 8th to Sunday 15th November 1914, when a film entitled *The Creation* was presented free of charge by an organisation called the International Bible Students' Association. The film was in four parts with a Grand Finale on November 15th at 3 p.m. and 8.15 p.m. This was the first time that the Globe had been permitted to open on a Sunday. The magistrates' leniency is clearly associated with the nature of the programme rather than a desire to see Sunday entertainment in the city.

The newspaper description of the presentation reveals that it told the Bible story in twelve reels of film and numerous coloured slides and panoramas. The reels depicting the Creation contain "imaginary pictures of the various steps taken in the preparation of the earth for human habitation."[151] Patrons could obtain tickets from the Globe management by sending a stamped addressed envelope. Children under 14 would only be admitted if accompanied by an adult. The dramatic depiction of Jesus Christ was officially forbidden by the then film censor, but, since local magistrates and police superintendents were the arbiters of what could and could not be shown an expression of the reverence of the scenes was often enough to allay criticism. Such appears to have been the case here, for the Chronicle reporter doubtless quoting from his publicity sheet declared, "Sacred subjects have been treated with becoming reverence, and there is nothing in the presentation to offend." In a later report, there is also the mention of a 'powerful gramophone' being used to explain the pictures. There were a number of mechanical compression devices available which could boost the sound generated by a gramophone pick-up. They had mostly been associated with synchronisers, but here a device appears to have been employed more for amplification than for synchronisation.[152]

The war was heating up. Newsreels at the Palace illustrated the evacuation of Ostend and Ghent. At the Globe *A Daughter of Belgium* depicted brutal acts by German soldiers in Belgium. This particular myth was repeated endlessly both during and after the war. The 22-minute film had been hurriedly put together by Barker's Film Company. Its late October trade release indicates the up-to-date nature of local programming.[153] Barker's Ealing Studio had been amongst the first to exploit the war drama with titles such as *Chained to The Enemy, The German Spy Peril*, *The Looters of Liege*, and *Your Country Needs You.* George Pearson at Samuelson's had rushed through a documentary reconstruction of *The Cause of the Great European War*, and Maurice Elvey at British & Colonial directed a war drama entitled *Lest We Forget*.[154]

The Royal Hippodrome, Langley Moor came out of its usual window card and hand-bill obscurity with a newspaper advertisement for its Christmas show. For a whole week including Christmas day they would be showing 'Star pictures including Drama, Comedies and War Pictures.' On Christmas night, there would be two shows at 6 o'clock and 8 o'clock instead of the usual one.[155]

Mr. Rawes at the Palace had also managed to persuade the magistrates of the Durham city police court that it was in order to have two shows on Christmas night. Permission was given on the understanding that the pictures shown would be 'perfectly harmless and more of an educational nature than anything else.' This popular music hall had been increasing its film content during the year. Continuity of patron attendance was clearly expected with the fortnightly introduction in November of one of the earliest serial films Selig's *The Adventures of Kathlyn*.[156]

The picture palace was now firmly established as the most popular form of general entertainment. Cinemas had been opened in the majority of the mining villages around the city, and, for the most part, they were making a modest living for their proprietors. During the next four years of war, they would take on an even greater significance if they could survive the man-power shortage.

* * * * * * *

The advertising hoarding for the Globe under the railway viaduct on North Road. The lettering is not clear enough to identify the films. *Courtesy of Durham University Library.*

Some local County Durham cinemas opened from 1910
Compiled by Frank Manders

Annfield Plain
Castle Picture Palace, Catchgate (9 November 1911)
King's Hall, off Main Street (25th April 1912)
Beamish
Beamish Picturedrome, Handenhold (18th Oct 1912 - 28th Jan 1914)
Bishop Auckland
Olympia, Railway Street 17 Oct 1910. "Despite the inclement weather, there was a fairly good company on the opening of the cinematograph exhibition at the New Olympia Picture Palace. Prior to the first picture being thrown onto the screen, the manager explained that before the weekend everything would be in full working order." *South Durham & Auckland Chronicle 20th October 1910)*
The original proprietor ceased to operate the cinema after 24th November, and it re-opened under new management on 26th December 1910. "Particular attention has been paid to warming the building and no effort will be spared to make the place more comfortable." *S. D. & A. Chronicle, Dec 29th 1910.*
Pavilion Picture Pal., Newgate St
Lyric Picture Hall, South Road (July 1912)
Burnopsfield
Derwent Pavilion (4 Oct 1911)
Butterknowle
Picture Palace /Miner's Hall (21 Sept 1912)
Byers Green
Globe (Dec 1913)
Chester-le-Street
Empire, Front Street (12 Jan 1911)
Hippodrome, Market Pl.(8 Feb 1911)
Star (1910 until 1912)

Consett
Daly's Hall/Daly's Picture House, Shakespeare St (5 Feb 1912) John Cottrell
Empire Palace, Front St (21 July 1913)
New Town Hall Cinema, Front Street/Middle Street (22 Jan 1912)
Olympia, Derwent Street, Blackhill (6 October 1913)
Coundon
Eden Pavilion (19 Sept 1912)
Coxhoe
New Electric Th. (29 Dec 1911)
Crook
Empire, Market Place (14 Nov. 1910) "The New Electric Palace at Crook is to be auspiciously opened on Monday night next. The Chairmen and members of the Urban District Council have accepted an invitation to the opening night. The building is one of the prominent architectural features of the Market Place and adjoins the well-known Temperance Hall, but it is a much loftier building and it has a much more imposing up-to-date appearance being entirely new. The interior has been modelled on the latest designs, both in regard to securing safety and easy viewing of the picture. Comfortable tip-up seats have been included, and Mr. Shepperd is deserving of every encouragement in his enterprise. During three nights in the week, the district people will have the advantage of a train leaving Crook 10.13 p.m." *South Durham and Auckland Chronicle Nov 10, 1910.*
Theatre Royal, Addison Street (licensed from 1910)
Dipton
Empire Electric Palace (15 Sept 1913)
Picture Hall/Royal Electric, Front St (29 April 1912)

Easington Colliery
Empire (21 Sept 1912)
Hippodrome (25 Jan 1913)
Esh Winning
Pavilion (14 Sept 1911)
Ferryhill
Dean Bank Hall (Cinema licence 1912)
Grange Villa
Coronation Pavilion, Alma Terrace (11
September 1911 ?)
Haswell
Palace, Front Street (25 Dec 1912)
Miners' Hall, South Hetton (24 August
1912)
Horden
Empress Electric Theatre (24 Dec 1910)
"At Castle Eden on Saturday,
cinematograph and theatre licences were
granted to Mr. Richard Thornton
managing director in respect of a new
theatre at Horden. The new building will
seat over 1,000 people and everything is
on the up-to-date principle. The first
performance will begin on Saturday,
December 24th." *S .D. and A. Chronicle.
Dec 22nd, 1910.*
Picture Palace/ Palace Picture Hall, Fifth
Street (10 Feb 1911)
Lanchester
Assembly Rooms (7 Dec 1911)
Langley Moor
Royal Hippodrome Film and Variety (11
Nov 1910)
Langley Park
Hippodrome (27 March 1911)
Meadowfield
Co-operative Hall/Central Palace (Oct
1913)

Murton
Empire, Woods Terrace (22 Nov 1912)
Olympia, off Church Street (Sept 1910)
Pelton Fell
Comedy Theatre (11 March 1910)
Shildon
Empire, Garbutt Street (1914)
Shotton Colliery
Empire Electric, Front St (10 Feb 1911)
Theatre Royal, Potto St (Cinematograph
licence - 10 Feb 1911)
Spennymoor
Cambridge Theatre (Cinema licence
from 1911)
Grand Electric / Arcadia Market Place.
(Licence from 1914)
Town Hall Cinema, James Street
(Licence from 1912)
Tantobie
Co-operative Hall (6 Sept 1911)
Thornley
Hippodrome (7 September 1912)
Theatre Royal (10 Feb 1911- 9 Feb 1913)
Trimdon Colliery
Imperial (31 May 1913)
Royal Electric (21 Dec 1912)
Tudhoe Colliery
Electric Picture Palace (1914)
Ushaw Moor
Empire (22 Nov 1912)
West Auckland
Picture House (22 Sept 1913)
Wheatley Hill
Miner's Hall/Royalty (10 Feb 1912)
Palace, Front Street (18 Oct 1913)
Willington
Empire, Commercial St (10 Feb 1911)
Wingate
Empire Electric Theatre (24 Oct 1910)
Palace Theatre, Front St (29 Nov 1913)

* * * * * * *

Chapter Three   The War Years

1915-19

The New Year began at the Globe with a presentation of Mary Pickford's *Tessibell of the Storm Country*. "This picture has been shown again and again in many towns," declared the advertisement, but, it was its first time in Durham and it had already been on release for a year. The Palace had a play *Bonnie Mary* followed a week later by the pantomime *Dick Whittington*. The Assembly Rooms were doing very good business with their series of Chaplin films, and in February they devoted a whole week to a programme of Keystone comedies, 'the latest craze in the cinema world.'[1] The Globe responded to this with its own inclusion of Keystone films. "*Fatty's Finish* is a highly diverting Keystone comedy in which the far-famed Fatty figured prominently. The building re-echoed with hearty laughter."

In April, the *Bioscope* magazine conducted a small enquiry into the state of the cinematograph trade during the first year of the war. The unsurprising finding for Durham was that there was no serious disruption of audience size, though all admitted that business could be better.[2] The needs of the war were dramatically signalled at the Assembly Rooms in April when the Harry Lauder's Famous Band of Pipers were present for three days to assist in a recruitment drive. The film accompanying the Call to Arms was *1914*. This 3,500 ft film was made by the London Film Company in their Twickenham Studio. It had been released in January 1915 and told the story of a dastardly German Captain who demands a woman in return for her husband's liberty. Fortunately the programme had its lighter moments with a Chaplin film *Those Love Pangs*.[3]

Whilst the Assembly Rooms Theatre was giving more and more prominence to the showing of each new Chaplin film, the Globe was steadily building up a reputation with its choice of big feature films: *Tessibell of the The Storm Country* was given a second showing; the 1½ hour Italian spectacle film *Spartacus* played to big audiences, and in August the epic British film *Jane Shore* played for the whole week. The Chronicle reviewer picked up the information that "Five thousand seven hundred and forty eight artistes took part in the production." It was certainly the prestige film of the year: "Interest in this film, which has been seen at no other picture hall in the city or district, continues, and there has been an almost unexpected rush for seats."[4]

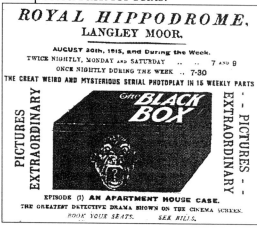

The illustrated advertisement for
The Black Box.

It was an exciting week for picture-goers in Langley Moor, too. The Royal Hippodrome commenced showing the serial *The Black Box* and clearly took advantage of the distributor's free publicity blocks by taking a large advertisement in both Durham newspapers. It was billed as 'The Greatest Detective Drama Shown on the Cinema Screen'. This 15-part film was made by the American Transatlantic Company. Several different publicity postcards were distributed to patrons before the first showing and in the subsequent weeks.[5] The Chronicle predicted a enthusiastic following for the serial and praised the manager Mr. Bury for "securing such attractive fare"[6]

Not far away from the Royal Hippodrome, a new picture hall was taking shape. Previously, one part of the site had been occupied by shops, and an open-ground section had been the occasional venue for a travelling theatre. The New Empire Theatre was being built for Messrs Wood & Briggs, two local miners. Their enterprise had almost been jeopardised by a court case in August. A Newcastle mortgage broker had claimed that the proprietors owed him £30 as commission for arranging the £2,000 mortgage. Wood and Briggs refused to pay a requested additional sum on the grounds that the broker had altered the initial agreement. The judge found in their favour.[7]

COPYRIGHT. TRANS-ATLANTIC FILM CO. LTD. 1915.

COPYRIGHT. TRANS-ATLANTIC FILM CO. LTD. 1915.

HERBERT RAWLINSON "The Black Box"

ANNA LITTLE "The Black Box"

Two of the *Black Box* postcards given away as publicity. *Author's collection.*

The buildings, dimensions and construction were fully described in the local press -

> The New Empire is a fine massive building measuring 100 ft in length and 66 feet in width, built of concrete blocks, interspersed with red and white glazed bricks and covered with a large dome. There is an arcade in front consisting of four lock-up shops. A large entrance 14 feet in width, leads to a stair case on the landing of which is the entrance to the body of the hall, and the ladies and gentlemen's lavatories. On ascending another flight of stairs entrance is gained to the large circle, upon either side of which a pair of select boxes are provided. [8]

Accommodation was set for 800 persons with tip-up seats provided in all parts. The circle and box seats were upholstered in velvet.[9] It was estimated that, with the four main exits provided, the hall could be cleared in two minutes. Electric light provided the illumination and a large ventilating fan in the roof would attempt to keep the air clear.

The proscenium was 30 feet wide and 29 feet to the back wall. Beneath the stage, there were dressing rooms for the artists.

The architect was Mr. Robson of Esh Winning; builders were Messrs Walton Bros. of Crook; fittings were supplied by Messrs Dinning & Co. and Messrs Murdock & Moody, both of Newcastle. The estimated cost of the building and fittings was c. £3000. The safety curtain or Act Drop, painted by the manager Robert McDonald, depicted Brancepeth Castle, at the time converted into a hospital: wounded soldiers were seen resting in the grounds. Other scenery was said to be similar to that at the Pavilion, Newcastle-on-Tyne.

The Empire, Langley Moor. *Durham Chronicle 24th September 1915.* A poor illustration, but the best that could be obtained. The main entrance is at the nearer end, with a parade of four shops beyond. There is a separate front stalls entrance and the stage door at the end. The roof rise at the far end is the fly tower over the stage, originally used for cine-variety.

The cinema was officially opened on Monday 27th September 1915 by the vicar of Brandon, the Revd. H. Hayward. He was quite sure the theatre was the finest place in the neighbourhood and he hoped that it would have an educative influence besides being a place of amusement. The building, he said, was a credit to Brandon and there could not be any finer place of the kind in Britain. He was glad that there was such good support for the enterprise of the two working men who had created it.

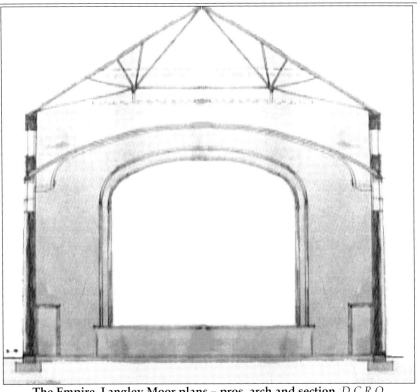

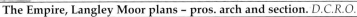

The Empire, Langley Moor plans – pros. arch and section. *D.C.R.O.*

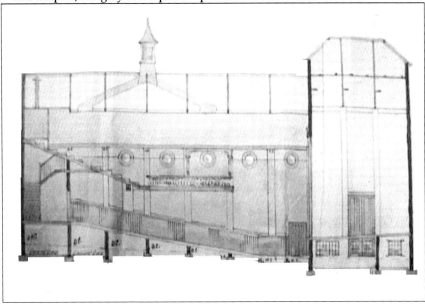

They had acted courageously in erecting such a palatial building. He thanked God that British pluck and British enterprise was evident here and all over the world. He hoped that those present might forgive any little mishap or shortcoming on the opening night. Everything, he had been assured, would be in full working order in a week or two. The Advertiser also made mention of the fact that the proprietors belonged to 'the working class community', and wished their enterprise every success.

The opening programme consisted of musical turns and films, and an orchestra provided the accompaniment. "The Sisters Sinclair in their singing and dancing turn were recalled, and as an encore gave an impression of high spirited school girl, which evoked rounds of applause." The main film was the 3,500 ft *Harbour Lights*.[10] This British film was one of the first features made by the Neptune Film Company at their Boreham Wood, Elstree Studios. It was directed by Percy Nash, a former stage manager turned film producer.[11] Though described as a 'Special' by the local newspaper, the film had been in circulation for over a year, however, it had not been shown by any other cinema in the area. Initially the programmes were billed for a week's run, but later this changed to a mid-week change of the films, and a special Sunday film programme. The newspaper advertisements often gave major prominence to the variety acts. For example 'Labas and El Chico, Marvellous Arab Tumblers and Jugglers direct from The Empire, London also the Two well-known comedians Ford and Lewis - The Fellow with the Kilt and the other Chap. Strong Pictorial Programme'.[12]

Durham Chronicle, 15th October 1915

The Globe was regularly showing a series of satirical animated cartoons involving caricatures of the Kaiser. There were several producers of these lightning-sketch animations. Both George Studdy's war studies, *Dicky Dee's Cartoons* and *John Bull's Animated Sketchbook's* were trade-shown at monthly intervals. The unidentified film shown at the Globe in the week of 25th October was concerned with 'the Kaiser's *gallant* attacks on defenceless children and wounded warriors.'[13]

The control that the county police courts exercised over picture halls was again demonstrated when the licence for the Empire, Ushaw Moor came up for renewal at the Durham County Sessions. The magistrates agreed to renew the licence to include two performances each evening, but stressed that in any future application they might restrict the licence to one house. Superintendent Waller thought that the theatre should not continue its performances later than 9.30.p.m. Mr. Ferens said that he did not know whether his clients would wish it but he thought they might come forward and suggest an earlier start and a finish at 9 p.m. or 9.30 p.m. He said that in his experience the second house was a very poor one. It might be possible that the bench would consider the matter and the licensees would ask them to grant permission for performances to start at 5 p.m. to 6.45 and from 7 p.m. until 9 p.m. Rather surprisingly, since the factor in question was opening hours, the Superintendent said that the halls could be open all day if they liked.[14]

The Central Palace, Meadowfield had been leased from the Brandon & Byshottles Co-operative Society as a variety and picture hall since 1913. In November 1915, they made the decision to run the hall themselves.

Opening night was Monday 8th November–

The President, Mr D. H. Pearson, said that this was a new enterprise that the Society had ventured upon, and he believed it was the first in the Co-operative movement. The hall was there for the members and it was to their advantage to patronise it. The manager's instructions were to provide good programmes of the best talent and pictures and secondly to see that proper discipline was carried out amongst the audience and the staff. There was another consideration, and that was profit after the payment of the artists fees etc., also a fair interest to be paid upon the preliminary expenses of the hall." [15]

The Society retained the services of the original manager, Thomas A. Young. His opening night's programme consisted of Hicks and Rose, acrobatic specialists assisted by two dogs, Wrangham and Gordon vocal and comedians and Rita Dilston comedienne. Only *The Bardon* was named in the film programme.

Christmas Day opening was treated somewhat differently between the town and the county. An application on behalf of the local cinema proprietors before the county magistrates sought permission to run film shows from 3 p.m. to 10 p.m. This was granted as long as the pictures shown were suitable. Superintendent Waller said that he was responsible for checking the suitability of the films to be shown, but that he could not visit all the halls to make sure that they were shown. The Ushaw Moor Working Men's Club made a separate application. It had been showing films on part of its premises since March or April.[16]

The Central Palace, Meadowfield advertised Christmas day performances of the 5,500ft film *The Jockey of Death* at 3p.m., 6p.m. *and* 8 p.m. whereas the Globe, Durham only had a 7 p.m. showing of the Hepworth drama *The Curtain's Secret*. The

Christmas Day opening
Central Palace Meadowfield.

Assembly Rooms had no performances. The Palace had a special Film Week leading up to Christmas. On Monday, there was *Vendetta*, on Tuesday, and Wednesday *In The Ranks*, on Thursday *Rupert of Hentzau,* on Friday *The Middleman*, and on Saturday, Christmas Day a 'specially requested' performance of *Quo Vadis*, a film it had shown two years previously.[17] On Monday 27th December, it opened with a play, *A Child of The Streets*. The advertisement, clearly wishing to allay public criticism, stated that no member of the cast was eligible for military service. In another gesture to the war effort, soldiers in uniform were to be admitted at half-price on Thursdays and Fridays to the pit and the stalls.[18]

Ushaw Moor Working Men's Club showing projection room extension to upper floor. *George Nairn Collection*

1916

The war, of course, featured strongly in the thoughts and minds of everyone at this time. Another Christmas had passed without any solution, and the casualty lists were growing ever longer. Registration and conscription were causing the forced enlistment of many local men. In an attempt to counter the horror of this reality, the Government

Durham County Advertiser
February 18th 1916

had made a series of sanitized 'official' army films. The first of these, *With the Indian Army At The Front*, was shown at the Assembly Rooms in the week beginning 23rd January 1916. The Globe included a Roll of Honour in its programming. "As the various photographs were projected on the screen and recognised by the audience, they were greeted with enthusiastic applause." [19]

The national need for a reduction in absenteeism and lateness at work led the county magistrates to consider again the schedules for cinema opening. "Houses of Entertainment, of which there are 17, on the whole have been well conducted," said Superintendent Waller. "At present the majority of houses have been having two shows nightly and closed down between 10.30 and 11 p.m. I suggest that they should close earlier each night at 9.30 except Saturday at 10.30." His reasoning was that since the public houses closed at 9 o'clock, many workers went from the public house to places of entertainment. This made them very late in returning to their homes, moreover, he went on, in the present darkened conditions it was very desirable that the risks to which women and children were submitted should be obviated as much as possible. He had circulated the managers of halls in his division and the majority were in favour of one house nightly with the exception of Saturday. He also ascertained the opinion of those in charge of children engaged in performing at halls, that they would only like one house per night.

Superintendent Waller said that he had an added difficulty in the Spennymoor district. There, half the place was in the Auckland division and half in the Durham division. The Durham division was willing to accept the proposal but the Auckland division was not. The magistrates said that they would make contact with the Auckland division on the subject.

Mr Ferens for the picture hall proprietors hoped that they would not make 9 o'clock a hard and fast rule because some of the big picture halls could not finish prompt on the minute. He also said that there was another point. Some halls had both cinema licences and dramatic licences. He quite understood the restriction on closing the cinema at a certain time, but wondered if it could be enforced upon the dramatic licence regulations. Would it be in order for a proprietor to put on a short play after 9.30 when the hall was closed under the cinema licence?" he asked. Superintendent Waller said he would object to drama taking place after the cinematograph performance. His concern was that the whole show should finish at 9.30 p.m.

Mr. Ferens was making a telling point here. The application of the dramatic licence did not give magistrates the same powers that they were given under the Cinematograph Act. It is probable that Mr. Ferens was only highlighting the anomaly as a debating point and that neither he nor his clients had any intention of pursuing it. The chairman announced that they would make enquiries further and that they would like to defer a decision until the adjourned Brewster sessions meeting on 23rd February.[20]

When that meeting took place, the magistrates resolved that in future halls should be closed at 9.30 from Monday to Fridays and on Saturday at the usual hour of 11 o'clock. All cinematograph performances would be prohibited on Sundays. Mr. Ferens expressed regret at the magistrates' decision and thought that the Sunday performances had a beneficial effect upon attendance at work on Mondays. He thought that the colliery owners and other employers would agree with him on this point. The Chairman said the police wished the streets to be cleared on Sunday nights at an earlier hour than at present and for people to be back in their homes in case of an air-raid. At any rate, they would see how the arrangement worked.[21]

Mr Ferens returned to the point of Sunday closure at the next Brewster session.[22] Acting on instructions from the proprietors of the picture halls in the division, Mr Ferens mentioned that they had asked again for the opening of picture halls on Sunday evening. Shrewdly cultivating the favour of the magistrates, he said that he felt himself to be a great difficulty since the decision against opening had so recently been taken by the Bench, and because he had not been able to give them much notice of the request. What he could say was that through these people being obliged to close on Sunday and at 9.30 on week-nights they would lose financially up to next September, since they had contracts for films which they were bound to comply with and pay for. The result will be that under present conditions that they would be unable to use films of 3,000ft in length and it was a most serious matter. Further, he wished to point out that complaints had been made by night-shift men that Sunday night was their only opportunity to have a little amusement by visiting a picture house, and they were now deprived of this. On the point of air-raids, he thought it might be relevant to draw their worships attention to the fact that the L.C.C. had a strong recommendation made to them recently in reference to the closing of picture halls on Sundays, and after hearing the evidence they allowed them to open on Sunday nights. So far as air-raids were concerned, London was more likely to receive them than other parts of the country. The chairman, Captain Apperley, pointed out that the decision of a county council was not law, and that they did not have to follow the L.C.C. Despite Mr Ferens re-stating his point about air-raids, Capt. Apperley said that the decision had been almost unanimous and that they would consider the application again in a month's time.

The condition of the Victoria Picture Hall, Queen Street, Sacriston had been the cause of some concern at a previous Brewster session.[23] Mr Ferens said then that Superintendent. Waller had visited the hall and was not satisfied that the public safety was sufficiently guarded. New plans had been submitted and subject to the addition of an extra emergency exit the police and the magistrates were now satisfied with the arrangements.[24]

Reports from the Military Exemption Tribunals featured regularly in the local papers. The names and places of employment of the applicants were never revealed. Applications from cinema employers revealed official attitudes to this form of entertainment.

One proprietor of a cinema hall applied for exemption of the operator and the manager. He said he had tried all round to find a man to fill the operator's place but without success. He feared that if he were taken the hall would close with the loss of the jobs of other people. Further, he said the appellant could claim to have done some service to the community as he had shown military and war pictures, and he had given performances for war funds and he also gave free admission to wounded soldiers. The operator had two brothers serving and one had not been heard of for many months. He had tried London, Newcastle and all around and could not get a man who was not only an operator but also an electrician and mechanic. Major White said his opinion of the case was that a picture hall was not absolutely necessary, but men for the army were. However, exemption was granted for three months.[25]

At another Durham tribunal exemption was claimed for a picture theatre employee. Four of the men on the staff as well as the operator were stated to have joined the colours, and the man applied for was now looking after the gas, the electricity and also operating. He was doing at least two men's work, and if he went the place would have to be closed up. "Would that be a serious matter? At least from the national standpoint?" asked the Chairman. "Yes," replied the applicant. "People must have some recreation. A woman cannot do this man's work. The man, too, is not fit for the army. I have a doctor's certificate to prove it." The chairman: "If we send this man forward you will get him back if the army doctors reject him. "Yes, but in the meantime, we will have to close the place." Another tribunal member said, "I don't think this board cares much whether the place is shut or open." The application was refused.[26]

The claim that women could not do the work was already being refuted by their employment in some London theatres and through the establishment of cinematograph operator training schools for women. Very few of the smaller provincial picture halls had motorised projectors and it was considered that women would not have the stamina to keep the hand-turned projectors in continuous motion. It was also felt that very few women had the electrical knowledge to sustain the arc lamps and the generators. By the close of the war, these opinions had been revised.[27]

In February, the Assembly Rooms had shown *The Rosary* to critical acclaim and to packed houses. Dubbed 'The Picture of the year' the advertisements carried a quotation from its originating poem. " The hours I spent with thee, dear heart, / Are as a string of pearls to me: / I count them every one apart, / My Rosary, My Rosary." According to the publicity, it was seen by 26,000 people in Newcastle. Its star, Kathlyn Williams, had already achieved fame with her first serial and now she was capping it with a great dramatic role. In April, 'by popular and repeated request' it played for another three days. In the same week, the film *Whoso is without*

Sin was presented. This film has an interesting history. The story was by May Sherman who won the Ideal Renting Company's £25 prize for the best script on the title's theme. The second part of the prize, to the obvious benefit of the Ideal Film Renting Company, was that they would film it. It was directed by veteran actor-director Fred Paul and starred Hilda Moore and Milton Rosmer, with screenplay written by Fred Paul and Benedict James. [28]

The Empire, Langley Moor was going through something of a crisis in the early Spring. Audiences had fallen away, and by April an acting manager, Welldon P. Stuart was in charge. He attempted to revive the fortunes of the theatre with some imaginative promotions. The star film for Monday 10th April was *The Lion Cubs,* so he invited the local Boy Scouts to a free viewing.[29] In April, he booked an exclusive showing of the Transatlantic serial *Greed*.[30] The cinema had previously shown the same company's serial *The Broken Coin,* but several weeks behind the showing at the Royal Hippodrome and the Central Hall Meadowfield. The efforts appear to have born some fruit, since the Chronicle reported in May that "Arthur Slater, the renowned Whistler, and His Master's Voice gramophone have been delighting audiences at the Empire".[31]

Audience loyalty was to be tested even more from 15th May by the increase of the prices due to the imposition of War Tax; thus, at the Empire, one half-penny was added to the 2d seats, one penny to the 3d 4d and 6d seats, and twopence was added to the 9d and 1/- seats. The Assembly rooms prices would now be 4d, 7d and one shilling and twopence.[32]

NEW EMPIRE THEATRE

LANGLEY MOOR, Co. DURHAM

Sole Proprietors ...   ...   THE EMPIRE CO

PICTURES.

MONDAY, TUESDAY & WEDNESDAY.

NURSE AND MARTYR.

The story of a devoted Nurse's supreme sacrifice in the cause of humanity.

THURSDAY, FRIDAY & SATURDAY.

GREED.

The Greatest of all Serial Photo Plays.   Filmed by the producers of "The Broken Coin."

AND OTHER FIRST CLASS PICTURES.

VAUDEVILLE.

CLARA COVERDALE'S NINE DAINTY DOTS

in their wonderful scena, entitled " Gipsy Revels," an act guaranteed to charm and satisfy the most fastidious taste.

WEE OLIVE in Songs and Dances. That remarkable Local Juvenile.

CHILDREN'S MATINEE AT 2 P.M.

TIME AND PRICES AS USUAL.

Durham Advertiser April 28th 1916

Entertainment in the city came under the scrutiny of a body calling itself the Durham Citizen's League. The main speaker, A. Beresford Horsley J.P. of Hartlepool, opened a discussion on 'Some Aspects of the Boy Problem'. He contended that education left off at a period when it was most required, namely adolescence. "The last thing many of them thought of doing," he said, "was going to church or chapel". He contended that instead they spent two or three nights a week at the picture palaces "one of the greatest social forces of the time."

"The picture palaces were a perfectly legitimate form of amusement for adults, "he said, "but what was proper for adults was ridiculously un-suited to the needs of boys in their adolescent period. Youths saw incidents on the screen that they thought were life and reality. This had a pernicious influence on them and it would eventually have to be stopped. Picture palaces might be used as an educational tool, but such pictures did not pay. Thus proprietors selected subjects that were not suitable for boys. Counter attractions were needed."

Canon Scrimshank, who was chairing the meeting, agreed with the lecturer regarding some cinema films. He had visited picture halls, and in a certain class of pictures he was astonished at the frequency with which the revolver was used.

The Reverend H. Hooper said that in their club, they did not debar members from going to the picture halls, but got them interested in reading and thinking for themselves, with the result that the boys thought that those exciting revolver films were rot.

The Reverend W. Bothamley had great sympathy with the boy who loved boisterous inane fun. At the same time he thought that many films were very harmful. He especially thought those showing the extravagancies of life were likely to cause class bitterness.[33]

Military exemption

At a Spennymoor Military Exemption Tribunal, the manager of a large picture hall and furniture business was refused exemption. This was probably Mr. Fenny of the Arcadia (Grand Electric). On the other hand, the proprietor of a picture hall in Tudhoe Colliery (obviously P. V. Morton of the Electric) was granted one month's exemption.[34] At a tribunal in the City, it was also possible to identify that T. C. Rawes' son had applied for exemption. He was described as a variety agent and the lessee of a place of entertainment in Stanley (the Victoria Picture Hall).

An unusual departure for the British cinema was the presentation at the Assembly Rooms of Hall Caine's *The Christian*. Part one of this almost three-hour drama was shown from Monday to Wednesday, and part two from Thursday to Saturday.[35] But, when the Globe showed the Italian epic *Cabiria*, which was of equal length, they decided upon one house nightly beginning at 6.45 pm.[36]

Patrons here would also have been immediately aware of the decorative changes made to the hall's interior during its annual fortnight's closure.

It was epic time all round. The Globe announced a showing of *Samson* with William Farnum in the title role. The Central Palace Meadowfield, now calling itself 'The House of Perfect Pictures', actually stole a march on the Globe by showing H. Rider Haggard's *She* a week previously, and the next week it beat the Assembly Rooms to a showing of *Tom Brown's Schooldays*.[37]

But things were not at all well at the hall. During its first quarter under the direct control of the Co-operative Society, it had accumulated a deficit of £100. The reasons given were the loss of its Sunday performances and the reduction in audience due to the War Tax price increases.[38]

Large audiences were guaranteed for the showing of *The Battle of The Somme*. So much so, that both the Globe and the Assembly Rooms gave it a simultaneous week's presentation. The advertisements and the reviews stressed its importance as a document on the destructive nature of war.

"The clouds of mystery that have hidden the war until quite recently pass away and reveal the dread spectre of war in its naked reality" wrote the Chronicle. Quoting from a London critic, W. G. Faulkner, the review continued, "War is a many sided thing, and this film shows us every side of it. The dead on the field give the casualty list in the newspapers a new meaning. We have lightly talked of bloodshed because we did not know what it was. Now we know. We see the blood our men have shed for us."[39]

Simultaneous advertising at the Assembly Rooms and at the Globe.

The film's impact on the city was immense: it played to capacity houses at both cinemas. Private shows were arranged for pupils from Durham School and students from St. Hild's College. On Thursday afternoon Archdeacon Watkins paid for the transporting of all the wounded soldiers in the district and their nurses, and afterwards entertained them for tea in the Town Hall.[40]

Dean Welldon seemed to possess the only dissenting voice. He had written to the Times newspaper on 8th September declaring his opposition to such a film being shown. His initial premise was that whilst there had been objection in some quarters to the portrayal of His Majesty's Cabinet in cinematograph form, the exposition of dead and dying soldiers had been greeted with acclaim. "A film of a few statesmen sitting together is held to be an insult to the self-respect of the nation – a film of war's hideous tragedy is welcomed! I beg leave respectfully to enter a protest against an entertainment which wounds the heart and violates the very sanctities of bereavement."[41]

In the Durham Chronicle of 22nd September, there is a report from Lieutenant Geoffrey Malins on how he took the film. We now know that, although Malins was a major contributor to the accumulated footage, the most famous scene in the film, as the men leave the trenches and go over the top, was re-enacted at the Trench Mortar Battery School.[42] Of course, as the 'official' war film,

The Battle of The Somme intentionally describes the events as a victory, when, in fact, with 57,470 casualties on the first day, it represents one of the worst defeats of any army in history.

Mr. Rawes' son made yet another attempt to gain exemption from call-up in the week of 18th September. The tribunal was told that since his father was 70 years old and was unable to manage the business without assistance, lack of exemption would mean the business would close with the loss of 60 jobs. He was granted a further month's exemption, but told that this would be his last deferment.[43] The effect on the Palace of Mr. Rawes' conscription was immediate, and advertisements ceased after 13th October 1916.

Losses continued at the Central Palace, Meadowfield, and concern was expressed at the quarterly meeting of the Co-operative Society. The President explained that of the £100 cinema deficit, £80 was payment to the Government in Tax. "There had been an increase in the cost of running such a show as that provided at the hall, and the lavish advertising in their attempt to build up a reputation. In future it was not intended to advertise so extensively as the place would advertise itself. Films were greater in cost and in addition the Sunday night performances had been abandoned, whilst many of their former patrons were now on war service." The President said the hall was not running at a continuous loss and that it would not be closed.[44]

In December at the University, the Durham Union Society debated the topic "That in the opinion of this house modern cinematograph entertainments are productive of juvenile crime". The Revd. R. V. Bainton, President of the Union, occupied the chair, but owing to the unfavourable weather there was only a small attendance.

The proposer, the Revd. H. H. Brazier (St. Cuthbert's Society) said that he did not attribute the whole of the increase in juvenile crime to the influence of the cinema, since it was clear that with the recruitment of many fathers into the army discipline at home had to some extent been withdrawn. "People sacrificed almost anything to go at least weekly to the cinema houses, and this rage amongst adults was equally keen amongst children." He thought that a new board of censorship should ensure that decent standards were portrayed in the pictures.

Miss N. Tunstall (Women's Hostels) believed that the cinema had been beneficial. It had created enthusiasm, and with its beautiful scenery and stories had elevated children. There were no doubt isolated cases of pictures producing crime, but she said, to accompanying laughter from the audience, seeing a drunken man on the screen did not mean that they should go out and get drunk.

The seconder, Miss D. M. Ruecroft, referred to the Manchester Commission that had concluded that the increase in juvenile crime could be attributed to a regular attendance at cinema shows. Further laughter occurred when she said that no one could imagine any good coming from viewing the pictures of Charlie Chaplin because he was vulgar in the extreme. The current censorship was hopelessly inefficient. F. D. N. Wynne (St. Chads) contended that the cinema was beneficial to boys who lived in an atmosphere of dull monotony. He refuted the contention that censorship was inefficient, since it was much more stringent than that applied to the stage or novels. When put to the vote, the motion was carried by 31 votes to 9.[45]

There were no Christmas Day shows at the Globe or the Assembly Rooms, and there appears to have been no application to the magistrates for this permission.

1917

Another official war film was the cause of simultaneous presentations at the Globe and the Assembly Rooms in February 1917. *The Battle of Ancre and The Advance of the Tanks* played to crowded houses.[46] Filmed by Lieutenant Malins and J. B. McDowell, it received critical acclaim, and according to the *Bioscope* did 'more good to the industry than thousands of pounds' worth of advertising'.[47]

When the New Miners' Hall was opened at Redhills, and the old hall became vacant, J. Dobson of Newcastle purchased it and surveyed the site for potential as a possible cinema and entertainments hall. On 7th February 1917, Durham city council approved plans for conversion of 13, 14, and 15 North Road and the old Miners' Hall. There would be a veranda and five street lights and shop fronts. The five lights were approved also if £1 per annum were paid. In March, Mr. Dobson applied for cinema and billiard hall and dancing licences for the old Miners' Hall. He stated that it was not intended to carry out the proposed scheme until after the war. The licence was granted subject to the plans being carried on to the satisfaction of the magistrates. There was to be a wait of 17 years before this could happen.[48]

A postcard of North Road, circa 1917. A sign next to the Miners' Hall reads 'Site for Picture Hall.' *Author's Collection*

A special cinematograph show took place at the Globe on Sunday 1st April at the request of the National Service Department. Admission was free and there was an address by the Mayor (Cllr. F. W. Goodyear). A series of Government-sponsored pictures were shown.[49] Another Government-sponsored programme appeared on Wednesday 9th May on Durham County Sailors' Day. The Assembly Rooms Theatre was handed over to Vice-Admiral Bearcroft, R.N., C.B. for a showing of the film *Glimpses of the British Navy in War Time*. This time however, admission was 1s 2d and 7d, and the orchestra was conducted by Lieutenant Cross.[50]

All efforts of the Meadowfield Central Palace management seem to have failed, and at the Co-op's April quarterly meeting it was proposed to discontinue the cinema operation immediately.

Simultaneous advertising again for *The Battle of Ancre*.

Mr. Cook, a member of the Society's committee, said that the picture hall had lost £266 4s 1d during the last four quarters and he considered it was a folly to carry on under such adverse conditions. Since the hall was opened by the society some years ago, they had lost practically £400. After lengthy discussion it was agreed to take a ballot of members as to whether it should close the place or not. The debate did not seem to include any suggestion that the opening of the nearby Empire had had an effect upon the hall's viability.[51] No report on the results of the ballot seems to have been published. By the time of the next quarterly meeting, the fortunes of the picture hall were not on the agenda, and it must be assumed that it had closed.

In April, the Palace suddenly emerged from its wartime retirement with a presentation of D. W. Griffith's *Birth of a Nation*. 'Exactly the same Picture as played at the Tyne Theatre, Newcastle and Broke all records', declared the advertisements.[52] Although completed in 1914, it was not

trade-shown in Britain until September 1915. Even then, it was only shown at selected major cities for special 'road shows'.

The Chronicle reviewer referred to it as 'the most amazing picture of its kind ever taken'. He made reference to the fact that many Dunelmians had already seen the film in Newcastle and he now urged those who missed it to visit the Palace. It was being shown twice daily at 2 p.m. and 7 p.m. for the whole week.

The following week *Dorian's Divorce*, a five-reel film starring Grace Valentine and Lionel Barrymore, was accompanied by the equally long *The Devil at His Elbow* starring Clifford Bruce. [53] The theatre seemed unsure of its role, as during June, it was host to John Ridding's Grand Opera Company with performances of *Faust*, *Rigoletto*, and *The Bohemian Girl*. It then closed again until it re-opened under new management on Bank Holiday Monday 6th August. The advertisement for the programme seems to be a throw-back to the Palace's original music hall days with variety acts and the Bioscope!

The new managers were the Messrs. Bolam Brothers & Pickering, and in the first week of September, the cinematograph licence was transferred to John Bolam. Before reverting entirely to variety acts, the Palace had a special showing of *The Dumb Girl of Portici*, an adaptation of the Auber Opera *Masaneillo*. It had had enormous publicity in America and in this country largely because Universal had paid its star, Anna Pavlova, the enormous fee, for the time, of £10,000 and a share in the profits. Audiences had to wait till the eighth and final reel before they could see Pavlova dance in a brief aerial ballet against moving clouds as she is whisked to heaven after being stabbed.[54]

The other cinemas in the town were well supported. The Globe seemed to be particularly linked with Fox films. They played *Romeo and Juliet* for a whole week in May and filled their advertisements with 'epic' details - "A Wonderful Production, 21 Characters 127 Minor performers. 2,000 supernumeraries; 413 Scenes with the action in 68 different places. And an entire moving picture studio with a replica of 14th century Verona."[55]

At the Assembly Rooms, their long-time chief operator, W. A. Waldie, was in no danger of call-up. He claimed to have been in the industry for 20 years, beginning with the pioneer showman A.

D. Thomas.[56] British feature films were particularly favoured by
Mr. Rushworth and in June he showed two prime examples.
Milestones, at two hours and 20 minutes, was so long that there was
only time for one house nightly. The film was produced by G. B.
Samuelson, directed by Thomas Bentley, based upon an Arnold
Bennett play, and starred Isobel Elsom and Owen Nares. *Masks and
Faces* was slightly shorter at 1 hour 40 minutes, but its cast
represented a major cross-section of the British stage - Irene
Vanbrugh, H. B. Irving, Gerald du Maurier, Dennis Neilson-Terry,
Gladys Cooper, Donald Calthrop, Lilian Brathwaite, Gerald Ames,
Helen Haye, Matheson Lang, Henry Vibart, and Ellaline Terriss.
And, in cameo appearances, G. B. Shaw, Sir George Alexander, J.
M. Barrie, and Charles Hawtrey.[57]

Newspaper critics, more familiar with plays than films, tended
to latch-on positively to anything that seemed rooted in stage-craft.
Thus, at first, they championed the exponents of 'legitimate'
drama. By 1918, the film star was a recognised functionary. A
generation of film-star postcard collectors had been created. Film
companies actively exploited this interest with publicity stories,
and distributors and cinema managers responded with give-away
portraits and souvenir sales. In 1917, the Wearside Film Agency at
Sunderland asked suppliers to send them pictures of film artistes
and pertinent literature. "It is the intention of the agency," said the
trade journal, "to devote a department to the sale of postcards and
novelties with a view to creating a keen interest in the players."[58]

Serial distributors were particularly
prolific with their promotional items, but
featured stars were also celebrated in film
scenes and in studio portraits. The
Chronicle, in declaring that Pauline
Frederick was very popular at the Globe,
even showed a picture of her, the first
such publicity in the newspaper.[59] Film
star names were given as much, and
sometimes more, prominence than film
titles and publicity blocks began to
appear in the advertisement.[60]

Occasionally, the cinema stepped into the field of controversy. In June 1918, the Palace switched from variety to show *Where are My Children*, a film advertised as approved by the National Council of Public Morals and described as 'A Propaganda Film of Paramount Importance'. Attendance was confined to adults and there was a special ladies only matinée at 2-30 on Wednesday. The newspaper was rather coy about the subject matter.[61] The film was made in America, by one of their few women directors Lois Weber, but it was drastically altered for its British presentation. Its plot advocated support for birth control but showed an abhorrence for abortion. It appeared in Britain at a time when the authorities were actively opposed to birth control because of a drastic drop in the birth rate and because of the huge man-power losses from the war. In the American version one of the main characters, Dr. Homer, is an advocate of birth control, but through an almost complete re-write of his inter-titles in the British version he appears to be in opposition to it.[62]

The *Bioscope* indicated that it was to be shown in Britain 'to adults only in special halls.'[63] It is difficult to see how the Palace was a *Special Hall*. It was a place of entertainment, and more likely to provoke an audience of *voyeurs* than concerned citizens. No figures are given for Durham attendance, and apparently there was no follow-up in the newspapers letters column: was this because the papers did not wish to be drawn into a debate on the subject.

The Palace continued with a film programme after this and included the Clarendon Drama *Ave Maria* with Madame la Claire 'the well known Northumberland soprano' supplying the voice accompaniment to the film.[64] This was followed by a six-day presentation of *Twenty Thousand Leagues Under The Sea*. Universal Studio's version of the Jules Verne novel was said to be the first film to use actual underwater footage. It had had a two-week run at the Tyne Theatre, Newcastle before arriving in Durham.

The Assembly Rooms had a particular event to celebrate in the same week. It was announced that Lt. Tom Rushworth had been award the Military Cross for conspicuous gallantry at the Battle of the Marne.[65]

In August, the Globe negotiated an exclusive booking of all the new Chaplin films. Billed as the 'million dollar Chaplin' after his move to the First National Studios from Essanay, patrons were advised to book their seats early for the first one, *It's A Dog's Life*. When it was shown, the Chronicle reported full houses. The programme changed on Thursdays but the Chaplin film was retained for the whole week.[66]

Though Cecil B. de Mille's *Joan, the Woman* told the mediæval story of the saint, it was given a contemporary framing story in the Flanders trenches, coming to the Globe for a week after being screened for a fortnight in the 1,250-seat Newcastle-on-Tyne Theatre Royal.[67] There had been a gradual shift away from war dramas, however, and cinema-goers were showing their preference for more peaceful fare. Thus, the film of Belle K. Maniate's *Amarilly of Clothes Line Alley* starring Mary Pickford could command a week's stay at the Globe, too.[68]

On Armistice Day, 11th November 1918, everyone at the Palace was given a holiday 'in view of the glad tidings', but there was business as usual at the Globe and Assembly Rooms. The latter was in the process of re-issuing the Essanay Chaplin films as an obvious counter to the exclusive showing of the First Nationals at the Globe.

The war years had taken their toll of cinema employees and new building had been severely restricted, yet, the prestige of cinema exhibition had increased. Cinema programme composition had changed: the picture hall was no longer a vaudeville of short subjects. Supporting comedies by Chaplin and other comedians might occasionally make top billing, but the feature film had arrived. Moreover, despite the submarine war, it was largely American films that were filling the screens. In the future, Trade magazines and local film reviewers would be at pains to praise home-grown products, but film fans knew the source of popular cinema. Soon, they would be demanding better presentation, better facilities, and a new standard in cinema building.

* * * * * * *

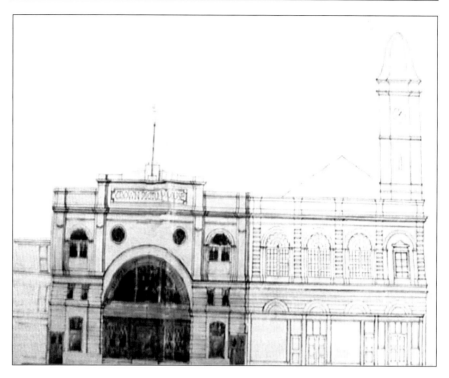

The Regal, Durham. The façade and longitudinal section, planned by S. Stephenson, of the cinema J. Dobson intended for the site he had bought in North Road, though it was not to be built for 17 years.

Durham County Record Office.

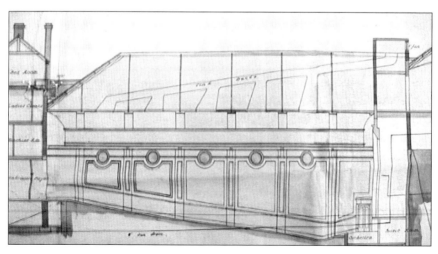

Chapter Four   Getting Back to Normal

1919

During the war, the opening times of the cinemas had been restricted. 6.30 p.m. and 8.30 p.m. had been the usual evening programme times. The original times of 7 p.m. and 9 p.m. were not authorised to be restored until 25th April 1919. For particularly long films such as *Cleopatra,* however, it was possible for the last performance to be extended beyond 10 p.m. By all accounts, Theda Bara gave a stunning performance in this film. The Chronicle reviewer observed that 'the raiment of the Queen and the Queen herself are the last word in regal magnificence. Much of it is daring but it is also dazzling.' Surviving stills and posters testify to his judgement. Prompted, no doubt, by the distributor's publicity, he almost ran out of superlatives in describing the cast of 30,000 people, Miss Bara's 50 distinctly different costumes, the 3,000 horses and 100,000 lunches that were consumed by the armies of Rome and Egypt. Durham audiences rushed to the Globe nightly for the whole week. [1]

Christie's East Auction catalogue *11th Dec 1995*

They were there in the same numbers the following week, but for a very different reason. Chaplin's three-reel war comedy *Shoulder Arms* was the main attraction; his longest film to date. The feature film alongside it was *The Awakening*, a forgettable 5-reeler starring Montague Love and Dorothy Kelly. The Chronicle reviewer makes no mention of it - the Globe manager was quite clearly balancing his budget with a cheap feature to offset the expensive Chaplin exclusive. The Assembly Rooms, too, were cashing in on the Chaplin craze at this time by re-playing all his Essanay comedies at the rate of one per week.

The Palace took a break from live theatre to show Chrissie White and Henry Edwards in *The Hanging Judge*. Interestingly, they emphasised the stage play origin of the story in their advertising. The Palace was the only venue in Durham at this time for live dramatic performances and the wording might be seen as an appeasement *and* an attraction for their theatre patrons.

WILLIAM
FAVERSHAM

in
"The Silver King"
A Paramount-Artcraft Special
By Henry Arthur Jones   •

"THE SILVER KING."
THE PICTURE OF 1919.

An illustrated advertisement announced the showing of the Paramount film *The Silver King* in April.[2] Although it was declared to be 'The Picture of 1919' neither its star, William Faversham, nor its title feature in any of the standard histories of American films. The extra publicity may have been linked with the fact that Faversham was an English stage actor starring in his first film at the age of 51, though the newspaper reviews don't mention this. The story must have had some appeal, because it was re-made in a British studio, also as a silent, in 1929.

In the days when the cinematograph was known as 'the flickers', because of the shutter-less projection of intermittent pictures, it was sometimes pointed out by opponents of the new entertainment form that visits to the cinema could result in eye-strain and headaches. A vestige of this opinion seems to be in a 1919 newspaper advertisement.[3]

'Do constant visits to the cinema induce lassitude? This question is provided by the fact that some people complain that after a visit to "the pictures" a weary languid feeling takes possession of them with a severe headache. The probable explanation is that the cinema is really a test of one's health. When a person is run-down or anaemic, a visit to the cinema produces the symptoms mentioned. Thanks to Dr. Williams Pink Pills you can get a complete recovery.'

In September, the Assembly rooms presented *A Peep Behind the Scenes* without making any reference to the fact that it starred Ivy Close, the Stockton girl who was winner of the Daily Mirror Beauty Contest in 1912. The film was made for the New Biograph

Company and was directed by Low Warren. Miss Close was to suffer tragedy when her film director husband Elwin Neame was killed in a car accident.[4]

When the Globe showed Mary Pickford's *Daddy-Long-legs*, their expectation of crowded houses was such that they charged a 3d. booking fee for advanced sales. The later reports of crowded houses suggest that their expectations were fulfilled. In the same week, the Assembly rooms had the G. B. Samuelson Film *Quinneys*. A set of 6 colourful postcards showing stills from the film were supplied to the cinema as publicity items.[5]

A publicity postcard for *Quinneys* 1920. *Author's Collection*

The Palace year opened with a week's performances of a musical play, *Kitty Grey*. The Palace's prices for live theatre were not much more expensive than those of the two cinemas. The pit and stalls were 6d and 9d respectively and the upper circle and centre circle only 1/- or 1/3.

There had been no Christmas Day shows at the cinemas, but the Globe was advertising a special New Year's Day matinée at 3 p.m. of Pauline Frederick in *The Woman on The Index*, and they were showing episode nine of the serial film *Elmo, The Mighty* with

Elmo Lincoln. The Assembly Rooms had *Kiss and Kill* starring Priscilla Dean and Alfred Allen, a film that was already over a year old. [6]

In the week of 19th January, the Palace had the musical play *The Movie Maid*. The star cast included Elsie Maynard and Mabel Graham, and there were spectacular dance routines by Doonan & Blackburn and 'The 8 Flickers'. The advance reports described the elaborate dresses, beautiful scenes and the work of the full chorus of 'Movie Girls'.[7] When this returned to the Palace in September 1920, it was described as 'Durham's Own Revue' and attributed to R. and W. Ainsley of the Gaiety Theatre, Houghton-le-Spring. During its Northern tour it was said to have broken all records at many theatres.[8]

The fire that damaged the Ushaw Moor Working Men's Club and Institute on the early morning of 19th February appeared to have started in the billiard room on the ground floor and spread with great rapidity to the steward's house adjoining. It then spread to the upper floor section used as the cinema. A slight breeze fanned the flames and threatened to engulf the whole building but Sergeant Jameson and local police officers were quickly on the scene and with other volunteers made strenuous efforts to stem the progress of the fire. The Rescue Brigade had to come all the way from Houghton-le-Spring. They arrived at about 8 a.m. and within the hour managed to check the flames. But the roof had collapsed and a lot of damage had been done.[9]

Elmo Lincoln had come to the cinemagoers notice in D. W. Griffith's *Intolerance* (1916) as the Mighty Man of Valour of Belshazzar's bodyguard. *Elmo The Mighty*, the serial being shown at the Globe, was not made until 1919. Between these films, he had starred as the screen's first Tarzan in *Tarzan of The Apes* and *The Romance of Tarzan*. The attention paid to him by the release of the serial obviously prompted the Globe manager to play both Tarzan films in February and March respectively.[10]

The magistrates would not allow the cinemas to open on Good Friday, but in the evening the cathedral moved into the audio-visual age before an 'exceptionally large congregation'. Dean Welldon presented the Passion of Christ by means of lantern slides. "It was all very wonderful. As we passed through the North door into the half-light of the great interior we cast our eyes along the nave, and away at the end of the avenue of massive pillars was the figure of the Crucifixion, the foundation of Christianity. The service was in reality an innovation for the Mother Church, and though the pictures were not so clear that they could be seen effectively by those at the rear of the Cathedral, they were none the less deeply interesting. The more modern vehicle of the screen has come into vogue." "In several respects, the service was in the form of an experiment. In the first portion of the pictures, the light from the pulpit detracted from the pictures, but this was soon rectified. The words of the hymn 'On Jordan's Banks' were thrown upon the screen and were sung by the congregation to the accompaniment of the organ." The slides that followed depicted the story of Christ's Passion with the Dean marking each one with a homily.[11]

John the Baptist (in the form of Albert Roscoe) was in evidence at the Globe the following week when Theda Bara's *Salome* was presented. "For Fox Pictures the creation of this great dramatic spectacle was a labour of love. The reproduction of Old Judea drew on their financial resources without reserve or hindrance. Five thousand players were engaged in this super picture - eight hundred artisans alone were employed in building a reproduction of the city of Jerusalem, one of several replicas on a large scale. Ten aeroplane propellers on stationary pillars produced the storm effects." The publicity handout obviously produced good copy for the Advertiser reviewer.[12]

Another controversial film made its appearance at the Palace in May, *The End of The Road*. The advertising announced that it was the only film authorised by 'the National Council', without adding that it was the National Council for Combating Venereal Diseases. There was a serious post-war crisis in the field of venereal diseases and the Ministry of Health approved the showing of the film. The British Censorship Board, however, refused to pass it. Its appearance in Durham, therefore must have received some kind of local authority approval.

In London, a group of medical students from the Middlesex Hospital voiced their resentment at the problem of venereal disease being used as public entertainment.[13] The Advertiser reviewer seems unable refer to it in any other terms. It was, after all, a fictional representation of a social dilemma.[14] "Visitors to the Palace this week are being entertained by the extraordinary film *The End of The Road,* which has achieved considerable notoriety. It is the world's greatest morality photo-play, as seen by a million people in London. The film aims at suppressing a menace to public health. Adults only are admitted to the Theatre." The showing passed off without any reported comment by the general public or the authorities.

In July, the Palace had an American Civil War film *Secret Service* and an unidentified Chaplin film, but its days of switching between films, plays, and variety were numbered. A newspaper advertisement in August indicated that it was closing for a short while for cleaning and re-seating. At the re-opening in September, again under the management of T. C. Rawes, elaborate new seating had been included *and* the cinematograph projector had been removed, 'for the time being'. A full report revealed the details of the 'much-needed improvements'. –

"Painters, decorators, upholsterers, joiners and electricians were speedily at work, and the result of their operations is seen in a transformed interior. Most noticeable, of course, to the casual visitor are the charming colour schemes which have been excellently carried out by Mr. Adamson and his staff of workmen. The proscenium forms a picture of great beauty, and by the skilful use of five colours, a most artistic effect has been secured. The flowering is one of the chief features of the decorations, and both these designs and the cherubs in front of the boxes have been cleverly treated. Three hundred tip-up new seats in red plush have been provided and fixed in the dress circle and a hundred in old gold in the orchestra stalls by Mr. T. Delicate. A new exit at the back of the dress circle secures absolute safety to the audience, and makes the theatre decidedly more accessible. The downstairs seats are newly arranged in red and green, the joinery work having been carried out by Mr. Arthur Mann. A new curtain is to be provided for advertising purposes. New scenery has been painted by a well-known scenic artist in the person of Mr Shepherd, London. Messrs Morgan and Saynor have installed a new system of electrical fittings. Linoleum has been laid the whole length of the ground floor, and the dressing rooms have been thoroughly cleaned, ventilated, painted and distempered. There will be a first class variety programme on Monday."[15]

In keeping with their usual practice, the Assembly Rooms had

GLOBE CINEMA,

NORTH ROAD, DURHAM·

Special Boy Scouts' Programme

(By kind permission of the I'n of p f f ANy

I N

WEDNESDAY, DECEMBER 29, 1920

at 3 o'clock.

THE PROGRAMME INCLUDES:

The Great International
Jamboree Film

ANIb

Scout Educational Film.

PRICES AS USUAL.

no Christmas Day show, but the Globe did. From its title the film *The Market of Souls* hardly seemed appropriate fare for a Christmas treat!! The plot of this Dorothy Dalton film, however, was more innocent than the title suggested. There were two performances on Christmas Day and a special matinée on Boxing Day. There was another special matinée on 29th December for the local scouts. The programme opened with film of the Great International Jamboree at Olympia, followed by an educational film about Scouting. The Chief Scout, Sir Robert Baden-Powell, was seen in the introduction to the film which went on to illustrate all the stages of scouting from wolf cubs to senior scouts. There were scenes taken at the popular scout camps. It was followed by a story film about how scouting converted a boy who had nothing to do into a dedicated scout. The *Pathé Gazette* and a Sunshine Comedy film completed the show. The surprising factor of the show was that it was 'Prices as usual.' [16]

1921

The New Year opened with an old debate in the Chester-le-Street Police Court.[17] John Turnbull applied for the renewal of the seven-day licences for the Pavilion, Grange Villa, the Grand, Newfield, the Empire and the Palace, Chester-le Street, and the Co-operative Hall, Birtley. Mr Lambert made a similar application in respect of a picture house at Wrekenton. Opposing the application in respect of Sunday opening were representatives of the local parish and non-conformist churches. The magistrates were clearly inclined to grant the licences from the outset. When one of the magistrates, J. R. Mole, asked why the Church group objected to the pictures when they didn't know the character of them, he received the reply that they objected to the showing of *any* films on

Sundays. Mr. Turnbull for the exhibitors, and sensing victory, repeated the magistrate's question and added that the objectors should not be casting aspersions upon the character of persons attending the performances without valid evidence. The objectors, he said, should visit the theatres and if they noticed anything objectionable they had recourse to complain to the police authorities. The Sunday shows provided wholesome entertainment for local people who because of the means of employment could not attend during the week. Moreover, young men attending the shows were better occupied than hanging about the streets. He drew the benches attention to the fact that in Middlesborough, a local vicar had been granted a cinema licence for Sunday night services. He also referred them to the complimentary remarks made by the recorder of Newcastle-under-Lyme, when assured by the police that attendance at the picture halls accounted for the diminution in crime. A police sergeant had expressed the opinion that pictures houses were as good as six policemen for keeping rowdy lads off the streets.

In granting the seven-day licences, the magistrates said that, though they had listened carefully to the honest points made by the objectors, they could not overlook the fact that there were a large number of people who stood about the streets. There was not the slightest doubt in their minds that if there were no picture houses these people would go to worse places. Their deliberations did not affect the cinemas in Durham city, but the arguments were bound to attract the attention of the local magistrates in any applications made to them. The two city cinemas appeared to be content with the situation of their six-day licences, however, and their respect for most Holy Days. They made no application in 1921 for films to be shown on Good Friday.

In March, the debate was carried to the south of the city, with applications for seven-day licences for the Ferryhill and Spennymoor Districts.[18] Deputy Chief Constable Waller reported that there were 13 theatre licences and 22 cinema hall licences awaiting renewal. The Revd. A. J. Courtney, Wesleyan minister, spoke against the Sunday Cinemas that had been open in the Ferryhill district. He had a petition signed by 1,765 persons against the proposition. Captain Apperley, from the bench, pointed out that it was invariably their custom to fix the terms so as not to interfere with church services. One of Mr. Courtney's arguments was that the opening of picture halls involved Sunday labour, and Mr Ferens on behalf of the cinema proprietors asked him if he did not consider that *he* worked on Sundays. Mr Courtney replied that, in his opinion, spiritual work was entirely different. Mr Ferens wanted to know if the pictures might affect the mind as beneficially as attending church services. Mr Courtney replied that psychology taught that a man was not only a thinking sentimental being but a moral being as well. On the question of Sunday labour, the magistrates maintained that employees must be free agents. It was also agreed that the doors would not be open before 7.45 p.m. on Sunday, and the performance would not start before 8 p.m. In a move that seemed additional to their normal powers, however, the magistrates decided not to renew the licences at that meeting until they could discover from the proposers if they might make some provisions for children and their parents to be in separate parts of the building.[19]

Vigilance in the operation of the 1909 Cinematograph Act occupied considerable police time, and in May resulted in an important prosecution. The proprietors of the Gaiety Picture Hall, Hamilton Row, Waterhouses were summoned for failing to take proper safety precautions under the Act. One co-lessee, Bert Whittaker, did not appear and the other, William Richard Bird, was represented by Mr Cooke because he was too ill to attend. The projectionist Patrick Rooney denied the offence. The evidence given by the police inspector was extremely revealing. Inspector Foster said that in the company of Sgt. Jameson, he visited the Gaiety Picture Hall, and found 230 people present (the cinemas capacity was 280). On inspecting the very small operator's box, they saw Patrick Rooney who was working the machine. Bert Whittaker was also present and said he was leasing the hall from Mr. Scott Elder. On the floor of the operating box, they found a lot of discarded carbon rods from the arc lamps and dozens of match-sticks. The box had evidently not been swept out for some time.

Immediately inside the door, between the entrance and the operator, were six un-boxed films which were not being used at the time. Altogether there was 5,000 ft. of films in the wooden operating box. The small hole through which the films were shown was not protected by a shutter. Near to it was the entrance door which led into the auditorium. The door was so lightly latched, that it would have given way under pressure. There was no railing between the operator's box and the auditorium and there was no fire-bucket filled with sand, there were no water buckets or wet blankets and no fire extinguishers in the box or any where around the place.

When the Inspector asked Whittaker why there were no fire-fighting appliances, he had said that he had been there eight weeks and had never seen any. He confirmed that Rooney, the operator, had asked for these to be supplied when he had taken over the building but that he had failed to fulfil the request.

Mr. Cooke, on behalf of Mr. Bird and the Picture Hall, said that the Hall belonged to Mr. Scott Elder, but as the tenants were continually changing he asked Mr. Bird, who was a practical electrician, to hold the licence. Mr. Bird unfortunately had been ill since February and Mr. Whittaker had been appointed as manager. It was intended to transfer the licence to him if he proved satisfactory. Mr. Bird had provided all the required appliances but with the exception of one lamp, everything had been stolen. The owner promised to provide a fireproof enclosure outside.

Detective Constable Waller said that Whittaker rented the place from the owner, not Mr. Bird, and paid £4 per week. It was clear that the licensee was shirking his responsibility. After a private consultation, the bench decided unanimously to fine Rooney 10 shillings and costs, and each of the other defendants £5 and costs in each case. The chairman added that because the hall seemed very unsuitable, the police should keep it under their observation. Plans for the rebuilding of the projection box were submitted to the licensing authority a few weeks later. The cinema had been opened in 1914, and after more troublesome years it finally closed on 4th February 1929. [20]

The Brandon & Byshottles Co-operative Society re-opened their meeting hall as the Co-operative Kinema, Meadowfield, shortly after the January quarterly meeting. In April, it was reported that the average attendance was now double that of its previous operation by the Society. The seats were priced at 5d, 8d, and 1/-.

A member of the Society objected to the manager's expenditure of £10 13s 2d. The chairman pointed out that this was incurred through journeys to film Trade shows in Newcastle in order to secure the best possible films for the cinema.[21] The July meeting of the Society confirmed that the Kinema was now paying its way and was well patronised. The expenses for the cinema were £865 15s. This comprised films, carriage, entertainment tax, wages and everything else. A member expressed his opinion that the pictures being shown were second to none in the neighbourhood.[22] When they showed the Dempsey-Carpentier Fight Film in August they were clearly expecting to entice some patrons from the city with their advertisement 'Buses from Durham Stop near the Door'.[23]

In July, the 'Women's World' column of the Durham Advertiser made some interesting comments upon cinema attendance. In an article headed 'How the Cinema Cultivates Taste in Melodrama', the writer suggested that the small stages of provincial theatres were no match for the wide canvases of the cinemas. Plays would do well to dispense with 'thrilling scenes' on the grounds that cinema did it far better. Nothing on the stage could match the escapades of Douglas Fairbanks, but the provision of colourful and engaging stage scenery was often a greater talking point than the hero's rights and wrongs.[24]

It was not the best of times for the area. The bitter miners' strike of earlier in the year had already caused the unemployment of over 25,000 miners. Feeding stations were in operation and though the strike was over by the summer a number of large collieries had still not re-opened. Attendances at the Palace had fallen substantially and in June it closed. It was estimated that it would be not re-open for some considerable time.[25]

The opening of the Coliseum cinema, Houghton-le-Spring, on Wednesday afternoon 3rd August 1921, prompted the Durham Chronicle reporter to reflect upon the recent history of entertainment in the town. "Some twelve years ago, (1909) Mr. John Ainsley at considerable cost built the Gaiety Theatre and three years later Mr. Wheatley built the Empire Picture Hall. Now Messrs John Lishman and Norman Robinson had provided the most up-to date of halls, decorated and seated in a way leaving nothing to be desired." The cinema, in Newbottle Street, was designed by the Newcastle architects Messrs Percy L. Brown & Glover, had accommodation for 800 patrons all with an uninterrupted view of the screen, and was officially opened by Robert Hunter, chairman of the Houghton-le-Spring Urban District Council.[26]

In September, the Secretary of the Durham Chamber of Trade, W. Hedley. said that he had been in communication with a film company with a view to their making an advertising film about the city. He had ascertained that a film of 700ft to 1000ft celebrating the historical features of the town would cost 2s 6d per foot with subsequent prints being made for 1s per foot. The President observed that the initial expense for the film (about £90) appeared heavy and he asked for information concerning the possible revenue if people were charged to see the complete film. No decision was taken at the meeting.

In Durham, the Assembly Rooms began showing a series of Sherlock Holmes films directed by Stockton-born Maurice Elvey. The great detective was played by Eille Norwood and Watson by Hubert Willis: eventually 15 self-contained 2000ft episodes were made by Elvey adding to his already prodigious output of films.

A neat bit of detective work by attendant Samuel Drain led to the police court appearance of 22year-old Edward Mews accused of committing a breach of the peace by discharging a catapult in the Empire Cinema, Langley Moor. The magistrates dismissed the charge after hearing details of a brawl between three men and another patron. [27]

After an eight-week closure, the Palace again tried to bring live entertainment to Durham. Chosen for the Bank Holiday re-opening was a show by Australian entertainers said to have been seen by over 550,000 people. Later reports indicated that there was good patronage in all the Durham places of entertainment.[28] The Palace continued to put on variety shows for the next three months, though on some weeks it was reduced to offering a £50 prize to induce 'Go-As-You-Please' contestants to fill the bill. Inevitably, closure again loomed.

When it re-opened in December, it was as a cinema not as a theatre. The Advertiser reported the change with regret - "For some time past the support accorded to stage productions has been much below that which the performances merited. It became evident that the cinema had the greater hold upon the people of the city. It should be noted that the pictures will be continuous – a system which has many advantages from 6.30 to 10.30 on weekdays and from 5.30 to 10.30 on Saturdays."[29] The new position of the screen was at the back of the present stage. There were crowded houses for the re-opening and the general opinion was that the continuous showing proved highly popular. The opening film was the Famous Players-Lasky film *Crooked Streets* with Jack Holt and Ethel Clayton.[30]

The Dean of Durham, James Welldon, again expressed some of his thoughts on Sunday observance in a sermon in September, entitled 'The Day of Rest'. "It is far better," he said, "that men and women should visit museums and libraries and listen to sacred music and lecture upon serious subjects that that they should hang about public houses." He didn't actually get as far as defining where Sunday cinemagoing fitted into this continuum.[31]

Later in the month, his sermon included a reference to the adulation of film stars such as Charlie Chaplin. On 9th September Chaplin had just made his first visit to London since 1910. He had been mobbed everywhere he went. "Hero-worship is good in itself," said the Dean, "in that it is important that the heroes should be worthy of the homage paid to them. And a nation which claims Charlie Chaplin as a hero may easily make itself somewhat of a laughing stock. He is only a pleasing figure on the films. I give all credit to the tenderness of his art, such as it is, but what is there in a pose, or a smirk, or a hat, or a pair of trousers to make a man a hero?"

In a clear reference to the previous year's rapturous London welcome to Douglas Fairbanks and Mary Pickford on their European honeymoon, the Dean said, "Yesterday, the heroine was Mary Pickford, I do not like to speculate whom the hero or heroine will be tomorrow." He continued his sermon on a more conciliatory note by saying that he wished Chaplin good luck. "There is something very natural and very human in his wish to re-visit the old scenes of his youth."

To some extent, he revealed his ignorance of the content of the Chaplin comedies by his concluding remarks. "I never forget that anybody who provides the people with clean fun is in some sense a benefactor, although I cannot profess to regard him as a hero in the national life."[32]

What people of Dean Welldon's class would regard as clean fun actually seems to be absent from most of Chaplin's two-reelers: domestic and public violence, drunkenness, infidelity, inappropriate behaviour and fraud are ever present.

The Little Tramp lives by guile rather than goodness. His virtue is survival.

1922

In January 1922, the Dean did have the opportunity to refer to the influence of cinema. In a criminal trial, a son had claimed that he killed his father because he had seen this at the cinema. The Dean said that such a violent incident could not fail to excite some reflection on the moral danger of cinema shows. It was his opinion, however, that it would be unwise to deny or disparage the educational value of the cinema. He hoped that teachers of all grades and in all classes would not fail to make use of the cinema. He thought that parents should not allow children to go night after night to exhibitions of an exciting, provoking or disturbing nature.

Zena Dare publicity postcard for 5 John Street. *(Author's Collection)*

He thought that the state was doing its best to prohibit film exhibitions that were immoral in themselves, and those of the sort that made heroes out of criminals. *The Bioscope*, in reporting his sermon, thought that the Northern Film Trade must have a warm friend in the Dean.[33]

Durham city cinemagoers now had three choices of programme. At the end of January the Palace was showing D. W. Griffith's *The Love Flower*, the Globe had the British film *The Way of The World*, and the

Assembly Room another British film *Married Life*.[34] This latter film was rumoured to have been based upon 'Married Love', Dr. Marie Stopes' book concerning family planning. In effect, it was a film adaptation of a play by J. B. Buckstone.[35]

Named comedians other than Chaplin began to occupy the local screens. Two-reelers by Harold Lloyd and by Buster Keaton made regular appearances at the Assembly Rooms, now affectionately known as 'the Semms'. Cinema was becoming an important part of the social and fashion life of the town. The Advertiser even carried a photograph of beauty and film star Zena Dare in the Astra production of *No.5 John Street*. The company had issued the same picture as a give-away postcard.[36]

Live theatre made a fleeting re-appearance at the Palace in February when the Durham Amateur Operatic Society staged its performance of *Tom Jones*. The booking was probably a long standing one completed before the Palace decided to convert to a cinema, since their next production in April took place at St. Margaret's Hall.

The link between other narrative forms and the cinema was observed by the Advertiser in reviewing the showing of the film *The Knave of Diamonds* at the Assembly Rooms. "Famous books are now adapted to the screen almost as a matter of course. Miss Ethel M. Dell's novels are no exception to the rule. Already there have been presented on Durham screens versions of *The Lamp in The Desert*, *The Knight Errant*, *The Way of An Eagle*, and *The Keeper of the Door* to mention but a few." All these films were produced by the Stoll Corporation between 1918 and 1922.[37]

Frugal programming was obviously a factor in the success of the cinema enterprise at the Palace. In May, they showed Mary Pickford's latest film *Little Lord Fauntleroy* on Monday, Tuesday, Wednesday and Saturday. Because of its length, special times needed to be arranged for the two showings each evening. No doubt the exclusive booking fee for the local showing had been excessive and on the other two nights of the week, they slotted in John Barrymore's *Raffles* first released in 1917! Varied programming must also have been a factor, for in the next week, they presented *A Thousand And One Nights,* an elaborate costume drama enhanced by the application of Pathécolor. In the same week, the Globe was attracting large crowds with another exotic film, *The Queen of Sheba*. Betty Blythe's costumes in this were considered to be quite daring (*see right*).[38]

BETTY BLYTHE AS QUEEN OF SHEBA

Animated cartoons were beginning to be a feature of most programmes during the twenties. Especially popular were those featuring *Felix The Cat*. The earliest Felix animations in 1919 were attached to a magazine short called *Eve's Review*. The Palace had been showing this for some time, even as part of its variety programme. In 1922, instead of advertising *Eve's Review*, Felix is mentioned separately. *Bud and Sue* cartoons, part of the magazine programme alternating with Felix appearances, were also included in the Palace advertisements.

The Globe showed the controversial film *Cocaine* in August.[39] In some places, this had been the subject of local censorship, and carried an 'A' certificate. The newspaper advertisements at this time ignored the British Board of Film Censors categories, and it seems that the local distributors also ignored the Board's request that the film should be shown under a different title. In May, it was Trade shown in London as *Cocaine*, and in July under its new title of *While London Sleeps*. No specific comment is made about its content in the local press.

On November 22nd, the Globe changed its programming to continuous performances between 6.30 p.m. and 10.30 p.m. on weekdays 5.30 to 10.30 on Saturdays, which exactly matched the times at the Palace. The Assembly Rooms persisted with separate performances.[40]

1923

The Palace Theatre began the year began with two spectacular productions. The Italian *Theodora, The Slave Princess* attempted to capture the earlier days of Ambrosio's classic magnificence, but its theatricality weighed heavily upon its length. *The Glorious Adventure* was a British production in a new colour process. Prizmacolor was a natural colour process achieved via bi-pack film. Its red and green colouration produced a variety of other colours through a subtractive process. A recent restoration of the only surviving print has demonstrated that it was only marginally successful in reproducing the rich colours of the period costumes. Since the film concerned the Great Fire of London, its red colours were particularly appropriate. Amazingly, the Advertiser reviewer made no mention of the colouring.

Controversy had surrounded the making and the showing of Erich Von Stroheim's *Foolish Wives*. "No picture yet produced," said the Advertiser reviewer, "has provided so much discussion. It is a film of tremendous interest and must be seen to be appreciated."[41] It was the Holy Week film at the Palace and the authorities seemed not to have objected to its showing on Good Friday.

The Palace, in fact, seemed to be getting all the most talked about films. *The Royal Divorce* was an unusually long British costume drama concerning the life of Napoleon. Its 10,000ft would have given it a running time of about two hours, and its week's showing was at special times in order that two shows could be accommodated into an evening. Gwylim Evans played Napoleon, and Gertrude McCoy played Josephine. [42]

A fire caused the enforced re-location of the cinema enterprise of well-known local showman William W. Turnbull. He had been using the upper floor of Bowburn Working Men's Club as the Olympia Picture Hall. In the early morning of Saturday 16th June an electrical fault in the fuse box of the cinema ignited the upper floor. As the fire took hold, the central heating reservoir water-tanks burst and saturated the walls of the adjoining steward's house putting out the flames and saving it from destruction. The first people on the scene were able to save a billiard table and a dynamo from the water and the flames. The uninsured projector and films valued at £100 were destroyed and the whole building was gutted. The report said that the building itself was insured and would be re-built.[43]

Undaunted by his misfortune, William Turnbull moved to Sherburn Hill and opened a cinema there on October 20 1923. The first film shown was a *Go Get 'Em Gurringer,* a 1919 Western drama starring Franklyn Farnum and Helene Chadwick. The actual location of the building is not made clear in the newspaper report.[44] It is possible that he took up temporary residence in the Co-operative Hall. When the Bowburn Working Men's Club was rebuilt, it would appear that William Turnbull re-opened the Olympia in February 1924.[45]

In the same month a cinematograph licence was granted to Mr. Turnbull for use in Sherburn Hill. It is not clear if this was for the new picture hall, which eventually came to be called the Unity and which remained open in the village until 1940.[46]

1924

Since 1922, the Cinematograph Exhibitor's Association had been campaigning for the removal of the entertainment tax introduced during the war period. They formed the Cinema Tax Abolition Committee. Little progress had been made until the formation of the Labour Government in 1923, since it was known that the Labour Party had been critical of the tax when in opposition.

In March 1923, the Entertainment Tax Abolition League, as it had now become, met the Labour Chancellor, Philip Snowdon. The eventual result of this lobbying was a minor remission of the tax such that it was removed from seats up to sixpence in price and reduced on those up to 1s 3d. The changes were to come in force from 2nd June 1924, on condition that the remission was passed onto the public in the form of cheaper seats.[47]

Locally, this was complied with and the Globe's new prices were advertised as 3d and 6d (no tax), 11d and 1s 2d (tax included). The Palace prices were listed as Pit 3d, Stalls, 6d and Circle 11d, and at the Meadowfield Kinema, they were 4d, 6d, and 1s. (Children half-price.)

The cinema programmes had now settled into a pattern of one feature film and several supporting shorts. Newsreels and interest magazines commonly filled this section, but cartoons were clearly attractive enough fare to be advertised in the forthcoming programmes. *Felix The Cat* was still very popular, but Max Fleischer's *Out of the Inkwell* series and the Bray Studio's *Colonel Heezaliar* comedies were also well received. [48]

The Palace showed Chaplin's first non-comedy film A *Woman of Paris*. "This wonderful picture was written and directed by Charles Chaplin but he does not appear in it," said the Advertiser reviewer.[49] By the time it was shown in Durham most film fans would have gathered from their fan magazines that Chaplin did make a brief appearance in the film as a railway porter, and they would also have noticed that it had not been well received by the public. The fact that it only played at the Palace for three days suggests that the owner Mr. Rawes recognised its lack of pulling-power. Buster Keaton was proving a much greater attraction with the presentation of *Our Hospitality*. "This is a screamingly funny picture with Buster Keaton supported by his wife, Natalie Talmadge, his father Joe Keaton and his son, Buster Junior."[50] *Hollywood*, a film that certainly would have appealed to ardent cinemagoers was shown at the Assembly Rooms in August 1924. In its story of 'star-struck girls searching for fame', it managed to include '30 stars and 50 screen celebrities'. The newspaper report didn't attempt to describe the difference between a star and a screen celebrity.

As a supporting film, the Globe had a novelty item by American star Florence Turner. In 1913, she had set up her own company in Britain, and her short films exploited her particular skill in parody and facial contortion. This 2,000ft film showed Miss Turner impersonating western star William S. Hart, comedians Larry Semon and Charlie Chaplin, dramatic stars Mae Murray and Richard Barthelmess, and the cartoon cat, Felix.

In the same week, the Meadowfield Kinema, mindful of its *clientèle* from the mining community, began to hold Wednesday morning special matinées for night workers. As had been intimated in a previous licensing court session, the opening hours of cinemas on weekdays was not a matter of concern to the magistrates or the police. There is no newspaper report of the success of these special matinées nor their period of operation.[51]

Westerns, detective dramas, and romances populated the screen, but there was still room for a dose of dramatic reality. The Wembley Exhibition was soon to open and provide 'theme-park' glimpses of the vastness of the Empire. Feature-length expedition films to exotic places provided the same kind of at-home travel, and they proved to be very popular. Some were hawked around the country by the expedition leaders themselves, often providing first-hand live narration via the new miracle of the sound amplifier. Dales-born cinematographer Cherry Kearton had pioneered the real-life animal expedition film before the war, and in the twenties he returned to the genre with some feature-length compilations of his early work. There was a particular fascination with films of human beings pitting themselves against wild animals and natural hazards. One such, *Hunting Big Game in Africa* was presented at the Assembly Rooms with cinema's usual superlatives – 'H. A. Snow's 5,000 mile expedition through the heart of the African Jungle.'[52] In Durham, it only stayed three days, but in London it had filled the Palace Theatre for several weeks.

The Empire Exhibition itself was of sufficient interest to generate a number of documentary films. In September, the Assembly Rooms advertised *Wembley the World's Eighth Wonder*, and attempted to draw the crowds with the information that 'The world's greatest exhibition has transferred to this theatre.' The report indicated that the audience would see a complete tour of all the exhibits, a valuable taster for Dunelmians who could take advantage of one-day trips leaving the railway station at midnight, or taking special six-day tours organised by the L.N.E.R.[53]

Adventure was clearly in the air at all the cinemas. Thrilling serials were again much in evidence. It was usual when one serial was coming to an end and another starting that the two ran concurrently, but, *Daniel Boon* and *Her Dangerous Path* at the Meadowfield Kinema were both only in their third episodes. The Palace was showing a British-made series of *Doctor Fu Manchu* episodes, and the Globe had a Hurricane Hutchinson serial *Speed*. The Assembly Rooms advertised that they were beginning a new serial *Ruth on the Range* starring Ruth Roland.[54]

Two cards of a series given away with the Stoll *Doctor Fu Manchu* films.
Author's Collection

In the same week, the newspapers and the town were paying tribute to the owner and founder of the Assembly Rooms Theatre, Thomas Rushworth, snr, who died at his home in South Street on 30th September 1924. Born in 1850, he was the son of Timothy Rushworth, who had established a fine art business in the city in the 1840s, and the brother of William Rushworth who had been an architect with the Durham Education Department. He was educated at the Model School in the grounds of Bede College and upon completing his schooling went into his father's business. He was a dedicated supporter of the Regatta and rowing, but his major cause for fame was his acknowledged authority in the field of British and Foreign artists. He was regularly called forth to identify and verify the provenance of paintings.

He had built the Assembly Rooms to his brother's design in 1891 on the site of a previous 'terpsichorean temple' and brought much-needed professional drama and opera to the city. He married a Miss Peele and had two sons, Walter and Thomas, and two daughters, Grace and Theresa. It had been his hope that the two sons would carry on the business, but Walter was taken ill and died in 1915, and Thomas, who had had a distinguished war-record, died from a war-related illness in 1923. Mr. Rushworth had appeared to be fit and well up to a few months before his death. Only his closest family knew that he was, as we can now assume, suffering from terminal cancer. At his own wish, the coffin was carried to the St. Mary-le-Bow Church for the burial service and interment in the "family shop-wagon draped in a purple cloth." [55]

The cinematograph licence was transferred to Grace Rushworth, but the adverts continued to say T. Rushworth & Son. The new manager's policy of showing innovative films continued Mr. Rushworth's tradition. In November, the Assembly rooms was showing a film made in Eire that also had the distinction, of being, according to the adverts, 'the first film to combine natural colour and underwater photography'. *The Innocent Sinner* starred Maire Flynne, Jean Tolley, Mary MacLaren, and William Bailey.[56]

A pattern was now clearly established in the cinema. What became known as 'Big' films usually played for a week, and, very rarely, longer. The more run-of-the-mill films or re-issues were booked for only three days. Thus Lillian Gish in *The White Sister* and James Cruze's *The Covered Wagon* came into the "Big" film category when they had their Durham debuts.

The dangers of flammable film stock were the cause of a singularly tragic Christmas Day accident in Sedgefield, ironically one of the few places in the county not then to have a picture hall. 11 year-old Herbert Ward, with his

FIG. 91. BUTCHER's EMPIRE HOME KINEMATOGRAPH.

A Butcher Home 35mm projector circa 1916

toy cinematograph, was entertaining his friends, 5 year-old Edith Cunningham and 11 year-old George Rennie, in the pantry of their house in Front Street. The cinematograph was placed on a stool and the pantry door was closed. The family heard screams from the pantry and flames 2ft. high emerged from under the door. When the children were rescued, Edith and her step-brother George were very badly burned, and Herbert less so. Two days later Edith died from her injuries.

At the coroner's inquest, it was revealed that the internal latch of the pantry door was defective and it was thus impossible to open the door from the inside or the outside once it had been shut. Henry Sinclair, who was in the house, forced the door with a poker, but by then the fire had extinguished itself. Mr. Cunningham explained that he had been wary of the safety of the machine and had, in fact given it away to Herbert Ward during the year. When a verdict of accidental death was reached by the inquest jury, the Durham Coroner, John Graham, said that toy cinematographs were dangerous things for children to possess and even experienced cinematograph operators had to take great care preventing fires.[57]

A number of home movie projectors had been available since the early part of the century. The 1912 Pathéscope 28mm. projector introduced in 1912 used acetate safety film, but there were a number of manufacturers in Britain and Germany making 'toy' machines which used standard 35mm. film clips often acquired from rental companies at scrap value. The Kodascope 16mm projector had been announced in cinematograph journals in 1923.[58]

1925

The New Year saw little change in cinema exhibition. The notion of seasonal films had disappeared in favour of up-to-date films. The Assembly Rooms, still operating two houses per night, had a film version of Robert W. Service's *The Shooting of Dan McGrew* starring Barbara La Marr and Percy Marmont, plus Buster Keaton's two-reeler *The Balloonatic*. The Globe had a British film, *Old Bill through The Ages,* a comedy based upon the war-time character. Made by the Ideal Company, it was a cavalcade film with Syd Walker dreaming that he was present at historic events such as the signing of the Magna Carta, the Armada and the Boston Tea Party. The management felt that it had sufficient popularity to command a special matinée on New Year's and a special children's matinée on the Saturday.[59]

January and February were 'Big' film months. The Palace attracted large audiences with Lon Chaney's *The Hunchback of Notre Dame*. To get in an extra show each day, the film was shown continuously from 4.30 p.m.[60] The Assembly Rooms attracted a more erudite audience with an Italian version of *Cyrano de Bergerac.* "This Pathécolor film gained first place at the international contest in Turin," said the Advertiser reviewer.[61] "The photoplay far surpasses the stage play, as scenes which would be in the confined space of the stage have been produced in an exceptional manner." This comment, no doubt, was aimed at the playgoer *clientèle* of the theatre. A stage version of *Cyrano* had played in London 2 years previously with a 10 month run and its impact had probably filtered through to Durham. A surviving copy of the film, in all its stencilled colours, very much supports the reviewer's comments.

Tinted and coloured films were in particular evidence during the year. *Captain Blood* at the Palace and the Kinema, Meadowfield, had a spectacular colour sequence of a sea battle.[62] *The Thief of Baghdad* at the Globe only had tinted sequences but the sumptuous sets and costumes persuaded the reviewer to declare that "It is the most beautiful of pictures ever to have been put on the screen."[63]

Zane Grey's *Wanderer of the Wasteland* at the Globe was Paramount's first outdoor Technicolor film. Its location shooting in Death Valley, California and the Painted Desert in Arizona gave it special interest.[64]

Death Valley was also the location for the finale of *Greed* shown at the Assembly Rooms in December. Hailed as 'Eric von Stroheim's dramatic masterpiece' and signalled as the film version of 'the celebrated novel '*McTeague*', it was only booked for three days. No mention was made in the reports that the tragic McTeague was played by Spennymoor-born Harold Gibson Gowland, and that he was related to the local picture hall proprietors of the same name. The reviewer recognised that it was a milestone in cinema history, however, and gave "striking evidence in support of the claim that the silent drama can portray the most subtle shades of character."[65]

Zazu Pitts, Gibson Gowland and Hughie Mack in a scene from *Greed*. Courtesy Peter Gowland.

There were other 'big' films in the year. *Monsieur Beaucaire* starring Rudolph Valentino, arrived in Durham during Regatta Week after its "triumphal success at the London Palladium", and the Palace management, mindful of a possible diminished audience, specially ended the final Wednesday evening performance at 10 p.m. so that patrons would be able to see the fire-work display.[66] Also at the Palace, Cecil B. De Mille's *The Ten Commandments* was originally scheduled for a six days, but such was the demand for seats that it was retained for an extra three days. The Palace reverted to two separate performances per evening and a matinee on Saturday. There were to be no reductions for children except at the matinee. The Advertiser reviewer accurately expressed his belief that 'no other film has had such a similar nine-day continuous showing in this city.'[67]

Moon of Israel, a British film made in the epic style, was scooped by the Meadowfield Kinema. The Advertiser probably using the press notes to describe the film declared, "Hitherto, America with its vast number of cinemas and its grip upon the film markets of the world has reigned supreme in the making of films of a really immense scale. Great Britain with fewer than 3,000 cinemas provides only a limited market for the home production and to spend enormous sums on a British production is to lose money. Sir Oswald Stoll, therefore, conceived the idea of co-operating with a continental film company and *Moon of Israel* a film which America cannot hope to eclipse, is the result. The picture was made in Vienna and Egypt and is a worthy adaptation of H. Rider Haggard's great story."[68] A week later, it also played at the Palace.

There were several novelty presentations in 1925. Norma Talmadge seems to have been particularly popular with Durham audiences, and in May, she was given a special week at the Assembly Rooms. On Monday, Tuesday, Wednesday and Saturday, a new film, *The Only Woman* was the main feature. On Thursday and Friday, fans could bathe in the nostalgia of consecutive 1922 re-issues, *Smiling Through* and *The Eternal Flame*.[69] *Father O'Flynn* at the Palace in July had a full accompaniment of singers. The lead baritone and presenter was T. F. Moss and the lead soprano was Mae Carr. Few details are available of this presentation, but in 1935 it seems that a musical comedy film of this same 'delightful story of the Emerald Isle' was distributed by Butcher's Film Service in the U.K.[70]

Positive encouragement of young people's appreciation of the cinema was made by William Turnbull at the Sherburn Hill Picture Hall. He had invited local schools to participate in an essay

competition concerning the film *The Covered Wagon*. The winners
were 5 year-old Doris Lister of Ludworth School and 9year-old
Henry Hill of Bowburn School. Runners-up, some of whom were
from Sherburn Hill Boys' School, received copies of a book telling
the story of the film *The Ten Commandments*.[71]

There had been a heavy blizzard throughout the city and
county on 19th December and Christmas Day performances took
place in fairly extreme weather. The Assembly Rooms had two
showings of Metro's thriller *The Way of a Girl* starring Eleanor
Boardman. The Globe was 'open as usual' on Christmas Night
with George O'Brien in the Fox film *Thorns of Passion*. The Palace
was the only one to offer what they called 'a seasonal picture': *One
Glorious Night*. It may have seemed too close to reality for comfort
as this domestic melodrama revealed how Elaine Hammerstein is
re-united with her child on Christmas Eve in a driving
snowstorm.[72]

1926

The Assembly Rooms began the New Year in comic style.
Marion Davies in *Zander The Great* was guaranteed to give patrons
an 'ideal entertainment of Love, Laughs and Thrills' according to
the publicity. The programme also advertised 'the latest screen
novelty - a Ko-Ko Song Cartune'. [73]

These short animations featuring the cartoon character Ko-Ko
the Clown, illustrated popular songs, and introduced the sing-
along system of the 'bouncing ball.' They were made by the
American Fleischer Animation Studios in 1924. Slide songs had, of
course, been very popular with audiences in both the Victorian and
Edwardian music halls, and the principle of pull-down printed
word-sheets survived into the computer age. The Fleischer
cartoons, whilst printing the words on the screen, also made
animated play of the words themselves and played visual tricks
with their alternative meanings. For many years, it was thought
that the 'bouncing ball', hovering for the right number of beats
over the words, was produced by animated drawings, but, in his
later years Max Fleischer revealed that the effect was achieved by a
employee holding a long stick with a luminescent white ball on the
tip, moving it up and down over the horizontally rotating lyrics.[74]

A year after these Song Cartunes appeared they were incorporated with Phonofilm, an experimental sound-on-film system. This process had been developed by Lee De Forest, inventor of the Audion valve, and Thomas Case, inventor of the glow-lamp. It enabled variations in microphone signals to be recorded on film. Some short films of singers and dancers and a speech by President Calvin Coolidge had been presented to the Royal Photographic Society in London on 17th February, 1925, but the audience was not very impressed by the sound quality.[75] De Forest and Case continued their experiments, both together and separately, and, as we shall see later, they had more success. Theatre organists and artists did have some problems with the silent versions of films. If they became damaged and there were missing frames, the ball would suddenly leap along the line, and disturb the continuity. [76]

 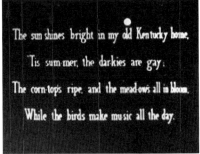

Frame enlargements from *My Old Kentucky Home* *Author's collection*

The Globe began the year in more serious mood with Pauline Frederick in *Smouldering Fires* at the beginning of the week and Mae Marsh in *Tides of Passion* at the end. There was, however, light relief with a Sunshine comedy *When Dumb Bells Ring* and a re-issue of Charlie Chaplin's 1922 film *Pay Day*. The Palace, opening at the earlier time of 5 o'clock on New Year's Day, played the epic adventure film *North of '36* featuring Jack Holt. Their advertisements assured potential patrons that it was better than *The Covered Wagon*. Critical opinion differed from this. Both were Westerns made by Paramount and both included Ernest Torrence and Lois Wilson in their cast lists.

January certainly was a momentous month for local cinemagoers. The Assembly Rooms had the epic French film *The Miracle of The Wolves* for just three days, whilst the Globe was showing one of Tom Mix's best-remembered films *Riders of the Purple Sage*. At the end of the month, the Globe recalled the war-time heroism of *Ýpres (Wipers)*. This was one of several reconstruction war documentaries made for British Instructional Films by H. Bruce Woolf and Walter Summers, using actual war footage, animated maps and re-staged items. The Advertiser report that 'individual acts of heroism' were being shown, falls into to the latter category.

The Palace had an unusual split week: on Monday and Tuesday they showed a re-issue of a 1920 film *The Virgin of Stamboul* featuring Priscilla Dean and for the rest of the week they had Paramount's much praised version of J. M. Barrie's *Peter Pan*.[77] This had filled the London Pavilion for weeks and the fan magazine had given it full publicity with feature articles on the choice of a *girl*, 17 year-old Betty Bronson, for the role of Peter Pan.

Animated cartoon producers in Britain had found the exhibitors particularly reluctant to accept their post-war efforts. There had been a number of attempts at cartoon series by Anson Dyer and Frank Zeitlin but they rarely progressed further than the titles indicated in their initial publicity.

Lancelot Speed's 26-episode series of *Pip, Squeak and Wilfred* in 1921 got reasonable reviews from the trade journals,[78] but there was no second series. A 1925 series seemed to have much more potential, based upon Bonzo, George Studdy's popular comic strip dog. The Kinematograph Weekly even suggested that it was 'a cartoon subject which will rival Felix the Cat'.[79]

CHEER UP DARLING, YOU'RE NOT SO RED AS YOU'RE PAINTED.
The film version of the Bonzo figure. *Author's collection.*

Certainly the surviving prints reveal well-observed movements and steady animation, but the story lines are rather plodding. The Globe showed its first Bonzo cartoon in the week of 8th March 1926 to the pleasure of the attending Dunelmians. Bonzo postcards were also very popular at this time. [80]

The Durham & District group of the National Council of Women held a special meeting in Durham in March. The main speaker, whose chosen topic was 'The Educational Value of the Cinema', was involved in an incident which itself could have emerged from a film drama. The large audience had to wait an anxious fifteen minutes for her arrival. The Honourable Mrs Franklin on her way from Edinburgh had unfortunately boarded a train that did not stop at Durham. She therefore had to charter a taxi at Darlington Station and make all speed to a lecture room on Palace Green.

She told her audience that the National Council of Women would be undertaking a survey concerning the effect of the cinema on children. "Everyone has an opinion on this," she said, "but what was needed was chapter and verse." She hoped that they would discover that cinemas were nothing more than good and wholesome recreation. She believed that films could not be considered educational, because viewing them did not require hard work. "Something that passes quickly in front of the eyes and requires no effort surely cannot be considered to be educational," she declared. She was also concerned that children as young as 14 and 15 were employed in the film-making processes, and she felt that another survey should investigate their working conditions.[81]

The Easter offerings were expected to attract large audiences. The Globe and the Palace were open at their usual times on Good Friday, and both managed an extra house on Easter Monday by opening at 5 o'clock. The Assembly had capacity houses for the six nights of the exhibition of *The Eagle* with Vilma Banky and Rudolph Valentino. And, the following week, they repeated the success with Eric Von Stroheim's *The Merry Widow.* The newspaper report drew particular attention to the spectacular settings, costumes and the Technicolor sequence. [82]

At this time, the Globe advertisements strangely reverted to the *New Globe.* There had been no change in management: the licence issued for the year was still in the name of Mary Jane Gray, and there had been no reported alterations. The Palace advertisements suggested that their programme contained a Crazy Kat Cartoon. The following week this was correctly reported as a Krazy Kat cartoon. These animations, based upon the George Herriman comic strip, first appeared in 1916 and had a chequered career of popularity. The 1926 series was produced for the same Winkler Corporation that gave Walt Disney his first animation contracts. English audiences found the slang of the American dialogue-bubbles both difficult to decipher and to understand, and they never achieved the popularity of the Felix cartoons.

Though Durham was virtually brought to a standstill by the General Strike of May 1926, film distribution was little affected. Supply dumps of films had been established in major towns and members of the Cinematograph Exhibitors' Association paid into an emergency fund. As things turned out, the brevity of the general part of the strike, precluded any need for the emergency plans, though the continuation of the strike by the miner's eventually reduced audience attendances, and greatly affected the community. In the 8th July issue of the Kinematograph Weekly, it was announced that the Pavilion, Grange Villa was closing temporarily because of the privations of the dispute, and that the closure of other halls in Durham and Northumberland was expected to follow. On the first day of the strike, 1500 miners from the Bearpark Colliery arrived in Durham with their banner flying and their band playing. "They proceeded to the Unemployment Exchange, deposited their unemployment cards, and returned home in an orderly manner." The Assembly Rooms seemed so certain of continuity that they embarked upon week one of a new serial *The Silver Streak* as an accompaniment to a Rin-Tin-Tin film *Below The Line*. The Palace had a double-feature programme of *Playing for Souls* starring Clive Brook and *The Cloud* described as 'an exciting picture of the air.' [83]

The following week the Meadowfield Kinema was claiming a 'picture of exceptional interest', *The Love Story of David Livingstone*. The newspaper advertisement declared it to be

"One of the most inspiring films ever produced. A Picture out of the common. Drama, Romance, Comedy, Adventure interwoven into a beautiful photoplay. You will see encounters with Lions, Buffalos (sic), Crocodiles and Hippos. Livingstone's fight with a lion, the discovery of the Victoria Falls; the Slave raids of Darkest Africa. It is a story of never ceasing excitement, of peril by day and night from wild beasts and hostile natives. The story that has thrilled and will thrill the hearts of all who respond to THE CALL OF ADVENTURE."

FIRST PRESENTATION IN DURHAM AND DISTRICT.

KINEMA MEADOWFIELD.

THURSDAY, FRIDAY, SATURDAY, MAY 20, 21, 22.

ONE OF THE MOST INSPIRING FILMS EVER PRODUCED.
A PICTURE OUT OF THE COMMON.
DRAMA, ROMANCE, COMEDY, ADVENTURE.
Interwoven into a beautiful photoplay.
THE LOVE STORY OF
DAVID
"LIVINGSTONE."
You will see actual encounters with LIONS, BUFFALOS, CROCODILES, AND HIPPOS.
LIVINGSTONE'S FIGHT WITH A LION.
THE DISCOVERY OF VICTORIA FALLS.
THE SLAVE RAIDS OF DARKEST AFRICA.
It is a story of never-ceasing excitement, of peril by day and night from wild beasts and hostile natives. A story that has thrilled and will thrill the hearts of all who respond TO THE CALL OF ADVENTURE.

ONCE NIGHTLY. AT 7. P.M. — SATURDAY. AT 2-30. 6-15. AND 8-45. P.M.

Although it was only shown once nightly on its four-day exhibition, there were two extra showings on the Saturday. M. A. Wetherell both acted the leading part and directed the film for his own company, Hero. It had been filmed in the actual locations in 1923, and released as a 6,500ft feature film. When it was trade shown in September 1925, the *Kinematograph Weekly* suggested that though it had plenty of wild animals, it lacked creative touches and was at least 10 per cent too long. Nevertheless, some inspired advertising helped it to reap good success in the provinces.[84]

In the same week, The Palace was thrilling its patrons with a different form of exploration, *The Lost World*. The special effects were particularly noted by the reports but the actual advertisement for the film was very low-key and it only had a three-day run. Even the biggest films were only presented for part of the week. A new version of *Quo Vadis* starring Emil Jannings, and John Ford's epic railway film *The Iron Horse* could only muster a three-day booking each at the Assembly Rooms and the Palace in June.

Leading up to the Bank Holiday weekend, the Palace provided a 'Song' picture for the seasonal crowds. *Rilka (The Gypsy Queen)* was accompanied by a group of singers. Leonard Williams, 'The

Popular Baritone', Renée Farrer 'The Eminent Soprano' and Lily Evans 'The Premier Contralto' synchronised their voices to the actors and actresses on the screen. The film had been made in Middlesborough for Thomas Thompson, the proprietor of six cinemas in the town. The actors were professionals, but the film appears to have been made by amateurs. It was shown in all the Thompson circuit cinemas, but it appears not to have had any bookings outside the northeast, and was not reviewed by any of the Trade journals. Thompson had ambitions to make more films, this was a reissue, his second and last was 'Neath Skies of Spain.[85]

They're joining the
GOLD (BAG) RUSH
by thousands !
**Meadow
Gold Bag (Small Leaf) Tea**
2/4 Reduced to 2/2 per lb.
A ½-lb. packet makes 90 good cups.

On the Monday, the Assembly Rooms re-opened after its annual week's closure for staff holidays and re-decoration. Its special attraction was a week's booking for Chaplin's *The Gold Rush*. An extra Wednesday matinée was provided for the entertainment of the holidaying school-children. The Kinema Meadowfield also had the same film for four days of that week. Its advertisements read 'This picture is for four days only. So get here early to avoid the Rush for the Gold Rush, Miss the Crush.' A cautionary note for its patrons, however, declared that 'owing to the enormous expense of this production, our usual prices will be changed. Our two-for-one prices will not apply.' The film even inspired a local advertisement for the Meadow Dairy Company in Silver Street!

The death of Rudolph Valentino in September was noted only by the reports of the newsreel film of his funeral. International news was rarely included in the local newspapers.[86]

The showing of *The Cobra* in October prompted the reviewer to declare that as a screen actor Valentino had "a lot of admirers in

Durham as elsewhere and consequently there are sure to be packed houses at the Palace for the remaining nights of the week."

His last film, *The Son of The Sheik*, was shown at the Assembly Rooms in December for six days.[87]

1927

The annual renewal of cinematograph licences rarely produced many changes, since careful inspection of the premises during the year usually revealed any impediments long before the licensing was due. In County Sessions for February, 1927, however, it was reported that that premises of the Empire, Low Spennymoor were not satisfactory, and that there was no request for a licence from the Club Hall, Ushaw Moor. [88]

Notable films for the early part of the year were *The Last Days of Pompeii,* an Italian spectacular with many Pathécolor sequences; and Alfred Hitchcock's *The Pleasure Garden.* 'This film has captivated audiences elsewhere and is sure to be a huge attraction.'[89] The Globe also showed Cecil B. De Mille's *The Volga Boatman* and provided the presentation with the musical accompaniment of *The Koslo Four*.[90] The most successful film at the Assembly Rooms at this time was King Vidor's *The Big Parade.*

The continuing popularity of Ivor Novello was further emphasised by the release of Hitchcock's *The Lodger.* "Ivor Novello appears with a famous review star 'June' in a thrilling mystery drama. A maniac is abroad murdering fair-haired girls, and London is alarmed. Into this atmosphere, there comes a young man who seeks lodging in a house. His attitude, his movements, his stealthy journeys at midnight are worked up by the producer to an intense pitch in a succession of guilty-looking incidents. But, is the lodger guilty? That is the problem which will hold the interest of the Globe audience to the last foot of film." [91]

In September, the Empress Cinema in Willington was completed for the Hately Brothers, the proprietors of the other Willington Cinema, the Empire. Conditions at the 500-seater Empire demanded an improvement. It was so close to the track of Bishop Auckland branch line that every passing train must have drastically disturbed the presentation. The new building was erected further up the road on the site of the old Parish Hall.

The Empress Theatre, Willington.. *Detail from a postcard in the George Nairne Collection*

For the opening, the proprietors had arranged a special concert and divided the entire proceeds between the Willington and District Nursing Association and the Oakanshaw Aged Miners' Homes. Mr Greener, the agent for Messrs Straker and Love's collieries, formally declared the theatre open and wished it every success. The concert performers were Madam Doris Cooper, (soprano), George Gibson of Birtley, (baritone), Tom Nicholson of Willington (comedian), the Willington West End Sketch Party, and the Brancepeth Colliery Silver Band conducted by J. B. Wright. No mention is made of any films being shown, but the newspaper report describes the ground floor projection room as being constructed of reinforced concrete conforming to the latest Government regulations. It was equipped with 'the latest machines for projecting pictures'.

There was accommodation for 1,000 people, 650 in the main hall and 350 in the gallery. The stage had an opening 25ft by 18ft and was equipped for theatrical and picture performances. The whole building, designed by Messrs Kellet & Clayton of Bishop Auckland and Darlington, was 121ft by 45ft. The entrance hall was surfaced with Italian marble with a doorway leading into the auditorium and two stairways leading to the gallery. The exterior frontage was of cream terra-cotta finished with an egg-shell glaze.[92]

Durham city cinemagoers were entertained to all the latest cinema crazes and major feature films. Harold Lloyd's *The Kid Brother* at the Palace was presented at a special matinée in aid of the Shaftesbury Homes. When *It* was shown at the same venue, the advertisement must have confused many citizens unfamiliar with its Americanese. It read, 'Flippant Flapper, and Dapper Naughty Haughty Chic Man Trapper.' [93] Rex Ingram's *Mare Nostrum (Our Sea)* and *The Battle of the Coronel and Falkland Islands* received high praise from the newspaper critic, and *The Flag Lieutenant* featuring Henry Edwards was described as 'The Greatest Entertainment ever screened.'[94] Vying for patrons in the week of 28th November were the film version of Jules Verne's *Michael Strogoff* and Fritz Lang's *Metropolis*. The Palace advertisements urged every man to see this film, which 'for sheer daring and imagination has never been equalled.' [95]

Amongst the Christmas festivities, the Old Folks' Trust Committee at Spennymoor arranged for an entertainment in the St. Andrew's Memorial Hall. Since it was not possible to accommodate all the old people at one time, the entertainment was in two halves. Firstly, Mr. Vasey of the Tivoli Picture Palace gave a cinematograph show from 12 o'clock until 2 o'clock, and then, after lunch, F. Gowland of the Arcadia gave a show for another two hours. There is no indication as to the origin of the films, or whether they were non-flam items suitable for showing in an unlicensed hall. [96]

1928

On January 5th, some Langley Park children were treated to a film show at the Empire through the generosity of the local Member of Parliament, Colonel Higham. He did not attend the show himself to see the special film presentation, the distribution of sweets and gifts, and the community singing and Christmas carols under the guidance of the resident pianist, Fred Burden.

The following week saw the arrival of *Ben Hur* at the Palace. A special booking office had been open for several days before the presentation and twice nightly separate performances were advertised. There were also to be afternoon matinées on Wednesday and Saturday. The film aroused so much interest that the vicar of the Claypath Congregational Church, the Reverend Harold Derbyshire, devoted the whole of his Sunday sermon to the topic of the Church and the Cinema. His case was so finely argued that it is important to quote it in detail. [97]

Ramon Novarro in " Ben - Hur."

One of a set of advertising cards for *Ben Hur*. *Author's Collection*

"The day has long past, if it ever existed at all, when the Church can afford to ignore the cinema, " he said. "Every week millions of people of all ages and classes watch the comedy, the drama and the chronicle of current events flitting across the screen. Their receptive minds are retaining an impression that is for good or evil. What should the church's attitude be? It would be futile, even were it desirable, to attempt to boycott the cinema on the grounds that the majority of films shown were injurious to morals. And surely the cinema is not evil in itself. On the other hand, it is an instrument which is capable of being used to accomplish mighty things for good."

"Christians could, I believe, by active support of good films even more than denunciation of bad ones, help to create a cleaner and saner cinema." "Unfortunately, a great many of the films shown in this country at present are not of a very high moral standard. Their general effect especially to young minds cannot be elevating. There are "crook" films, which may too easily familiarise children with crime. There are a great many war films, the sole motive of which seems to be to foster militaristic ideas, to glorify war and to hide its bestiality. And there is a great mass of picture drama from Britain, as well as from Hollywood, which lay an unhealthy emphasis on sex, and seem to assume that marriage, the most sacred of all human relationships is either a matter of temporary convenience or of selfish passion, or of both."

He then turned to his own review of the *Ben Hur* film -

"An example of the cinema's art at its best was exhibited in this city last week. A great subject has been treated in a manner that is on the whole beyond praise. Themes and incidents about which Christians are justifiably sensitive have been dealt with reverently and sympathetically. Nowhere in the film is the face or figure of Jesus portrayed. We see a hand stretched out to heal, an arm raised in exhortation to prayer, but that is all, and on the whole, perhaps it is wise. It is at least doubtful whether the figure of Christ can be shown reverently on the screen. There have been many objections to the film *King of Kings* which has been shown in London recently, although there have been other expressions of approval from well-known people. I have seen the Passion Play at Oberammergau, and that is not only a great spectacle, but a wonderful inspiration. But I am afraid that the atmosphere of Oberammergau is not too easy to produce in a photographic studio."

The original censorship precepts drawn up by the British Board of Film Censors in 1913 did decree that there should be no portrayal of Christ on the screen, re-affirmed in the Cinema Commission Report of 1917.[98] Although it had been granted an 'A' certificate by the B.B.F.C. in 1926, De Mille's *King of Kings* was refused a showing in a number of provincial towns.[99]

During his sermon, the Revd. Mr. Derbyshire also suggested that his 'line of argument' applied equally to the stage. He hoped that the proprietors of the proposed theatre to be built next door to his church could work with him in an amicable relationship.

The building was initially designated to be exclusively a theatre. Indeed, the share flotation also gave this impression. An advertisement offering shares in the project was placed in the Durham Advertiser of 2nd February. £20,000 capital was to be raised in £1 shares for the establishment of The Palladium (Durham) Ltd. 'to construct an up-to-date Theatre in Claypath, Durham.' At registration in January, the directors were Thomas William Holliday of Southlands, Durham (Chairman), Thomas Thompson, proprietor of the Hippodrome, Middlesborough, G. L. Drummond of the Hippodrome, Bishop Auckland, W. S. Gibson of Middlesborough, and J. W. Wood of Western Lodge, Durham. The share application was quickly oversubscribed by the closing date of 8th February, amidst denied rumours that the directors acquired most of the shares themselves.[100] Land clearance and building began in February 1928 with a proposed opening date of October in the same year.

Durham County Licensing February session supplied some valuable evidence of the operation of some of the cinemas close to the city. The Ushaw Moor Working Men's Club had not been used as a cinema since May 1926. According to Superintendent F. Foster it had only been open on 55 days during 1925 and during 1924 there had been similar restrictions. The obvious reason for this was that the Empire Cinema was only 100 yards away, and there was really no need for two cinemas. In fact, the club had adopted a policy, which he did not think was illegal, of renting the hall to the proprietors of the Empire for £5 a week in order, apparently, to keep the place closed. There were two cinemas at present in course of construction at Ferryhill and Gilesgate Moor.

In the Superintendent's opinion, these two cinemas were not needed. "It is my experience," he said, "that where you get a reasonable number of cinemas sufficient to provide for a particular area, there is reasonable income for money expended, and the public have a well-conducted place of entertainment. When an extra hall is erected the income drops and the licensee cannot reduce his expenditure or his staff and the only other method is to reduce expenditure upon his films or shows. This is going to happen in Ferryhill where there are already two big halls."[101] The newly completed Pavilion, Ferryhill with 901 seats, was granted a magistrates' licence in August 1928. The Dean Bank, Ferryhill with 900 seats, had held a cinematograph licence since 1924, and was sited in the former Miner's Hall. The owner was none other than Richard Monte, the former travelling showman still trading under the name of Randall Williams. The Gaiety Electric Theatre in John Street, Ferryhill is listed as having 1000 seats in 1914.[102] The Gilesgate Moor cinema, Marshall Terrace, Durham was licensed as the Crescent on 14th March 1928 under ownership of George Lamb. The plans had been submitted for approval in June 1927.[103] Notwithstanding Superintendent Foster's pessimism both new cinemas and their neighbours survived into the 1950s and 60s.

The frontage of the Crescent Cinema. Gilesgate Moor.
From original plans at D.C.R.O.

After recovering from its fire damage, the Ushaw Moor Workingmen's Club revived its interest in cinema in March. They applied for a licence on the understanding that they would abide by the rules. The club had a membership of 700 and they received no subsidy from a brewery. Losing the revenue from the cinema would seriously affect their finances. The Licensing chairman, in considering the application, said that competition in the cinema business had become very keen, and it had been observed that the cruder pictures drew the biggest crowds. It was the magistrate's job to uphold the moral tone of the people.

Superintendent Foster, in his statement about the running of the cinema, included interesting statistics concerning the varied cinema-to-population ratios. At Spennymoor they had six cinemas for 20,000 people; at Sacriston, three for 5,000; at Coxhoe, one for 4,000; in Durham City, three for 20,000, in Darlington 11 for 65,000, at Brandon, three for 10,000 and at Ushaw Moor two for 3,500, with three more in nearby Esh Winning. He had no quarrel with the way that the Club cinema was run. The working population of the village had diminished since the closure of the colliery in 1927, and there were only 242 employed at Sleetburn. The magistrates then granted the licence for one year, "when they would consider the question of the cinemas from the moral *and* the financial aspect."[104]

The Gem, Coxhoe (circa 1918)

The Superintendent's objections to a new cinema in May, 1928 were again very harsh.[105] Fred and Thomas Iseton applied for a provisional cinematograph licence for a cinema they proposed to erect at Blackgate, Coxhoe. Their solicitor, H. E. Ferens, said that the area served a population of almost 10,000 people and that there was at present only one cinema in the area, (the Gem) 200 yards away from the proposed site. This cinema could only accommodate 300 and it had been open for about 18 years. The new cinema was to cost between £4,000 and £5,000 and would have seating for 600.

The site of the proposed new cinema in Coxhoe. *George Nairn Collection.*

Superintendent Foster asked if the proposers were aware that the former tenant of the other cinema had been summoned for non-payment of his local rates and that he had asked for time to pay because he was losing heavily on the business. The new owners of the cinema had made proposals for an extension of the premises. Was it their intention to close him down?

Mr. Ferens said that they were interested only in proper competition, and the chairman of the magistrates said that they must guard against monopoly. F.A. Carline contested the application on behalf of the Coxhoe Cinema Company.

He said that his client had only been in ownership for six weeks and that after much hard work, the cinema was now just beginning to pay its way. When circumstances further improved, he would make the required enlargements. Superintendent Foster further supported his objection and urged the magistrates to take a tour of the district cinemas prior to granting licences in the next year, since he was sure that some of the premises should be condemned. After a short private deliberation, however, the magistrates granted the application for a licence.

In Durham city, itself, there was still quite a dilemma in relation to *continuous* or *separate performance* programmes. The management decisions appeared to be quite arbitrary, though the popularity of the film or its inordinate length appeared to be limiting factors. For example, in the week of 13th February, the Palace was showing Norma Talmadge in *Camille* with continuous programmes, and the Globe was showing *What Price Glory* with two separate performances at 6.15 and 8.30. The advance publicity suggesting that there would be crowded houses for this 'greatest motion picture ever conceived' was probably the reason for the change of marketing, but there is no indication that seats were bookable in advance.

Programmes with a single feature film were the norm. When a double-feature was presented, the advertisements usually made much of the occasion. For three days of the week of 20th February, the Palace announced a 'Grand Double Feature Programme', *Mountains of Manhattan* with Dorothy Devore 'A fine sports picture' and *Wanted a Baby* with Helen Chadwick, 'a scream from start to finish'. Neither film could be classed as first run. The first had been made in 1926 and its star, though once the highest paid actress in Hollywood, was nearing the end of her career. The second had been re-titled from its United States original of *The Bachelor's Baby* and was only listed as a "B' picture in the Columbia catalogue. The programme was no doubt a fairly cheap package by the booking agency.

The occasional special film attracted the attention of the public and the newspaper reviewer. The Palace presented the film *The Somme* 'the best war film ever made', at the end of February. This was not a re-issue of the 1918 War Office film but a documentary by M. A. Wetherall using newsreel footage, maps and reconstructions. [106]

The Kinema, Meadowfield had a special four-day presentation of *INRI, The Life of Christ*. Its single nightly performance was duplicated on Saturday night and there was narration by J. Lisle, of Durham Cathedral, and choral accompaniment by the Brandon Male Voice Choir.[107] The film had been made in Germany by UFA, and directed by Robert Wiene but this fact was not indicated to the British public. It was based upon a novel by Peter Rosegger and Christ was played by Gregori Chmara. Henny Porten's films were regularly advertised in Durham with her star name, but no mention was made for this presentation that she was playing the part of Mary, nor that Danish actress Asta Neilsen was to be seen as Mary Magdalene. The controversy surrounding the presentation of Cecil B. De Mille's *King of Kings* does not appear to have affected the showing of this film.

Ever the critic of the new and untried, Dean Welldon's sermon on 22nd April 1928 gave a prophetic assessment of the new

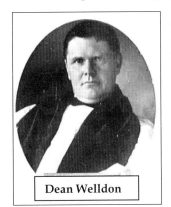

Dean Welldon

television medium. "New mechanical inventions destroy or impair the virtue of privacy," he concluded. "Photography is leading to vulgarising certain solemn functions of life, say of funerals [and] threatens to complete the work of photography, making an end of secrecy which has in many senses beautified and sanctified human life. The most saintly lives have often been the most silent. And sometimes I think if it were possible there should be a new beatitude, "Blessed are the silent for they shall be heard in Heaven." [108]

In July, the Palace reverted to an old pattern of including variety acts with its films: possibly with the advent of talking pictures, the management felt that they needed to have something other than the silent screen to fulfil their patrons' needs. In October the Assembly Rooms, too, included live entertainment by means of a British novelty song film, *The Corner Man*. Operatic vocalists, Leon Williams, Renée Farrer and Tom Liversage, provided the accompaniment. The release date was 1921, but the Advertiser report makes no mention of age.

"Hugh E. Wright, Britain's well-known character actor is now starred in a novel song film entitled *The Corner Man* which will form an outstanding attraction for the rest of the week. This picture tells in dramatic sequences the love of father for his child, who through the tragic working of fate lives her life in ignorance of his being. But apart from the intensely human narrative contained in *The Corner Man* mention must be made of the specially prepared music, songs and ballads with which the picture is embellished." [109]

Patron loyalty was again encouraged at the Assembly Rooms in August with the showing of *The Masked Player Film*. "A fascinating newspaper competition, with £325 to be won. For five weeks several famous film stars will be shown masked or disguised, and prizes will be awarded to those identifying most of them." [110]

It was a time for gimmickry. New technologies were around the corner. The cinema had become part of daily life and film stars had become icons of fashion and appearance. This was the last

silent Christmas, and the Globe was showing Chaplin's *The Circus*. The Assembly Rooms had Anna Q Nilsson and Lewis Stone in *Lonesome Ladies* and patrons could see themselves as others see them in a Pathécolor documentary *The City of Durham.*

* * * * * *

The somewhat uninspiring and very old-fashioned entrance of the Kinema, Meadowfield. Originally the Central Hall of the Brandon & Byshottles Co-operative Society, the departments can be seen on either side.

Chapter Five   O.K. for Sound

1929

The New Year opened with a portent of things to come. The Durham County Advertiser devoted a whole column to an innovative cinematic event; the arrival in the district of a modern form of the sound synchronised film.[1] Some extracts from it reveal the content and origin of the films –

> "The talking film is the marvel of the year, and Bishop Auckland has taken the lead in the North in this astonishing development. It must be intensely gratifying to J. G. Drummond, the lessee of the Hippodrome to know that he is being so well supported in what must be regarded as a revelation in the art of the cinema."

> ....

> "A succession of scenes depicting incidents in the London Zoo is fascinating enough at any time, but when the sounds that emanate from the lion's den, from the tiger's lair, from the polar bears, elephants and other weird and wonderful occupants of the zoo, not omitting the parrots and the monkeys, are reproduced at precisely the same instant as the pictures are thrown on the screen is, to say the least, sensational."

> "Many people are naturally of the opinion that sounds are, and can only be, reproduced on gramophone records, and that under such a method synchronisation could not be obtained. That would be true enough, but it is not the method that obtains at the Hippodrome.

HIPPODROME, BISHOP AUCKLAND.
WE LEAD FOR OTHERS TO FOLLOW.
SEE AND HEAR THE
TALKING FILMS.
THE MARVEL OF THE NORTH.

This Week
OLLY OAKLEY, World-Famous Banjoist;
OWEN NARES, in "Sentenced to Death";
A VISIT TO THE ZOO, with all the Sounds

Next Week :–
THE NEW PARIS LIDO CLUB BAND;
LESLIE SARONY (of the "Show Boat", in Comedy Numbers;
HAL JONES, in Comedy Numbers

SPLENDID FEATURE FILMS IN SUPPORT.

Three Hours' Show. Nightly at 7.
Saturday, 6.15 and 8.30.
Sundays at 8 p.m.

Box Office:

Telephone: 121 Bishop Auckland.

Scenes are photographed at the same time as the sounds are recorded, and both sound and sight are on the same strip of film, so that synchronisation cannot be avoided. By view of the fact that a strip is allowed for the sound, the picture is reduced in size by the smallest possible fraction."

...

"Sound waves are transmitted from the photo electric cell to a 12 valve wireless amplifier which converts the light waves into sound and reproduces them on the latest pattern of moving coil loudspeaker."

The report goes on to declare that the operation of the sound producing equipment has been faultless, but it is known that on the opening night a fault prevented the amplifier from working. Besides the Zoo film there was also a musical item with comedian Olly Oakley. "Every time his fingers touch the strings (of his banjo) the music is instantly broadcasted [sic!] quite clearly and distinctly, and, what is more important, the strains from the instrument lose none of their charm in the process." A dramatic item was also shown. "In *Sentence of Death*, an emotional play with Owen Nares as the chief figure, every word that passes between him and the 'doctor' is reproduced perfectly naturally."

The reviewer's prediction concerning the continuance of cinema orchestras was clearly not fulfilled in the long term. "The idea has long been pooh-poohed and it was even suggested that the innovation would ultimately cut out the orchestra. So far from being the case the orchestra at the Hippodrome has been increased and improved."

The films were produced by the De Forest Phonofilm system, and the films referred to were first given press showings in April and November 1927. The Phonofilm Company loaned the sound producing equipment and the films to cinemas during the promotional period for £16 10s per week with 3,000ft of film.[2] The opening night problems were resolved and, for the rest of the week, full houses enjoyed the synchronised musical items.

The patents for this sound-on-film system were disputed and eventually it was continued in Britain by the British Talking Pictures Co. In America, its co-inventor Thomas Case developed an improved system and sold the rights to the Fox Film Corporation from whom it eventually emerged as Fox Movietone.[3]

Coxhoe cinema bankruptcy

The examination for bankruptcy was a sad end to the career of Gordon Gray, the theatre name of the former proprietor of the Electric Theatre, Coxhoe. He appeared in the court under his real name of Archibald Boxwell Muirhead Gray of Hallgarth Street, Durham and his present occupation was described as film renter's traveller. He had debts of £490 11s 10d and a bank balance of only 10s. He declared that his failure in the business could be attributed to the depression in the trade arising from the coal strikes of 1921 and 1926. He had been a cinematograph operator in the South of England and had come to the North to take up a post in Sunderland.

Mr. Henderson had built the Electric Palace Theatre for him in 1911, and with a capital of £100 he had taken the lease at a rental of £3 per week. The theatre had paid fairly well until the miner's strike of 1921. After this, the takings declined from £35 per week to about £20 per week, and he gave up the lease in May 1928.

Between 1911 and 1921, his average weekly profit had been £11. During this period he had been able to save about £100. He had invested this in a film company, which went into liquidation. He told the court that he was not able to show them any account books for the period because they had been destroyed in a flood when the boiler in the theatre burst.

During the 1921 strike, they had been forced to lower their prices and as a consequence the takings dropped. In February 1928, he had offered to pay his creditors 12s 6d. in the £1 but this was refused. In July, he offered them £50 down and £1 per week, but this was also refused. As a film traveller, he was earning £529 per annum. Currently this amounted to £2 10s. per week plus a 5 per cent commission.

S. Parish, for the creditors and the Kinematograph Renters' Association, attempted to show that, with the commission, this amounted to £17 per week, but Mr. Gray denied this. Mr. Parish further asked what the most expensive film had been that he had shown at Coxhoe, and Mr. Gray replied that it had been *The Ten Commandments* at £20 for the week. Mr. Parish thought that such an amount for a film for Coxhoe might not have been justified, but Mr. Gray replied that it was.[4]

Sunday Licences

In March, when the Palladium opened its doors for the first time, the licensing magistrates gave it a seven-day licence.[5] This factor seemed to be more important than the actual opening in the eyes of some. Sunday licences were available to all the cinemas in the county districts including the tiny Crescent cinema in Gilesgate Moor, but they had never been granted in the city before. This kind of anomaly had been questioned at the Lanchester, Consett and Stanley Licensing sessions in February.[6] Mr Aynsley on behalf of Fred Storey, proprietor of the Pavilion, Esh Winning, asked that the prohibition on Sunday opening should be removed from his theatre since 400 yards away the Memorial Hall cinema licence, which came under the Durham county police division, was not thus prohibited. His application was actually supported by the Revd. Father Beech of Newhouses. He was in favour of Sunday opening after church opening hours if suitable pictures were shown. In his experience, the pictures afforded innocent recreation and helped prevent many evils. The Revd. M. J. Burgess, Vicar of Waterhouses, was of the same opinion. The magistrates rejected the application but requested the clerk to write to Durham County Council and suggest that there should be some kind of uniformity of conditions for Sunday opening throughout the administrative county. The newspaper report found its way into the hands of Basil Brunning of the Lord's Day Observance Society in London, and the Durham Advertiser printed his rejoinder. He was particularly incensed that clergy had given their support to 'Sabbath desecration'. "It seems incongruous," he went on, "for clergy to support an effort to secularise a day which God has commanded to be kept sacred, that the number of 'evils' in Esh Winning might be restrained in their growth."[7] When H. E. Ferens presented his case for a seven-day licence for the Palladium before the magistrates at the Durham city police court, he said that he thought the time had now come for the city to follow the practice already adopted in the county. He asked for the cinemas to be open from 8 p.m. to 10.30 p.m. on Sundays.

Canon Lillington opposed the application on religious grounds and contended that Sunday opening was quite unnecessary. It would add to the difficulties of the clergy in their attempt 'to try and elevate the masses'. He added that 68 leading towns had consistently refused to grant Sunday licences. Canon Bothamley said that if the licence was granted to the Palladium, the other cinemas would also follow the example. It would tend to break down the solemn observance of Sunday, and the idea of religion and morality in the mass of the people. The Revd. C. J. Thurlow, also opposing, said he enjoyed a good picture, but that this application would retard not enhance religion, and furthermore it would mean the employment of men on Sundays. The Revd. H. Derbyshire said that Sunday was a day of rest and quiet and the opening of cinemas would disturb this. The Revd. D. Sharp, secretary of the Council of Christian Churches for Temperance, said that since Durham was a cathedral city it should uphold the Christian tradition of Sunday.

Superintendent Foster, whilst not supporting or denying the application, said that there was a lack of provision for people after eight o'clock on Sunday evening. He also turned to the oft-stated argument that in colliery villages where there were Sunday cinema openings, attendances at work were better on Monday mornings than before the openings.

Following a lengthy consultation by the magistrates, they decided to grant the application. The cinema could not be opened until 8.15pm and should close by 10.30 p.m. The Sunday programme would have to be submitted to the police for approval. Canon Lillington remarked that he had had only one day's notice of the application, and asked if it should have been advertised more widely. The clerk of the court said that no such regulation was in effect. The Revd. Harold Derbyshire's earlier hopes for co-operation with his cinema neighbours had clearly been dashed by the magistrates' decision. As President of the Durham Free Church council, he was obviously required to take a particular lead in the matter.[8] There was little new in the opposing arguments, but in his sermon at the Claypath Congregational Church on 10th March the Revd. Mr Derbyshire was particularly vigorous. Taking as his text, 'They shall be afraid of that which is high', he said -

"I cannot help making a special reference tonight to our own city - this Cathedral City of Durham. It is a city with ancient and honourable traditions. It was born so the legend tells us out of the faithfulness of pious monks to sacred charge. While formerly its rulers and people played leading parts in the temporal affairs of this realm, its chief glory has always been in its spiritual possessions and influence. I wish I could say that this was true today. For all its outward show of piety, and in spite of the position that it occupies in the eyes of the world, the spiritual life of this city is at a low ebb."

He dealt cleverly with the judicial situation by stating that he did not wish to criticise the magistrates "since it was necessary to abide by their decisions however much one deplored them." He was also careful not to alienate all libertarians, by stating that he had never been a narrow Sabbatarian, but he did feel that "the Christian Sunday was too precious to be lightly cast away." He saw Sunday as a physical, mental and spiritual necessity. Whilst recognising that some public services needed to be performed on Sundays, he thought we had no right to require others to render us a service "merely administering to our own pleasure."

He was on firmer ground when he questioned the amount of public demand that there had been for the Sunday opening. "I feel sure," he said, "that the majority of people if they had been asked for an opinion would have been strongly against it. This is not an effort to supply a want; it is an attempt to create one. I have reason to believe, also that the existing picture halls of the city have been most unwilling to see Sunday opening. They feel now that they are obliged to fall in line." Again his oratory avoids direct confrontation: "I do not want to excuse their action, but, at any rate one can understand it. I am sure they would not suffer in the long run if they stood out."

In the same edition of the newspaper, an un-named director of the Palladium questioned the minister's authority in speaking for the general public. "There is a law of supply and demand," he said, "and if there is no demand for Sunday performances then the directors are not likely to run them."

In another portion of his sermon, the Revd. Mr Derbyshire included a rebuttal of some of the pro-opening arguments. "It is all humbug to talk of the need to keep young people off the streets. If that is all the applicants were anxious about, they would be opening their cinemas free of charge. But they are out to make money. Are they not endeavouring also to tempt young people who might otherwise be in their own homes?"

The approved content of Sunday programmes had exercised

the ingenuity of showmen and managers from the first granting of seven-day licences. Mr Ferens had told the magistrates that the cinema would show "suitable and educational pictures and not trashy films" and that the programmes would be submitted to the police before each Sunday. The Revd. Mr Derbyshire said that they would be watching to see if this was carried out to the letter. He further declared that he was sure that the application would not have received approval if some senior members of the Anglican and Roman Catholic churches had not 'sold the pass'. He was certain that in the long run the promoters' proposals would once again be defeated. "We can kill it, if only we try hard enough," he said.

In a later report of the actual application for the Palladium licence Superintendent Foster said that, though the titles for Sunday programmes were required to be submitted to the police, he wanted to make it clear that the police were not censors.[9] He had suggested to the Mayor that he should form a committee to inspect and decide upon the suitability of a film. He thought it was most likely that the position of Sunday night *film censor* would not be a peaceful one. Alderman Ferens said that it was up to the proprietors to see that the licence conditions were carried out, and if they foolishly disobeyed them, then they must take the consequences that their licence would not be renewed at the end of the year.

The letters column of the Advertiser of the 14th March edition was completely taken up with the pros and cons of the Sunday opening decision. The majority of the writers clearly wished to hide behind noms-de-plume. One correspondent 'Let There Be Light' felt that the names of the eleven magistrates who 'for good or ill' had granted the licence should be published. Another writer signing as 'Delos' hoped that there would be space for his letter amongst the expected protests. The granting of the licence was "a shrewd blow struck at the old habit of coward and repressive Puritanism". 'Merry England' took up the cause of Roman Catholic support for the decision. "The common-sense views of the Vatican do not condemn reasonable enjoyment on feast days and Sundays." He concluded his witty letter with a postscript - "Needless to say Sunday Cinema going is not an essential part of the Roman Catholic faith". 'Objector's' letter began with an economic argument and ended with a homily: "Tradesmen claim that there is no money about and yet the cinema proprietors believe they can get the public to part with more of what does not exist". Suggesting that the adoption of a Continental Sunday will eventually lead to employers demanding longer hours, he warned that "Sabbath breakers should look ahead to see where their action will eventually lead". Canon Bothamley in *his* letter regrets the decision and believes that most citizens of Durham would also express their objection if they were enabled to do so. He compared the law-abiding attitudes prevalent in Britain with the criminal chicanery of the police in Los Angeles, the city officials of Baltimore and some crooked bankers in Paris apparently attributing their downfall to a general public malaise. Many towns in England had now re-established Sunday closing and he hoped Durham would follow their principle as quickly as possible.[10]

Palladium opens

The opening of the Palladium was given a special advertising section in the same edition of the Advertiser. Banner advertisements by the contractors and outfitters endorsed the cinema, and their own involvement. The initial editorial, however, dwelt upon the entrepreneurial aspect of the opening. "The familiar and perhaps somewhat threadbare statement that there is a lack of enterprise among the people of the City of Durham is gradually but surely disproved. Durham is fortunate just now to have in its midst men of industry who will bring the City into the very forefront. Perhaps a public library will be the next step."

The special report continued: "Durham is excellently served by its picture halls which have brought real happiness and pleasure into the lives of citizens, generally, and with the addition of the new structure in Claypath another great stride has been taken. The building will be a revelation to citizens. It occupies what was formerly the site of two shops and slum clearance, and from this foundation has risen one of the finest buildings of its kind in the North of England. There is seating accommodation for 1,065, and there is in addition standing room for many more. The interior is 60ft by 80 ft [18.2m.x24.3m] deep and the seats both in

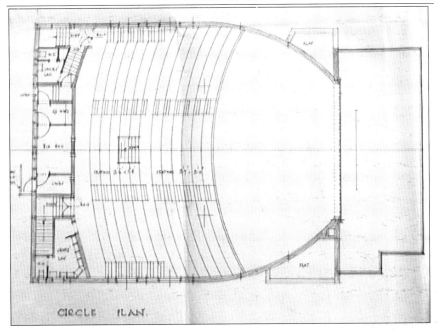

Palladium circle plan. *Durham County Records Office*
Palladium Longitudinal elevation. *D.C.R.O.*

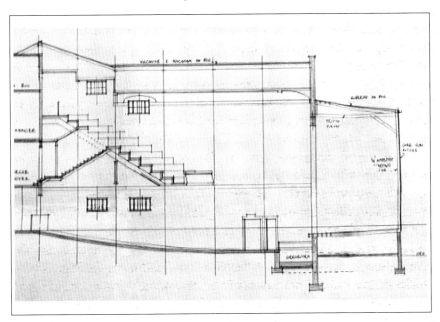

the spacious circle, stalls and pit are so arranged that a clear view of the stage or screen may be had from any angle with the utmost freedom. This last has been obtained by reason of the sloping ground on which the structure has been erected. The theatre is designed both for pictures and for theatrical purposes, the stage being 20ft [6.1m] deep and the screen 20ft by 17½ ft across [6.1 m x5.1 m]. The criticism that there is no hall large enough for public gatherings can no longer be urged by the large organisations who wish to meet and hold their demonstrations in the city."

The stalls *(Durham County Record Office)* **and the entrance in 1975.**

The contours of the site meant that the main entrance was on a floor level between the stalls and the circle. The extensive foyer contained two rooms that could accommodate patrons waiting for entrance. In the stalls, there was a large orchestra pit. The carpeting was one of the latest designs by Hugh Mackay & Co. At this time, 'Durham Carpets' were being ordered for numerous new cinemas and theatres. There was tip-up seating throughout. The commissionaire's uniform was obtained from Fred Doherty's of Durham. The major construction work was carried out by F. W. Goodyear & Sons to the architectural designs of W & T. R. Milburn of Sunderland. Interior decorations were the work of E. Hodgson & Co.

PALLADIUM, DURHAM.

Proprietors PALLADIUM (DURHAM) LTD.   Manager H. GATT

6-30   TWICE NIGHTLY   8-30
Doors Open 6 p.m.

OPENING DAY, MONDAY. MARCH 18, 1929.

MONDAY, TUESDAY and WEDNESDAY MARCH 18, 9, 20

REX INGRAM'S
GREAT NEW PRODUCTION
" THE GARDEN OF ALLAH."
All Star Cast includes ALICE TERRY and IVAN PETROVICH.
TOPICAL.   EVE'S REVIEW.   COMEDY.

THURSDAY, FRIDAY, and SATURDAY, MARCH 21, 22, and 23.
RAMON NOVARRO and NORMA SHEARER
IN
" THE STUDENT PRINCE."
TOPICAL.   EVE'S REVIEW.   COMEDY.

Prices   -   -   -   1/3, 1/-, 6d and 4d.

SUNDAY, MARCH 24TH, AT 8-15 P.M.,
" KING OF KINGS."

The official opening on Monday afternoon 18th March was fully reported in the 21st March Durham Advertiser. Cllr. Holliday, the chairman of the directors, in introducing the Mayor, Cllr. Wilkinson, said that he was certain that at the end of the year those who had opposed the seven-day licence would become its supporters. The Mayor congratulated Cllr. Holliday in the care with which he had approached the enterprise of creating this 'super' cinema. The cinematograph theatre trade was a problematic one, and independent picture halls were faced with keen opposition from 'the great combines'. The Palladium directors were well positioned in the cinema world and their knowledge would contribute to the success of the venture, and enable them to obtain the best in high-class pictures. The Mayor concluded his speech with a rejoinder to the criticism that he, as a shareholder, had had an influence on the decision to grant the cinema a seven-day licence. He issued a challenge that if anyone could prove the contrary he would give £1 to the Durham County Hospital fund for every shilling that he could be proved to own in the company. Cleverly employing a biblical quotation, he said that he was surprised that "people of his own faith should be led away by false reports from people whose relationship to Ananias must be very close." It is clear that the Mayor did distance himself from the decision, since, as chief magistrate, he absented himself from the licensing session in question.

Cllr. Wood, in proposing a vote of thanks to the Mayor, said that there was a real need for a theatre of this sort in the town, especially one run by local enterprise. He had no doubt that within a short time one of the theatre circuits would have looked to Durham for a similar project. In seconding the vote, Cllr. Goodyear said that the hall could provide a large enough venue for public meetings. The Miner's Hall was too far out of town for this purpose. The architects presented the Mayor with a piece of solid silver plate inscribed "Presented to Cllr. W. W. Wilkinson, Mayor, on the occasion of the opening of The Palladium Theatre, Durham."

After the speeches, Rex Ingram's *The Garden of Allah,* the film for the first three days, was shown. Alice Terry and Ivan Petrovich were in the leading roles. The film and the musical accompaniment by the orchestra were heartily applauded. Many of the guests then moved on to the Three Tuns Hotel for a celebratory tea. The main film for the second half of the week was Ernst Lubitsch's *The Student Prince* starring Ramon Novarro and Norma Shearer .

The first Sunday film was Cecil B. De Mille's *King of Kings.* This might seem to have been an apt choice were it not for the controversy it had aroused throughout the country. Although the British Board of Film Censors worked according to general principles rather than a prescribed code, in 1913 they had created two specific rules that there should be no nudity and no portrayal of Christ.[11] *King of Kings* was given an 'A' certificate but the licensing authorities of a number of towns banned its presentation, and others approved it only after a special viewing. There appears to have been no protest in Durham before the film's presentation, and only one recorded protest sometime afterwards. Canon Bothamley preached a sermon on the subject of 'The King of Kings'. He was particularly incensed at the idea of the Christ figure being employed merely for entertainment purposes. For this reason, also, he objected to cinemas being open on Good Friday. "Is it a right thing to try to attract people away from the churches to see *Red Hot Love* and *Red Hot Hate*?" [12]

The Sunday opening controversy continued for several weeks more. The Revd. Mr Braley, principal of Bede Teacher Training College and chairman of the Durham Diocesan Society for the

Protection of Young Women and Girls, welcomed the decision along with other senior members of the Society. "I think it is bordering upon hypocrisy for people to tilt against the opening of cinemas on Sunday, so long as there is Sunday golf, Sunday motor riding and all that sort of thing. There is a new conception of the Sabbath day. It is no longer a glorified policeman saying *Keep Off The Grass*".[13]

Dean Welldon had his say a week later. His issued statement observed that the opening of cinemas on Sundays was fraught with much difficulty, not least the disruption of the feelings of the Puritans and their descendants. He was obviously in a somewhat perverse mood when he suggested that, having thrown off the previous rigidity of their lives, they were now attempting to impose restrictions upon their neighbours. "It is impossible in the twentieth century to retain the old Sunday", he said. "After all, there are many thousands of people who do not, and will not, attend church on Sundays. I could not oppose the use of parks for recreational purposes, and it is better to spend part of Sunday in a music hall or a cinema than in a public house." He still thought, however, that it was the duty of every man to worship God on Sunday, and that it was not incompatible to engage in worship *and* recreation on the Lord's Day.[14] Even whilst Dean Welldon was writing his statement, Canon Wesley Bothamley was delivering a Sunday night sermon at St. Nicholas' Church, Durham on the subject of 'Christ and The Pictures'. The Advertiser quotes his address at length.[15] Basing his text upon the action of Christ against the priests of the Temple courts of Jerusalem, he remarked that "money sets most moral questions". He observed that a few years ago, a cinema trade journal stated that if they could get the law changed on Sunday opening there was five million pounds to be shared amongst the proprietors. Critics had observed that by refusing to have Sunday cinemas, Durham was behind the times. "In earlier years when Durham was behind the times, it was an honest town", he said. "The latest bank to be built has had to put a grill in front of the cashier's counter!" He saw Sunday opening as a further erosion of the Christian Sunday. He opposed the open-air band concerts on Sunday because they did not stick to their appointed times and their performances flowed into Church

Service times. "How many people will keep up the practice of going to Church first and the pictures afterwards?" he asked.

The newspaper reported that the congregation dispersed a few minutes before eight o'clock by which time many hundreds of people were lined up outside the Palladium to see *The King of Kings*. Others were waiting for admission at the Globe to see a re-issue of Buster Keaton's *Steamboat Bill Junior* and, only yards away from St. Nicholas Church, the Palace was showing a 1928 comedy *Love and Learn* starring Esther Ralston. The Assembly Rooms Theatre was the only cinema not to apply for a seven-day licence.

The second Sunday's offerings seemed hardly different from those of the week, apart from their dates of release. The Palladium showed *The Lovelorn*, a 1927 romantic drama starring Sally O'Neil, Molly Day and Larry Kent. During the same week, the theatrical facilities at the Palladium were loaned to the Durham Amateur Operatic Society for the presentation of *The Belle of Brittany*. The Palace had a re-issue of a British-made Paramount film *Madame Pompadour*. The advertising placed Lillian Gish in the leading role, when in fact it was her sister Dorothy who had been brought to England by Herbert Wilcox to star in the film.

The Sunday presentations for 21st April were particularly noteworthy. The Palace showed the Danish film *The President.* This had been made by Carl Theodore Dreyer in 1919 and must have bemused Dunelmians gathered for a Sunday evening's entertainment. No doubt it was part of a cheap one-day rental package and it fitted the re-issue pattern of the Sunday films at each of the venues. As time went on it is clear that little regard was paid to what might be termed suitable Sunday films, if there ever was such a definable category. *The Whip Woman* starring Estelle Taylor (Palladium 28th April 1929) and *Shingled Gowns* (Palace 5th May 1929) would surely have been questioned by the Police Superintendent in earlier times. If the detractors were taking note, there was good ammunition here for objection when the licences came up for renewal.

Indeed, the Revd. Mr Derbyshire was unceasing in his pursuit of redress against the magistrates. The clerk of the justices had told him that no notice needed to be given of an impending change to the licensing conditions. He had therefore asked the local Durham

M.P., J. Ritson, to verify the situation with the Home Secretary. His reply was published in the Advertiser along with an explanatory letter from the Revd. Mr Derbyshire. The letter is, in fact, rather inconclusive, though Revd. Mr Derbyshire claims that it supports his protest. "The Act does not specifically require any notice to be published. It is however within the power of the licensing authority to require that public notice shall be given and, as the Reverend Mr Derbyshire points out, the London County Council have adopted some such requirement. I have no authority to issue instructions to licensing authorities in this matter." As in a number of clauses and requirement in the 1909 Cinematograph Act, then, the final decision rested with the licensing authority. Although it might have been equitable to the objectors for notice to be given, the Clerk to the Justices was quite right in not giving it.[16]

In the midst of all the arguments, the Palladium advertised what it called 'a mystery film'. This method of marketing a programme seems particularly puzzling. Since there had not been any attempt to demonstrate this ploy before, the management must have been pretty confident that it would work, especially since it was engaged as the main film for seven days. From the reviews in the next week's paper it becomes clear that the film was *Baby Mine* starring Charlotte Greenwood in her first film role. "The Karl Dane / George K. Arthur team combination of laughter makers and the lanky comedienne are responsible for a solid hour of chuckling, giggling and guffawing."[17]

There were other sound innovations in the first week of May. The Empire, Langley Moor was advertising some talking films. There is no clear indication of their origin, but since they are listed as 5 distinct items, it is more than likely that they, too, were showing the Lee De Forest Phonofilms. In the North East, the Mayor of Durham could be heard extolling the virtues of the city via the Newcastle radio station.

The Palace showed a war film with a difference towards the end of the month. *The Guns of Loos* was accompanied by a personal appearance of Piper David Laidlaw. "With his original bagpipes, he will re-create the deed of valour that won him the V .C. at Loos." The film was made by the Stoll Company in 1928 and, besides David Laidlaw playing himself, it starred Madeleine Carroll, Bobby Howes, Hermione Baddeley and Henry Victor.[18]

The switch-over to sound was hanging in the air in Durham. Hints of it were everywhere. At the Stoll Cinema, Newcastle, *The Singing Fool* began a ten-week run on 11th May 1929. In the first week of July, the Palladium showed the silent version of *The Jazz Singer*. Much of the film was, of course, silent, but the newspaper report doesn't make specific reference to the absence of Al Jolson's singing voice. For six weeks in July and August, the Havelock Cinema in Sunderland showed *The Singing Fool* to packed houses. Estimates put the total attendance for the presentation at 120,000.[19] In August, the Assembly Rooms showed *Motherland* advertised as 'a sound film (not mechanical) synchronised by Human voice'.[20] This was a British film set in the war and made by the Samuelson company and originally released in October 1927. The 'sweet singing and special effects' were arranged by Leonard Williams, and the show promised a revival of all the popular songs of the war period.

The vigilance of the local constabulary was in evidence again in midsummer when John George Manders was summoned for an offence under the Cinematograph Regulations 1923. The Cinematograph Act of 1909 was still the actual statute, but a number of Home Office regulations had been added to bring its clauses up-to date. One of the new regulations was that no person was allowed to stand in the gangways between the seats. P. C.s Burdon and Bayles had visited the Memorial Hall cinema in Esh

Winning on Sunday evening 18th August and found that there were nine chairs on one side and eight on the other and that in the balcony there were seventeen people seated on chairs between the aisles. Patrons who wanted to leave their proper seats had great difficulty in getting along the gangway. P. C. Burdon said that if there had been a rush there would have been 'serious state of affairs'. In answer to a question from Mr. Ferens representing the defendant, he also said that he was not aware that 250 patrons had been turned away before the start of the performance. With this line of questioning, it would seem that Mr. Ferens was trying to justify the overcrowding as an act of charity on the part of the manager. Clearly disturbed by this, Superintendent Foster intervened to state that it was clear to him that seating the patrons where they were was an intentional act by the cinema assistants and not a chance occurrence.

Mr. Ferens, seeing that the game was up for his client, then offered his apologies for the misdemeanour and the rightness of the police in bringing the prosecution. Mr. Manders had been in the box office instead of 'going about the hall', and whilst he was there the chairs were utilised to accommodate the large audience. He would make sure it did not happen again. He had had a trouble-free history as manager of the hall. Between 1925 and 1927 it had been managed by the Welfare Committee. Then, for a time, it had passed out of their control. It was now back in their control and Mr. Manders had been re-engaged. There had been a tremendous rush of patrons that evening and he had attempted to accommodate them even though the numbers exceeded the capacity of the hall. The magistrates found the case proved and in fining the defendant £2, the chairman, Brigadier-General H. C. Surtees, said that the safety of the public had got to be considered.[21]

The Memorial Hall had been opened on Brandon Road, Esh Winning in 1924 and the cinema was part of a complex of meeting and function rooms. The first manager had been Joseph Wood of Browney Colliery followed by John Manders. General mismanagement by the Miners' Welfare Committee seems to have occurred in 1927 and Fred Heslop took over the running of the cinema. In 1929, John Manders returned as manager and Fred

Heslop became the long-term manager of the Pavilion Theatre, Waterhouses.[22]

In Bishop Auckland the *real* Talkies had arrived. For the whole week beginning 2nd Sept 1929, the Hippodrome began showing Morton Downey in *Mother's Boy*. This 1929 film was made by Pathé in the R.C.A. sound-on-film system, but both it and its star appear to have sunk without trace.[23]

EMPIRE, LANGLEY MOOR.

WEEK COMMENCING SEPTEMBER 9th., and all the week.

SEE AND HEAR

WILLIAM FOX presents his 100% TALKING PICTURE—

" SPEAK EASY "

(DIRECT FROM STOLL PICTURE HOUSE, NEWCASTLE).

TIME AND PRICES AS USUAL.

A Western Electric Disc and Sound-on-film Projector

A Kalee 8 mounted on a Western Electric Universal stand with sound-on-disc and on-film attachments.

In September, the Empire Langley Moor began their Talkie era with *Speak Easy* starring Lola Lane and Paul Page.[24] Fox were using the sound-on-film Movietone process, but no indication is given in the report of the sound system the Empire was using. It would seem that initially they had sound-on disc, but many machines were altered to play both disc and edge-track systems.

In August 1930, the man from the Newcastle distributors who delivered the discs for 'the talking apparatus' was fined £1 for smoking in the projection room during his delivery.[25]

THE PALACE THEATRE, DURHAM.
PROPRIETOR ... ... T. C. RAWES
THURSDAY, FRIDAY, SATURDAY, NOVEMBER 28th, 29th, 30th.
TWICE NIGHTLY at 6.30 and 8.40.
THE ALL TALKING and ALL SINGING PICTURE.
" CLOSE HARMONY,"
Featuring CHAS ROGERS and NANCY CARROLL.
NOTE — SATURDAY at 2,30 6.30 8.40.
SUNDAY, DECEMBER 1, at 8.15 "SOMEONE TO LOVE," and
"SLIM FINGERS."
(At our usual Silent Picture Prices 3d ; 6d ; 11d.)
MONDAY, TUESDAY, WEDNESDAY, DECEMBER 2nd, 3rd, 4th
AND ALL THE WEEK
THE GREATEST TALKIE YET,
" SYNCOPATION."
Delicious Songs — Superb Dancing — Fascinating Story.

After a short closure, the Palace switched to sound with the Paramount film *Close Harmony*. This back-stage story starring Charles (Buddy) Rogers and Nancy Carroll had as its one enduring feature the musical number 'Twelfth Street Rag'.

The first British sound feature film to be shown in Durham was Alfred Hitchcock's *Blackmail*. The Palace advertisement for 9th December 1929 called it 'an all-talking super-film', when, in fact, it was a re-shoot of a film already partly completed without a sound track. The silent version was shown at the Assembly Rooms in February 1930.[26]

1930

The New Year began with news of a dreadful cinema tragedy. A fire in the projection room of the Glen Cinema, Paisley during a Hogmanay children's matinée had caused a panic. As the children rushed down a staircase to the emergency exits they fell on top of each other. 69 were killed and 150 needed hospital treatment. After an investigation, the manager was charged with culpable homicide.[27] Local authorities were quick to look into the safety systems of their

Glen, Paisley.
Author's collection.

own licensed picture halls. In the Durham Police Court on Monday 6th January 1930, the Mayor (Councillor Murdoch) asked Police Superintendent Foster if he could give an assurance that the cinemas in Durham were in perfect order. Without naming names, the Superintendent declared that he was not able to give that assurance.

There were four halls in the city, one of which had just recently opened. He indicated, somewhat loosely, that three of the halls had

been licensed in 1909 or shortly after. The 1910 licensing of the
Assembly Rooms and the Palace, and the 1913 licensing of the
Globe hardly fitted this description. His statement was, however,
merely a preamble to the indication that two of the halls were
converted into cinemas and had previously been licensed for some
other purpose. The additions in the 1923 regulations were largely
concerned with the management and safety in new buildings, and
the older buildings though licensed annually, had managed to
survive with very few modern additions.

He regarded one of the halls (we can assume this to be the
Palace) as being unsafe because the upstairs patrons could only
leave by one inadequate staircase. The re-wind room was not only
unsafe but also dangerous. Its defects would be discovered if there
was an occurrence in the projection box. The operator would have
to leave directly into the audience, an action condemned in the
1923 regulations since it would certainly produce a tragic panic in
the audience. Superintendent Foster suggested that the justices
should meet specifically to look into the safety aspects of the City
cinemas, because, as far as he was aware there had been no
inspection since 1909.[28]

Ironically, the same court session included a summons for the
manager of the Palladium, the only cinema opened since the new
regulations. Twenty-five year-old Harold Gatty was charged with
offences under the Cinematograph Regulations. Superintendent
Foster said that he had visited the Palladium on New Year's Night
and on going up stairs found that nine people were occupying
chairs placed behind the seats between the gangways. The chairs
were of a spindle-legged type that could easily tip over. They were
not normally kept there but had been brought in from another
room. He said that he had the unfortunate task of removing the
people from their seats. It was the job of the manager to do this and
it was not fair that 'the police should get the opprobrium of the
people for moving them'. The maximum penalty for the offence
under the regulations was £20 and he hoped that this case should
carry a substantial penalty as a warning to other managers that the
safety of the public should come first.

Mr. Ferens for the defendant attempted to show that though
the seats were illegally placed, they did not actually constitute a

clear danger to the large audience. Under questioning, Superintendent Foster said that he did not think the manager had sold more tickets than the capacity of the hall, but this was the first house, and there was plenty of room in the second house of the evening. Mr. Ferens said that the manager was at fault, that he expressed his profound regret over the offence and that he had been instructed by the directors of the cinema not to let it happen again. The magistrates, clearly more influenced by Mr. Ferens than by the Superintendent, imposed a fine of only £2.[29]

The safety precautions already in place at the Central Hall cinema, Meadowfield, and the cool action of the projectionist, averted any danger to the audience on the night of 25th January 1930. The film *Cardboard Lover* was being screened when it ignited. Almost immediately the smell of the burning film was apparent in the hall. The operator dropped the protective shutters, attempted unsuccessfully to tackle the fire with the available sand and then left the box. He was able to tell the engineer of the problem and almost before anyone had realised what had happened, they were informed without panic that they were in no danger and should vacate the building in an orderly fashion. As the audience left, the orchestra struck up a march. The film was still burning in the box but because it was fireproof nothing more escaped into the hall. The loaded reel of film was destroyed but the rest of the damage was not extensive, and the cinema was in operation again the next night. Mr. Kenworthy, the projectionist, escaped via a safety rope. The Co-operative committee had recently submitted plans to the authorities for a new projection box with a separate entrance and exit from outside the building. These plans were approved at the County Police Court a few days later on 29th January 1930.[30]

The Paisley disaster also prompted the Durham County Petty Sessions Division to debate the current state of safety in the 21 cinema halls under their licensing control. Superintendent Foster observed once more that hall conversions and recently built cinemas were very different in their safety aspects. Modern cinemas had projection rooms, and rewind rooms which had ventilation systems and access entirely separate from the auditorium. During the year, a sub-committee of the court had visited some of the halls he was unhappy about, and he now

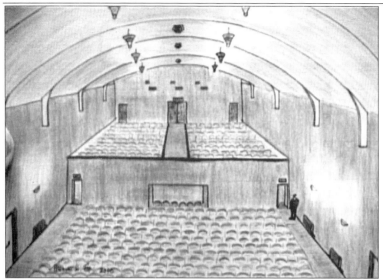

The Central Hall, Meadowfield as remembered by Tom Fox. The new projection room was prefabricated in the Co-op yard with a steel girder frame. This was then demounted and reconstructed behind the balcony. An alcove was created where the old projection room had been. The ushers normally reserved its six seats for courting couples.

The Regal's *art deco* organ console up on the pit lift.

recommended that two of them, Sherburn Hill and the Bowburn Club should be found unsuitable for licensing. During the year, he had closed down two un-named halls for breaches of regulations and obtained convictions for the misdemeanours. He suggested that children's matinée performances should be confined to the ground floor of halls, and that where the hall was situated upstairs that such performances should be prohibited.

The magistrates considered the superintendent's report and observed that the cinema proprietors were just as keen to follow the regulations as the magistrates were in administering them. They were unable to make it a condition of the licence that the owners should take out a third party insurance for any accidents or injury to patrons, but they thought the cost of no more than £3 or £4 was not beyond the resolve of the managements. There were minor irregularities in some halls, but the problem of Sherburn and Bowburn Halls could only be solved by the provision of entirely new premises. The Bowburn Hall was to be closed immediately. H. L. Swinburn, representing the interests of the Sherburn Hill Cinema Hall proprietors, asked whether it could remain open for adults only whilst alterations took place. It had been operated for years without any mishaps, and if it closed now it would take away the lessee's livelihood. He admitted that the building was out-of date but plans had been submitted for a two-storey façade. Even so, the present operating box was entirely outside the building, so that there was no danger of fire. It was merely an inconvenience at the moment rather than a danger. The chairman, T. F. Brass, said that it really was a wretched building and he was surprised that the proprietors allowed it to remain as it is. But, as a gesture to the lessee and the public he would allow it to stay open for adults only as long as the alterations were completed within the month. A certain amount of leeway must have been given since the work was not started until 25th March 1930 and was not completed until 17th August. The loss of the Club Cinema at Bowburn was not such a disaster for the local population, since the Picture House (formerly The New Electric Theatre) was situated not far away.[31]

The opening of the Avenue Cinema at Blackgate, Coxhoe, only a quarter of a mile further on, was an added compensation. Building had commenced on 18th June 1929 and was completed on

3rd February 1930. The main contractor had been A. Elcoat of Bearpark to the design of Messrs. Hays & Gray of North Shields. The Iseton brothers, Thomas and Fred, members of a well-known Coxhoe family, were the owners and managers. The opening ceremony took place on Monday night, 24th February when a full house watched the Colleen Moore film *Love Never Dies*. The building, at the important Blackgate junction, was well placed for travellers from all parts of the district.

The Avenue Cinema front *(above)* **and decorative proscenium detail** *(below)*

There was accommodation for 800 patrons, 526 on the ground floor and 265 in the balcony. Its spacious hall was approached from a wide covered foyer. The newspaper report seemed keen to stress that the decorative scheme was simple rather than elaborate, the ornamentation being confined to the proscenium and the front of the balcony.

The safety aspects were particularly emphasized. The projection room was of fireproof construction and entirely separate from the main hall and the circle was approached by a fireproof staircase. There were four emergency exits. The seating was made-up principally of tip-up seats in mohair velvet. The screen measured 12 feet by 6 feet. It would appear that the Kalee No.8 projectors were not adapted for sound films at this time.

The opening ceremony itself was performed by Michael Wandless, a ninety year-old Coxhoe resident, who had lived in the village for over 70 years. Tom Iseton presented Mr. Wandless with a couple of treasury notes as a memento of the opening, and then spoke to the audience about the safety features of the hall. So perfect was the fireproofing of the projection room, he said, that they would have time to walk to Newcastle before it could reach the main building.[32]

The cinema must have proved popular because, in November 1931, Thomas Iseton was summoned by Durham County Police Court for allowing a fire exit to be blocked by additional seating. The magistrate, W. Green, regarded the occurrence as a serious breach of the Cinematograph Act and imposed the maximum fine of £2.[33]

The City Brewster sessions in February had promised to be somewhat stormy given that the local church representatives had felt themselves to be out-manoeuvred the year before. Canon Lillington and the Revds. Mr Thurlow, T. Harrison Burnett and H. Derbyshire, represented the case for the church denominations and Alderman Ferens represented the cinema proprietors. As usual, the proceedings opened with the report by Superintendent Foster. He informed the chairman of the bench, the Mayor (Cllr. Murdoch), that all city cinemas were quite safe, or would be when all approved alterations had taken place. He said that Sunday cinema performances offered something of a problem, since there was a shortage of appropriate pictures. During the year he had, however, managed to create a sub-committee of experienced film men who could co-ordinate the selection and approval of all Sunday pictures. He praised the local proprietors for their co-operation in this matter, and for their patience in accepting the verdicts of this sub-committee. He was also of the opinion that whatever the disadvantages of Sunday cinemas "they keep men from public houses" and younger people from "parading up and down the streets and lanes and forming promiscuous acquaintances with often disastrous results."

Canon Lillington outlined his objections to the granting of cinema licences for Sunday performances. He contended that there was no public demand for Sunday cinemas, and that it was mysterious why Durham should grant it when Newcastle, Middlesborough, Gateshead, and Sunderland had refused. The church representatives asked the magistrates to help them to foster in the present secular materialistic age the spirit of worship. Every introduction of that kind into the city constituted a danger to the religious principles of the inhabitants. If the city was to prosper, there must be a moral basis, but, after Alderman Ferens outlined his case in support of the application, the magistrates decided not to change the current situation and approved the licences for seven-day operation.[34]

In the same week, it was announced that the Assembly Rooms Theatre had been sold to the University. Film shows and variety would take place at the Theatre until the transfer of ownership took place. The closure of the city's first cinema hall was not long in coming however. The last programme was advertised on 13th March 1930. The Advertiser said, "Citizens will regret the passing

of such a popular place of amusement. They will be ill advised to miss the last film *The Emerald of the East*. Made for British Pacific films and starring Mary Odette, Joshua Kean and the actor/director Jean de Kuharski, it told the story of a maharajah's daughter rescued from bandits by a British Lieutenant, and had been released in January 1929.

The Palladium burst into song with its first Talkie in the week commencing Monday 17th February. They had installed the Western Electric Sound System on their projectors and were able to show the M.G.M. musical *The Broadway Melody.*

The Globe was closed for four days in February to allow the required alteration to exits to be carried out. In April, the licence for the Globe Cinema was officially transferred to John William Peacock, the former Director of Music at the Gaiety Theatre, Newcastle. He had actually been the manager since 6th February when Mary Jane Gray had retired. Unfortunately, there was no newspaper report of her departure though she had been the lessee of the Globe since February 1918.[35]

The Globe had still not converted to sound. In June, it showed a film, *Meet The Prince,* which was advertised as having music and effects produced by an all-British sound producing apparatus. This was actually an American silent film. Besides being the only silent house, the Globe was also the only local cinema still showing a serial - *Ace of Scotland Yard.* Unfortunately, Globe advertisements

cease after those for the week of 30th June 1930 and do not re-
appear until October with an obscure silent Francis X. Bushman
film *The Reckoning*. Then advertising again ceases until February
1931, when *Alf's Button*, a British sound film with a colour
sequence, was shown. Thus the precise transition period from
silent to sound for this cinema is obscured by the lack of publicity.

GLOBE CINEMA,
DURHAM.
Lessee and Manager:
JOHN W. PEACOCK, A.T.C.L.
THURSDAY, FRIDAY; AND
SATURDAY.

"AT DEVIL'S VALLEY"
featuring HELENE ROSSON and
MAX ASHER.
Serial:
ACE OF SCOTLAND YARD,

▲ John Peacock at his Newcastle Offices.   The first advert with his name ▲

The loss of the Assembly Rooms Theatre and the conversion of
the Palace to a cinema had deprived Durham of its live theatre
venues. Occasionally, these two theatres had engaged out-of town
companies, or leased the premises for local amateur productions.
The Advertiser posed the question 'Does Durham need a
Theatre?'[36] A nameless leading citizen reported to the newspaper
that though

> "cinemas are quite all right in their way, there must be a
> substantial proportion of the community that wants something - shall
> I say - a little higher. The novelty of the talkies has worn off, and,
> speaking personally, I must confess that I am wholly fed up with
> them. Apart from the cheap jargon and Americanisms which
> characterise most of the synchronised films, music, the sweetest and
> most delicate of the arts is being ruined."

He deplored the situation, which had put so many cinema
musicians out of work, and longed for live rather than "canned
mechanical jazz".

But, there were supporters for the talkies. Clearly with a vested interest, the local cinema managers thought that Durham was well catered for with up-to date varied and attractive entertainment. "The talkies," said one, "have enabled us to see and hear many famous plays. Plays are very expensive to produce and to engage, and local theatres are not able to afford high class drama companies." "For my part", he continued," I can see a day when except in the biggest towns stage plays and the variety theatre will almost die out and the Talkies will hold the field supreme."

Overcrowding on the first night of the Talkies at the Empire, Wingate caused it to be in breach of the regulations. John Barton, the manager, was charged with allowing the gangway to be blocked. Sergeant Luke told the court that there were chairs and people standing, but Mr Charlton, defending, said that there was no real obstruction since there were only two chairs and 8 people in the gangway. Colonel Rowland Burdon, the chairman of the Castle Eden magistrate's court, told Mr Charlton that he would be fined 5 shillings this time, but if it happened again he would not be let off so lightly.[37]

The year ended with further cinematic controversy. A High Court ruling under the Sunday Observance Act of 1780 had re-affirmed that Sunday entertainment for which a charge was made was prohibited. Alfred Smith, secretary of the Northern branch of the Cinema Exhibitors' Association, said that he thought it would not make any difference to the showing of Sunday films in the North-east. Canon Lillington, sub-dean of the Cathedral, replied that they had known all along that they were right in opposing Sunday cinema shows. Canon Bothamley, the former vicar of St. Nicholas Church, had often reminded everyone that the Sunday Observance Act had never been repealed. The new Mayor of Durham, J. W. Pattinson, councillor and local Salvation Army treasurer, said that he was overjoyed with the decision. "I am broadminded in most things," he said, "but I cannot agree with the Sunday opening of cinemas." The outgoing Mayor, Cllr. Murdoch, who had been chairman of the magistrates when the licences were last granted, said that he was in favour of Sunday cinemas after 8 p.m. "I view this matter from the standpoint of the mass of the people who have nothing to do on Sundays, and not from the angle of the armchair critic who has a comfortable home and wireless music. Most of the people who want Sunday cinemas are the workers who are not in too comfortable circumstances. They are only too glad to get out. And since there is a general suspension of work I see no justification for the magistrates to deny this form of entertainment."[38]

The cause of the cinema was taken up by none other than the Governor of Durham Gaol, Captain Scott. Whilst recognising that highly sensational films may have a harmful effect on the temperament of the young, he thought that it was unfair to single the cinema out as the prime cause of crime amongst adolescents. There were much more reprehensible ways of the young using their time than attending the cinema. One of its main assets was taking the poor out of their "drab comfortless environment" and enabling them to forget for a space of time "the dumb miseries of life in a slum dwelling".[39]

The Licensing Magistrates moved swiftly on the subject of Sunday Observance and announced on Wednesday 25th January that they would not consider Sunday cinema opening when licences came up for renewal on Monday 2nd February. The two advertising cinemas, therefore adopted the same policy of playing their Saturday film for an extra day. Thus for their final Sunday offerings, the Palace showed the colour musical *Rogue Song* starring Lawrence Tibbett, and the Palladium, the similarly coloured *Song of The West*, a film version of Oscar Hammerstein II's operetta.[40]

Opinions were divided. Canon Lillington congratulated the authorities on their wisdom and courage. "It will certainly make for the righteousness and prosperity of the people as they learn the importance of respecting the law." "No doubt," he continued, "we shall hear of the matter again and in a very prominent manner - at the next General Election - when candidates who wobble over the question of Sunday Observance may find themselves in a precarious position." James Robson, president of the Durham Miners' Association, and also a member of the city bench, strongly deprecated the move. "It is my experience," he declared, "that the opening of these places of entertainment on Sunday is one of the greatest agencies for temperance that can be conceived." The deputy Mayor, Cllr. Murdoch, repeated his support for the benefits of Sunday cinema opening after 8 p.m. He hoped that new legislation would amend the Sunday Observance Act to meet modern requirements. Cllr. Holliday, whom it must be remembered was a director of the Palladium Cinema, considered that Sunday opening had been 'a boon to the city.' He hoped the Government would take early steps to repeal the Act of 1780. The newspaper reported that a private Member's. Bill to that effect would be put before Parliament in the present session.[41]

The following week, the Advertiser published three comments on the subject. D. Clark of Darlington felt that the decision of the King's Bench could not be allowed to stand. Its logical conclusion would be that all forms of transport would be illegal on Sundays since they are paid for. The kill-joys in the name of Christianity have gained a hollow victory. He concluded that outdated laws should be amended.

Joseph Close of Brandon Colliery, Durham was of a similar opinion. The 1780 Act ordered that, "No carrier with a horse or wagon man with a wagon or cart man with a cart or drover with any cattle may travel upon the Lord's day". He deplored the fact that Britain had become a slave to religious opinions and actions, and that clerics such as Canon Lillington should realise that they are in the twentieth century and not the Middle Ages.

'Layman' suggested that the Church should find some other activity for the youth of the town on Sunday evenings. In Sunderland the Free Church ran Sunshine Services from 7.30 until 9.30 in the Victoria Hall with talented musicians and singers. He thought that Alderman Goodyear might be able to secure the Palladium for similar services.[42]

When the Licensing Session was held at the Durham police court, there was little new to be said. H. E. Ferens, on behalf of the Cinematograph Hall proprietors in the division, actually made an application for Sunday opening, but he realised that the bench were in a difficult position. Not ever the man to let a good point go to waste, he did manage a few parting shots. "I am glad to hear of the good conduct of licence holders generally and also of the cinemas during the year, and that these have carried on to the satisfaction of the Bench, and the public. It is not through fault nor mine, nor that of the general public, but an old Act of Parliament, that the position is rendered so difficult this morning. Part of the sobriety which has been alluded to is due no doubt to the Sunday opening of cinemas and places of entertainment. They have the effect of keeping the people from frequenting and staying in public houses longer than is wise. If the privilege is 'decktied', it may have a detrimental effect on that respect, but the Act of Parliament advises us on that point. There are now two Bills before Parliament and something may come of them. If that is so, it may be a solution and give us a way out of the difficulty, but at present. I cannot see any way until the law is amended." The Chairman agreed, and said that in the present circumstances they were bound to reject the application until the law was amended.[43]

An indication of the nation-wide interest in the ruling is that the Advertiser printed three letters, which had obviously been syndicated. Maurice Whitlow of the Lord's Day Observance Society wrote concerning the claim that the Sunday ban would discontinue the charitable donations made from the proceeds. He thought the Cinematograph Exhibitors' Association's claim that the £180,000 that was sent yearly to London Hospitals from the proceeds of Sunday was greatly exaggerated. Many places received nothing from the showings, and there was no provision in Mr. Isaac's Bill before Parliament for such a donation. Jack Jones, M.P., said in his letter that he saw no reason why the people of this country should not have the right to rational recreation on Sunday providing that those employed to serve them were properly paid and had received one day's rest in seven.[44]

The letter from a Miss Dodo Watts referred to the newspaper report that a petition against the Bill had received signatures that together would stretch to 6 miles. She pointed out that at its lowest estimate the combined queues of people waiting to enter cinemas on a Sunday evening would stretch for at least 21 miles. Though her letter does not reveal it, Miss Watts was a minor British film starlet currently doing the rounds as a glamorous representative of the British Film Industry. It is perhaps disparaging to her memory to point out that on a planned visit to Leicester in October 1931 to open the Trocadero Cinema, she went to catch the train at Victoria instead of St. Pancras!! [45]

The dilemma of local licensing regulations and the issue of

entertainment on 'Holy Days' was clearly upsetting everyone's rational thought. The City licensing authorities had refused to accept an application for the usual opening of cinemas on Good Friday after three p.m. Mr Ferens, on behalf of the Durham Cinematograph Exhibitors, then made a second application asking to be able to open the cinemas from 6.30 p.m. to 10.30 p.m. instead of from 2 p.m. to 10.30 p.m. There was a clear precedence for such opening since all the other magistrates courts in the area and in Newcastle had granted licences. He wished to point out that the ban was particularly harmful to the proprietors who had to guarantee to the film renters a certain amount from three performances. The picture which had been booked for Good Friday weekend would be subject to the same cost whether it was shown two nights or three. The application was again refused.

On the same day, however, in a neighbouring courtroom, a meeting of the County Court bench agreed that since Bishop Auckland had granted permission for Good Friday opening to two of the Spennymoor cinemas that came under their jurisdiction, the other three Spennymoor cinemas would be at a disadvantage if it was not granted to them. Two local vicars and a Roman Catholic priest had endorsed the application. Mr. Ferens then made a third application to the city magistrates who, by a majority decision, allowed opening on Good Friday from 6.30 p.m. to 10.30 p.m. So, the Palladium and the Palace were able to show their advertised films *The Big House* and *Paramount on Parade.* [46]

The Durham Advertiser carried an editorial on the occasion of the second reading of the Sunday Performance (Regulation) Bill. He makes his views clear on the absurdity of the antiquated Sunday Observance Act and welcomes the provisions within the current bill that do not force Sunday Cinema opening on reluctant communities. County and Borough Councils will be able to make their choices according to the demands of the electorate of each locality. He hoped that the new provisions would also take away the anomaly of different divisions of local justices arriving at different decisions.[47]

Another more local storm was brewing in the correspondence columns of the paper at this time. Three students from St. John's College drew the readers' attention to what they considered to be some objectionable behaviour during the screening of the film *Young Woodley* at the Palladium during the second house on Saturday 2nd May. They said that the picture was notable for its exceptional plot and distinguished by splendid dramatic acting. "The action throughout was interrupted by inane, stupid laughter whilst one of the tensest moments of the whole piece was greeted by an uproar that amounted to little less than hooliganism." They praised the Palladium management for including British films in their *repertoire*.

In another part of the newspaper, the theatre and screen reviewer commented that this was not an unusual manifestation in Durham cinemas when any scene of 'tender passion' is exhibited on the screen. He suggested that, though laughter may be irrepressible at times, verbal comment such as that reported on should be promptly checked. [48]

Three of the culprits from University College defended their position in a later letter, which displayed the usual college and academic rivalry and must have astounded or bemused the locals.[49] They began with a gibe at the ecclesiastical foundation of St. John's College.

"Far be it from us to dispraise the efforts of certain gentlemen with theological leanings to castigate the manners and morals of their age. Rather do we admire them for their own exemplary lives and unimpeachable tastes." They continued with a particularly interesting demolition of the output of British studios. "We sympathise with the audience which saw cause for laughter in the film version of *Young Woodley*. To us it was just another Elstree abomination. Of course, we know what we ought to have done; we ought to have sat and simulated aesthetic pleasure at this sickly prodigy of the sex drama; applauded when Mr Van Druten's characters were being slaughtered before our eyes. We must endure the galling massacre of stage dramas that are adapted for the film, as if the techniques were the same for both."

With further stabs at Elstree and at the young trainee clerics, they concluded: "The salvation of Elstree lies not in the morbid; however much its films may tickle the salacious instincts of certain young gentlemen who uphold worn-out doctrines under the guise of patriotism and effete platitudes."

Another letter from 'Three Citizens' suggested that their

criticism might have found greater support if it had come from a source other than students. Mr. Cowley from Sherburn Hill sympathised with the original writers but he also drew attention to the regular disturbance of dramatic moments in films by student patrons. He deplored their behaviour and suggested that they should be the ones setting an example to all.

The editor allowed the original three a reply before closing the correspondence. They said that they had expected the general criticism of students from citizens of the town, and they accepted the view that certain sections of the University could be more boorish and objectionable than the general public. They deplored this behaviour, too. They regarded the defamation of the film as particularly at fault since it had been "universally praised by competent critics." They wondered if the University College gentlemen equated their standards with those of the typical American all-talking, all dancing travesties with 100% American accents. There was mystery in their denouement. They were sorry that the lady who wrote them (they assumed it was a feminine hand) did not include her name and address, so that they could discuss the point she put forward more fully.[50]

The Sunday saga continued to run. Chester-le-Street magistrates did not withdraw Sunday opening from the existing licences, but Houghton-le-Spring magistrates heard eight police summonses against the Hetton-le-Hole Picture House Co. Ltd. Their representative, F. J. Lambert of Gateshead, entered a technical plea of guilty and gave an undertaking that "the halls managed by the company (the Imperial Picture House and the Pavilion Picture House) would not open again on the Sabbath." The bench considered the case the first of its kind before them and said that they would let them off the charges on the payment of costs for each case and a solicitor's fee of five guineas. Superintendent R. Harrison explained that the position of Sunday opening locally was very diverse. In the Castle Eden area there were seventeen picture halls open on Sundays, and Sunday opening was allowed in three out of the eleven divisions in the County.[51]

Whilst all this was taxing the minds of the authorities, the Sacriston Institute Cinema changed over to Talkies. There was a large audience for the opening night. Sacriston had three entertainment halls at this time. The biggest, at almost 700 seats, the aptly named Victoria Theatre in Queen Street, was opened in 1921 as a variety hall and cinema. The Institute Cinema in part of the Front Street Memorial Institute was opened in 1924 to hold 450 people. The Royal or the Theatre Royal in Church Street was also opened in 1921 with accommodation for 550. This did not convert to sound and closed in 1930/1; not re-opening until 1954. The cinemas were known collectively as the Top, Middle, and Bottom houses.[52]

The Emergency Act allowing places of entertainment to be licensed for Sunday opening was given the Royal Assent on 7th October 1931. On that same day, W. Hateley J.P. of Willington and chairman of the Durham county branch of the Cinematograph Exhibitors' Association made an application to the magistrates of Durham county police court on behalf of the 22 cinemas in the area for permission to recommence Sunday performances. They decided that the safest course of action would be to defer a decision until the following Wednesday. When this arrived, the chairman was about to give his assent to the request under the old terms of opening at 8 p.m. and closing by 10 p.m. when one of the magistrates suggested that all the J. P.s in the other court should be invited to attend. The request was sent to them, but only one other appeared. This bit of manoeuvring by one of the church groups clearly failed, for when the application was made again, it was granted by a majority of the Bench.[53]

The picture was entirely different when the city magistrates met to consider an application on Thursday, 29th October. As expected, strong opposition was voiced by the Canon Lillington for the cathedral, the Revd. Mr Pickering for St. Nicholas Church, and the Revd. H. Derbyshire for the Free Churches. Mr. Ferens pointed out that all the cinemas around the city would be operating on Sunday evenings and that it was most unfair that they would have to go out from the city for their entertainment. Canon Lillington made the shrewd observation that if, as had been suggested, the populace would be attracted into the public houses if the cinemas were not open, why were the publicans not here to oppose the Sunday opening.

The Revd. Mr Derbyshire was of the opinion that most of the people queuing for admittance to the city cinemas on Sundays were from outside. The police had made no objection to the application, and Mr. Ferens was clearly very much put out when a unanimous decision against the application was given. He felt out-manoeuvred by the fact that the application was destined always to be heard by the full bench and not the usual three justices.[54]

The decision was followed by one letter in the newspaper. 'Young man', as he signed himself, had noticed that the opposition to the application consisted solely of 'religious gentlemen'. He was disappointed that the Revd. Mr Pickering, himself a younger man than the majority of his colleagues, should have declared that it was better for the youth of the city to walk the streets and "meet in the eyes of men, than in an atmosphere of seducing darkness." He thought it was clear that the vicar had not experienced a well-run Sunday cinema, nor the 'seductive darkness' of North Road and its darker places on a Sunday night. Young people, he concluded, could hardly be encouraged into the church by vicar and curates who used silly objections to deter them from harmless pleasures.[55]

In November, the new Mayor, Councillor J.W. Wood, took up his office. Although as a director of the Palladium Cinema, it was clear that he could have been an ally of the cinema proprietors, at his first appearance as chairman of the magistrates, he said that he would not take his seat on any Bench considering cinema matters.[56]

The picture hall site (for what was to become the Regal) on North Road gave rise to a letter of complaint in the Advertiser on 27th November 1931. New plans for the cinema had been submitted in January 1929, and demolition work had been begun next to the former Miner's Hall.

The excavations for the new building had revealed gathering waters, probably the remnants of the diverted Mill burn, and construction had been halted whilst a solution was found. The complainant wondered when the "hideous gap in North road would be 'stopped up'. "

He still had some time to wait.

1932

The home cinematograph and the ciné-camera had become more available in the late twenties and early thirties. There were feature films, comedy shorts and documentaries available for showing in the Pathé 9.5mm gauge. Kodak 16mm projectors were being produced for industrial and educational exhibitions. 35mm safety film was also available for non-licensed premises. The Hugh MacKay Carpet Company produced a ten-minute 35mm film on safety stock showing all the processes of Durham Carpet manufacture, for presentation at the North East Coast Exhibition in 1929.[57] The headmaster of Brandon County Junior School applied to the Director of Education for permission to use a cinema projector in the school for the purpose of illustrating lessons. There is no indication concerning the kind of projector envisaged, but permission was granted provided that all the films shown were non-inflammable and that there was no danger to the children. [58]

There were no surprises when, in February, the magistrates once more refused to grant Sunday opening licences to the three city cinemas and the proposed cinema in North Road. The licensing session had again been conducted by the full Bench of ten magistrates. Their decision was reached by a majority. Mr Ferens produced figures to show that the Sunday opening had been popular; the average attendance at the Palladium on Sundays being 752. The Reverend Mr. Henderson thought that Mr Ferens had been very selective in his choice of figures. His figures might be true for the winter months, but in the summer they were more like 3 to 4 hundred. Canon Lillington also countered with his opinion that the streets of Durham had been unusually quiet since Sunday opening was discontinued.

The debate, however, took a new turn when the Revd. Mr Derbyshire objected not only to the kinds of films being shown but also to the posters used to advertise them. He made reference to the disgusting posters for the films *Seed* and *High Queen* and had drawn the attention of the police to their 'grossly indecent' images. Superintendent Foster took exception to his use of language. He had received a note from the reverend gentleman concerning indecent posters, and three members of the bench and he himself had been to look at them. They thought that they might not have been in good taste, but they were no more indecent than a draper's shop where there might be a dressed model of a woman." The poster," he said, "was objectionable from one point of view, but it was not indecent from the point of view of the law."

Posters for the films referred to by the Revd. Mr Derbyshire have not survived but film reviews reveal something of their content and demeanour. *Seed* released in 1931, starred John Boles, Lois Wilson, Genevieve Tobin *and* Bette Davis in an early role. Its story is described as 'a turgid drama based upon the novel by Charles G. Norris in which a would-be author deserts his wife and five children for a high-powered employee of the publishing firm where he works as a clerk.'[59] The Revd. Mr Derbyshire revealed his lack of knowledge of poker by confusing the film title *High Queen* with its correct title *Queen High.* It was also released in 1931 with stars Charles Ruggles, Frank Morgan, and Ginger Rogers, described as a musical comedy about a garter manufacturer who, having lost a game of cards, has to become the servant to his partner. It was a screen version of a stage play. One of its songs was 'I love the ladies in my own peculiar way'.[60]

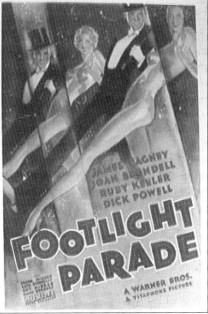

Posters of the kind that must have displeased the Revd. Mr. Derbyshire.

A reader's letter the following week indicated the writer's anger with the tiresome outbursts of ill-informed local clergy. He was particularly incensed by the Revd. Mr Derbyshire's accusation that the films that had been shown on Sundays were worse than those shown in the week. He wondered how this information was gathered. If it was hearsay, then he was surprised that it was able to used as evidence at the justices' court.[61]

The Synod of the Sunderland and Newcastle district of the Methodist church was held at Hetton-le-Hole in May. As part of his address, the Revd. J. J. Alderson of Newcastle suggested that in contemporary life "the film had created a great social problem." He considered it to be a specious argument that the Hollywood producers were only giving their audiences what they wanted. "Hollywood," he said, "provides the world with a silly and shameful vulgarity which disgraces a vast art. Producers are wrong in their belief that the public want the worst type of film. If they were given the chance to see the best type of film they would respond to it at once. We want a man like Sir John Reeth [sic] who controls the broadcast programmes of the BBC, at the head of the film industry. We pray that the church will provide such a man. Then the film industry will be used for the good of the race and not for its ill."[62]

It was very rare that local newspaper advertisements made any reference to the classification system employed by the British Board of Film Censors, though it was a necessary part of the licensing legislation of most local authorities that the film categories should be displayed in the cinema entrance. When the Palace showed *Frankenstein* for the whole of the week starting 4th July 1932, however, the publicity indicated its ADULTS ONLY status.

The film had actually been given an 'A' certificate when it was reviewed by the British Board of Film censors on 24th December 1931. Some scenes had been cut from the film but it should have been possible for persons under the age of 16 to have seen the film if accompanied by a *bona fide* adult. A wide interpretation of methods of recognition resulted and ingenious strategies were adopted by adolescents and younger patrons for evincing an entry. The Leicester Branch of the Cinematograph Exhibitors' Association in 1930 had objected to the fact that some *adult* films had had the word *only* added without any regulation. Several local authorities had arbitrarily banned all children under the age of 16 from their cinemas when an 'A' certificate film was being shown. The British Board of Film Classification in the 1990s gave the film a PG (Parental guidance) rating.[63]

The Globe Cinema in the week of 25th July 1932 played a repertory programme of musicals. Durham had come late to the talkies, and there was quite a backlog of 'unseen' films to clear before up-to-date releases could be the main menu. *It's A Great Life* (1930) on Monday was a showcase for the Duncan Sisters (Rosetta and Vivian). The film's bad reception by the critics was fair proof that vaudeville dancers were not necessarily great film stars. Things looked up a little in Tuesday, with Bessie Love in *Good News* (1930); a film version of the stage play that most of the trade press thought was bad news. *New Moon* (1931) on Wednesday starred Lawrence Tibbett and Grace Moore in the Romberg-Hammerstein operetta. It could hardly fail, and there must have been a rush for the seats at the Globe for its twice-nightly showing. On Thursday, *Show of Shows* (1929), with its two-colour Technicolor sequences, must also have been popular in North Road. Warner Bros had brought together an amazing array of film and vaudeville talent in a plotless review. There was even a touch of Shakespeare with John Barrymore playing a scene from Henry VI, Part Three!! On Friday afternoon there was a matinée for John Boles in *The Desert Song*. This 1929 film had been seen before in Durham, but no doubt its continued popularity and its position in the film week would have produced good audiences.

Saturday was reserved for *Viennese Nights*. This Warner Brothers' Romberg & Hammerstein musical was made in the same year as *New Moon*. Its enduring songs and its Technicolor photography would have ensured good houses for all three performances. The main stars were Alexander Gray and Vivienne Segal with Walter Pidgeon as the other man. Mr. Peacock had put the Globe back on the map.

Newspaper reports indicated the cancellation of some Christmas parties. Even the calendar seemed to be against the celebrations since Christmas Day was a Sunday, and no cinemas were open. One party that did go ahead was at Wingate. The manager of the Palace Pictures, Mr. Harrison, with the aid of a local charity, put on a special show for the old people of the village

and afterwards they were provided with 'a knife and fork tea'.

An end of the year bonus for film fans was the visit of Harold Lloyd to Washington Old Hall (see left). He had visited Blyth earlier in the day. There was a big crowd to see him and 'an outburst of wild cheering upon his arrival'.[64]

The population of the county certainly needed some cheering up, since this was a period of lay-offs and pit closures.

Applications for Sunday cinema licences were on the agenda for the city Licensing Sessions in December 1932 and again in February 1933. The Palace Theatre did not even include itself in the application and, as Mr. Ferens had anticipated, there was no change in the strength of the church opposition, the arguments put forward or the final decision. One clause of the Sunday Entertainments Act of 1932 did allow for public opinion to be tested by a citizen's vote. The problem was that the authorities had to be convinced first that there was a public clamour for the vote. No-one in Durham outside the trade seemed keen enough to pursue this course of action. Indeed, the Revd. Mr Derbyshire at a Free Church conference in Durham in February 1933 was of the opinion that "Durham was one of the areas to which the provisions of the act for a plebiscite did not apply".[65]

In the following week the county bench also disallowed Sunday opening applications. They had consistently allowed seven-day licensing for the previous 14 years, apart from the break whilst the Sunday Entertainments Act was considered. There was no opposition from the local clergy, but a new element had been introduced, the non-payment or the late payment of the charity contributions that were required under the new regulations. Mr.

Ferens on behalf of the Durham and District Cinema Holders' Association volunteered that he was aware that the rates decreed in this county division were less than those in other divisions and only half those levied in Chester-le-Street and Houghton–le-Spring. He said that if the new licences were granted he would appeal to the licensees to be prompt with their payments. But Mr Gibson, proprietor of the Gaiety Electric Theatre, Ferryhill, said that any increase in the charity levy would be very detrimental to his business. The Clerk of the Court pointed out that Mr. Gibson's levy based upon the seating accommodation of his theatre amounted to 4 shillings and 2 pence. Mr. Gibson attempted to declare the extent of his losses for the year, but the justices would only allow him to speak of his accounting for Sunday performances. He was told that he would not have to pay any dues if he was closed on Sundays. Mr. Gibson was thus in something of a dilemma. He was able to make up for some of his losses in the week with good houses on Sunday, but had to pay some of those takings to the charity fund. The chairman of the Bench, T. F. Brass O.B.E., was clearly not very sympathetic to his pleas, since he had been told that within the last fortnight attendances on Sunday consisted of more people than his theatre could hold.

Mr. Tinsley of the Victoria Theatre, Sacriston tried a similar tack. He said that with a seating capacity of 700 he had to pay ten guineas per year in charity fees, and this was "a stiff item in a small place like Sacriston". Mr. Brass, who lived in Sacriston, would have none of it. "I know you have full attendances on Sunday nights," he said. "I do not go to them because I have my own books and smokes at home." Mr. Tinsley agreed that he had good houses on Sunday because it was the only night that the night shift men could attend the cinemas. He had suffered a loss of £750 during the year because of the depreciation on the machinery.[66] Superintendent Foster also seemed un-moved by the hardship stories by saying that the total amount to be collected from the three Sacriston Cinemas was 6 shillings and 9 pence. Mr. Turnbull of the Sherburn Hill Picture House said that for four months last summer, his takings on Sunday nights had amounted to no more than 30/-.

Just before the magistrates retired to consider the applications, the clerk of the court said that a good many of the licensees had not paid their charges for the last year. On their return, the magistrates declared that Sunday licences would be withdrawn, and that the cinema proprietors would need to make separate applications for licences to open on Good Friday and Christmas Day.[67] The ban lasted less than a month. On 1st March, the magistrates reinstated the Sunday licences on the understanding that the cinemas would pay £3 per annum for each hundred seats; double the amount they had previously paid. Mr. Ferens said that the cinema proprietors had been shocked by their withdrawal of the licences, since they felt that they had performed their obligations under the regulations without error. There had been no complaints concerning the films shown and there had been an increase in the use of educational films. Mr Ferens cleverly concluded his address to the magistrates by drawing their attention to the sums of money that had been contributed to the Police Boot Fund from the Sunday performances. Prior to the magistrates reversing their decision on the licences, Superintendent Foster said that the amount handed to charity in the last quarter had been £50 10 shillings.[68]

There was a minor reference to cinema in the tragic death of a Mr. Ringwood in Millburngate, Durham. The victim had been to the first house at the Globe cinema in nearby North Road. When he returned home, a heated argument ensued, during which Mrs. Ringwood stabbed him to death. Though originally charged with murder, Mrs Ringwood, who had suffered years of physical abuse from her husband, pleaded guilty to manslaughter and was sentenced to nine months imprisonment. Mr. Ringwood had just seen the film *The Doomed Battalion* starring Victor Varconi and Tala Birrell.[69]

In June, the Durham diocesan conference in the chapter house of Durham Cathedral paid particular reference to film and film production. The subject was introduced by the Revd. Dr. Charles Budden of East Mildred, Croydon. In his diocese picture halls were open on Sundays. He said that he personally regretted the passing of the old style Sunday and that the question of Sunday opening bristled with difficulties. He thought that the primary issue was that the church should have some control in film production because the effect of the cinema on public morals and public opinion was incalculable. He attacked the die-hard Sabbatarians who no doubt bought their Monday morning newspapers that had been produced on Sunday. "What did the church provide for the population on Sunday evenings?" he asked.

In Croydon, their selection committee was comprised of two cinema managers, two churchmen and four members of the local authority. Under the chairmanship of the Bishop of Croydon they had devised a system of operation for the Sunday opening of cinemas. No employee should work more than six days and a proportion of the Sunday takings should be given to charity. The programmes consisted of two feature films and three 'shorts'. All the films must definitely be wholesome and uplifting and refreshing. They did not rule out comedy films because there was nothing wrong with a good laugh on Sunday. They attempted to encourage the showing of British films and believed that the reign of Hollywood was coming to a close.

"We definitely rule out gangster films, and crime and horror films as well as those dealing with sex. We rule out also those films that are simply silly and stupid," he said. A survey had shown that the cinemas in the poorest parts of town were better attended than those in the mainly residential areas. It was clear that the cinema was providing shelter for those who had no decent homes to go to. 90 per cent of those attending the cinemas on Sunday were young people who might otherwise have been roaming the streets. He thought that many films were shown that were a good deal better than some of his sermons. There was clear opposition to his discourse. Canon A. Silva White of Monkwearmouth proposed that they should adhere to a resolution passed on 2nd November 1929 by 95 votes to 41 that they should resist to their utmost any encroachment on the Lord's Day. He thought that the argument that young people were at risk roaming the streets was a bogey. They were in the open air not in the dark unhealthy atmosphere of the cinema. Canon White thought that if Sunday were destroyed Christianity would be destroyed. The Revd. R. Rumney of Bishopwearmouth in seconding the motion said that what was inevitable in Croydon was not desired in the North. He didn't think even the best cinema proprietors were fit people to interpret the deep things in their faith.

The Archdeacon of Auckland, Dr. Rawlinson, moved an alternative motion commending the Croydon experiment and suggestion co-operation with the cinema industry. He was supported by the Reverend F. S. Myers, Rural Dean of Lanchester. He was sure that pictures could be utilised in a way that would be beneficial to the public.

There was further opposition from Canon Lillington. When there were pictures in Durham City on Sunday, he said, amongst the attendees were young people from Sunday Schools and Bible Classes. The Revd. Mr Pickering declared that in acquiescing to Sunday films they would be seriously jeopardising their spiritual work. They were not ordained to sit on committees to select suitable films. The final resolution proposed by the Bishop of Durham, Dr. Henson, considered what they had heard from Doctor Budden but reiterated their concern regarding further encroachments on the Sabbath. The church in Durham thus remained unmoved. [70]

In the same week, the death was announced of Alderman H. E. Ferens *(pictured right)*. Both he and his son had represented the City and County cinema managers at the licensing courts since 1910. On their behalf he had been a staunch advocate of Sunday opening. He had been born in Gilesgate in 1844 and he had continued his practice up to his death.[71] Ironically, the death of one his greatest opponents occurred shortly afterwards.

Canon Bothamley, formerly the vicar of St. Nicholas Church, had been outspoken on many issues of church and civil practice, but he had been especially vociferous on Sunday cinema opening, and the extension of the opening hours of public houses on Miners' Day.

His successor at St. Nicholas Church, the Revd. Mr Pickering was no less keen on these subjects and in the same week as the Canon's death, he had written a further strong condemnation of the arguments for Sunday entertainment in the parish magazine. "There is sufficient evidence from public behaviour here in this city that far from keeping young people off the streets on Sunday, Sunday cinemas bring them onto the streets, and after entertaining them for two hours they turn them out on the streets at a perilously late hour."[72]

Film fans were now, however, a part of everyday life. A large throng of female admirers waited on Palace Green for Anna May Wong, when it was rumoured that she was going to visit the cathedral on 5th September. Unfortunately, although she only had to come from Newcastle, where she was appearing on stage, she didn't turn up.

Encouragement was also given to the young cinemagoers of the Advertiser who were asked to vote for their favourite film stars from Janet Gaynor, Norma Shearer, Joan Crawford, Constance Bennett, Jean Harlow, Jessie Matthews, Laurel and Hardy, Clark Gable, Jack Oakie, Tom Walls, Ralph Lynn, and Ronald Colman. The result published on 22nd September was surprising. In order of popularity were Janet Gaynor, Norma Shearer, Joan Crawford, Jessie Matthews, Jean Harlow, Laurel and Hardy, Clark Gable, Tom Walls, Ronald Colman, Ralph Lynn, and Jack Oakie. Of the six prize winners in the competition, five were girls.[73]

An Amateur Film Society was formed in Houghton-Le-Spring, with 22 year-old Edward Gilderoy as its secretary. Initially they had 22 members with an average age of 22 years, and their aim was not only to make amateur films but also to encourage the study of the art and science of cinematography through a book library. Nationally, the British Film Institute had been formed for a similar purpose. [74]

When the Palladium showed *The Sign of The Cross* for a week in October, it included a dramatic prologue by A. Delman, formerly of the Durham Amateur Operatic Society. There was only one performance each evening and it was possible to book all seats in advance. A rumour had circulated that all seats were booked. The newspaper report indicated that there was ample room for all who wanted to see the film.[75]

"KINEMA,"
MEADOWFIELD.
NOVEMBER 27th, 1933. All the week.
Monday and Saturday at 6.10 and 8.40.
Remainder of week at 7.30.

"KING KONG,"
By EDGAR WALLACE.
This picture has to be seen to be believed.

Here are some of the exact measurements of **"KING KONG,"** the prehistoric gorilla, which is the dominant figure in the picture:—
Height—Fifty feet.
Face—Seven feet.
Nose—Two feet wide at nostrils.
Mouth—Six feet.
Legs—Fifteen feet.
Arms—Twenty-three feet.
Reach—Seventy-five feet.
This is the first time of showing in the district, and nothing has ever been been like it before.

The Central Palace, Meadowfield, now appearing under the name Kinema, had a busy week with *King Kong* at the end of November. Though the newspaper advertisement gave full details of the dimensions of Edgar Wallace's invention, no 'Adults Only' classification was included.[76] The film was eventually shown at the Globe cinema in the city on 11th December.

The Palace, since July, had been alternating film programmes with variety turns and revues. There is no indication concerning the popularity of the variety programmes nor any editorial comment upon the re-appearance of professional live entertainment in the city. Live entertainment of more sinister kind was provided at the Palace on Saturday 9th Dec. when Sir Oswald Mosley spoke on Fascism. Free tickets were obtainable from the British Union of Fascists at 85, Claypath, Durham, and the sound was relayed to the Town Hall. The report described how the curtain was raised and Mosley and his black-shirted bodyguards stood on the stage. There was a large curious crowd, but no interruptions. [77]

1934

The Palace opened the New Year with a week of the American mystic, Dr. Raymond, and followed it with a pantomime of *Babes in The Wood*. On 22nd January a split week of films was again on the bill. The Palladium had Buster Crabbe in *King of The Jungle* and Mickey Mouse in his only 'A' certificate cartoon *The Mad Doctor*. They also had Arthur Furby's Grand Cinema Orchestra to play musical interludes at each evening performance. Cinema orchestra musicians had been made redundant by the talkies, and these *interlude* performances were the last vestiges of live orchestral music in cinemas. Record players (the 'non-synch.') linked through the cinematograph amplifier were mostly used in intervals and between houses, though the cinema organ was still a popular fixture in the new generation of super cinemas.

At about two o'clock on Tuesday morning 16th January, a fire was discovered at the Palladium cinema. Police Constable Snowdon was the first to see the blaze. He quickly contacted a director, Joseph Wills, who lived nearby and they entered the building to find thick smoke. The fire brigade were on the scene very quickly but they found that the fire

Palladium fire damage. *Photograph in Durham Advertiser Friday 19 July 1934. Courtesy of Durham Advertiser.*

hydrants within the building did not have enough pressure for the hoses. After transferring these to the street hydrants they were able to tackle the blaze on the stairs and in the roof. Deputy fire-chief Pawson attempted to tackle the blaze in the circle, but was slightly affected by the fumes and smoke from the burning seats. The Houghton-le-Spring brigade arrived shortly after this to find that the fire was mostly under control. Great volumes of water had been poured onto the flames and this had run down from the balcony into the stalls.[78]

The ceiling was blackened and the circle was in ashes. An inspection of the electrical circuits of the cinema found nothing amiss, and it was therefore assumed that the blaze began with a carelessly discarded cigarette end. Fortunately, the cinema had adequate insurance cover and it was expected that renovation would begin immediately after the clean-up operation. There was apparently only minor damage to the projection room.

The following week, the Globe had a two-day film programme. There is no link here with the reduction in screens since the films were a job-lot of Columbia releases all over a year old. On Monday and Tuesday, there was Jack Holt in *Soldiers of Fortune* (1932), on Wednesday and Thursday Walter Huston in *American Madness* (1932) and on Friday and Saturday Lillian Miles, Jack Holt, and Gavin Gordon in *Man Against Woman* (1932). The experiment seems to have been successful, since they repeated it for the next few months.

In the county cinemas, Sunday opening had obviously been very popular. Superintendent Foster reported that the charity charge had raised £353 for the year. There had not been the increase in educational films that the Bench had hoped for, but the committee had been able to eliminate those that were termed undesirable. He was sure that constant and regular

supervision was necessary to achieve the aims of the Bench.[79]

The Palladium re-opened on 5th March 1934 with Leslie Henson in a British comedy *It's A Boy* and Mickey Mouse in *Ye Olden Days*. Pattison's supplied the new Durham carpets and the original contractors for the cinema, F. W. Goodyear & Son, carried out the reconstruction work. The newspaper reported that almost everything in the cinema was new except the 'very courteous manager, Mr Harwood and his staff'. A new lighting system had been installed and new curtains had been hung. Four artistic panels were set into the walls representing Variety, Drama, Travel and Romance.[80] The re-opening was just able to capture the publicity before Durham's new cinema opened its doors.

Detail from a postcard photograph of North Road showing the cinema under construction. *Author's collection. Below illustration courtesy of the Durham Advertiser.*

The old Miners' Hall and the adjacent houses had been translated into the Regal Cinema and Ballroom. The official opening was on Tuesday night 27th March 1934, but before then the Advertiser had fully described the new structure.

The water problems on the site had been eliminated by the use of pumps, and there was little possibility of it returning. The construction had been undertaken by Messrs G. Gradon & Son of Durham to the plans and designs of S. Stephenson. A particular attraction was the

Christie organ with its gold console. It was to be played by Herbert Maxwell, an accomplished organist well-known throughout the country, and a long-time friend and associate of the proprietor, Joseph Dobson. Besides the cinema, the site also included a ballroom and a billiards hall.

The opening night was attended by the Mayor and Mayoress, Alderman and Mrs. J. Lynch, personalities from the university, the civil authorities, the contractors and the architects. The Mayor, Cllr. Fowler, in declaring the building open, said that the cinema would be an asset to the community. Besides all the modern amenities of a cinema, it had the potential to house live theatre productions as well. Durham was proud of its ancient buildings and it could be proud of its new ones as well. Mr. Gradon on behalf of the builders presented the mayor with a silver cigarette case as a memento of the occasion from an old school friend. To the amusement of the audience, he said that the Regal's illuminations would enable Alderman Lynch (whose shop was opposite) to save on lighting for his own premises. Mr. Dobson, who was suffering from a severe cold, made a few remarks and presented bouquets of flowers to the Mayoress and to Mrs. Lynch. A fanfare of trumpets then followed, and the curtains opened to the accompaniment of moving coloured lights and the Christie organ. The manager, Herbert Maxwell, demonstrated the versatility of the organ with a medley of folk, jazz and classical tunes. "The Blaydon Races gave way to Jazz and the Jazz gave way to Handel's Largo. At the end, he had the whole audience joining in 'Daisy Bell'."

As the lights faded, the opening film *Her First Mate* was shown. This minor comedy directed by William Wyler starred Slim Summerville and Zazu Pitts. At only 66 minutes long, it was clearly chosen to fit in with the timing of the opening ceremony. It was replaced by the hit musical *Gold Diggers of 1933* for Wednesday, Thursday and Saturday. On Good Friday, it was thought to be more fitting to show the film *Heroes For Sale*, a drama about the problems of a returning World War Veteran, starring Richard Barthelmess and Loretta Young. It was one of Warner's 'social consciousness films', and in some quarters it proved quite controversial because of its treatment of drug addiction.

REGAL, DURHAM.
GRAND OPENING,
TUESDAY, 27th MARCH, at 8 p.m.,
By the Right Worshipful
THE MAYOR OF DURHAM
(Coun. James Chisman Fowler).
FOR OPENING NIGHT ONLY—
SLIM SUMMERVILLE and ZASU PITTS in
"HER FIRST MATE."
WEDNESDAY, THURSDAY, SATURDAY,
Nightly 6 and 8.30 p.m.   Matinees 2 p.m.
"GOLD DIGGERS OF 1933."
SPECIAL GOOD FRIDAY ATTRACTION,
6 p.m. and 8.30 p.m.
RICHARD BARTHELMESS in
"HEROES FOR SALE"
At all performances HERBERT MAXWELL
at the Great Christie Organ.
Prices of Admission: 7d. to 1/6
(including Tax). Children Half-price.

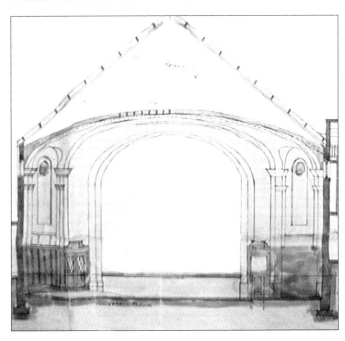

(*above*) **The unconverted Miners' Hall and the Regal's opening advert.**

(*left*) **The architect's drawing of the Regal's proscenium arch.** *DCRO plan 000841.*

(*below*) **Press advertising block for** *Moonlight and Melody.*

Initially, there was some cause for complaint that the cinema had separated rather than continuous performances. They were instituted later in the year. [81]

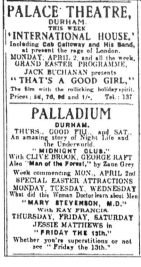

In the first week that Durham had four cinemas, the film programmes showed a wide range of British and American productions. All the films had release dates in 1933, and were showing in Durham for the first time. Although *International House* was a W. C. Fields film, the Palace chose to emphasise the musical elements. *That's A Good Girl* continued the singing and dancing with a Herbert Wilcox film.

The Palladium did not bow to Good Friday sensitivities, and continued with their underworld drama *Midnight Club*. The full programme, including the Henry Hathaway western *Man of the Forest*, would have been over 2½ hours in length. There was no advertised second feature for the following week's three-day presentations of *Mary Stevenson, M.D.* and *Friday the 13th*. If the cinema had played the later film on the next week, it *would* have been Friday 13th. An opportunity missed!

The Globe played *The Past of Mary Holmes,* an overacted remake of the Clarence Brown 1925 classic, *The Goose Woman*, and followed it with two down-market Monogram films *The Phantom Broadcast* and *Black Beauty*, both directed by Phil Rozen.

The Regal's second week featured a frothy musical from the Universal stable, *Moonlight and Melody*. Glamour cards vaunting the leggy young ladies from the original American title number *Moonlight and Pretzels* were used as publicity devices. The Hayes code was about to descend upon the American cinema and such revelations would soon be rare.

In April, the Palace surprisingly featured a whole week of live variety in the form of 'Gandy's Comic Circus'.[82] The accompanying film was The *Ace of Trouble,* the first film in a series of twelve two-reelers forming part of a competition advertised as giving away £100,000 in prizes. The audience were asked to observe deliberate mistakes planted in the films and to register their findings on forms supplied by the cinema. Each episode was to be shown twice nightly. The films were British-made by the New Era Company. Later in the month, they advertised 'One Night of Variety - 7 Good Acts' and in May they had a week of 'Levanti - the illusionist'. [83]

The Regal advertisements now gave evidence of the complete programme. Monday, Tuesday, and Wednesday - Bette Davis in *The Bureau of Missing Persons* with *Nothing But The Tooth, The News* and *Sea Devils.* Thursday, Friday and Saturday - Paul Lukas in *The Secret of The Blue Room,* with *Big Benefit, The News* and *Palsie Walsie.*

Competition for patrons was clearly heating up. In May, the Globe, with the new rival cinema on the opposite side of the road, renewed its policy of changing its programme every two days, and the Palladium and the Advertiser combined in a film promotion. They asked readers and patrons to state whom they thought were the best actress and the best actor in the film, *Dinner At Eight* being shown that week. Alongside some tie-in advertising for Greenwell's Wine Shop, and Porter's Grocery store, there was a coupon for readers to complete. 12 pairs of free tickets were on offer to the winners. The winners, to be decided by ballot, would be those who most nearly selected the pair chosen by the majority!! Six male actors and six female actors were included in the list.[84] The published choices were Lionel Barrymore 422, Marie Dressler 436, Wallace Beery 419, Jean Harlow 319, John Barrymore 318, Billie Burke 157, Edmund Lowe 52 and Madge Evans 26. It would appear that Lee Tracy, Jean Hersholt and Karen Morley received no votes. The winners came from Browney, Gilesgate, Bear Park and Framwellgate Moor. [85]

An unusual departure for the Globe for three days in July was a live stage performance. The group of entertainers calling themselves 'The Cinema Players' were Rolls and Roye - the inimitable Car Comedians; Phyllis - the phenomenal Soprano;

Guiseppe - The Wizard of the Accordion; and Jimmy - the renowned ventriloquist. The minimal stage facility would have been sufficient for this kind of performance. The supporting film was *Jury of the Jungle*, a 55-minute adventure film (US Title *Fury of the Jungle*).

Members of the 1st Battalion, The Durham Light Infantry attending a special performance of *On Secret Service* at the Regal, Durham. *Durham Advertiser.*

"Mae West with her new style of acting will keep audiences interested from start to finish", declared the Advertiser reviewer in recommending *I'm No Angel* to Palace patrons. "Come Up and See Me Sometime", implored the advertisement. "The Picture you have all been waiting for." It was certainly a week for blondes: the Palladium was showing Jean Harlow in *Blonde Bombshell.* [86]

Mr. Dobson, proprietor of the Regal, demonstrated an enterprising piece of showmanship on Monday 23rd July by inviting some members of the Durham Light Infantry to a special afternoon showing of the film *On Secret Service*. Herbert Maxwell, the organist, led the audience in the singing of war-time songs. The actual connection of the film with British troops is somewhat mysterious since the film starring Greta Nissen and Carl Ludwig Dahl was concerned with the spying activities of an Italian girl and an Austrian officer and was an adaptation of the novel 'Spione Am Werk'.

It was to be one of Mr Dobson's last activities, for on 17th August 1934, he died at his home in Monkseaton. Although he was the owner of a number of billiard halls, his main occupation had been as an estate agent. He was also the proprietor of the Crown Electric cinema in Newcastle. The building of the Regal had occupied his mind and his time for many years since his purchase of the original Miners' Hall in 1917. There had been many structural problems connected with the building alterations and the Advertiser obituary suggested that the completed cinema would stand as a monument to his endeavours. [87]

Photo: Durham County Advertiser

The Advertiser reported an unusual occurrence on Palace Green in August. Two cars arrived on a Sunday evening and unloaded 'a quaint contraption'. A curious crowd gathered and it was soon ascertained that this was a film crew. Shortly before

seven o'clock, one of the visitors was seen looking at his watch, and seconds later one of the men declared that they were recording the sound of the cathedral bells chiming seven. When this had happened, they packed up their gear and drove away.[88]

New Talkie apparatus was installed in the Palace during August. The reviewer reported that there had been good houses for the first film employing the Photophone system and that it would be bound to attract many new patrons. Photophone was an R.C.A. patent from 1927. It used a variable area optical track to reproduce sound. The Palace had previously been equipped with a sound-on-disc and sound-on-film combined projector, and after

four years use it must have been in dire need of replacement.

Another local theatre manager died during September. Charles Robinson, Tower Cottage, The Avenue, Durham had been the manager of the Meadowfield Kinema for 15 years, and died in Wolsingham Sanatorium at the age of 41. His whole working life had been spent in the cinema industry. He was an apprentice in Loftus, Whittington and Guisborough. He became head electrician to Moss Empires in West Hartlepool. After service in the Mechanical Transport Corps in 1914-1918, he returned to Hartlepool, but soon was offered the managership at Meadowfield. For many years, he was secretary of the Durham City and District Cinema Licence Holders.[89]

The Regal's resident organist, Herbert Maxwell, had been a regular broadcaster when he was a theatre organist in Sunderland. Twice a week for five years he had broadcast from the Havelock Cinema. He was now renewing his association with the BBC at Newcastle and his first broadcast of a series went out on Saturday 20th October between 6.30 and 7p.m. A large audience had gathered in the cinema before the time of this first broadcast from a Durham cinema. The Mayor gave a short address saying how pleased he was that the city had 'resources that could meet the exacting needs of the BBC.' Then a slide was projected onto the screen telling the audience that in a minute or two they would be 'on the air'. They were asked to maintain silence throughout the performance part of the

Both photos: D. Advertiser

broadcast, and were told to watch for the red light on the stage, which would mean that the broadcast had started. The red light went on and Mr Maxwell's fingers crashed onto the giant instrument with 'The Blaydon Races', his signature tune. The other items were an intermezzo from Faust, a fox-trot, 'Leaning', 'Classical Memories', a tango fox-trot 'Café in Vienna', 'Smiling Through', 'Savoy Scottish Medley' and in conclusion 'Auf Wiedersehen'. The applause was heard 'all over the North-east'. Then the audience settled down to watch the picture *Behold We Live*, an RKO film starring Irene Dunne and Clive Brook. This was the British title for the American *If I were Free*. There were further broadcasts on 9th November and 14th December.

On the latter date, Mr Maxwell announced his departure from Durham. The Regal had been his first managerial post and he was pleased that 10 months of hard work and endeavour had produced a thriving cinema. He had started the Saturday evening sing-songs and his broadcasts had been excellent publicity for the cinema. He had no immediate plans but a move South was contemplated.[90] In March 1935, he took up an appointment at the prestigious Paramount cinema in Newcastle with its three-manual 19-rank Wurlitzer, the second largest in Europe. [91] His successor as organist at the Regal was to be George Carr. The assistant manager, W. H. Harriot, would take over as manager. He had had experience in cinema management in Margate, Morecambe, Whitley Bay and Spennymoor. [92]

The Christmas programmes presented local cinema-goers with a varied fare. Christmas Day fell on a Tuesday and the magistrates made no objection to the presentation of evening shows. The Regal had *Baby Take a Bow* featuring, as the advert put it, 'Shirley Temple, the five-year old sensation of the talkies'. The Palladium presented *Evensong*, a British musical drama starring Evelyn Laye. The Globe had *A Modern Hero* with Richard Barthelmess giving one of his best ever performances. In his only American film, German director G. W. Pabst juxtaposes the perils of the circus ring with those of the stock market. The Palace offered De Mille's epic *Cleopatra* with Claudette Colbert and Frederic March. All the glories of Egypt and Rome for 5d, 7d, 9d or 1/- !

1935

At the Palace, Mr. Rawes was determined to keep some vestige of live theatre operative in the city, and he began the year with a week of the pantomime, *Little Red Riding Hood*. The Palladium was showing, for the first time, the 1930 United Artists film *Raffles*. Some of the design work for this film had been supervised by local celebrity Lady Maureen Stanley, daughter of the Marquis of Londonderry, the Lord Lieutenant of County Durham. A report of her visit to Hollywood to declare on the authenticity of the turn of the century décor of the film had been printed in the Durham Advertiser in September 1930, but the current newspaper reviews made no mention of this. [93]

Cinema, the young, and censorship

The influence of the cinema on the minds of the young was the central topic of the annual general meeting of the Durham County Federation of Women's Institutes in February. The main speaker, Miss Norah Balls of Tynemouth, spoke with the authority of her membership of the National Cinema Inquiry Committee. She informed her audience that current cinema attendances were around 20 million weekly, and that 75 per cent of these were by the under-25 age group. She was concerned that the educative possibilities of the cinema were being undermined by the poor standard of the films. She had been appalled to see hundreds of children waiting to enter a cinema hall for a matinée, the subject of which was a picture called *The Broadway Cocktail*. The film's 'glaring poster depicted a scantily-attired young lady sitting on a glass of pink coloured liquid.'

No such picture seems ever to have been made, but, whatever its title, the speaker thought that parents should be more aware of what their children were seeing. A recent survey in Birmingham had shown that the majority of 10 to 14 year olds went to the cinema at least once a week, and that some children went five or six times a week.[94]

A questionnaire had asked the young people what their impressions of cinema were. A great many had answered that the cinema taught them 'what life really is.' A number said that they learned 'the art of love'. Some said they learned 'how to murder and one boy said he learned 'how to shoot from his pocket'. Miss Balls seemed to accept that these statements were short-term responses, but she felt that young people faced with unemployment and financial problems should be brought up with a 'clean and decent outlook'. Yet, she observed, the films they see are about 'irregular sex relationships, crime and cruelty'.

She thought that film censorship was a very 'make-shift job' and then, somewhat straying from her remit, she turned to the way that animals were portrayed on the screen. "Animals, it had been proved in one film, had been brought together to butcher each other for the amusement of millions." Losing her way a little in her argument, Miss Ball's concluded that "Women's Institutes across the nation should inform the Chairman of the Censorship Board that they were not going to stand for that sort of thing."

In March, the Palace devoted a whole week to the showing of the film *Forgotten Men*. This American compilation documentary contained scenes of battle from the 1914-1918 War that, in some cases, had proved to be too harrowing to show whilst the war was on. The reviewer urged everyone to see it and to understand the terrible results of modern warfare.[95] It was considered to be a timely film in this era of appeasement.

The King's Silver Jubilee celebration was the occasion for most cinemas in the area to deck themselves with bunting, and Jubilee insignia. The Palladium showed *The King, God Bless Him*, a special film containing newsreel episodes from his life.

The Globe's special occasion was a complete refurbishment of its seating and over the next few months its projection and sound equipment. It highlighted its role as the New Globe (typing error and all) in a number of advertisements in October.

The new management by the Stanley Rogers circuit and competition with the Regal was clearly the motivating factor. With the obvious success of its re-launch, it returned mostly to twice-weekly programming. 'Have you seen Durham's New Cinema?' its advertisements asked during June.[96] Its films were not always the latest offerings and sometimes with special promotions they were decidedly ancient.

The Globe's British Week consisted entirely of old Gainsborough films; Monday and Tuesday *Falling For You* (88 mins 1931*)*; Wednesday and Thursday *The Ringer* (75 mins 1931) and Friday and Saturday *There Goes the Bride* (Jessie Matthews 79 mins 1932).[97]

An innovation for politics was the appearance of the talking cinema van in Durham. The National Government had sponsored a series of films on various aspects of national and international policy and they could display them at selected venues by means of a daylight screen and rear-projection cinematography. The films to be shown in Durham on July 15-17th were speeches by the Prime Minister (Stanley Baldwin), the Home Secretary, (Sir John Simon), the Chancellor of the Exchequer (Neville Chamberlain), the Minister of Agriculture (Walter Elliott), and Ramsay McDonald. A little dramatic film *Without Prejudice* of conversations in a coffee shop was also included. Later in the summer, the exercise was repeated in Seaham Harbour, Easington Lane and Blackhall, where the large crowd meant a van movement to a more spacious location behind the Co-op Store.[98]

A number of films using new colour processes began to appear in Durham's cinemas. At the Regal in August, there was *Radio Parade of 1935*, a British film featuring over 40 radio stars and a musical finale shot in the Dufaycolor process that was supposedly showing the innovation of colour television. Also at the Regal in November was Eddie Cantor's *Kid Millions*. "The girls are gorgeous, the scenes are breath taking, the songs are terrific, the comedy is side-splitting and the climax in Technicolor is the greatest thrill ever to be held on any screen. Book Your seat early," declared the advertisement. The Palladium's offering in the first week of December was the first feature film in three-colour Technicolor, *Becky Sharp*.

The Christmas treat for over 400 pupils of the Gilesgate, Bluecoat, St Godric's and St Oswald's Schools and the Crossgate Moor Cottage Homes and Durham Poor Institution, was a free film show at the Globe. The Shirley Temple film *Bright Eyes* headed the bill after community singing led by the Mayor (Cllr. W. R. H. Gray). The Mayor, Edward J. Hinge, managing director of the Stanley Rogers cinemas, and Robert Conlon, manager of the Globe, each welcomed the children with a few words and at the close of the performance toys and sweets were handed out by the deputy manager W. L. Moffitt.

By 1935, the Stanley Rogers circuit had virtually become the E. J. Hinge circuit. Stanley Rogers had founded the circuit in the 1920s and with 'Teddy' Hinge as general manager had acquired numerous run-down North Eastern and Cumbrian cinemas and turned them into profitability. When Stanley Rogers died in 1933, Hinge took over the ropes completely and by the end of the thirties, the circuit had thirteen cinemas and two theatres, the Grand, Byker and the Hippodrome, Darlington. E. J. Hinge had begun his show business career as an actor and profits from his cinema circuit were pumped into the two theatres in a vain attempt to keep variety alive.[99]

1936

The year began with a new organist for the Regal. There is no indication of the reason for Mr. Carr's contract not being renewed. His replacement was Jack Fenner, former solo organist and orchestra director of the Stoll Theatres Corporation.

A particularly ruthless prosecution of a local cinema manager had a fairly gentle conclusion. Sergeant Coats had visited the Majestic cinema, Esh Winning on Sunday night, 8th December at 7.30 and discovered there were 50 people in the auditorium. The Sunday opening regulations stipulated that cinema doors should not be open before 7.45p.m. Although pleading guilty to the breach of the regulations, in his defence the manager, Robert Edwards, stated that it was a cold night and some old people were standing outside. He sympathised with their condition and opened the doors early. The magistrate ordered him to pay £2 into the poor box, and no conviction was recorded against him.[100]

The severe weather continued well into the New Year and caused considerable damage to buildings. At Byers Green, the Globe cinema, closed for several years, was completely destroyed in the gale. It was opened in 1914 with a seating capacity of 700. In 1933, its owner, Herbert Derdle, had been charged with starting alterations to the building before planning permission had been granted, and the closure appears to date from this time.

The wrecked Globe cinema building in Byers Green, near Spennymoor.

In Spennymoor itself, a chimney on the roof of the Cambridge cinema crashed through the operator's box. The operator had a remarkable escape as over 200 bricks fell around him. The boy who was assisting received slight cuts. The second performance had to be abandoned: "There were 40 people in the cinema at the time and although the sound of the crash created some alarm, there was no panic and the people left in an orderly manner."[101]

The death and funeral of King George V provided the cinemas with distinct opportunities to show their worth as popular communicators. Wars and rumours of wars also enabled the authorities to use the local cinemas as recruiting stations for the armed services. In the first week of January, the Regal showed the Air Ministry recruiting film *The RAF*.

Sunday cinema openings had been well established in the county both before and after the 1932 Sunday Cinema Regulations, but there were still attempts from some sections of the church to call the practice into question. It is unclear why a city vicar, the Revd. F. H. Pickering, vicar of St. Nicholas, should be pursuing his oppositional line with the County Licensing Magistrates, as his arguments did not convince them and seven-day licences were granted in all the cases of application.

Superintendent Foster said that Sunday performances continued to attract good audiences and he was particularly gratified to receive the donations from Sunday cinema opening for the Police Boot Fund. Every penny was used for the purchase of boots where there was a demand, and nothing was used up in expenses or administration. Since the previous September over 1000 pairs of boots and shoes had been distributed amongst poor children in the division.

In an almost perverse snub to the opinions of the Revd. Mr Pickering, Superintendent Foster remarked that they received no donations from city cinemas though there was more necessity for the fund there than in the county. £340 17s 6d had been collected and £323 16s 7d had been paid into the Police Boot Fund. The remainder had been handed to Durham County Council to be credited to the Cinematograph Fund in accordance with the Act.

Superintendent Foster also reported that the committee representing the cinema proprietors have again carefully examined the lists of films to be exhibited at these performances. There had been no complaint against the type of film being shown. On occasions during the year, three cinema licence holders had been neglectful in submitting the names of the films they proposed to exhibit in time for the committee to consider the same before forwarding the list to him. He suggested that this requirement should be written into the conditions of the licence.

The presiding magistrate, Mr. Brass, declined to include the clause in the licensing regulations but warned the cinema managers of their agreed obligation.[102]

The Little Boy That Santa Claus Forgot

CHILDREN ONLY

SHIRLEY TEMPLE & BORIS KARLOFF   KIDDIES XMAS TREAT

Readers can help the fund for giving poor children a special Christmas treat at the cinema by sending subscriptions to Newspaper House, Durham.

The popularity of Shirley Temple amongst the young readers of the Advertiser resulted in her being chosen as their favourite film star in the newspaper's poll. Just behind her was Gracie Fields. When 'Uncle Tony' of the Joymates column of the paper had communicated this fact to the young film star he received a letter 'in her own hand' thanking the boys and girls of Durham County for their choice.

One of the films at the Esh Winning Majestic in July was *Building Bridges*. Patrons were surprised by the appearance on the stage of a young lady from Durham to introduce the film. It was made by the Oxford Group and was concerned with building bridges in Denmark not only between island and island but also between man and man. In 1938, the Oxford Group re-named itself Moral Re-armament. The newspaper reported the item under the title of 'Christianity on the Screen' but gave no indication of how or why the film came to be on the programme.[103]

1937

The abdication news of Edward VIII provided the newsreels with opportunities to show more pictures of the shy new king, George VI, than they had been inclined to take when he was Duke of York. The year opened with the Palace playing Chaplin's *Modern Times* for an extra week. The Palladium had Nova Pilbeam in *Tudor Rose* for the first part of the week and Spencer Tracy in *Fury* for its close. The Globe had Steffi Dunn and Stanley Morner in *I Conquer The Sea* and Herbert Marshall in *Forgotten Faces*, and the Regal presented Francis Lederer in *One Rainy Afternoon* and George Arliss in *East Meets West*.

The second annual poor children's treat took place at the Globe organised by the manager of the cinema R. E. Conlon, by permission of Edward G. Hinge. The special programme of films included *Old King Cole, The Blue Streak* and a cartoon. The 400 youngsters each received fruit and sweets from the Christmas tree.

Durham's motorists had a free film treat in store at the Three Tuns Hotel. Leslie Henson was the star of one of the advertising films, *Honeymoon Trail* and there were several others. The popularity and portability of the new 16mm. sound projectors made exhibitions of promotional films much more common. No cinematograph licence was needed for these performances.[104]

At a meeting of the County Durham Discharged Prisoners' Aid Society also attended by the Mayor of Durham, and the Bishop of Durham, the Marquis of Londonderry was critical of the part played by the arts in assisting the improvement of morality in society. "I wonder if we are being helped by films, theatre and most importantly books. I am inclined to think these agencies with their terrific powers are not moving in the right direction," he said. His accusations seemed particularly vague, however, and in another part of his address, he was willing to grant that there were many excellent contributions made by the arts.[105]

In May, the city was fully decorated for the Coronation celebrations and the cinemas, too, were be-decked with flags and bunting. Children from the Belmont Junior Schools were transported to the Crescent cinema for a special show. Afterwards they had a Coronation tea at the school and were presented with a commemorative beaker and a new pencil. Despite the reporting of all the street parties and parades in the newspaper of the following week, there is scant mention of the presentation of Coronation newsreels at the cinemas.[106] Interest in cinema stars was again promoted by the Joy Mates children's column in the newspaper. Top film stars for the year were Clark Gable, Gary Cooper and Jeanette MacDonald.[107] The adult reader's list placed Clark Gable, W. C. Fields and Jeanette MacDonald as leaders.[108]

The newspaper's subscription list for special film shows for poor children gained momentum during the year and five venues were announced. In Stanley at the Victoria Cinema, 800 children would be entertained. In Houghton-le-Spring at the Empire another 800 would see a special show. The New Cambridge at Spennymoor would take 600 and the Palace Cinema at Chester-le-Street a further 800. In Durham, on 28th December 800 children would see a special Western drama and cartoons at the Palladium.[109] The Mayor of Durham, and the newspaper's 'Uncle Tom' attended this show and received tumultuous applause. The staff of the Palladium was cheered and the children received fruit, sweets and new pennies. The first cartoon featuring Donald Duck was greeted with great delight. Then the children watched the newsreel and the Western drama with 'intense interest'.[110]

1938

The New Year saw the promotion of Superintendent Foster from the Durham County constabulary to the new post of Detective Superintendent. He had been in charge of the Durham County division since December 1922 and his involvement with the licensing magistrates was almost legendary. His concern for the safe running of the cinemas in both city and county had been exemplary and many managers had benefited from his advice *and* admonition. He had joined the police force in 1900 and had also served for two years in the Southern Rhodesian constabulary. His post was filled by Superintendent J. R. Johnson of Darlington, another long-serving police officer. The newspaper described him as a "strict disciplinarian, like the officer that he has succeeded".[111]

Another change of personnel occurred at the Regal. The new organist was to be Mr. Joseph Davenport. Before coming to Durham, he had composed several musicals.[112]

The entertaining and informative output of the Post Office Film Unit had been particularly influential in the British documentary movement. On Monday 31st January, a number of their films were shown at a promotional evening in the Durham Town Hall. The free show proved to be so popular that large numbers of people were turned away. and the organisers quickly arranged for another show on the following evening. The listed films were *6.30 Collection, Air Post, Night Mail, The Calendar of the Year, Weather Report*, and *Cable Ship.*

Cinemagoing was referred to in a city parish magazine and in the Public Court. In his monthly report, the vicar of St. Cuthbert's Church Durham, the Revd. Joseph Maughan, M.A. was concerned by the lame excuses his parishioners made for not attending church. He said even thought the weather had been bad in recent weeks it didn't seem to stop people "battling against wind and rain if there was a good film to be seen or an exciting game of bridge to be played". In the Durham Assize Court during the hearing of a case of breach of promise the plaintiff was asked "Did Mr. Nichols seem to you to be fairly generous?" "Yes and No", came the reply. "Sometimes I suppose you went to the six pennies rather than the eight pennies", asked the lawyer. "Yes, often to the shilling seats and then we would transfer to the 1s 6d seats after the dark without paying the extra."[113]

The opening of the Majestic Cinema, Sherburn Road was overshadowed by the opening of the Essoldo Super cinema on Westgate Road in Newcastle. In the trade and local papers a description of the Durham cinema was almost totally absent. The

Advertiser of 20th August reported only that the Majestic had been completed and would open on Monday. Since there was no official opening ceremony, there appeared to be nothing to report.

The cinema was built and opened by the same consortium of individuals that opened the Palladium, and according to the 1938 Kinematograph Year Book, it had a seating capacity of 906. It occupied a prime site opposite the new council housing estate: clearly expecting to benefit from this population, also attracting clients from Sherburn Village and Sherburn Hill.

Mrs Tate of Sherburn Hill (86 years old in 1996) remembered walking three miles from there to see the opening film *Maytime*, even though there was the small Unity cinema in Sherburn Hill itself. The cinema was built on the grand scale, with a very attractive frontage.

Proscenium elevation and (*overleaf*) **the façade of the Majestic.** *Plans in D.C.R.O.*

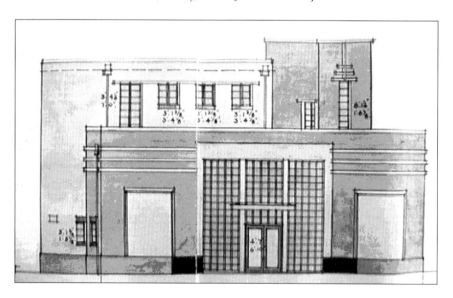

Manager I. M. Drummond initially provided two separate houses nightly at 6.20 and 8.30 with a children's matinée on Saturday afternoon at 2.30. In October, this policy was changed to continuous showings from 6 p.m. until 10.45 p.m. everyday. Since the theatre stood just outside the city boundary it was granted a seven-day licence, the first Sunday offering being John Wayne in *I Cover the war* (1937).

For the most part, programming was separate from that of its Palladium partner. Occasionally, the film for the second half of the week would be duplicated – examples in October and November were the simultaneous showing of *Rebecca of Sunnybrook Farm* and *Everybody Sing*. In the week of 2nd November, both programme changes were duplicated.[114]

The Palace at this time was attempting to ring the changes on screen and stage presentations. In October, it presented two weeks of the International Grand Opera Group. A different opera each night over 12 nights and two different Saturday matinées must have seemed overwhelming for city and county opera fans, but they turned up in good enough numbers to please both the management and the newspaper reporter.[115] Variety programmes and Royal Bengal Circus were also profiled. The latter gave rise to a number of spectacular parades in the city as cast and animals were transported from Durham Station to the Walkergate theatre. The animals were housed in the Co-operative Society Stables on Claypath between performances.

Signalled for several weeks in their advertisements, the first presentation of *Snow White and The Seven Dwarfs* proved to be a popular event. "From the moment that film fans in Durham knew it was to be presented bookings began," said the Advertiser. So speedy was the uptake of bookings that the management felt obliged to include 10 a.m. screenings on Monday, Wednesday and Saturday, and to suspend its free list.[116]

Cinema Manager embezzles

The sad end of the cinema career of the Globe manager was reported in the Police Court columns. 23-year old Robert Earnest Conlon was charged with the embezzlement of £27 17s belonging to the cinema. Evidence was given by the cashier Ruth Elliot that she had given him various sums of money on three days in April 1937, which it was eventually discovered had not been taken to the bank.

Conlon rapidly left the city before an arrest warrant could be activated, but eventually gave himself up at Felixstowe Police station on 11th November 1938 and was transported to face the charge before Durham Magistrates. It was stated that he had been appointed probationary manager at the Globe on a wage of £3 p.w., increased to £3 10s when he was appointed permanent manager. His solicitor stated that he had been living beyond his means and had got into debt. He had been prolific in his charity work amongst the unprivileged in the city and his rash act was not in keeping with his character. The magistrates said that he was a young man who deserved another chance to prove his value to society, and bound him over for two years in the sum of £5 on condition that he repay the embezzled money from his future earnings. [117]

In December, the Palladium had an interesting split week, with Nelson Eddie and Jeanette MacDonald in *Rosemarie* on Monday and Wednesday, and Jeanette MacDonald and Allan Jones in *Fire Fly* on Tuesday. The Globe chose to re-issue *King Kong* for three days and the Palace put on the pantomime *Babes in the Wood* for one week. Since Christmas Day was on a Sunday, even the Sunday licence cinemas were not given permission to open. But the Majestic put on the Special Christmas Eve Attraction of Paul Robeson and Leslie Banks in *Sanders of the River*. This 1934 film had been re-released in 1938 564ft shorter than its original length, but it is doubtful if the Christmas Eve revellers would have noticed this. The same cinema followed this with a Special New Year's Eve presentation of the 1937 Monogram Pictures' *Boy of the Streets* with Jackie Cooper.[118]

1939

There must have been a number of Leslie Howard fans in the city because *The Scarlet Pimpernel*, originally been released in 1935, was shown by special request at two cinemas at either end of the same week! The Palace had it for three days from 23rd January, and the Majestic for one day on Sunday 29th January.

A serious interest in the art of cinema was heralded by the announcement that it had been agreed to form a Film Society in Durham during the year. The film society movement had been originated in London in 1925 by Ivor Montagu and Hugh Miller. It numbered amongst its members distinguished artists, critics, film-makers and writers who wished to view films that might not otherwise have received a showing in Britain. The Society was often the centre of controversy because it wished to show films from the Soviet Union that the censors had refused to certificate because of their overt political propaganda. The Durham Film Society stated that its aims were 'to bring to a local audience outstanding continental films which have been characterised by intelligence and imagination.' They also pledged to do all in their power to encourage the development of a critical and intelligent attitude towards the cinema by promoting discussion groups.

The prime mover of the announcement was N. Gillespie Cox, assistant manager at the Palace, who had been concerned with the establishment of the Tyneside Film Society and was actively connected with the Newcastle People's Theatre.[119] The Durham Film Society held its inaugural show at the Palace Theatre on Thursday 4th May when a programme consisting of two short films *Zoo and You*, and *Czechs Prepare* were shown with the 1931 German feature film *Kameradschaft* (Comradeship). This had particular relevance to the area because it was concerned with a mine rescue that was resolved by co-operation between Belgian and German miners. The two performances were well attended by town and gown and a large number took up membership. By the time of the next performance in June, there were 500 members.

The Palace Theatre presented *Un Carnet de Bal* (The Dance Card) on 14th June 1939, a 1937 French film directed by Julien Duvivier, bringing together several romantic stories in the context of a society ball. Seats could be reserved at 1/6 and 1/- in the circle, and 9d. in the stalls, unreserved seats were priced at 6d.[120]

Before the talkies, film had been truly international. English inter-titles and references enabled the dialogue and the culture to be understood. Even during the early sound period there had been a co-production work with sound originating in a number of different language versions. But, by the end of the decade, with the European situation being so uncertain, this had ceased.

Preparations for war were clearly indicated in the national and local press. Plans for urban evacuation were reported on, and major air-raid shelter constructions were taking place in strategic mining and urban areas. When war with Germany was declared on 3rd September 1939, one of the first edicts under the Emergency

Powers Act ordered the closure all places of public entertainment as a precaution against mass population destruction in air-raids. Therefore, during the first week of September, cinemas became more silent than they had ever been before.

* * * * * * *

The Meadowfield Kinema (ex-Co-op. Central Hall) between the wars as it is remembered and drawn by Tom Fox.

Chapter Six   War Again

It was, of course, correctly predicted that air raids would be a constant threat to the civilian population. During the next six years, some cinemas would be damaged or completely destroyed by bombing and some audiences would become casualties both during and after performances. But, the initial reaction to close all places of public gathering, except churches and other places of worship, was somewhat precipitate.

In the first week of the emergency, the Advertiser reported that the titles of some of the films to be shown in Durham had a prophetic ring to them; *Trouble Brewing; Let Freedom Ring;* and *Sword of Honour.*[1] The closure order was fairly swiftly lifted in areas that the local Chief Constable had decided were not expected to be immediate targets for enemy action. Accordingly on · 14th September, it was announced that for the city of Durham and its districts, places of entertainment could re-open on Monday, 18th September within strictly controlled hours and under blackout regulations that required all outside and foyer lights to be switched off or shrouded. Performances would not be permitted to continue beyond 10 p.m. and whilst the auditorium was occupied a warden would need to be posted outside to warn of any air raid. Gas masks would have to be carried by all patrons and none would be admitted without them.

In Durham city, the Globe and the Palladium reverted to separate performances at 5-45 p.m. and 8 p.m., but the Majestic would be continuous from 5-45 p.m. until 9.50 p.m. and the Palace would also be continuous from 3 p.m. to 10 p.m., and in order to attract daytime patrons prices were reduced to 6d in the circle and 4d in the stalls before 5 p.m.[2]

A local reporter quizzed city inhabitants and cinema managers about their attitudes to cinemagoing in the context of possible air raids. The manager of 'one Durham's most popular halls' said that business was good, but audiences were 'way below normal even though in the first week of the war they were showing a film of one of Britain's top actors'. His takings were approximately £100 down on what he would have expected in peacetime. We can assume that this was the view of the manager of the Regal which was showing *Trouble Brewing* with George Formby. Another manager said that during the week his audiences had grown and that this was a justification for the Government's action in re-opening places of entertainment and sport. Young and old were delighted that the cinema was available to them. One young man well below call-up age said that they couldn't be expected to stay in the house at night, and that the B.B.C. programmes lacked the variety and sparkle of pre-war days. The cinema provided a welcome retreat from the blacked-out streets. A middle-aged lady said that many people of her age group dared not go out at night. She was glad that there were early performances to attend. A third opinion was obtained from a young man in his thirties whose visits to the cinema rarely exceeded once or twice a month. He said that he would not be unduly worried if the cinemas remained closed for good. But he thought that if people took proper precautions like carrying their gas masks, keeping the cinemas open would be good for general *morale*. Another interviewee thought that the blackout would cause more road accidents to people leaving the last cinema performance, but that the cinemas had a part to play in relieving the strain that war imposed upon people.[3]

The editor remarked that the emergency had arisen just as the season for concerts, dramatic productions, dances, and whist-drives was about to begin. Cancellations had been inevitable but it was not long before some normality returned to the entertainment scene. Adjustments had to be made but these only seemed to make people keener to try to 'carry on, regardless'. Some of the cinema adverts themselves contained timely reminders. When the Regal showed the British Technicolor film of *The Mikado,* it urged those who could to come to the 2 o'clock matinée and avoid the blackout.[4]

The Palace had a variety show entitled *Leon Dodd's Wartime Tonics* with Dodd & Dean, the Radio Girls and Bunty & Bijou.[5] Very unusually, for the week before Christmas both the Palace and the Regal programmed Alexander Korda's semi-documentary about the R.A.F., *The Lion Has Wings.* 'Its roar awakes a New Britain,' proclaimed the Palace advertisement.

The Majestic was in more sombre mood with a double bill of 1931 thrillers. They wheeled out *Dracula* and *Frankenstein* under the banner 'The Horror Show of the Century'. The innovation was that they listed them both as 'A' certificate films, when on their first appearance they had been ranked 'H'. It is probable that there had been a re-classification on their second release. In 1942, the British Board of Film Censors decided that it would not pass any more 'H' films. There had already been complaints from a number of local authorities concerning this type of film during wartime, and the ban stayed in force until the end of hostilities.[6]

Despite wartime problems, Durham Film Society was able to present their third film in December in association with the Palace. The film they had chosen for showing during the whole week was *Professor Mamlock,* a Soviet Russian film highlighting the repressive qualities of Nazi Germany. It had been made in 1938 before the infamous Russo-German pact. It had been running for three months in London. The secretary of the Film Society, A. P. Rossiter, hoped that there would be sufficient interest in the showing of such films so that regular performances could be organised. There must have been enough support because their next show was a three-day engagement of Fritz Lang's *The Testament of Dr. Mabuse.* Made in 1933, it was a sequel to his classic 1922 film *Dr. Mabuse, the Gambler.* The exploits of the film director himself were almost as thrilling as the film. Lang had cleverly included anti-Nazi propaganda in the film, and it had not gone un-noticed by the German propaganda minister Dr. Goebbels. He decided to ban the film but at the same time offered Lang a job making Nazi propaganda films. Lang, who had one Jewish parent, decided that an immediate departure for France with a copy of the film was the safest course of action for his survival. The Film Society announced that their next film would be *Mayerling*, a 1936 French film directed by Anatol Litvak. His American film *Confessions of a Nazi Spy* had received very favourable notices in Britain. The society also announced that there would be a special meeting on Sunday 19th June at the Durham House Settlement for an address by Ivor Montagu, the co-founder of the London Film Society.[7]

The Sands Easter Fair did not take place in 1940. For the showmen, Mr. Hoadley said that the wartime restrictions concerning movement and heavy vehicles did not currently permit the shows to be transported. His own indoor amusements in Darlington were able to continue.

The Sherburn Hill Unity Theatre did not renew its licence in February 1940 but there is no newspaper report concerning its reasons for closure. It is known that many Sherburn Villagers made the journey to recently opened Majestic on Sherburn Road, and it is possible that the Sherburn Hill residents did the same.

The question of Sunday cinema opening in the city was being discussed 'in many circles today' suggested the newspaper in March.[8] Some men on leave from France and several correspondents in the district asked why it was that a few people on the bench said that picture halls on the outskirts of Durham could be open on a Sunday evening and those in the city remained 'locked, bolted and barred'. 'Wartime presents an altogether different outlook' and 'no-one could contend that because of magisterial injunction everyone should spend their Sundays in a state of unmitigated gloom'.

Although the Sunday Entertainments Act of 1932 already gave councils permission to ballot their electors on Sunday opening, Defence Regulation 42b eventually made provision for Sunday opening in areas where there were significant numbers of troops, or where there was sufficient local electorate support. By July 1945, 305 new areas of the country had obtained Sunday opening by this regulation.[9]

The importance of National Savings was promoted by a series of visits by a mobile cinema van in April. 'Come and hear about Savings Groups and Save Your Way to Victory', announced the advertisement. Shows took place in the Market Place, Elvet, Neville's Cross, and Gilesgate on Saturday 13th April before moving out for a tour of the rural districts.[10]

A perceived increase in juvenile crime since the beginning of the war prompted the newspaper to ask a number of prominent people for their views upon it cause and its possible solution. Will Lawther, President of the Mineworkers' Federation of Great Britain, thought that the teachers' lack of use of direct punishment was a part cause of this, and he thought that there was no question that films that portrayed 'dead-end kids' and 'black-faced angels' had a melancholy effect upon the minds of the young. "I am all in favour of films for the young," he said, "but they ought to be of the type such as *Abraham Lincoln, Stanley and Livingstone* and *Pasteur.*"

William Green, chairman of the Durham county juvenile magistrates thought that, amongst other things, lack of parental control with fathers away in the services was a contributory factor. But he, too, observed that more suitable films should be produced for young people. Another magistrate, Malcolm Dillon of Seaham, was more circumspect regarding the influence of films. Even in the isolated case where it was claimed that processes depicted in a film crime had resulted in a real-life crime, he concluded that it was 'the means that was to blame and not the motive.'[11]

Call-up demands had put great pressure upon the management and recruitment of trained projectionists. The physical demands of the job were not so great as they were in the 1914-18 war, and it is surprising that women were not more widely employed in projection rooms.

The difficulty in maintaining proper standards is highlighted by a case brought by the police in Esh Winning. Robert Edwards, the 50 year-old manager of the Majestic Cinema, was fined £5 for 'leaving a person under the age of 16 in charge of the cinematograph apparatus.' Sergeant Guthrie gave evidence that he had visited the cinema on the night of 8th July, and saw the chief operator standing in the canteen of the dance hall. He then saw two 14 year-old boys operating a machine in the box. The chief operator said that he had left the box for two minutes to get some sweets for the boys. He said that his assistants were both efficient and intelligent. Superintendent Johnson said that it was perfectly in order to leave the box in the charge of someone over the age of 16.

The operator explained that he had had difficulty in recruiting assistants over the age of 16. The cinema had lost four assistants since the start of the war. The Superintendent thought this was a strong reason for *not* leaving the box. Upon hearing the magistrates' ruling, Edwards, who had several convictions for breaches of the rulers, indicated that he was not prepared to pay the fine. When the Superintendent asked him if he required time to pay, he replied that he did not.[12]

Wartime conditions of employment had prompted some cities to offer temporary seven-day licences to their cinemas. Durham had, not surprisingly, remained distant from the pressures. That there would be an audience for the additional performances is evidenced by the packed house at a single Sunday charity concert at the Palladium in aid of the Mayor's Ambulance fund. Local artists filled the bill which included lightning sketches of 'Hitler and his gangsters' by the headmaster of Neville's Cross School, Cecil Wheatley.

In October, the Palladium announced a price rise linked to the increase in Entertainments tax. Seats were now 8d in the stalls, 1/- in the circle, and 1/6 in the dress circle, an increase of twopence all round. *Pinocchio* was the key attraction that week and from the report of good attendance it would seem the patrons stumped up the difference.[13]

Durham Film Society presented *The Magic Bullet* on Monday Tuesday and Wednesday at the Palace. The subject matter of this new American film had affected its general release. Edward G. Robinson played Dr. Ehrlich, the man responsible for discovering a cure for syphilis. The society had hoped for large audiences to justify their continued existence. The president of the society, Clifford Leech, gave further evidence of an informed film culture in the city. Whilst praising the management of the Regal for obtaining *The Grapes of Wrath* in the week of 18th November, he criticised them for showing a truncated version. He had seen the film in London, and knew that the opening scenes had been deleted. These were essential for the development of character and plot, and without them the progression of the film was difficult to follow.[14]

1941

A new cinema opened in Bowburn in January. Plans for the Crown cinema had first been given approval in April and June 1939. Two alternative façades had been suggested, though the auditorium had a common plan. The architects were Browne & Harding for the proprietors, Iseton Brothers, owners of the Avenue Cinema and the Gem, Coxhoe. Building had commenced in July 1939. It was interrupted by the declaration of war, and there must have been

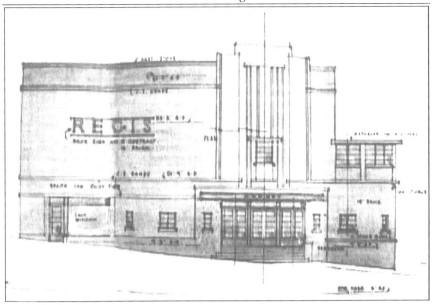

(above) The proposed front elevation for the Crown Cinema, Bowburn, approved in April 1939, and *(below)* the second elevation approved in June 1939. The change of name is not explained. The proscenium width 35', and the sound system was Western Electric. Film programmes were booked at the Avenue Cinema, Coxhoe. In 1945 seats were 6d – 1/6. Performances were once-nightly, with two performances on Saturday.

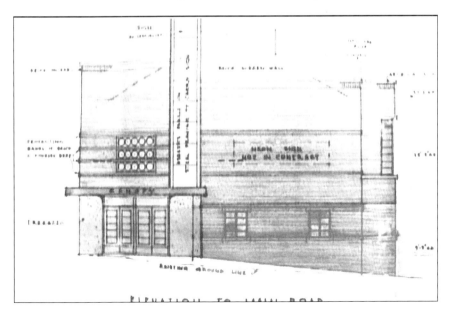

building material regulations which caused it not to be ready for opening until January 1941. Its capacity is given as only 481 seats. There is no mention in the local papers of an opening date, though the Cinematograph licence was granted on January 15th 1941.[15]

Despite Mr. Leech's criticism of the Regal management, or perhaps because of it, the Durham Film Society had negotiated the use of the Globe cinema for its shows from January 1941. The Hinge circuit was now in overall management of both houses. It would seem that their choice of films could not sustain a three-day Palace, but could adequately attract members and non-members to Saturday afternoon performances. The first film under the new arrangements was Sacha Guitry's *Remontons Les Champs-Elysees*. Its success was followed in February by Jacques Feyder's *Les Gens de Voyage*, and the acclaimed American documentary by Pare Lorentz, *The River*.

Cinema halls proved to be ideal places for the transmission of public notices and public appeals. The Trade had agreed that up to ten minutes of any programme could be appropriated by the Ministry of Information for their films. The Mayor of Durham also received the agreement of the city cinemas management that he could make his appeal for the Durham Spitfire Fund from their stages. [16]

An unusual programme parity occurred in March. The Palladium and the Palace both had *The Great Dictator* as their main feature. The Palladium, by arranging for matinées at 2.30, was able to present three separate daily showings of the film. The Palace had a single showing nightly at 6.30 and a Saturday matinée at 2 o'clock. Reported business was excellent at both venues.[17]

In May, there was a special showing of Air Raid Precaution films at the Pavilion Cinema, Esh Winning, at which there was an almost capacity attendance of 600 people. No doubt some of the fire-fighting methods suggested in these films would have been useful in Sacriston on the night of Wednesday 30th April when the Victoria cinema, Queen Street was burned to a shell. An on-duty police constable first noticed the fire and reported it to the Daisy Hill Auxiliary Fire Service. Leading Fireman W. Hardie and seven men arrived inside five minutes and connected their hoses at the hydrants in John Street, 400 yards away. The blaze was very fierce at this time, and residents in Lower Queen Street and King Street were advised to leave their homes. James Clamp, the general dealer, whose shop was opposite the cinema, took his stock into the back room as a precaution. Eventually, Chester-le-Street and Houghton-le-Spring brigades arrived on the scene, but the building was beyond saving.

The manageress, Mrs Fred Tinsley of Sacriston, who had not seen her cinema for the past six months because of an injury to her foot, visited the scene of the fire the next day. She said that she had been told of the fire, but could not believe that it could be as bad as it was. Everything had been destroyed. The hall had only recently been decorated and fitted out with new seating. She estimated the total damage to be as much as £10,000. W. W. Smith the projectionist said that he had, as usual, examined the building before leaving, and everything had seemed in order.[18]

Durham Film Society presented their tenth programme at the Globe on Saturday 24th May at 2.30 p.m. Their last film of the season until the autumn was the 1938 French film *Education de Prince*, a satire on the political situation in Eastern Europe before the outbreak of war. It starred Louis Jouvet, Charpin and Elvire Popesco, and was accompanied by one of Dr. Massingham's short comedies *Tell Me If It Hurts.* The performance was also open to the public, and it was hoped that some of these would become members by paying the one shilling subscription to the secretary and treasurer Mrs. P.M. Rossiter. At the annual general meeting of the Society, Mr. Jude, the manager of the Globe Cinema, was thanked for his invaluable help.[19] On Saturday 15th November, they began a new season with the *Amphitryon*, a German film made in 1935 by Reinhold Schünzel. The film could be justified in the war situation by the fact that Schünzel was a Jewish director who left Germany in 1938 to go to Hollywood. His film starring Willy Fritsch was a comedy musical adapted from the Plautus classical play.

A somewhat less positive interest in the films was cause for concern in some of the pit villages. The cinema played a big part in the lives of some of the miners and absenteeism was often attributed to cinemagoing. One mine spokesman said that some miners would rather miss a shift than miss certain pictures. Some of the cinemas associated with miners' welfare halls presented morning shows in an attempt to halt the malpractice.[20]

The actress Jeanne de Casalis addressed the Durham Ladies' Tea Club in the Town Hall in November. Though her topic was the survival of live theatre against its many rivals for public attention and entertainment, her description of the power of the cinematic image was the strongest part of her speech. "It is a form of optical hypnotism; the film concentrates upon the face to the exclusion of everything else. After 30 or 40 close-ups, I become fascinated - in fact, hypnotised. I cannot get rid of the impression. Undoubtedly, the film has the power of forcing into people's minds images which in saner moments they must know are utterly unworthy of their preoccupation." "It is not necessary for a film star to be an actor, but an actor can become a film star. There is something 'phoney' about the art of films, though undoubtedly it is an art. I say it with no bitterness because I love the film....There is a fallacious belief that the camera never lies. I can tell you that it never stops lying. The art of film is not the art of acting it is the art of photography."[21]

Durham Ice Rink was slowly increasing its patrons. Professional ice-skaters had been engaged, and with the arrival of some Canadian troops in the area, some Ice Hockey matches had been arranged. In November, it further attempted to swell its numbers with a film session. If skaters turned up between 2.30 and 3 p.m. on Sunday November 9th, they could be part of a film being made as an advertisement for the rink and for ice-skating in general.[22]

One of the city fathers, Alderman Nicholson, spoke at a conference of the Durham County Association of Boys' Clubs about what he called the regrettable state of films. He harked back to the beginning of the film industry when, he said, many films of an educational nature were shown. These soon gave way to 'lines of Western Shows'. The Alderman's logic seemed to go astray as he declared that, "ever since the motor car there had been a large amount of shooting and tragedy in films which could not be of the slightest use in educating anybody." He thought that some present day films of the Royal Air Force and the Royal Navy should be recommended. He suggested that the youth of the country for the moment should give the cold shoulder to films that provided no other object than exciting amusement. His argument became more and more out of touch as he suggested that one of the greatest disadvantages of modern life was speed. Perhaps his final statement summed up his attitudes. "Verify your statements, and having verified them, fear no one." He clearly believed he had done this during his speech.[23]

1942

America had now entered the war and the New Year began with standard fare films. There was now no neutral process by which the films could cross the Atlantic and end up on British screens. It

was expected therefore that the number of new American films would be reduced and that re-issues would have to fill the bill where new British film production could not. The Palace had the 1938 Nelson Eddy Jeanette MacDonald all Technicolor musical *Sweethearts*. The Globe, not known for being a first-run house anyway, hauled out James Cagney's 1934 film *Here Comes The Navy*. The Palladium paraded the Nelson touch with the *Lady Hamilton*; a 1941 American-made film with two British stars. The Regal regaled Durham with *40,000 Horsemen*,

a 1941 semi-documentary made in Australia and telling the Great War story of one of the last great cavalry charges. The Majestic fell back upon a 1940 'B' picture Denis O'Keefe film *Girl from Havana* as their main feature.

In June, the Hippodrome, Langley Park was the venue for a free Sunday showing of some Ministry of Information films. A crowded house saw two films showing the devastation that had come to Poland and whole areas of Russia as a result of the

German invasions.[24] An information film of a different kind was included in the programmes of the Palladium and the Majestic in July. Oxydol's advertising film featured Vic Oliver the Austrian - born comedian (real name Victor von Samek), who was also an accomplished pianist and violinist, and had made his reputation as a radio broadcaster. At this time he was best known for his membership of the Bebe Daniels, Ben Lyon 'Hi Gang' team and had just completed a film with them. His marriage to one of Winston Churchill's daughters also gave him an extra popularity.[25]

The Palace still adopted a week's closure for its annual cleaning. It was a difficult hall to keep clean. Its origins as a warehouse seemed to leave it with a legacy - patrons recall that the stalls area was not the most salubrious place in town, and that the air filtering system required the regular intervention of Mrs. Rawes with her deodorant spray. The re-opening on 11th July featured *Ships with Wings*, a 1941 Ealing war film starring John Clements, Leslie Banks and Ann Todd.

The Crescent cinema, Gilesgate Moor had changed its name to the Rex in January 1941 when its management was taken over by Carter Crowe.[26] Its normal advertising was by window cards and posters outside the cinema, though in November 1942 it ventured into the newspaper with an advertisement that revealed a rare glimpse into its programming. That particular week, it had four changes of programme. Its position just outside the City boundary allowed it to open on Sunday with *Wise Guys*, a British 'Quota Quickie' dating from 1937, and a supporting western from 1935 *Between Men*. On Monday and Tuesday there was *Magic in Music,* an 80 minute 1941 musical starring Allan Jones with a supporting comedy *Galloping Hoofs* starring Jane Withers and Charles Rogers. On Wednesday and Thursday, a reissue of the

1940 Jack Benny and Fred Allen film *Love Thy Neighbour* had a 61-minute gangster film *Queen of The Mob* as support. The end of the week fare, which was bound to fill all 320 seats of the little cinema, was George Formby's 1939 film *Trouble Brewing*. At this time, too, the Kinema, Meadowfield also had four changes of programme weekly.[27]

1943

A local airman was involved in the making of one of the Crown Film Unit's morale boosting films about the armed services. The newspaper report suggests that Pilot Officer Navigator Henry Morton of Hetton-le-Hole gets the biggest laugh of the show with his completely unexpurgated comment as he sees a squadron of Lockheed Hudson bombers closing in on a German raider. The film *Coastal Command* was shown at the Palladium on 15th - 18th March.[28]

The diminutive entertainer and occasional film star 'Wee' Georgie Wood addressed the Durham Ladies' Tea Club and recalled that the last time he had visited Durham was in December 1910 when he stayed at the Big Jug Hotel. He regretted that Durham had not turned out in their multitudes to see him. He was aware that Durham was now practically without a theatre. In wartime, he said a live theatre was essential. "Pictures cannot give you the same reaction that an actor can give you." He was at the time touring the country with a forces entertainment called *Tommy Get Your Gun*.[29]

Price changes at the Palladium were implemented at the same time that 'Wings For Victory Week' was inaugurated. The stalls would now be 10d, the circle 1 shilling and the dress circle 1 shilling and nine pence. The official opening of the week was held at the Regal on Saturday morning 29th May 'by kind permission of Mr. J. Dobson.' There were speeches by Capt. Harry Crookshank, M.P., the Postmaster General, the Mayor, Cllr. H. Gradon, and the Marquess of Londonderry. There was a march past with the saluting base at the County Hospital, and the novelty of a 'pigeon post'. Special events and collections raised a total of £253, 072.

1944

Local interest was shown in issue number 17 of the film series *Calling Blighty*, when it was screened at the Palladium in April 1944. All 25 service personnel featured in the edition came from various parts of the county, and they were all sent invitations to attend. Durham County Army Welfare paid half the cost of return fares for the next of kin and one other member of the family and the Palladium reserved them seats at reduced rates. The audience was overjoyed at the prospect of seeing and hearing from their relatives and many even returned the next day at their own expense for a repeat performance. The Advertiser included the full list of participants.[30] A second film featuring local men should have been shown in June but unfortunately the wrong film was sent. By the time it was finally shown in March 1945, some of the participants had already been home on leave. But there was still a buzz of excitement as the film was announced, and a hushed silence as each soldier delivered his message. The film was shown again at the end of the performance for some relatives who had arrived late.[31]

Audience participation of a different kind was reported in June. A conference of Youth leaders at the Bishop Cousins' Library, on Palace Green heard that a group of young people had staged a walkout at a Seaham Harbour cinema in protest at what they considered to be 'bad entertainment'. The conference chairman, the Revd. T. Bullock, representing the Free Churches, said that he thought no children should be taken into films with an 'A' certificate. Mr. Battle of Washington was more circumspect with his implication that educational establishment should include discussions about what constituted good films so that the youth of the country had some basis upon which to base their judgements. Reference was also made to J. Arthur Rank's Film Clubs, which were providing special films for young people's matinées.[32]

It was a time for concerns about influences upon the youth of the land. A 'Brains Trust' held at the Club Hall Sacriston, as one of its subjects considered the good or bad influence of the cinema on young people. B. W. Abrahart, secretary of the North-east Council of the Workers' Education Association, thought that the cinema was both good and bad. The highly capitalized film industry, he

Cinema entertainment in the Durham
Advertiser for 22 September 1944.

said, had to make films on which they could get the best returns, restricting them to highly emotional films that romanticised an unreal world. He said that he would like to see something of the Russian method of having films for children made by children. Will Lawther, the miner's leader, felt that the cinema was often blamed as a bad influence when there were many more areas of bad influence.[33]

Four youngsters from Esh Winning had been fined in the previous week for stealing film valued at £20 17s from the Pavilion Cinema. It seems that the manager, Fred. Heslop, had packed the film spools into a container and left it in the entrance hall ready for film transport. When the container was checked at the *depôt* two 1000ft reels were missing. Police recovered sections of the stolen film rendered useless by being cut-up. The 9-12 year-old boys were ordered to pay 30s each in compensation and 10s each costs.[34]

No doubt, the manager was glad to begin his retirement two months later. Mr. Heslop, described as 'jovial and jolly', had been manager and lessee for 15 years. As tenants for the Crowe & Thompson cinema circuit, the enterprise had been a family affair. Mrs. Heslop looked after the box office, R. A. Heslop was the chief operator, and their married daughter was the usherette. Fred Heslop was born in Crook, and had served in the 21st Royal Fusiliers during the 1914-18 war, being one of only 32 survivors of the 5,000 strong battalion. After demobilisation, he became part of the entertainment business at Shotton Cinema Hall. After this he took over the Majestic for two years before transferring to the Pavilion in 1929. Mrs. Heslop had trained as a teacher.[35]

In November 1943, the County Council Education Committee had received a request from Easington District Education Sub-Committee to restrict the attendance of elementary school children (up to 14 years) from attending cinema second houses. Before any action could be taken, the local authority sought clarification of their powers. In July 1944, they returned to the subject: it was felt that enforcement would be a problem even if they had the power. A decision was deferred pending the result of a Somerset case before the High Court.[36]

As part of the national centenary celebrations of the Co-operative movement, the Brandon & Byshottles Society held a special Sunday film display at the Kinema Hall, Meadowfield. Prizes for a poster and essay competition were awarded to local children, including Magdelina, a Spanish refugee. After the audience sang 'England Arise', several Co-op. films were shown - *Postman's Knock*, *Co-operette*, and *Too Busy to Work*. The special centenary film *Men of Rochdale* was to have been shown but unfortunately the print had been destroyed by 'enemy action'.[37] The Kinema itself, with four changes of programme a week, was still showing a profit for the Society.[38] Patrons were always praising the cleanliness of the cinema, but there were often complaints about the proximity of the Co-op Butchery Department abattoir. Livestock was brought down from the railway yard and housed in an adjacent field prior to slaughter. The stench was often to be experienced within the cinema itself.[39]

VE day in May was celebrated in most cinemas with bunting and patriotic symbols, though none of the displays was illustrated in the papers nor seems to have been preserved in photographic collections. Despite U-boats, new American films had managed to appear regularly and still held sway in the eyes of the fans. The cinema's appeal had even been enhanced by wartime conditions. Despite price increases, average weekly audiences grew from 19 million in 1939 to over 30 million in 1945.[40] Youngsters, too, declared American stars to be most popular. A June Children's Corner competition asked youngsters to order their favourites from a prepared list. The results showed the leaders as Deanna Durbin, Bing Crosby, Shirley Temple and Margaret O'Brien.[41]

* * * * * * *

Chapter 7   Riding for A Fall -- The Post-War Boom

The Regal had new owners in September 1945, when the Essoldo circuit acquired it. The first film under the new management was a full week's showing of *The Thin Man Goes Home*.[1] There was no newspaper report on the changeover. Sol Sheckman, the founder of the circuit, began his theatrical career in County Durham. He gave up boxing promotion in 1922 to take the lease on the Palace, Blackhall Mill in 1923. At about the same time, he formed a company called North Eastern Theatres Ltd, obtaining the leases of the Hippodrome, Crook and the Co-operative Hall, High Spen. By 1925, he also controlled the Queen's Cinema, Crawcrook, and the Picture House, Rowlands Gill. In 1926, from the offices in Bath Lane Newcastle, further expansion began with the acquisition of Crook's two other theatres, the Empire Palace and the Theatre Royal. Various changes of name and compositions of the circuit took place before the final Essoldo logo was adopted around 1932, deriving from a combination of parts of the names of Sol's wife Esther, his own, and that of his daughter Dorothy.[2] His 2,018-seat flagship cinema in Westgate Road, Newcastle in 1938 was the first to bear the name ESSOLDO, and, as we have seen, its high-profile opening took all the publicity away from Durham's Majestic, which began its presentations on the same day.

The Brandon and District Debating Society probably reflected the feelings of many local people when the motion before them was 'That Children should not be permitted to visit adult cinema shows.' Mr. Paulin proposed the motion with his own statistical evidence that "75 per cent of films were American production featuring 'boy meets girl' situations, 15 per cent were horror films, 5 per cent were drivel and trash, 3 per cent were pornographic and 2 per cent were sob stuff. Sex," he said, "had become mixed with sensuality, and some of the titles of films were enough to undo in themselves the work of the Sunday School." His further description of the undermining of proper values by the excesses of cinema concluded with an invocation written long ago concerning the employment of children underground: "Be canny with the bairns man, Ye once was one yurself."

Appropriately, the opposition was led by T. H. Vayro of Browney Colliery. He agreed that children under seven and babes-in-arms should not be admitted to cinemas catering for adult entertainment. He believed that parental control could counter all the objections of the proposer. Cinema was made a scapegoat for many of society's ills, he contended. Cinema-going was a family affair and it was not possible to exclude children from films they had gone to see with their parents. The cinema industry should be prevailed upon to provide more films suitable for children. The motion was eventually lost by 59 votes to 22.[3] In Durham, both the Palladium and the Majestic had children's matinées at 2 o'clock on Saturdays.

In January 1946, Miss D. R. W. Carr of the County Education Authority presented models of a proposed Arts Centre for Durham. Since Durham now had no drama theatre it was suggested that the venue should be able to stage plays, exhibitions, concerts, lectures and *even* films.[4]

Although it was generally stated that in 1945, war films had declined in popularity, the Daily Mail poll decided that the most popular British film of the war years was *The Way To The Stars*. It didn't arrive in Durham until February 1946 when it played for a week at the Palladium. Because of the expected attendance, the continuous performance policy was suspended.[5] The question of Sunday cinemas was still a contentious one in the city. Countering a plea for Sunday closure by the Revd. Hugh Corden of St. Andrew's Church, Stanley, in August, the editor of the Advertiser said that he could not understand why a handful of people were able to decide this matter. Perhaps, he said, that some films were more uplifting than some sermons.[6]

The issue was further contested by the Vicar of St. Nicholas Church, Durham in his parish magazine. Although this was reported on in the newspaper as 'Vicar on Sunday Cinema', it was more a comment upon the ethics of cinema in general.[7] He wittily attempted to turn the question on its head by re-applying many of the points made by people concerning their non-attendance at church. "My parents made me go too often when I was young. No one at the cinema speaks to me. Every time I go someone asks me for money. The Manager never visits me in my home. The people who go do not live up to what the films teach them." In questioning the reasons for better attendance at cinemas than at churches, he suggested that the cinema gave people what they wanted to see, but the church gave them what they needed to know, but what many did not want. He had heard people say that if churches had cushioned tip-up seats, adequate warmth and canteens in their foyers people would pour in. The vicar thought this was nonsense. It was not the churches' job to entertain and to copy cinemas in the hope that queues will begin to form, he concluded.

In his sermon on 6th October 1946 his argument became more challenging when he suggested that Christian people should 'draw the sword with Hollywood'. "Sometimes," he contended, "the Church is called a killjoy, but the cinema is the greatest killjoy since it gives an utterly wrong idea of joy, and has done more than anything else to lower the standard of marriage." He was particularly dismissive of the film *The Wicked Lady*. Many women were shocked by it. "The cinema covers fornication with a veneer of glamour and hides adultery under the veil of romance," he declared.[8]

The appointment of the new organist for the Christie at the Regal Cinema must certainly have raised a few eyebrows. T. W. Gasgoine, described as a music dealer of North Road Durham, had until recently been the organist of the North Road Bethel Chapel and the conductor of the City Methodist Choir.

Bad behaviour at the cinema was referred to in a letter to the Advertiser in October. 'Regular Patron' was disgusted by the hooligans that visited the cinema on Saturday nights. Their appalling noise, especially at the beginnings of films, was an annoyance to other patrons, he wrote. He also reported that they spoilt sad sections of films with giggling. In the same week, the Advertiser gave front-page treatment to a meeting of the self-styled Northeast Women's Parliament held in Newcastle. A resolution requesting that local licensing authorities should ban all children under the age of 16 from 'A' certificate films was forwarded to the appropriate authority. Miss Enid Atkinson of the National Council for Women said that she had seen hundreds of children admitted to a cinema for a film in which the principal characters were a prostitute and a murderer. An adult, she said, did not accompany the children. Enigmatically, considering the earthiness of her previous statement, she said that she was not surprised that there were large numbers of juvenile delinquents when the 'unreal world of cinema put before them all the gilded trappings of that enormously wealthy industry.'

The Advertiser editor in a lengthy editorial questioned the dour picture that the meeting had painted. There *were* certainly films produced that it was undesirable for even older persons to see, but it was difficult to select any age group that might not be excited by the unhealthy passions depicted. If 16 year-olds were banned, why not 21 year-olds, he queried. Life was full of undesirable things to which there was free access; overcrowded dance-halls, the dirt and squalor of poor housing, and the effect of bickering parents. Not all 'A' films were undesirable for youngsters, and they were not always able fully to comprehend their content.[9]

In November, a front-page story of a different kind praised the children's cinema matinées at the Palladium. Mothers from Durham and the surrounding villages could leave youngsters between the ages of three and sixteen in the care of the manager, Mr. Harwood, and his staff. "No adult," the report contended, "not even a fond parent, is allowed to be present at the show. And the children jealously guard their private gathering." The shows were normally full and the general fare was a western, a Donald Duck, another cartoon and the Three Stooges. The concluding item each week, clearly attempting to seek continuity of attendance, was the very popular serial. Other incentives, such as ticket lucky-dips and spotlight prizes provided interval entertainment and interest.

For obvious safety reasons, only the circle and the stalls were open. The dress circle with its balustrade was thought to hold too many possible dangers. The emergency exits were easily opened by the push-bar. After each performance, the children were always assisted across the busy Claypath by the staff. The children's behaviour was mostly in order and usually better than some of the usual adult audiences. At that time over 200 seats were under repair because of damage caused during the week. Mr. Harwood said that none of it could be attributed to children.[10]

Another attempt to bring a drama theatre had been signalled in October with much oratory but little clear indication of ways and means. Mary C. Glasgow, secretary-general of the Arts Council of Great Britain, indicated at a meeting in the Town Hall that if a theatre was to be built in Durham it should have a capacity of 1,450 and incur a capital expense of £150,000 and a possible annual overhead of around £30,000.

The meeting was chaired by Dr. J. F. Duff, vice-chancellor of the University, supported by the Mayor, Cllr J. L. Robson, the chairman of Durham county council, Cllr T. Benford, the Bishop of Jarrow and G. E. Bull, Town Clerk and convenor of the meeting. Miss Glasgow said that she thought that Durham was a suitable centre for such a theatre because of its University and its music, drama and operatic groups. The vice-chancellor said that the students would strongly support such a theatre. Oxford and Cambridge took the presence of a theatre in their midst for granted, he said, and so should this university with its growing number of students.

The motion was also strongly supported by W. Welton of the Dramatic Society. C. Boffrey Cole, chairman of the Durham County Drama Association, felt that an Arts Centre would be more in keeping than a theatre.

Canon Braley, Principal of Bede College, thought that the theatre could also supply a much-needed conference hall for the city, but he wondered where it was going to lay its hands on

£150,000. Cllr. Benfold said that he hoped local industry would provide some funds since the county council was not able to pledge financial assistance.

The meeting decided to set up an exploratory committee representing all the interested parties: nothing more was heard of the project.

In February 1947, the first advertisement changing the Regal's name to the Essoldo was published.[11] Show times indicated that programmes were usually about two and half hours in length.

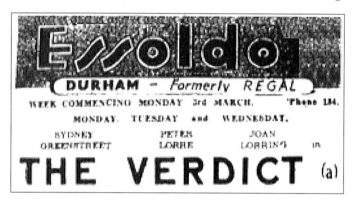

The Sunday cinema anomaly in Esh Winning still persisted, with the Pavilion unable open because it was listed in the Lanchester licensing division. A Bench decision in March failed to resolve it, when the 22 cinemas in the Lanchester, Consett and Stanley districts were refused seven-day licences. The application was made on behalf of the proprietors by Colonel Hugh Swinburne. His main argument was that most other places had granted seven-day licences without any problems. Polls conducted in the county had shown that 86,000 people were in favour and 34,000 against. Cllr. J. Robertshaw, president of the local Durham Miners' Association Lodge, said that it was generally felt that the Sunday opening of cinemas kept the youngsters in the villages. Bus stands were crowded on a Sunday night as the youngsters sought to attend cinemas elsewhere. Whilst it might be regretted, the old-style Sunday was no longer desired by young people. His case was supported by John McGuire, chairman of the Langley Coke Union, who said that it was impossible to get on a bus for Esh, Sacriston, or Chester-le-Street on a Sunday between 5.30 and 7 p.m. for the crush of cinemagoers. The Revd. Mr Ferguson of All Saints Parish Church, Langley Park also supported the opening after 7.30. He said that he did not provide a whole evening's programme in his church and that those who desired cinema entertainment should have it. Churches were places of worship for those who wanted it, and cinemas for those who wished to see a show.

There had, in fact, been a public ballot in Stanley in which the majority of those who voted wished cinemas to be open. Defence Regulation 42b, by the Emergency Laws (Transitional Provisions) Act of 1946, was to remain in force until 31st December 1947, but unfortunately, the provisions of the regulation also allowed the licensing authority to have discretionary powers to withhold the licence if they so wished, saying that the decision must be arrived at "according to reason and justice and not in accordance with private or personal views and must not take into account extraneous matters."[12] This makes the Lanchester Magistrates' decision appear to be somewhat questionable. In the same week that they were deliberating, Sunderland voted to request an order for Sunday opening as a permanent arrangement.[13] By the end of the 1947, 75% of licensing divisions in England and Wales were operating Sunday opening.[14]

The Revd. Norman Hall said that the young people in his church youth clubs went to the cinema at least twice a week, and that they were 'enthralled' by it. "You see how they grow up in this atmosphere," he declared, "talking, walking and dressing in the way of life portrayed by American magazines which they read as much as they attend the cinema." Revd. H. E. George, Vicar of Annfield Plain, asserted that the experiences at Shotton Colliery and Hetton-le-Hole showed that Sunday performances did not clear the streets of 'louts'. On the other hand, he said that Sunday cinemas had not been known to empty the churches.[15]

Cinema Glamour fraud

The attractions of the cinema stardom were central to a false pretences and fraud case at Durham police court a week later. George Kirby, from East Barnet, a 26 year-old window cleaner and former naval rating, was accused of the offences whilst falsely posing as an exploitation officer for Gaumont-British Pictures.

When Kirby arrived at the Royal County Hotel to take up residence in the pre-booked room, he signed his address as Lime Grove Studios, Shepherd's Bush. He said that as representative of Gaumont-British Films he was in the area for the purpose of collecting material and local colour for a film about a miner's daughter. He intended to be in residence for at least five weeks, and that as part of the publicity he would be holding a dance and cabaret in Durham. He booked accommodation for the stars of the show: Felix Mendelssohn and his Hawaiian Serenaders, the Western Brothers, the Ashcroft Sisters, Derek Roy and Ray Ellington, indicating that Gaumont-British would cover the costs.

He had met Sam Watson, general secretary of the Durham area of the National Union of Mineworkers, and had sought his co-operation for the making of the film in an old colliery. Brandon Pit had been chosen for the location, and he had discovered a family whose daughter Monica was the type for which he was looking because she resembled Margaret Lockwood. Mr. Watson was convinced of the man's genuineness and gave him a letter of introduction to various people in the mining industry. The same day, he met George Metcalfe, a teacher at Durham Johnston School, who was writing a history of the Durham Miners' Association. Mr Metcalfe, also convinced of Kirby's authenticity, lent him a typewriter. At the same time, Mr. Kirby offered Mr. Metcalfe the appointment as historical officer on the film, at a salary of £1,250. The following day a telegram purporting to come from Gaumont-British films confirmed his appointment. Tickets for the Dance and Cabaret were printed and, at 5/- each for such an impressive array of artists, they were quickly snapped up.

George Kirby, who is charged with false pretences. With him is Miss M. Mains, Browney, who is a witness in the case.

No bills had been paid, and creditors began to get a little worried. The police discovered that Kirby was not employed by Gaumont-British, and he was interviewed on 21st February. He admitted his deception. At the hearing, each of the creditors gave evidence of the depth of the deception and Monica Maines of Browney Colliery appeared to confirm that she was offered a role in the film at £5 per day. She was taken to the Edis photographic studio where Kirby told Daisy Spence, the proprietress, that he had found 'a budding film star'. As part of his confession to the police, Kirby said that it was his intention to leave Durham with the money collected for the dance and not to pay any of his bills. Nevertheless at the close of the hearing Kirby pleaded 'Not Guilty' and reserved his defence.[16]

By the time the Quarter sessions were convened in April, Kirby had changed his plea to 'Guilty'. His biographical details were much more dramatic than the film he had pretended to be preparing. His defence lawyer described how he had been left on a doorstep as a baby and had been reared by a foster-mother. He had been bound over after threatening to burn a cinema in Barnet in 1938. At one time after stealing an Admiralty document whilst a naval rating, he had been suspected of being a German spy. He was given a three-month prison sentence and discharged from the navy. Other prison sentences for deception and arson had followed. After hearing psychiatric evidence, the judge ordered that he should be bound over on condition that he was to be resident at St. George's Hostel, London for three years of psychiatric treatment.[17]

In the city, there was only limited concern about the effect of cinema going upon Good Friday church attendance, or film suitability, but application still had to be made to the magistrates. In 1947 permission was granted for opening between 5 and 10 o'clock on the understanding that the programme was submitted in advance to the overseeing policeman, Superintendent T. Hetherington. In the event, each cinema made no changes from the Thursday, Friday and Saturday programme, except the showing times. The Palace presented Marjorie Reynolds in the Columbia musical *Meet Me On Broadway* (1946). The Essoldo had Ida Lupino in *The Man I Love* (1946). Cashing in on the school holidays, the Globe was showing an inexpensive double-bill of Laurel and Hardy in *Saps at Sea* (1940) and a 1937 William Boyd western *Rustler's Valley*. The Palladium included two showings of the 1946 British musical film *Spring Song*. Cinemas still needed to include a quota of British films in their annual programmes and it would seem that the locals all chose to select the usually poor business of August Bank Holiday week for part of their commitment. The Palace gave three days to the 1943 Jack Warner film *The Dummy Talks*. The Essoldo had a first-run full week of David Lean's *Great Expectations*. The Palladium also devoted the whole week to a first Durham showing of Carol Reed's *The Odd Man Out*. The Globe presented a re-issue of Frank Randle's 1943 film *Somewhere in Civvies* for the last three days of the week, and the Majestic chose Tom Walls in *This Man is Mine* (1946) for the first part of the week. The Rex normally closed for its annual staff holidays for one week in August and this year chose to re-open with a British week of three re-issue programme changes - Monday and Tuesday Jimmy Hanley in *For You Alone* (1945); Wednesday and Thursday *The Private Life of Henry VIII* (1933); and Friday and Saturday Frank Randle in *Somewhere on Leave* (1942).

The fare did not truly reflect the quality of contemporary British production. The Advertiser's Children's Corner selection of favourite film stars for 1947, however, for the first time had a majority of British stars. The selected order was James Mason, Margaret Lockwood, Bing Crosby, Pat Roc and Ingrid Bergman.[18]

The first edition of the Advertiser in 1948 carried a front-page article on 'The Influence of Children's Cinemas'. It began by declaring that the cinema was the most popular form of entertainment for both adults and children, and in this capacity it was considered by some sections of the population to be a possible wayward influence upon young people because of the types of films produced, but its main theme was the establishment of national cinema clubs in Odeons by the J. Arthur Rank organisation. The editor had been invited to the Darlington Odeon where Sheila Holmes, formerly of Durham, outlined the philosophy of the clubs. Besides the selected entertainment films the programmes also contained public service items on such things as road safety and safety in the home.

The Rank Organisation had been influential in establishing the Children's Film Foundation and one of their films, *The Little Ballerina*, was included in the press show. Although there was no Odeon in Durham City itself, the editor was clearly giving his support to other forms of children's film shows.[19]

The Majestic Cinema's Christmas Party show was reported with enthusiasm. Over 1,000 children were entertained in this second annual event organised by the manager, Mr. Drummond. The programme began with a documentary *A Modern Coalmine* and continued with Roy Rogers and Trigger in *Romance on the Range*. The film quiz and spot prizes included autographed film star photographs presented by Santa Claus (John Corbett). The afternoon's celebration was completed with the singing of Christmas carols.

Boom-time for Durham Cinemas. The first advertisement for the Palace as an Essoldo Theatre. March 26th, 1948.

When the Consett Brewster sessions decided that Sunday opening could take place on and after 4th April 1948, the magistrates imposed the conditions that no children under 13 would be admitted unless accompanied by an adult, that there would only be one house nightly beginning at 8 p.m., and that the programmes should finish by 10 p.m. Mr Swinburne, for the proprietors, attempted to negotiate the obligatory contribution to charity at one farthing (¼d) per seat, but the magistrates were in no mood for bargaining and had already decided that 5% of the gross takings should be delivered to the court for that purpose.

Durham Advertiser 4 June 1948   **Durham Advertiser 11 June 1948**

In June, the Essoldo circuit expunged the last vestige of the Regal's original name. The circuit itself was expanding both nationally and locally. During 1948, in the North-east, they had acquired the Empire Gateshead, the Roxy Blyth, the Picture House Shildon and the Savoy Benwell.[20]

Nationally, attendances were in a nervous position. From a peak in 1946 of 1,635 million admissions, there had been a fall to 1,462 million in 1947. This had picked up to 1,514 million during 1948, but 1949 with only 1,430 million saw the beginning of a twenty-year continuous decline.[21]

Proprietress Agnes Knowles closed the Empire Theatre Langley Moor, for cleaning in the week from Sunday 25th July. During the closure, in addition to this annual renovation, a new Gaumont-British 'Duosonic' sound system was added. *Blackwell's Island* starring John Garfield and originally released in 1939 was the usual Sunday fare for the re-opening. Durham residents denied Sunday cinema entertainment could easily correct this with a short bus journey. The Empire management, aware of the situation, indicated that the theatre was on United routes 42, 49, and 47.

In the same week, film cameras were present in the cathedral for the Miner's Gala Service. Some remarkably old-fashioned editorial comment was nevertheless favourable. "Though the film-makers with their apparatus and arc lamps perched against the font introduced a sort of American atmosphere to the sacred edifice, we felt that if the result of their work will convey something of the spirit of the service to the millions who might see the film then even this seeming desecration was worth while. They filmed the procession of the banners and choir along the nave to the chancel and took 'shots' of the stained glass windows." The editor added that he would very much like to see the film, but there was no indication as to its eventual destination.[22]

In September, the town was shocked to hear of the death of Mrs Laura Rawes, the wife of Frederick Rawes, owner of the Palace up to its take-over by the Essoldo Group earlier in the year. Mrs Rawes was well known to the patrons of the cinema with her picture hats, her considerate and sometimes embarrassing guidance of young couples into the double seats at the back of the circle, and for her habit of discharging sweet-smelling spray just as the curtains opened. She had lived in Durham for 30 years.

Portraits of Mrs. Laura Sylvia Rawes by her brother-in-law and Durham photographer Ernest Rawes.

Born Laura Sylvia Lodge in Newcastle, she had lived for a time in British Columbia with her mother. She was an accomplished dancer and on her return to England, she succeeded in juvenile parts for the Frank Benson Company. At the age of 11 she went to John Tiller's dancing school in London and became one of the famous 'Tiller Mites'. After she had completed her training at the school, she danced under her stage name of Laura Vane in Geneva, Paris, Bordeaux, Brussels, Lyons and Berlin.

Back in England she appeared in pantomime and theatre all over the country. She was with George Formby senior's company and also with Harry Weldon. In 1916, her mother died, and she returned to the North-east where she met and married Charles Rawes, the son of the proprietor of Durham's Palace Theatre and a theatre manager and theatrical agent in his own right. Her presence as front-of-house manager at both the Victoria Theatre Stanley and the Palace is remembered fondly by her contemporaries. Her funeral at St. Giles Church was attended by members of the family, representatives of Durham cinemas and her many friends.[23]

A newspaper report that films on religious topics were to be shown in local schools prompted a response from a local resident. Under the pseudonym of 'Teacher', a correspondent delivered a lengthy and somewhat fanatical warning. "Quite apart from the view that all films of whatever kind tend radically to harm the moral and intellectual development of children," he began, "there arises the specific question of what impression the children will receive of the significance of the Bible." He argued that 'so-called religious films' would only vulgarise spiritual understanding, and that attempts to reduce the message of the New Testament to photography would be a 'degrading travesty' of its true meaning.[24]

The following week's newspaper gave space to a very long and personal reply from one of the teachers involved in the operation of the scheme. Mr. Spikings, of Whinney Hill Boy's Modern School, wondered what experience 'Teacher' had of showing any kind of film in schools. Whilst agreeing that indiscriminate film viewing might be seen as a drug on the mind, he felt that the careful selection and study of the content of cinema and radio output could serve a useful purpose. The films in the experiment had been shown to parents, and had received their approval. Religious films, the writer contended, could have as much spiritual effect upon their viewers as the written word. He himself had witnessed the showing of religious films on Sundays at an RAF camp at St. Athan in 1942, and could vouch for the whole-hearted concentration for the overflowing audience. He concluded by saying that it was the duty of teachers to give film a 'full and fair trial' as a teaching medium in schools. "Time alone can prove us right or wrong."[25] Before closing the correspondence, the editor allowed 'Teacher' a further statement, but by then the argument had moved away from pedagogy into Theology.

The contemporary opinion of the local clergy in respect of Sunday opening was also more doctrinal than practical. Prior to the reconsidering of an application for Sunday opening from the Cinema Managers Association, the Revd. J. W. Wenham, vicar of St. Nicholas Church, launched his attack in a letter to the editor of the Durham Advertiser. Under the startling headline 'Headlong To The Materialistic Hell', his argument seemed at first conciliatory. "Superficially the issue looks simple. It is the Merrymakers against the Kill-joys, the advocates of a brighter Durham against the dog-in the manger advocates of perpetual gloom." But he goes on to argue that it is not a simple issue. "The issue in the world today is whether man is to be de-humanised and reduced to the level of the beast or whether he is to achieve the purpose for which he was made to find the indescribable joy and friendship of his All-Loving, All-Good Creator." Seemingly, from later paragraphs, the opinion of the reverend gentleman was that the act of going to the cinema on a Sunday provided individuals with a short-term pleasure that played into the Devil's hands.[26] His strong irritation over Sunday cinemas seems particularly strange since the New Year in his own church started with evening service, in which the sermon was replaced by the showing of a Church Pastoral Aid Society film of the activities at a boys and girls camp, presented by the Revd. F. Pickering, a former incumbent of St. Nicholas's, and now a representative of the Society. In his time in the early thirties, Mr Pickering had been a strong opponent of Sunday cinemas.

When the issue was put before a special sitting of Durham city licensing justices, for the third time in twelve months, permission for Sunday licences was again refused. For the managers of the Essoldo and the Palladium, Colonel H. L. Swinburne seemed to present a telling argument. The applicants, he said, appreciated that Durham was a cathedral city, and their application was for only one performance on Sunday evenings. Such a practice was already in operation in York and Canterbury. Within a radius of ten miles from the city, there were 42 towns and villages that were allowed to show films on Sunday evenings. The demand for Sunday evening was beyond question and under the clauses of the 1932 Sunday Entertainments Act the magistrates had the power to grant seven-day licences. The Essoldo circuit, he went on, had set up a special department in their organisation for the selection of films that they thought suitable for Sunday showing. A recent charity concert at the Durham Essoldo had been sold out without any publicity away from the theatre.

In his evidence, the Town Clerk, G. R. Bull, said that the City Council had no objection to the application on condition that performances should not start before 8 p.m. and that only appropriate films would be shown.

The representative for the Durham and District Council of Churches was none other than the Revd. J. W. Wenham. He contended that he represented the opinions of over 2,000 parishioners and voters, but on a point of fact, he admitted that the population of the city was 18,900. His argument varied only a little from that in his letter to the newspaper. He suggested that he was speaking as a citizen as well as a clergyman, and pointed a finger at the growing menace of world communism that was filling 'the void in men's minds.' He attacked the profit motive of the cinema proprietors, the commercialisation of Sunday, the erosion of their employees' day of rest, and harmful effect of poor films. He was supported by the Revd. W. H. Ivatt of the Temperance and Social welfare committee of the Durham Methodist circuit, Mr. W. McIntyre, and the Revd. J. R. Kay of the Claypath Congregational chapel. This latter objector with his own chapel adjacent to the Palladium drew attention to the Sunday bedlam that was experienced in Chester-le-Street where a church was directly opposite a cinema. Durham Ice Rink was permitted to be open on Sundays and its proprietor, Alderman J. F. L. Smith, spoke in favour of Sunday cinema licences being granted. The magistrates were not required to state publicly how they arrived at their decision, nor did they.[27] The Revd. Mr Wenham was clearly not antagonistic to all films, since on Sunday evening 6th February, a film called *Indian Village* was shown in his own church rooms.

Majestic Esh Winning *above* **Newcastle City Libraries** *(Percy Harding Collection)*
below - **Durham County Advertiser** *4th March 1949*

The re-opening of the Majestic Cinema and Ballroom under new management in March presents something of a mystery. Robert Edwards had been listed as the previous manager from 1935. In January 1945, he had been heavily fined for allowing a dance to continue after midnight and in subsequent years he was several times at odds with the law. The magistrates' court fined him £10 for causing bricks to be stolen from the site of the old picture hall in Hamilton Row, Crook.[28] After this, he wrote an allegedly libellous letter to the magistrates who decided the case, and he was committed for trial at Durham Assizes on a charge of criminal libel in November.[29] When this came to court in January 1947, Edwards, in his own confession as 'a very bellicose little man' was bound over to maintain good behaviour for two years.

A new manager, Theophilus Lee, appears in the licensing book without an appointment date. In December 1950 the licence was transferred to Kenneth Wilson of Gosforth. Admission prices in the new enterprise were listed as 10d, 1/6 and 2/-, and there were four changes of programme weekly. The management may have been new, but the films were not. In the first week, the Sunday film was *Fag End* starring Claude Allister and Gene Gerrard, the British title for a 1945 American film *Dumb Dora Discovers Tobacco.* The Monday and Tuesday fare was *Dinner At The Ritz* (1937) with David Niven and Paul Lukas and *Windjammer* (1937) with George O'Brien. Wednesday and Thursday offered *I was a Criminal* (1945) with Mary Brian and *Borderland* (1937) with William Boyd as Hopalong Cassidy. Friday and Saturday concluded the week with *The Moon and Sixpence* (1942) with George Sanders and *The Roar of the Press* (1941) with Jean Parker and Wallace Ford.

On Sunday, there was a single house at 8 pm. On weekday nights the programme was continuous from 5.30, but on Saturday, the advertising suggested that there were two performances with doors open at 5.30 p.m. Since the Saturday programme on 12th March was at least 2½ hours long and the licence permitted the cinema to stay open only until 11 o'clock at the latest, it is possible that the projectionist did a little bit of trimming on one or both of the films. This practice was not unusual and a number of projectionists have indicated that they selected and excised dull moments in some films to make them fit the schedule, and then replaced them for onward transmission.[30]

The nearby Waterhouses Drift Mine was host to the young film starlet Pamela Davis in August 1949. She was making a personal appearance to promote the film *The Perfect Woman* during its week's showing at the Palladium. Accompanying her on the visit was the Chief Constable. Col. T. E. St. Johnston, Sam Watson, the Miner's Union leader, Roy Penny of the J. Arthur Rank Organisation, and W. Harwood of the Palladium Cinema. On Tuesday night, she was introduced to the enthusiastic audience at the Palladium. She told them of a number of incidents in the making of the film and pointed out that she could be seen again in the recently completed film *Trottie True*. She was presented with a bouquet of flowers by eight year-old Olga Jeffrey of Gilesgate, Durham; a little girl with an appropriate name since in *The Perfect Woman* Pamela Davis plays the part of Olga the Robot.

Pamela David and some young admirers at Esh Winning Mine.
Durham Advertiser August 12th 1949 Page 1

In November, the Town Hall was the venue for the showing of two Fact and Faith films by the Durham & District Council of Churches. Since their success in blocking Sunday opening, they probably thought it necessary to make some positive acknowledgement of film. *God of Creation* was a nature documentary and *God and The Atom* investigated the mysteries of atomic energy including film of a test explosion in New Mexico. Admission was free, but entrance was restricted to those over 13.[31]

In December, the Majestic Sherburn Road management held their third special Christmas party. Although there was no newspaper report, advance announcements suggested that the programme consisted of cartoons, comedies, westerns, carol singing and competitions.

In Sunderland, a hint of competition to come. On Sunday 16th December Messrs Rose Brothers, by an experimental 23-valve receiver, had been able to pick up a TV transmission from Sutton Coldfield - only occasional fading marred the reception.[32]

In June 1950, the Durham Methodist Big Meeting was the subject of a film produced by the Methodist Home Mission London HQ. Camera crew were in Durham to shoot scenes of the procession, the services and the meetings. The Durham Division of the National Coal Board arranged for scenes to be shot at Vane Tempest colliery, Seaham and Murton colliery canteen, locals at Dawdon colliery were on hand to demonstrate their achievement in creating their own swimming pool, and Wheatley Hill miner and Methodist lay preacher 82 year-old William Snaith was filmed talking to George Walker, a National Coal Board welfare officer. Communion service at St. John's Church, Easington Colliery was also to be part of the film.[33]

In August, an unexpected film star visitor to Durham was recognised in Saddler Street as he walked from a visit to the cathedral. It was also a lucky break for one of the Advertiser reporters who was approached for a light even before he had a chance to take out his notebook. Puffing on his American cigarette, Sir Douglas Fairbanks told him that Durham was one of the best places in the world. "I am on my way to London with my wife after a visit to the Edinburgh Festival and I thought that I must visit this fine city," he said. He also indicated that he had just completed a picture due to be released around Christmastime.[34]

For the first time since they had taken over the Palace, Essoldo carried out a *décor* renovation. It closed on 15th September for a fortnight, re-opening 2nd October with *C-Man* (1949: Dean Jagger and John Carradine) as the main feature, and the Fredric March 1939 *Trade Winds* as support. Essoldo ownership was not on the adverts.[35] In the same week, Dryburn Hospital was the venue for a special Round Table film show. The Deputy Mayor, just returned from a holiday in the South, brought with him several hundred feet of film. This and the 1941 feature *The Common Touch* was shown on the 'Carpenter' 16mm projector.[36] In December, the Essoldo presented three days of film nostalgia with a special showing of the 1930 *All Quiet On The Western Front* and Charlie Chaplin in *The Vagabond*.[37] The Majestic once again put on a grand Christmas party for local children with special films, "lucky dips" and presents from the Christmas tree.

1951

Hollywood musicals of the late forties and early fifties were attempting to keep Americans away from their small-screen black and white television sets. Big stage musicals were bought up for translation to the screen with ever-bigger budgets and enormous publicity. Ethel Merman had performed the role 1,159 times on Broadway, and MGM originally assigned Judy Garland for the film. Betty Hutton's dynamic performance made it the studio's best money-maker of the year. 'At last on the Big Screen' screamed the posters for *Annie Get Your Gun*. Its arrival in 'Durham was greeted with the tag line "The Greatest Musical Under The Sun' and lots of column inches. For weekdays, the film was to be shown with continuous performances, but for

the final Saturday four separate bookable performances were announced. It would have been a very busy day for the staff, with the children's matinée in the morning; a mixed fare of *Silver on The Stage*, a 1939 Hopalong Cassidy Western and a re-issued Chaplin.[38]   The cinema industry itself was predicting further falls in audience attendance as the number of television licence holders increased. Through the Cinematograph Exhibitors Association, they launched a 'Let's Go to the Pictures' campaign. The Globe was the only local cinema to

attach the slogan to its newspaper advertising. In July, the Essoldo, whilst trying to increase its audience with its advertised newsreel of the Turpin v Robinson Boxing Match, also had a 'mind-reader', 'The Great Nixon' on stage. The newspaper failed to report on the event, however.[39]

A somewhat tongue-in-the-cheek feature article in the newspaper in October suggested that television as a form of entertainment had its drawbacks. The first concern was the expense of the original purchase. The second appeared to be the disfiguring of the rooftops with the 'H' aerial. The third impediment was the fact that you couldn't do anything else in the house but watch

when the programmes were on. The last and, perhaps, the most irritating factor is that once your friends know that you have a set you will be constantly disturbed by their visitations.[40] Advertisements for Palmer's department store in Sunderland show that 12-inch table-top sets ranged in price from £71 to £88. Payment-out-of-income arrangements were negotiable.

The 1951 Festival of Britain provided a national focus for British achievements and numerous local pageants and historic vehicle rallies were organised. The Majestic Cinema, Sherburn Road, held a Festival of British Films in July. Herbert Lom and Phyllis Dixie in *Dual Alibi* (1947) and *Old Mother Riley's Circus* (1941) were shown on the Sunday though they were not actually listed in the Festival's offerings. The Festival proper featured Glynis Johns in *Miranda* (1948) on Monday, David Lean's *Oliver Twist* (1948) on Tuesday, Powell and Pressburger's *The Red Shoes* (1948) on Wednesday, Margaret Lockwood's *Madness of The Heart* (1949) on Thursday, Alexander McKendrick's *Whiskey Galore* (1949) on Friday, and Jean Simmons' *Blue Lagoon* (1949) on Saturday.

In the cinema exhibition world, a new classification system had been devised by the British Board of Film Censors to accommodate the showing of films with an adult theme. The first mention of an 'X' certificate appeared in the Kinematograph Weekly in 1945. A youth leader suggested that this category should be for 'mild thriller films and detective pictures where children were admitted with an adult.' Films in the existing 'H' certificate should be for those over twenty years of age, and 'A' certificate films should be for adults only.[41]

A year later, the National Council of Women at a branch meeting of the Edinburgh Cinematograph Exhibitors Association, advocated that there should be an 'X' certificate for films from which children were excluded.[42] In May 1950, the report of the Departmental Committee on Children and the Cinema (Wheare Report), suggested the implementation of a new 'X' certificate for adults only. Discussion took place with the industry and in January 1951, eight films, all foreign language imports, were given the first 'X' certificates.[43] Not all local licensing authorities accepted the category and refused to allow 'X' certificate films to be shown without their approval.

J. Arthur Rank's Odeon and Gaumont circuits were also reluctant to include 'X' films in their programme since they denied access to the regular patronage of their family audiences.[44] In November 1951, when Rank tried out *Detective Story*, it confirmed their belief and when Gaumont found the same happened with *Murder Inc* in January 1952, they jointly decided to show no more 'X' films. Initially, therefore, their exhibition was left to other circuits and the independents. *Detective Story* was shown for three days at the Essoldo, Durham on Thursday 14th February 1952 without special publicity and without any published protests, and *Murder Inc.* appeared at the same cinema on 10th March. The Palace had its first 'X' on 28th February with the American re-make of classic

German film *M*. It followed this in March with *Manon*, one of the first batch of foreign imports to be designated 'X'.

On the day of the funeral of King George VI cinemas remained closed until 6 p.m. In the following few days, newsreel presentation began to appear in the cinema. The Advertiser thought it worthy to mention that the newsreel companies and the cinema managers had presented the pictures in a sincere and memorable manner.[45]

In April 1952, the Globe set out on a brave filmic adventure. For the most part, its programmes had deteriorated into re-issues of undistinguished British and American films with the occasional thirties classic. The re-run of Flash Gordon serials attempted to re-gain patron loyalty, but the programming was clearly no competition for the first run films of the neighbouring Essoldo. The management took a gamble on showing a season of foreign films.

The initial offerings were three-day bookings for two Carmine Gallone opera films clearly aimed at Durham music lovers. *Faust and the Devil* (1948) and *Rigoletto* (1947), as with the films for the whole season, were shown with the original soundtrack and English sub-titles. In the following weeks, *La Traviata* (1947), *Die Fledermaus* (1945), and a dubbed version of *Addio Mimi* (1947) (re-named *Her Wonderful Lie*). Classic dramas were fitted around them. Julien Duvivier's films *Panique* (1946), *Au Royaume des Cieux.* (1949) and *Sous le Ciel de Paris* (1951) were selected. Edmond Gréville's *Passionelle (Pour une Nuit d'Amour)* (1947) and Yves Allégret's *The Wanton (Manèges)* (1950) were the only 'X' certificate films in the eleven week season; a clear indication that the management were seeking a discerning *clientèle*. There was even a special request showing of Powell and Pressburger's Scottish drama *I Know Where I'm Going*.

Occasional Advertiser correspondent Alan Maitland praised the Globe for its enterprise. He began: "The Globe is so small a place that someone unacquainted with Durham might go past it and never know it was there. It bears a name honoured in the sphere of dramatic entertainment and, true to its association, it is now the scene of an interesting experiment." He selects his favourites from the season, Cocteau's *La Belle et La Bête*, Sjoberg's *Miss Julie* and Moguy's *Domani e Troppo Tardi*, 'the cream of

European Cinema', he avows. In praising the integrity of these films and congratulating the Globe manager for his efforts, however, he makes a general criticism of Hollywood films, comparing unfavourably their 'superlative-ridden publicity' system with what he considers to be the artistry of the European product.[46]

His attack provoked a carefully argued rejoinder from J. Brian Smith of the Avenue, Durham. He pointed out that whereas we see most of the American output good and bad, we only see carefully selected examples of the European product. He wondered what cinema would be like without the creative force of film-makers such as Walt Disney. He celebrated also the fact that the America has produced two 'particular contributions' to cinema: the musical and the western. His well-informed review of the current American cinema compared the gentle charm and freshness of films such as Vincente Minelli's *Under The Clock* with that of a film seen in the continental season, Jacques Becker's *Edouard et Caroline.* He concluded by suggesting that the Globe manager might mount an American classics season, 'a project every bit as desirable as the present one.'[47]

An American film star was in town on 6th June. Katherine Hepburn, accompanied by ballet dancer Robert Helpmann, appeared on Palace Green in her shiny American limousine at around noon. The event was observed by students waiting to enter the examination rooms, and many workers on their lunch break. She called in at the Saddler Street Antique shop. Mrs Appleton, the mother of the proprietor, turned to Robert Helpmann and said "Doesn't she look like Katherine Hepburn?" Miss Hepburn replied, "I ought to," but she asked that there be no photographs or requests for autographs. The report thought that Miss Hepburn's reputed retiring nature could hardly be supported by the startling nature of her clothes. "There was a trilby hat that had a 'sat-upon' look, a donkey brown coat with an exaggerated swagger effect that billowed out in the breeze and there were her brown slacks hiding a pair of white socks. She wore flat brown suede shoes with *crêpe* soles." By the time she emerged from the cathedral the news had got around and quite a crowd had gathered. She was appearing that week with Robert Helpmann in a production of *The*

Millionairess at Newcastle's Theatre Royal.

In October, after a summer of minor American and British films, the Globe manager, mindful of the start of the university term, began a second European season. Its even more adventurous programming may have contributed to its lack of success. Though well-known festival winners such as *Bicycle Thieves, Un Carnet de Bal* and *Vivere in Pace* must surely have attracted adequate audiences, the choice of more obscure offerings such as *All Roads Lead to Rome,* the 1937 Emil Jannings' film *The Broken Jug* and the 1943 Raimu film *Le Colonel Chabert* must have puzzled all but the most knowledgeable. The manager probably bent to the request from Mr. Smith for a showing of John Ford's 1935 film *The Informer* and Orson Welles' 1948 screen adaptation of *Macbeth.* No doubt, the curious

would have attended the screenings of Martine Carol's X certificate romp *Caroline Cherie* and the opera-lovers would have turned out for Tito Gobi in *The Love of a Clown,* but three nights and a matinee for Jean Cocteau's *Ruy Blas* and Leontine Sagan's 1931 *Mädchen in Uniform* would have left a lot of seats empty. Not surprisingly in a review of the year, the Advertiser film critic considered the Globe experiment, despite its lack of support, as one of the most important aspects of the city's film presentations. His forecast for the New Year was the popular presentation of colourful Musicals, Westerns and Costume Dramas.[48]

Long-service Manager

In November 1952, William J. Harwood, who had been almost born into the cinema business, celebrated twenty years as the manager of the Palladium. He had actually been absent from the theatre for five years during his wartime service in the RAF. "As the father of two daughters," the report observed, "he had always been interested in children and for the last six

▲ The Palladium auditorium from the rear circle, showing the 27′ wide proscenium. The Academy-ratio screen is set well back on the stage, with a pair of screen tabs. This must have been before CinemaScope was installed. The concealed lighting badly needs re-lamping.

◄ Box-office or hanging card for the Globe, w/c 18th April 1949. ▼ The Palace re-opening after a fortnight's renovation under Essoldo – 1950.

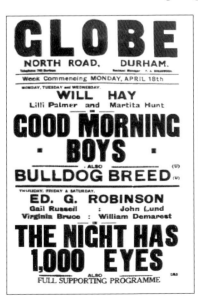

GLOBE
NORTH ROAD, DURHAM.

Week Commencing MONDAY, APRIL 18th

MONDAY, TUESDAY and WEDNESDAY.
WILL HAY
Lilli Palmer and Martita Hunt
in
GOOD MORNING BOYS
• ALSO •
BULLDOG BREED (u)

THURSDAY, FRIDAY & SATURDAY.
ED. G. ROBINSON
Gail Russell : John Lund
Virginia Bruce : William Demarest
in
THE NIGHT HAS 1,000 EYES
ALSO
FULL SUPPORTING PROGRAMME

PALACE

WEEK COMMENCING MONDAY, 2nd OCTOBER, 1950.
MONDAY, TUESDAY and WEDNESDAY,
"C - MAN"
(Cert. A).
Featuring—
DEAN JAGGER and JOHN CARRADINE.
Also TRADE WINDS (a).
Featuring FREDERICK MARCH and JOAN BENNETT.

THURSDAY, FRIDAY and SATURDAY,
"ANGEL WITH THE TRUMPET"
(Cert. U)
Featuring—
NORMAN WOOLAND and BASIL SYDNEY.
Also WILD ANIMALS AT LARGE (u).
MATINEE SATURDAYS AT 2.0 O'CLOCK.

years had provided Saturday morning shows for the youngsters."
He was born in South Shields and had spent a short time with the
merchant navy in 1918. For many years he had helped to run the
old Cosy Cinema at Shildon which was owned by his father.
Before he came to the Palladium, he had been manager of the
Empire Whitehaven. The whole family had been involved in the
cinema industry and his brother Joseph C. Harwood was Northern
Area representative for General Film Distributors. His staff at the
Palladium were also long serving; the chief operator F. Parker had
been there 17 years, Mrs. P. Everard in the pay box 11 years, and
Miss E. Hall had been head usherette for almost seven years. His
favourite film stars all dated from years gone by; Ralph Lynn and
Tom Walls, Jeanette MacDonald and Nelson Eddy, Greta Garbo,
Clark Gable, Jack Hulbert, Greer Garson and Wallace Beery.

Contemporary likes were expressed in the Advertiser's
Annual film star poll for its child readers. Lassie, Anna Neagle and
Jean Simmons got the most votes. Anna Neagle's portrayal of
Florence Nightingale had been shown earlier in the year at the
Essoldo and the manager had enterprisingly invited nurses and

their recruiting
officers to be
present at a special
showing at the
Essoldo showing of
*The Lady with The
Lamp*.

In November
1952, a 250ft
temporary tele-
vision aerial had

been erected at Pontop Pike, for the transmission of 425 line BBC
TV. The signal was to have horizontal polarity at 66.75 megacycles
for vision and 63.25 megacycles for the sound. The previous
transmissions from Holme Moss were not well received in the
county, but now the signal would be adequate for good local
reception.[49] Before the Coronation in June, there was a tremendous
increase in rental and hire-purchase installations of television sets.
During 1951 and 1952, the slide in national audience figures had

actually slowed down to about 1%. Attendance figures for Durham are difficult to gauge, but the results of a collection for the George VI Memorial Fund could give some indication of the popularity of each cinema during the first week of 1953. £124 was collected at the Essoldo, £64 at the Palladium, £29 at the Majestic £12 at the Palace and £10 at the Globe.[50] The economic circumstances of the environs of each cinema could also have been a variable factor as well as the popularity of the particular film being shown.

3-Dimensional!

Previous cinema experiments with stereoscopic films had needed red and green anaglyph decoders from a single film-strip projection to achieve their results. A new system called Natural Vision could be viewed through vertical and horizontal polarized glasses via locked twin projection and a special reflective screen.

As a process, it had been around for a number of years but no-one in Hollywood was interested in it. At the Festival of Britain's Telekinema, a series of short films in a similar process had proved very popular, but the special projection equipment and screens meant that they were difficult to promote elsewhere. In 1952, however, with American audiences deserting the auditorium for the living-room, film producers and distributors took desperate measures to keep solvent. Arch Oboler's independently produced

Natural Vision film *The Lions of Gulu* was renamed as *Bwana Devil* and released in November 1952. It did such great business that studios previously uninterested in the process announced their own programmes of 3-D production. *Bwana Devil* was released in Britain in May 1953.

Warner Brothers' *House of Wax*, which had exceeded the box office takings of *Bwana Devil*, played for a week at the Essoldo from Monday 3rd November 1953. Although it was an 'X' rated film, its reputation as a sensational spectacle had gone before it. The Advertiser reviewer thought that it provided a novel entertainment and that it would be the 3-D gimmicks that people would really be watching. Indication was also given that the polarized glasses sold for the first presentation could be used for the other 3-D films that would be presented.[51] The Columbia film *Man in the Dark* was shown in the week of 6th November. This swiftly-made black and white thriller had an exciting roller coaster ride (albeit shot against a 2D back-projection screen), and some effective shock effects. The third 3-D presentation at the Essoldo was a double bill with *Fort Ti* and a 16-minute Three Stooges comedy *Spooks*. *Fort Ti* was one of America's best box office hits in 1953 and its out-door scenery and dramatic action made it one of the most effective of all the 3-D films. *Bwana Devil* was eventually shown in May 1954 with a re-issue of Harold Lloyd's *Feet First* supplemented by a music and sound effects track.

In December, the Majestic, Esh Winning fell foul of the regulation that required Sunday opening cinemas to pay a charity levy from the takings. When the Durham county licensing magistrates met to consider applications for cinema opening on Christmas Day, the court clerk revealed that despite warnings the Majestic management had failed fulfil their obligation. As a result, the magistrates refused to allow them to open on Christmas Day. [52]

CinemaScope

The independent nature of the Palladium probably prevented it from spending money on the presentation of 3-D films in their stereoscopic form. During the year, the theatre did show *Inferno* and *Kiss Me Kate* in 'flat' format, but its major coup was being the first cinema in the area to show a CinemaScope film. *The Robe* had been shown at Blacks' Regal in Sunderland for four weeks during January, and its arrival in Durham was something of a cinematic occasion. No details are given of the dimensions of the screen at the Palladium or its location under the proscenium arch. The ratio for full size CinemaScope screenings was 2.55:1 against the standard 1.33:1. From a plan of the Palladium stage it is possible to see that this ratio could have been managed by moving the screen further back on the stage.[53]

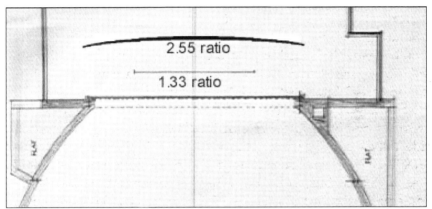

The CinemaScope-size screen placed on the Palladium stage plan.

The Robe was shown in separate performances but without any pre-booking arrangements. It was retained for a second week, from 10th May. A month later the second CinemaScope film was *The Flight of The White Heron*, the documentary of Queen Elizabeth's Commonwealth tour.

At the beginning of June the Globe had announced a temporary closure 'for renovation and re-decoration and the installation of the latest and greatest sound and projection equipment'.[54] It re-opened on 2nd August with a new wide screen, but without the facility to show CinemaScope. It was to have three changes of programme per week, and a slightly changed price range; front stalls, 1/-, rear stalls, 1/3 and the circle 1/6. Children would be admitted to the front stalls for 9d. Children accompanied by adults could be seated in rear stalls for 9d also, and in the circle for 1/-. Ominously, at the bottom of the advertisement was the warning 'The Management reserve the Right to refuse Admission.'[55] The Pavilion, Esh Winning had been advertising itself for some months as 'The Only Cinema in the North with a Panoramic Screen Floating in Colour', whatever that meant. It, too, was showing standard films with wide screen masking probably in the ratio of 1.66:1.

A new cinema

A new cinema in the region was created at a time when cinema closures around the country had reached significant numbers. The Royal Cinema in Church Street, Sacriston was opened on July 26th, 1954 by Mrs. P.Bartley, wife of the M.P. for Chester-le-Street. Until 1952, it had been the local dance hall, but before this it had been a skating rink, a live theatre and between 1924 and 1929 a cinema.

(left) **Mrs. Bartley and children at the opening.** *(right)* **The Royal Cinema in 1964 after closure.**

The original maple floor had been retained, and was jacked up from underneath to make a slight gradient from the back of the house to the front. There were 382 seats in red cushioned leather and a small balcony was included. The admission prices ranged from 9d to 1s.6d. There would be two houses nightly beginning at 5.30 p.m. Films were not to be shown at the cinema until three or four months after their general release, and after they had circulated in Newcastle, Sunderland, Durham and Chester-le-Street. The proprietors were A.H. Aaron and R. Armstrong who were partners in A & F Entertainments Ltd., and also owned the Palace Cinema in Haswell. The manager was Harold Smith, who had previously been manager of the King's Theatre, Pelton. The projectionist was Mr. Wilkinson of Langley Park. Mrs. A. Guy, wife of Councillor Joseph Guy of Sacriston, was the cashier. Her father, Robert Hall, had been employed there when the hall was a skating rink.

The opening programme was Chaplin's *Limelight*, and displayed in the foyer of the cinema was the telegram received from Chaplin himself wishing the new venture well. Mrs. Bartley spoke of the profound influence of the cinema, and hoped that the people of the locality would support the venture.[56]

In December, probably for head office organisational reasons, the advertisements for the Essoldo and the Palace were combined under the heading Essoldo Theatres, but in Durham itself, the main cinematic interest was at the Palladium, the only cinema in the Durham area showing the latest CinemaScope films.

Gradually, more cinemas saw the need to compete in this field. In January, the Sacriston Memorial Institute Cinema converted to CinemaScope and unusually for this venue showed *The Robe* for a whole week. In February, the Durham Essoldo showed its first CinemaScope film, *The Egyptian* and later in the month the Kinema, Meadowfield began their CinemaScope era with a week of *The Robe*. The Pavilion, Esh Winning opened their true wide screen era with *King of The Khyber Rifles* on 10th October 1955. The Majestic, Esh Winning celebrated its conversion to the wide screen on 30th April 1956 with three changes of programme in three different processes; *Seven Brides For Seven Brothers* in Cinemascope, *Vera Cruz* in Superscope, and *Deep In My Heart* in Metroscope. The Royal, Sacriston announced on 18th May 1956 that it was now equipped to show films in CinemaScope, Superscope and VistaVision and promptly did so with *The*

Kentuckian. It was December 1956 before the Majestic, Durham was able to follow the Palladium with wide-screen films, ironically with a presentation of *The Tall Men*!

The VistaVision advertisements for the Palladium and the Essoldo in March 1955 for *The Ring Circus* and *White Christmas* were misleading. They used the original VistaVision posters for the tiny number of cinemas that were equipped with the special projectors to transport the film sideways through the film gate. In practice, the enhanced VistaVision image was printed in a wide screen ratio onto standard 35 mm stock. The improved image quality enabled it to be projected on to screens up to 50 feet wide without observable degradation via a mask and a standard lens. After 1957, VistaVision prints were optically squeezed onto a normal 35mm frame and then projected via an anamorphic lens.[57]

At the annual licensing magistrates meeting in Durham on 2nd March 1955, the application for seven-day licences for the four Durham cinemas was granted. Colonel Hugh Swinburne for the Durham Cinemas Association seemed quite surprised when no objectors stepped forward when given the opportunity. Previous objections had hinged upon the fact that since Durham was a cathedral city it should strive to preserve Sunday as a day of rest and worship. Since most other cathedral cities now had Sunday opening the argument seemed to be lost. The cinemas would only be open on Sundays between 7.45pm and 10pm and they would contribute £3 per annum per hundred seats to charities. The contribution by the Palladium and the Essoldo with 1,075 seats each would be £33, the Palace with 800 seats, £24 and the Globe with 533 seats, £18, whilst the selection of the films would be made by a special department.[58]

Clerical reaction to the licensing came not from any Durham minister but from the Revd. Kenneth R. Brown, Methodist minister of Ferryhill. He refuted all claims made by Col. Swinburne, mostly on questions of fact rather than questions of ethics. Sunday films were in no way different, he claimed. "They offer no intelligent creative improvement on week-day films." He opposed the notion that because one place did something, everyone should do it. "Are we like sheep?" he questioned.[59] The following week, a single letter on 'Keeping the Sabbath' was the only other published objection.

The Palladium was first to take advantage of the new licence on Sunday 4th March with Debra Paget in *Bird of Paradise*. On Sunday 13th March, the Essoldo joined in with Doris Day in *Starlift*, and on Sunday 20th March, the Palace, Essoldo and Palladium were all open. No Sunday films were shown at the Globe in this initial period, but since it ceased to advertise from 1st April 1955 until 9th November 1956 it has been difficult to determine its policy. When it did re-advertise, its avowed programme of adults-only continental and special films precluded Sunday showing under the terms of the magistrates' ruling.

On the night of Wednesday 25th January 1956, the Pavilion, Esh Winning was burned to the ground. About an hour after the audience had been watching *Valley of Fury*, a fire raged through the wooden structure and totally destroyed it. The alarm had been raised at 11.15 p.m. but by the time the fire engines arrived the structure was beyond saving.

▲ The ruined Esh Winning Pavilion cinema covered in a snow-fall.

A dramatic photograph of the Pavilion in flames taken by W.B. Hannon of Esh Winning. ▶

The fire had started at the screen end of the cinema, and quickly enveloped the roof and side walls. John Sayers, the projectionist who lived at New House Avenue close to the cinema, went into the blazing building but only managed to retrieve the boxes containing the film reels *(see left)*. The cinema lessees were Carter Crowe & Co. of Newcastle.

The manager, J. Studholme, was lying seriously ill in Dryburn Hospital, and the news was kept from him.[60] On 3rd February the Advertiser printed a story that on the night of the fire, in a delirium, he had told his daughter he could see flames. Mr. Studholme did not recover from his illness and died on Saturday 28th January 1956, unaware of the cinema's destruction. He was an electrical engineer by trade and had previously managed the Majestic, Esh Winning, the Rex, Gilesgate, Durham and the Durham Globe. These three cinemas at the time were advertising under one blocked column. The newspaper report also said that 14 years before arriving in Durham he had managed the Rex, Coxhoe. This reference may be a misprint for the Gem, Coxhoe, since no cinema called the Rex has ever been listed for Coxhoe.[61]

Fire at the Majestic

In August another fire caused widespread damage at the Majestic, Durham. George Dixon of Cuthbert Avenue telephoned the fire brigade at 5.32 a.m. on Sunday 26th August to report the outbreak. Engines were quickly on the scene and firemen gained entrance by breaking down the door of the sweet shop at the side of the cinema. Station Fire Officer Armstrong said that the men managed to fight against the terrific initial heat and eventually brought the fire under control. The source of the fire is thought to have been cigarette stubs. Harry Coates, the manager, assessed the damage and said that without the warning telephone call it could have been far worse. Beside him stood a pile of jars holding boiled sweets from the cinema shop. The worst affected area appeared to be the rear stalls on a raised part at the back of the auditorium and the part of the foyer where the door gives access to the seats. The woodwork and paint were scarred and covered in bubbles. The seats in the front were practically undamaged but the stage and screen were badly burned. With such a gap between the two worst affected areas, it seemed that several fires had broken out. But, the fire officer's explanation was that the fire had started with such fury in the auditorium that it reached the ceiling and then swept along nearly 100 feet before reaching the stage.

The chief projectionist, Edgar Denham, said that he had left the cinema on Saturday night at about 10.30 after the last showing of *The Lady Killers*. His reels for the Sunday performance *Fear in the Night* and *Caged Fury* were already made up for projection. Mr. Coates said that repairs to the cinema would take place as soon as possible.[62]

The cinema was closed for three months and re-opened on Thursday 6th December 1956 with Kenneth More in *Reach for The Sky*, advertising itself as Durham's most modern cinema. All 900 seats were pulled out and rows of red and gold replacements were fitted. Matching Durham carpets replaced the damaged flooring, and the walls were re-lined in fawn with a brown speckled decoration. The roof was re-painted maroon with silver stars and light blue surrounds. Wall fittings replaced the ceiling lights.

The stage area most affected by the fire had been completely replaced with a new steel framework and a new wide screen. The stage curtain was now cream and maroon. A new pay-box and confectionery shop had also been added.[63]

The Majestic's exterior and the projection box.

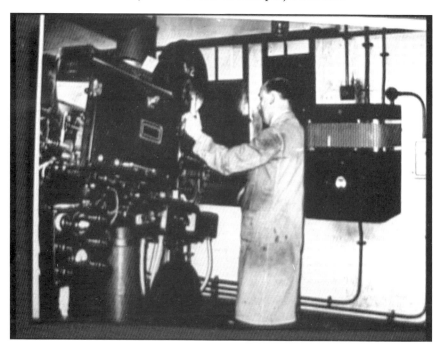

The Savoy, Sedgefield in 1964.

Another new cinema
Cinema closure was not a universal factor in the area. Sedgefield, 9 miles south of Durham had never had a permanent cinema until the war. With army camps and R.A.F. stations around, W. W. Turn-bull, that stalwart of cinema enterprise in South Durham, clearly believed there was a demand for and rectified the situation by opening the Savoy in a converted building. It remained in operation until 1970.

The re-opening of the Globe as a venue for continental 'X' certificate films had its good and bad elements as described by a correspondent to the Durham Advertiser in February 1957. He accepted that running the cinema with its current policy had its obvious financial risks and that bringing films to Durham that were 'off the beaten track' was a service to the community. But, he felt that better attention could be paid to presentation. "They could make sure that the light in the projector does not keep dimming throughout the film." He also felt that they could restore the 'square' screen. Showing standard films on a wide screen meant that some of the picture was missing, and when the bottom section of the screen had to be in view so that the sub-titles could be displayed, the heads of the actors were cut off at the top. He thought that allowing this to happen was absurd. Another irritation had occurred the previous Monday: there were only three people left in the audience during the last ten minutes of the film, and in that time the caretaker noisily walked up and down the rows with his torch tipping up the seats.[64] The film being shown then was Clouzot's 1949 film *Manon des Sources.*

The following week, the Globe manager, N. Johnson, replied. He said that they did not intend to continue showing 'square' films. "There is considerable expense involved requiring not only a change of screen but of a lens also." He said the incidence of the fading light was not the fault of the projectionist but of the mains voltage, and that on the night it was reported 'it was rising and falling in waves'.[65] It was the older films that did not fit and he was already embarking on a season of newer films designed for the wider screen. The manager's strange parting shot was "I won't say the students aren't a good audience, but they are apt to pass comments."[66] The films he refers to didn't seem forthcoming, since that week the Globe was showing Kurosawa's *Rashomon* (1950) and Max Ophül's *Madame De...*(1952).

Another correspondent thought that the original criticism was unfounded, and the detractor had acted in haste. "I haven't noticed the light fading," he said. "I wear glasses and am sensitive to that sort of thing. His final remark was somewhat insensitive to the problem. "If he wants a bigger screen, he should go to a bigger cinema." A week later, another letter supported the original writer. He also objected to the practice of showing square films on wide screens, and said that this was the reason why he had stopped going to the Globe despite their offering of a wide selection of foreign films.[67] In March, the manager of the Essoldo was also featured in the newspaper. In an interview, B. Theaker recounted one of two of the patron requests he had encountered. One lady wanted him to remove a person from a particular seat, because she had been using it for years. On another occasion, he had received an irate letter from a gentleman who had an L.P. record of the soundtrack wanting to know why he had cut out a particular song from *The King and I*. In actual fact, said Mr. Theaker, three songs were missing from the original presentation of the film, and the version shown in Durham was the one that had been given a general release. Other correspondents voiced their opinions about films they thought should never have been shown.[68]

'X' certificate films were largely confined to showings at the Globe, but occasionally a clutch would turn up elsewhere. In the week of 18th March, the Globe was showing *I Vitelloni* (The Spivs), the Rex had *The Quatermass Experiment* and the Palace *The Werewolf*. In April, the Palace was the venue for *Birth of a Baby*, an adults-only film sponsored by the National Baby Welfare Council.

Audiences at the Globe did not improve enough to make it a viable proposition and in the week of 29th July 1957, it showed its last programme. Ironically, the final films were not for adults only despite the familiar advertising banner. *The Sin of Anna (Peccato di Anna)* was an 'A' certificate 1952 Italian film. *Secret Conclave* was starring Henri Vidon, and the supporting film was an English dialogue version of the 1949 French film *The Dancer of Marrakesh*. Norman Johnson explained that the showing of continental films was only really successful for the first three weeks. "Then audiences began to tail off," he said. "The cinema was doing well with westerns and thrillers up to about a year ago." He said he was very disappointed when the proprietor, Carter Crowe, told him the cinema would be closed at the end of the week. Mr. Crowe still had the Majestic, Esh Winning and the Rex, Gilesgate under his control. The leaseholder of the building, Mrs. M.J. Burns, said that there was still eight years to run on the present lease, and that no one had approached her to take it up.[69]

New Cinema

As the Globe was closing, builders were putting the finishing touches to a brand-new cinema in Sacriston. In 1937, the Trustees and Committee of the Sacriston Memorial Institute had set the project in motion. Films had

The exterior and interior of the New Cinema Sacriston on opening day.
Courtesy of Karl Snowdon.

been shown on the upper floor of the Institute since 1924, and they had only recently equipped the hall for showing the latest wide-screen films. George Graves, secretary for the Institute, said

that the war, post-war restrictions and the 'credit squeeze', had prevented progress being made, but when it seemed it would never be built, restrictions were lifted. The architect was C. Lowes. On the evening of 30th September 1957, C. R. Harvey, chairman of Chester-le-Street RDC introduced Dr. Gavin Millar of Sacriston and asked him to declare the cinema open. Dr. Millar spoke of the stimulus that the cinema would bring to the village, enhancing the lives of the old people, and they could now enjoy their filmgoing in considerable comfort. The auditorium held 800 seats and the cinema had been equipped with the latest CinemaScope screen and stereophonic sound. The first presentation was Yul Brynner and Ingrid Bergman in *Anastasia*. Performances were continuous from 5.30 on weekdays, but initially on Saturdays there were two separate houses at 5.30 and 8.15.

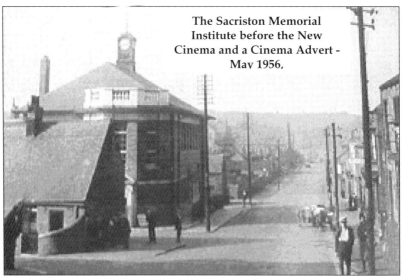

The Sacriston Memorial Institute before the New Cinema and a Cinema Advert - May 1956,

The Cinema room in the Institute itself continued to show films in competition with its own enterprise next door. For a time, with the Royal, there were again three cinemas in the village.

The Advertiser asked Mr. Theaker, manager of the Essoldo, for his opinions on the state of cinema exhibition. He thought that television was responsible for a drop in attendance. When questioned about the possibility of cinemas including live variety acts, he was certain that this was no solution to the problem. Audiences still supported particular special films; high quality productions such as *The King and I,* he said, but they could no longer be relied upon 'just to come and see anything.' The cinema had been a family entertainment in the past, but now the family could be together in front of the television set. He did not think that audiences had diminished because of the cinema's sales interruptions. These were an essential part of the cinema's income, he said.

Part of the audience on the opening night of the New Cinema, Sacriston, and one of the weekly triple cinema advert. afterwards.

Durham Advertiser

The downward audience trend was fairly general. In 1957, national audiences figures had fallen to just over half those of the peak year of 1946. Between 1956 and 1957 alone there had been a loss of almost one hundred and fifty million tickets sales, and this was to be repeated the following year.[70]

The boom was well and truly over.

* * * * * * * *

Ecce Signum!
The Essoldo neon sign on the tower of the former Miners' Hall in the circuit style of lettering – with the running 's'.

The projection box showing one of the pair of projectors. The spool-boxes are open – illegal with the arc running in the days of flammable nitrate film and the film is threaded through the gate. A Westar mechanism and sound-head with a Peerless Magnarc lamphouse. The base is a very old contraption.

Chapter 8:   Going, Going, Gone!

The New Year of 1958 saw the closure of another of Carter Crowe's houses, Durham's smallest cinema, the Rex, Gilesgate Moor, with 346 seats. It had always had a loyal audience from the local housing estates and it was these people who came to the final show. The 'Rex' sign was illuminated above the green swing doors for the last time. The faithful stepped out of the melting snow and filed through the red-painted foyer to see the last films *Fall-in*

(1943) and *Eagle Squadron* (1942). They exchanged their usual pleasantries with the lively grey-haired manager Mrs. Emily Studholme. Many of them were children when they first visited the cinema.

▲ Mrs Emily Studholme in the paybox on the last night. Projectionist Tommy Atkinson ▶

As the two war films got under way and amid the noise of gunfire and marauding aeroplanes, she explained that the cinema lease had run out and it was no longer viable to renew it from the owner Freddie Lamb. "We used to get £19 on a Saturday night," she said, "but now we are only get £7 to £8. Coke for the heating costs £14 per month. There are the electricity costs, entertainment taxes, staff wages, and film rentals. All this has happened over the last two years. Television has killed the cinema".

Two years before, Mrs. Studholme's husband had died. *(see Chapter 7 – Esh Winning Pavilion fire.)* In his time, he had been manager of the Globe, and two cinemas in Esh Winning. He had done all the odd jobs

in the cinema, but since his death, Mrs. Studholme had had to pay maintenance men to fix them. She and the staff of three had managed the cinema alone. Her daughter, Mrs. Connie Jackson, was in the pay box. She had been employed in the cinema since the age of twelve when she used to sell ice-creams. 17 years later, she now had two children of her own and had brought them along to the last show. She could not believe that it was the end. They had tried to keep the prices down. When she first came to the cinema, prices were 7d to 1s 3d. They were only 9d to 1s 6d now.

A section of the audience on the final night *(Durham Advertiser)*, **and** *(top right)* **the Rex exterior after closure.** *(Newcastle Libraries)*

The 36-year old projectionist, Tommy Atkinson, had been there for 16 years. Until the year before, when the Rex stopped Sunday performances, he had hardly ever had a night out.[1] He was un-married and reckoned he had seen five thousand films in his time as a projectionist. He would no longer climb up the iron ladder to the projection room and he would be now unemployed.

The youngest employee for the evening was 15-year old Isobelle Oliver. She had only been working there for seven months. Two members of the audience, Mr

REX   -   GILESGATE MOOR
WEEK COMMENCING JANUARY 13th, 1958
MONDAY and TUESDAY (January 13th and 14th)
PAUL LANGTON and JEAN ROGERS in
FIGHTING   BACK   (a)
Also MR WISE GUY (a)
WEDNESDAY and THURSDAY (January 15th and 16th)
JEAN ROGERS and RICHARD TRAVIS in
B A C K   L A S H   (a)
Also GOOD GIRLS GO TO PARIS (a)

FRIDAY and SATURDAY (January 17th and 18th)
JON HALL and DIANA BARRYMORE in
EAGLE SQUADRON   (a)
Also FALL IN (u)
PATRONS PLEASE NOTE
OWING TO TERMINATION OF LEASE THIS CINEMA WILL CLOSE
AFTER THE FINAL SHOW ON SATURDAY, 18th JANUARY, 1958.

and Mrs Lambert, said they had been coming to the cinema every Saturday night for 13 years. Mrs. Lambert said that she always went for the groceries before heading for the cinema and her husband went for a drink. She said that she had liked this cinema better than any other she had been in. Another member of the audience, Henry White, said that he had been coming to the Rex for 26 years. He remembered the days when they held local talent shows and the admission charges were 1d and 2d. Before a local catholic church was built, a curate from St. Godric's would bring up a table on Sunday mornings and celebrate Mass. Mr. White said that he continued to come to the cinema even though he could see television at his daughter's house.[2]

Around the county, the closure of local pits was another pressure upon the survival of the small village cinemas and Miners' Welfare Halls. The Club Hall cinema in Ushaw Moor discontinued film shows on 28th February 1958, and on 10th May, the Miner's Welfare Hall at Burnhope Colliery, not far from the intended site of the new commercial television aerial, discontinued cinema performances. The nearby Empress, Lanchester also fell victim to the audience recession and closed on 6th December 1958. Other cinemas managed to survive rather than to prosper.

1959 brought further competition with the opening of Tyne-Tees Television from Newcastle on 15th January. Over the next three years, closures followed thick and fast despite sterling attempts to delay them; the Hippodrome Thornley, a 1912 cinema; the Co-operative Hall, Craghead, run by the Society since 1915; the Empire Electric, Dipton had been providing local entertainment since 1913; the King's Theatre, Pelton had only been in new ownership for three years; the Pavilion, Grange Villa switched to bingo. The Empire, Langley Moor brought seasonal cheer and nostalgia to the district for one week by reverting to live theatre and staging a professional pantomime. But Ben Knowles, the proprietor and manager, saw it as a singular celebration and had no illusions about it providing an answer to other forms of entertainment.[3]

Television rentals and sales had greatly increased and when the Pavilion Cinema at Hetton-le Hole closed down in May 1959 the manager, Robert Ferguson, blamed the competition with television and the warm Spring weather. The Hippodrome, Thornley closed. The Royal, Sacriston had done well to stay open since the New Cinema opened but at the end of June it played its last programme of film with Disney's *Cinderella*. Ironically, the other film in the final week had been *Too Much, Too Soon*.[4]

The Hippodrome, Langley Park closed on 6th February 1960. It had been the only cinema in the colliery village since the King's was gutted by fire in 1953. The manager, Tommy Wilkinson, observed that television could take some responsibility for the loss of audience, but he also blamed the growing bingo craze. There were four regular bingo sessions in the village every week in four different venues. The cinema had originally opened as a variety theatre in 1911, and had converted to a cinema after World War I. Mr. Wilkinson had been at the cinema since 1939. In 1948, he had spent a short time at the Newcastle News Theatre and later at a Sacriston cinema. He returned to Langley Park in 1949 with himself as manager and his wife as cashier. He said that he had tried to keep the price of admission down to one shilling and sixpence at the 'posh' end and one shilling for the rest of the house. Pensioners could see a film for as little as threepence and yet local people were willing to pay five shillings for a night at bingo.

For a very popular film patrons were also willing to pay more. When the Palladium showed *South Pacific* in July and August 1960, it increased its prices to 6 shillings in the dress circle, 4 shillings and sixpence in the circle and three shillings in the stalls. There were two separate houses nightly with bookable seats in the circle and the dress circle. The prices were clearly no deterrent since it was retained for three weeks.[5]

The Memorial Institute, Sacriston had managed to maintain cinema programmes for three and a half years after the opening of the New Cinema next door. In its penultimate programme week in February 1961, it even played a repertory week with a double feature change of programme for each of six days. It finally closed on 18th February 1961 with *Battle Inferno* and *The Beatniks*. In December, a disastrous fire severely damaged the building.

During the year, the Empire, Langley Moor closed as a cinema. It had actually ceased advertising in the newspaper in May 1959. The final Cinematograph Licence was valid until 2nd February 1961, and was not renewed on 9th February. The building was used for bingo for some years afterwards. It was demolished in 1987 and replaced with a Kwik Save super-market. The Kinema in Meadowfield played its last house on Sunday 16th July 1961 with no announcement in its final advert.

In November, after a split week of the Oscar winning musical *Oklahoma* and the Elvis Presley film *Flaming Star*, the Majestic Sherburn

Last newspaper advertisements for three of the long-serving local cinemas.

The Empire Cinema Langley Moor after closure. *(Newcastle Reference Library)*
Bingo takes over at the Majestic, Sherburn Road. *(Author's collection)*

Projectionist Robert Swainston on the Meadowfield Kinema projection room balcony (the only entrance), and in the box with Gaumont-Kalee machines and arcs.

Road, ceased operating as a cinema and opened exclusively as a bingo hall. For some months, the bingo club had used the cinema on Thursday evenings and the membership list had 1,600 names. Bingo sessions operated under British gaming laws and in there only signed-up members could take part. Casual visitors were not allowed.

J. H. Forester, the chairman of directors of the owning company, Palladium (Durham) Ltd., said that the Majestic had competed quite favourably with television, but during the current Bingo trend attendances had dropped.[6]

By the end of the year the Ritz Thornley, the Empire Easington Colliery, the Empire Willington, and the Palace, Tow Law had all closed their doors or converted to bingo.

In January 1962, the cinema came to Durham in a novel way. Allied Film Makers were taking location shots for their film *Life For Ruth*. Stars Michael Craig and Patrick McGoohan spent Sunday afternoon and evening in the city filming a sequence in which a man throws himself in front of a bus in Old Elvet. 20 local people were recruited as extras at the Durham Employment Exchange. One of them, 62-year old retired Detective Chief-superintendent Richard Hall described the experience as 'very interesting' as he viewed the procedures from the top of a double-decker bus. Shooting began at 3.30 p.m. and lasted for four hours.[7]

Four location shots for *Life For Ruth* **by cameraman Otto Heller**

Michael Craig in Old Elvet   Patrick McGoohan rescues Michael Craig
Two action scenes from the film. (Allied Film Makers)

The film told the story of a miner's family who, for religious reasons, were refusing to allow their dying daughter to have a blood transfusion. Directed by Basil Dearden, it also starred Janet Munro and Lynne Taylor. It was released in the summer and shown at the Durham Palladium on 26th November 1962 for 4 days.

As Mr. Theaker had predicted, big films were still supported by big audiences even when special prices were charge. At the Essoldo in February *Ben Hur* was shown for a week to packed houses. The length of the film with its interval meant that there was only one show per evening. So, all seats were bookable at the considerably increased prices of 3/6 and 5/6 in the stalls, and 6/6 and 7/6 in the circle. A concession of 2/6 was made for pensioners only at the Wednesday matinée and there were special prices for group bookings of ten or more.

Interest in the art of the cinema may not have been sufficient to support the efforts of the Globe management in bringing foreign films to Durham, but there was still an enthusiastic number of people willing to form their own film society. The Durham Arts Film Group, chaired by architect Peter Tong, held performances at Neville's Cross College. They had a special showing of a film featuring the *Bolshoi Ballet* in January 1962 and asked the 200 people attending to fill in a questionnaire about the sorts of films they would like to see. Not surprisingly, some parts of the audience selected dance films and musicals as their favourites. The voting was *American in Paris* (20), *Seven Samura* (16), *The Defiant Ones* and *The Red* Shoes (14), *Hamlet*, and *Les Enfants Du Paradis* (13) and *Clochmerle* (8). The next film in the 1962 season was announced as Ingmar Bergman's *The Seventh Seal*.[8]

Academic interest was also on the increase. Attitudes towards cinema and the media in general had begun to shift from the condemnatory to the investigatory. A conference on the teaching of Film and Television was held at Bede College during the Easter vacation. Organised by Roy Knight, a lecturer in Drama at the College, the four-day event attracted 38 teachers and lecturers from the North-east. The tutors were Paddy Whannel, Education Officer of the British Film Institute and Stuart Hall, a sociologist who had written authoritatively on teenage tastes and attitudes. The Principal, Gerald Collier, and Brian Shallcross of Tyne-Tees Television also contributed to the sessions. Some of the liveliest sessions, it was reported, were concerned with the presentation of violent incidents in television drama. The feature films *Living* (by Akira Kurosawa), *My Darling Clementine* (by John Ford), and *On The Town* (by Gene Kelly and Stanley Donen) were shown with an introduction indicating how they might be used in schools to promote positive discussion. The Headmaster of Ushaw Moor Secondary Modern School, R. S. Gibbon, was present to introduce extracts from a film that was being made at his school by pupils and visiting students from Bede College.[9]

Pupils of IIIA filming a sequence for the film in Ushaw Moor.

The progress of this film-making was reported in the following week's edition. *Harry's Half-Crown*, as the film was eventually to be called, won the secondary school section of the 1963 Young Film-makers Festival organised by the National Union of Teachers. The scripting, filming and composing of the percussion music track were the work of a third-year class at the Ushaw Moor School with the assistance of Bede College students and tutors Roy Knight and Louis Pearson.[10]

Further recognition of the importance of the art of cinema was made by Durham University at the July Congregation. An honorary Doctorate of Letters was conferred on Charles Chaplin. The public orator, Dr. Karl Britton, began by saying it was his honour to welcome to the congregation a man who through his art had become the most familiar figure of our lifetime. "To most of us," he continued, "Mr. Chaplin is the Charlie of early films and

strip cartoons. Seeing him today in theses old silent mimes, we find that the enchantment is still there." Dr. Britton managed to include a sarcastic gibe aimed at Oxford University's conferring of a similar honour a few days before, "in a language that Mr. Chaplin could not understand." It seems that Durham University were the first to approach Charles Chaplin with the honorary degree but Oxford University held their congregation a week earlier.

Dr. Britton and most of the newspaper reports seemed to be celebrating Chaplin's return to Durham after a 74-year absence. His performance on any Durham stage is a myth. He had appeared in Newcastle, Sunderland, Darlington and Hartlepool during 1904 and 1906 in the play *Sherlock Holmes*. Between 1906 and 1907, he had been in *Casey's Court Circus* in Newcastle, South Shields and Hartlepool. In 1908, Durham did not possess a variety theatre which would have attracted *Casey's Court Circus*, and in the autumn of that year, Chaplin was with Fred Karno's troupe in Paris.[11] The Palace, which everyone seemed to think was the venue for his visit, was not opened until 9th August 1909. Moreover, Chaplin himself says that he never played here. In an interview for the Durham Advertiser, he said that he had no recollection of visiting Durham with the Lancashire Lads, a troupe he had left before 1908. In 1908/9, he was in France. He had clear recollections of playing Newcastle and Sunderland as a young boy.[12]

A letter to the Advertiser in November drew attention to the unemployment caused by cinema closures. The correspondent indicated that over 1,800 cinemas of the original 6,000 had already closed and, in Durham, the new road scheme would add the Palace to that number. He asked readers to spare a thought for the plight of cinema workers who had fallen victim to the 'eye-sight destroying monster, television'.[13] The Regal, Tantobie played its last house in February 1962, and the tiny Gem Cinema, Coxhoe closed during the year and was converted into a café in 1970.

Going
and
Gone:

(above)
The
Palace,
Durham
in 1962

(below)
The
Gem,
Coxhoe
in 1994

When *Spartacus* was shown at the Essoldo in November 1962, the programme note was very much a prediction of the future of cinema presentation. "Owing to the length of the film, there will be no supporting features." The second feature film, and the 'supporting programme' were slowly disappearing from schedules as cinemas tried to cut costs, and as more 'blockbusters' began to appear.

In January 1963, the Essoldo replayed *Ben Hur* to full houses once again. They had reduced all their original seat prices by sixpence. The policy of showing big films for seven days was becoming fairly normal. The Palladium made a big showing of *The Guns of Navarone*, and *El Cid* was given the epic treatment at the Essoldo in March. Adverts for its showing at the Queen's Hall in Newcastle in a 70mm. version had appeared in March 1962.

'Pop' music films were proving a considerable attraction for young people, and the film industry on both sides of the Atlantic tried to keep pace with the demand. *It's Trad, Dad* enjoyed a popular run at both the Essoldo and the Palace in 1962. These posters, for the week of 19th October, were on a site next to the Railway Hotel, Sidegate (now demolished) which is offering Cameron's of West Hartlepool Strongarm bitter. *Photograph by courtesy of Michael Richardson.*

A rising film actor paid a very brief visit to the outskirts of Durham in September 1962, but it seems that only the local constabulary noticed. At a magistrates' court in January 1963, Sean Connery was fined £3 *in absentia* for speeding at Neville's Cross. It seems that he was doing 44 m.p.h. in a 30 m.p.h. zone whilst driving North. He gave a London address and pleaded guilty by letter.[14] The first James Bond Film *Dr. No* was not shown in Durham until 28th October 1963, so the reporter may be forgiven for not making more of the incident. Sean Connery's film achievements before this had been very undistinguished.

In February, the New Cinema, Sacriston attempted to cash in on the interests of both cinemagoers and bingo fans. On two nights a week, a bingo session was included within the cinema programme. On Wednesdays and Fridays, the evening film began at 6.15 p.m. and the bingo session began at 7.30. By March, the cinema was advertising the programmes as Cine-Bingo.[15]

The interest engendered by *The Longest Day* in 1963 can be seen in the left-hand photograph (*Newcastle City Library*), **and the Palladium when the Malthouse pub was next-door.** (*Michael Richardson*)

Anxious to get the best possible audience for its showing of *The Longest Day,* the Palladium had begun advertising it several weeks before the actual presentation. It had a special booking form printed in the newspaper and an advance-booking position in the theatre foyer. There were to be no telephone bookings. Prices were increased to 6/-, 4/6, and 3/6. Seats were bookable, but in the dress circle and circle only.[16] From Sunday 1st September, the film played for two weeks.

The Advertiser saw need to make reference to the unusual nature of the film programmes for the week on 21st Sept 1963. Under the heading 'SIX 'X's' NEXT WEEK' the editor observed that the presence of "Profane acts, monsters and vampires and lots and lots of murder. All this and more is part of the 'bumper fare' being offered to Durham City's adult cinemagoers next week under the guise of entertainment." The Essoldo was adventurous with a showing of *Phædra* starring Melina Mercouri and Anthony Perkins but conventional in the supporting choice of *Dr. Blood's Coffin* as the opening offering of the week. At the same time, the Palace had *Something Wild* and *The Fantastic Disappearing Man*. The Palladium had *Frantic* and *Seddock, Son of Satan* for Thursday, Friday and Saturday. The editor accepted that not all 'X' certificate films were rubbish, but he thought that none of the films on show had any chance of Film Festival Awards. (*Phædra* had been nominated for an Oscar for its costumes, and for Best Foreign Film and Best Aactress for British Academy Awards.) At all events, however, he thought that six 'X' films in one week was too many.

Esoteric interest in cinema in the city had been increasing, however, and in November, Peter Tong, the chairman of the Durham Arts Society Film Group reported that membership had almost doubled and now stood at 174.

Some aspects of cinema presentation had not changed, and the three Durham cinemas managed to provide Christmas entertainment with 'U' films.

Documentary

Though it was quite usual for the newsreels and the Mining Review magazines to include brief items on the Miners' Gala, longer documentaries by professional groups were rare. Earlier, in July, two films had been made. One, called *The Big Meeting*, by Data Films for the National Coal Board was given an exclusive première at the Durham Essoldo. H. Rogers, the manager, said he was honoured to be getting the film first. "It will be shown," he said, "at all houses for a fortnight, beginning on 8th January with the James Bond film *From Russia With Love*." The B.B.C. owned the performing rights and they intended to show it on television later in the year.

The second film, *Gala Day,* had been made by a former native of Durham, J. C. G. Irvin and his film co-operative. It had been financed by the British Film Institute Experiment Fund and was given its première at the National Film Theatre also in January. It was shown on B.B.C. television on Wednesday night, 19th February 1964. The Advertiser reviewer thought that it was not as good as the film shown at the Essoldo, because it lacked a commentary. Dean Wild, however, thought that it was the best film of the gala he had ever seen. He thought that it gave everyone a good idea of what the gala was like. His only criticism was that there were far too many close-ups.

The Palace entrance on closure week *(Durham Advertiser)* **and the extremely seedy exterior of the projection box at the time of demolition.** *(Ray Middleton)*

The expected closure of the Palace took place on 1st February 1964. Throughout its entire existence as a music hall and a cinema, a member of the Rawes family had been involved in its ownership or management.

Its final film programme was a re-run of two 'X' certificate films, *The Pit and The Pendulum* and *Premature Burial*. The newspaper reports of the final show repeated the myth that Stan Laurel and Charlie Chaplin had played there.

The other cinemas were apparently having a fairly good year of it. In April, the Essoldo had *Zulu*, and *Lawrence of Arabia* for 14 days each. The Palladium had good support for seven days for *The Great Escape*, and a return week of *The Longest Day* just as the demolition men began tearing down the Palace. But, all was not well behind the scenes. The Advertiser reported that there were to be major changes in Claypath with the Gas Board seeking new premises and the Palladium closing. The owners had approached the city council about the possible purchase of the properties by them.[17]

The University

The University increased its potential as an area of film culture during the year. At Bede College, the first year of a main course in Radio, Film and Television was begun. It was Britain's first such course in a teacher-training establishment. During its first year of operation, it attracted the attention of documentary film-maker, Denis Mitchell. His film for Granada Television *The Dream Machine* compared the work and philosophy of T.V. producer Paul Fox and the Bede College course tutor, Roy Knight.

The Appleby Theatre and Lecture Hall in the new science block of the university was opened in South Road. It was equipped with 35mm. projectors and soon became the venue for the University Film Society. The University also indicated that it was prepared to fund half the cost of a theatre planned to be built within the new Milburngate Complex.[18] Its initial cost was projected as £185,000. Annual running costs were expected to be £16,000 per year and a daily hire fee of £56 would be needed to recover costs.[19]

In October, two well-known actors visited the city. Film star and dancer Jessie Matthews, famous at the time as radio's Mrs. Dale, was the guest of the Durham Ladies' Lecture Club at the Three Tuns Hotel. In the same week, David Kossof, stage and film actor, gave his one-man show at the Durham Technical College.

For the close of the year no application had been made to the magistrates for the city cinemas to open on Christmas Day even though it fell on a Friday. By the rules of the licensing authority, proprietors were required to pay employees double time and offer them an alternative day's leave. It is possible that this increase in the overheads was sufficient reason for the closure. On the Sunday after Christmas, the Palladium attracted seasonal audiences with a four-day re-issue of *Seven Brides For Seven Brothers* followed just over a week later by three weeks of the epic *Cleopatra* with Richard Burton and Elizabeth Taylor. Seat prices were increased to 8/6 for the dress circle, 6/6 for the rear circle and 5/- for the stalls.[20]

Unusually, an acclaimed documentary on the life of Winston Churchill, *The Finest Hours*, was shown for a week at the Palladium. Television had created a willing audience amongst the older age group for epic compilations and reconstructions of historical events, and the producers of several such films clearly hoped to lure this category of patron back to the cinema. But for the most part cinema programmes in general seemed largely directed towards youthful audiences.

A spate of 'X' certificate horror films emanating from the Hammer Studios and Roger Corman occupied a number of weeks in the early part of the year. One such in May 1965 at the Palladium even advertised itself as 'Nervo-rama' for the showing of *I married A Werewolf* and *Where Has Poor Mickey Gone?* Their titles and subject matter became ever more lurid; *Dr. Terror's House of Horrors*, *The Black Torment*, and *Trauma* could all be seen in the city within months of each other.

Durham Arts Film Group provided a world-view of cinema production with its 1965/66 season. *Never on Sunday*, *Shane*, *The Seven Deadly Sins*, *The Idiot*, *Wild Strawberries*, *Billy Liar*, *Black Orpheus*, *The Life of Adolf Hitler*, *The Asphalt Jungle*, *Ugetsu Monagatari*, *La Strada* and *Clochmerle* were amongst the host of films on the programme. Most of the films were shown at Durham Technical College, but two were scheduled for the Cædmon Hall, Bede College under the sponsorship of the college's Film and Television Department.

In the Durham village of Evenwood an attempt was made to revive local cinema-going. James Etherington and his brother were granted a cinematograph licence for the former Empire cinema. For the previous two years it had functioned as a teenagers' dance hall under the name of the Jiro Club. The original cinema was opened in January 1912 with a seating capacity of 398.[21]

The Palladium had a special single performance of the film of *Der Rosenkavalier* on Sunday 20th February. The newspaper advertisements gave it a fortnight's advance notice and indicated that seat prices would be 4/- in the stalls and 5/- in the circle. This 1962 German production directed by Paul Czinner was in Estmancolor and had a running time of 195 mins. There was no newspaper report on the success of the venture.

Palladium refurbishment
The Palladium seemed sure of its continued viability in carrying out extensive refurbishment in the second half of 1967. On 30th September, after a successful two-week run of *My Fair Lady*, it closed its doors until November. The re-opening was given extensive press coverage with before and after photographs.

A new ceiling, new décor, new seats, a new screen and proscenium and new projection equipment brought the cinema up-to-date. The Palladium (Durham) Ltd had as its chairman John Holiday Forester, the nephew of Alderman T. W. Holiday, one of the original board members at the cinema's opening. The Forester family built the original Albany Theatre that once stood on the site of the Savings Bank building in Millburngate. Another director, W. S. Gibson, nephew of the late Thomas Thompson, was the only surviving member of the original directors and still the managing director of Thompson Enterprises of Middlesborough.

The cinema manager was Denis Simpson, then living in Lanchester. He had begun his cinema career with the ABC circuit at the Majestic Newcastle, and had also managed the Ritz Wallsend, the Savoy South Shields, and the Haymarket Newcastle before coming to Durham in 1964.

Chief projectionist was 38 year-old Wallace Langley, a Durham man, previously a projectionist at Black's Regal in Sunderland and who came to Durham in 1954 as a projectionist at the Majestic on Sherburn Road. His assistant was Gerald Nyland, a newcomer to the trade.

(Before) **Palladium facelift showing steep floor rake and projection angle** *(After)*

The re-furbished projection box contained controls for the lighting, curtain movement, and the audio system. The new projector had a 2000ft spool capacity and could run continuously for twenty minutes lit by its 3000watt carbon arc. The foyer had been re-designed with a combined sweets and tobacco sales kiosk, and advance booking office. In charge of this was Bessie Barron assisted by Katherine Houghton, also doubling as an usherette. Other part-time usherettes were Doris Beecham, Kathleen Bussey, M. Kallandra, Geraldine Kehoe, Mary Lowes, and Beryl Wilson. The doorman was Thomas W. Parry. In the redesigned pay box, the cashier was Elizabeth Wilkinson, who had been at the theatre for two years.[22]

Cashier Mrs. Wilkinson Projection - Wallace Langley Manager Denis Simpson

The local group of the National Council of Civil Liberties quickly expressed their opposition to any attempts to ban the film. They said that it had always been the city council's policy not to interfere with the control of films passed by the British Board of Film Censors. "The only objection to the film is that some Christian might find the film offensive," said Jean Rogers, the local N.C.C.L. secretary. "We feel that it is a pity that the Bishop did not confine himself to warning his flock that they might find it offensive. The adults of Durham are capable of deciding for themselves whether they want to see it, and if they are afraid of being offended, they should stay at home."

Easington council condemned the film whilst still allowing it to be shown. Many members spoke fiercely against it, although no one had actually seen it. Durham city councillors would see the film at the Classic at a date to be arranged.[38] When the council did see the film at a special showing in May, they agreed that it should be shown with its 'AA' certificate. Their stated reactions to the film were in the range of 'a load of filth', through 'disgusting' to 'absolutely marvellous'. By a majority of 27 to 6, the city was saved the embarrassment of banning it.[39]

The former Majestic Cinema in Sherburn Road was set to take over from the ex-Palladium as the local bingo hall. There had been objections to the continued use of the Palladium by the northern area traffic commissioners. The licences for bus operators bringing the patrons to the congested area of Durham Claypath were being re-considered. It was hoped that the Majestic would be fully functioning by the end of the year. £150,000 would be spent on its renovation. Shortly after its closure as a cinema in 1961, it had been a bingo hall, but later it had been converted into use as a Skateboard Bowl. When this venture failed, it had been used as a furniture warehouse.[40]

Controversy again centred on the city council concerning the showing of a film celebrating the 800th anniversary of Durham's Charter made by Michel Gough. Jean Middlemass, the organiser of the Charter events, said that it would be shown over and over again along at the University New Arts Block auditorium along with film taken of the visits to the city by the Queen, and by American President Jimmy Carter. The newspaper report said that city councillors had turned down their invitation to the event because it might mean that they would have to pay for refreshments. It is not clear whether the report meant that they would have to pay for their own refreshments or those of everyone else![41]

The Community Arts Centre at Castle Chare temporarily occupying buildings next to St. Godric's Junior School was keen to attract film enthusiasts to its programmes. With the catchy title, 'Electric Chare' it proposed a series of film events. In January 1981, it showed the North East premier of the heavy metal film *This is Spinal Tap*, and in February it showed the Spanish ballet film *Blood Wedding* and a programme of silent films with piano accompaniment.

The first hints that Durham might be losing its remaining commercial cinema appeared in November 1983. The Classic circuit had been acquired by Cannon Cinemas and now operated as Cannon Classic Cinemas Ltd.

At a council meeting, Cllr Mrs Sue Watts quoted a 'non-authoritative source' that indicated the Classic would soon be closing. The cinema head office said that this was a surprise to them, but it is clear that there had been hints that the property was to be put on the market again. Prospective developers had made enquiries of the city planning office and this had fuelled speculation about its possible change of function. Maurice Pinto, of Cannon Classic Cinemas Ltd., said that there were no plans for closure and that the Classic was a 'reasonably profitable cinema'.[42]

On January 19th 1984, the advertising for the Classic underwent a slight change with the inclusion of the Cannon logo.

Classic advert DA January 12th Cannon logo Classic Ad. DA January 19th 84

There was a small celebration for the 50th anniversary of the Regal in February 1984. Miss Bilton of Framwellgate Moor was its first cashier and she remained in the job for '12 of the happiest years of my life'. She recalled that when the cinema opened there were 21 staff including four operators, and a front of house commissionaire. She was certain the Regal's position as the most popular of the four city cinemas in Durham was because it did not have an extra charge for seat booking. She admits to the fact that on Saturday nights she used to hold a few seats back so that the nurses from Dryburn hospital could get in at 8 p.m. when their shift finished. Miss Bilton also sang with a succession of resident organists; Herbert Maxwell, Jack Feather, George Carr and Joseph Davenport. In 1946 a serious traffic accident incapacitated her for seven years and her association with the cinema ceased.

Newspaper photographs of Hilda Bailey and Joan Morton (manager), Miss Bilton and projectionist Tony Smith.

Now, with its newspaper advertisements and its exterior sign changed to CANNON, the North Road cinema applied for a cinematograph licence extension, attempting to increase its student and other patrons with late Friday night shows. A short-term improvement was observable, but in November 1989, as part of a nationwide asset-stripping process, the Cannon Circuit put the cinema up for sale - 16 of its 150 sites had already been sold. In 1988, they operated 143 sites /380 screens throughout the U.K. By 1990 sites had decreased to 137, but with the further development of multiplexes the number of screens had increased to 392.

Britain's first multiplex had opened in Milton Keynes in November 1985 and its initial combination of improved presentation, programme variety, and ancillary services began a slow increase in cinema going.

In 1988, cinema complexes with five screens or more accounted for 12 per cent of all screens in the U.K. By 1990 this had risen to 30 per cent. The number of cinema seats had fallen by 13 per cent between 1983 and 1988, but increased by 7 per cent between 1988 and 1990 largely due to the development of out-of town multiplex sites.[43] 12 miles away, the 10-screen UCI multiplex in the Gateshead Metro Centre was capturing some of Durham's audience potential.

No buyer came forward for the Durham Cannon and the company gave one week's notice that the cinema would close after the last performance on Thursday June 28th 1990.[44]

The final programmes had ironic titles. Cinema One showed *Look Who's Talking* **and Cinema Two** *Hard to Kill.*

The last night frontage and Cinema One projector and Peerless arc-lamp.
Photographs by John Lackenby, the final projectionist.

Durham was without a public access cinema for just over one year. The College of St. Hild & St. Bede installed a 35mm. 'cake-stand' projection system during this time and their Film Society was able to show contemporary releases to its student audience. The North Road site was purchased by Troveworth Limited for £500,000 in 1991. At this time, there were plans afoot to re-open the cinema with a certain amount of very necessary structural refurbishment, and an increase in the number of screens. £250,000 was said to have been expended on the alterations. The interior was in a dilapidated state and required entirely re-seating. The upstairs Cinema Two was divided down the middle to make Screens Two and Three. It was also planned, with £25,000 from Durham City Arts, Northern Arts, and the British Film Institute, to provide a small Screen Four auditorium for general use and as an Art House screen. This was to be carved out of the right-hand side of Cinema One's auditorium.

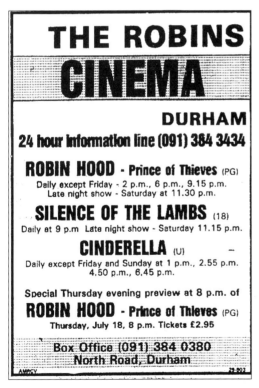

The Robins cinema chain, an independent company, with other cinemas in places such as Burton-on-Trent and Deal, emerged to operate the cinema. Generous rental and contractual terms were agreed with the owners and on July 19th, 1991 the Mayor Cllr David Bell cut a reel of film at the main entrance and declared the cinema officially open. 200 children from local schools watched a performance of the re-issue of Walt Disney feature animation *Cinderella*. A 'Cinderella' was flown over from America by the Disney Corporation.

The cinema actually re-opened the night before with a sneak preview showing of Kevin Kostner's *Robin Hood - Prince of Thieves*. There had been a north-eastern interest in the film, since some scenes were shot on the Roman Wall and in Northumberland. Ticket prices were £2.95 and £1.95. The manager Penny Edwards said that she was so pleased to be bringing a 'terrific building back to life'.[45]

With programming based mostly on current releases, and limited but valued request programming in the 66-seat Screen Four, the cinema showed a modest profit. Water-level problems and drainage at the proscenium end of Screen One were still present and occasionally the sumps overflowed into the cinema. Plaster surfaces in the ceiling of Cinema One were also in a parlous state and required fairly constant observation. The purchase of Chinese projectors had also given a few problems, but an eventual replacement for Cinema One and an updating of the sound system provided patrons with better than average presentation.

But, six years into the management, there were ominous signs for the cinema and the Robins circuit. A number of their cinemas were deemed unviable in places where new multiplexes had captured their audience, and the company already on narrowing margins needed to re-organise. The same threat surfaced in Durham in 1997, when plans for the development of the site of the former McKay's carpet factory in Walkergate, included a ten-screen cinema and theatre complex.

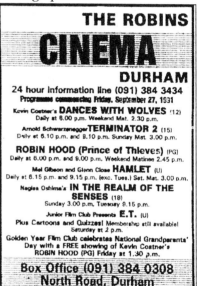

THE ROBINS
CINEMA
DURHAM
24 hour information line (091) 384 3434
Programme commencing Friday, September 27, 1991

Kevin Costner's **DANCES WITH WOLVES** (12)
Daily at 8.00 p.m. Weekend Mat. 2.30 p.m.

Arnold Schwarzenegger **TERMINATOR 2** (15)
Daily at 6.10 p.m. and 9.10 p.m. Sunday Mat. 3.00 p.m.

ROBIN HOOD (Prince of Thieves) (PG)
Daily at 8.00 p.m. and 9.00 p.m. Weekend Matinee 2.45 p.m.

Mel Gibson and Glenn Close **HAMLET** (U)
Daily at 6.15 p.m. and 9.15 p.m. (exc. Tues.) Sat. Mat. 3.00 p.m.

Nagisa Oshima's **IN THE REALM OF THE SENSES** (18)
Sunday 3.00 p.m., Tuesday 8.15 p.m.

Junior Film Club Presents **E.T.** (U)
Plus Cartoons and Quizzes! Membership still available!
Saturday at 2 p.m.

Golden Year Film Club celebrates National Grandparents'
Day with a FREE showing of Kevin Costner's
ROBIN HOOD (PG) Friday at 1.30 p.m.

Box Office (091) 384 0308
North Road, Durham

A typical programme with
special club features *(DA)*

The notion of a 'proper' theatre for Durham had been the dream of some people for many, many years, but the prospect of this had proved both elusive and unviable. Even in the live theatre days of the Assembly Rooms in the early 1900s continuous theatrical presentations were possible only through the generous subsidy provided by Mr. Rushworth and his son. The flotation of a company for the proposed theatre on the corner of Claypath and Providence Row was under-subscribed in the 1902. The dual role of the Palladium as a Cinema/Theatre was disturbed by the arrival of sound films. In 1965, the theatre proposed for the first phase of the Milburngate development as a joint development of the city, the county and the university was dropped eventually because of its rising costs. In 1985 an article in the Durham Advertiser was headlined 'Why Durham might never get a Theatre'. [46] It reminded readers of the previous attempts and suggested that lack of commitment at all costs was the reason why no theatre had ever emerged. "Where there is no will, there is no way," the article concluded.

In 1997, the will and the way seemed to present themselves in the form of the Millennium Commission. The cost of the £28 million project for a multi-function Millennium Hall and a new library grouped round a Millennium Square was to be met by £12½million from the Commission and £15½ million from the City.

Alongside this development, the city council formed a joint venture company with AMEC for the development of the Walkergate site. A section of the planning application stated that

'The anchor unit is an eight-screen multiplex cinema, seating 2100 people. As the largest single building, it is located adjacent to the existing flyover in order to minimise its overall impact on the existing townscape. Similarly a 368 space car park is situated at the rear of the development, hidden from view by other buildings within the scheme. The Walkergate development is based on three primary levels; ground level at Freemans Place comprising of a family entertainment centre, music venue and multiplex cinema.'[47]

By April 2000, it was reported that Warner Villages who were first expected to operate the cinema complex were now considering withdrawal. AMEC indicated to council officers that 'as a result of a downward turn in the commercial leisure market (particularly in relation to multiplex cinemas)' they were unable to make 'the minimum commitment that had been previously proposed.'[48] It would appear that Warner Villages required a subsidy in the order of £1 million to continue their involvement in the project. In order to make the overall project viable, AMEC proposed the inclusion of a large nightclub in March 2001, along with the licensing of the several restaurants. They still had not found an operator for the cinemas.

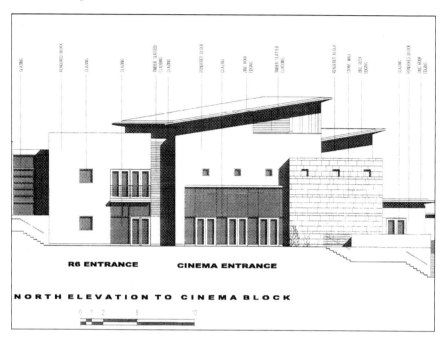

Part of the plans for the multiplex . *(Courtesy of Ellis Williams, architects, Runcorn)*

At the same time plans were submitted by Regent Inns to convert the Robins cinema into an Australian theme bar. Part of their 'Walkabout' chain, it would be open between 11a.m. and 2 a.m. offering food, dancing, televised sport and live music. The proposal was objected to by the Durham City Trust, local residents, the operator of the North Road Club Elysium and the Police.[49]

Although the Robins Cinema still retained the name, the Robins Company had gone into receivership in November 1999, and its cinemas that could not find alternative operators had been closing. The operation of the Durham Robins Cinema was carried on by Bill Freedman Limited, but the lease for the cinema was now on the basis of one month's notice. Under the new management and new terms of operation, a small but steady profit was reported to have been achieved.

Negotiations for the discontinuance of the building as a cinema continued to undermine any long-term plans for its operation. On 28th September 2002, the building owners placed a two-column inch notice in the Durham Advertiser stating their case for its closure. Their major claim was that the cinema could not have operated profitably at all without the generous rental terms offered by Troveworth. Negotiations with Regent Inns plc would provide a 'much needed facility in the centre of Durham' and provide a 'welcoming atmosphere to residents and visitors to Durham alike.' They did not seem to countenance the fact that an unused building would lead to no rental at all or that the liquor licence for the building was not fully assured.

Severely vilified for their decision by some, the council felt justified in not pursuing their objection to the building's change of function as it had become clear that, after expensive litigation, their previous objections to similar facilities had been overturned on appeal. They were keen the populace should know that their previous involvement in the Robins re-opening and their continuous interest in the Walkergate multiplex indicated their positive attitude to main-stream cinema in the city.

Sharon McCourt puts her sign in her newsagency window. *Durham Advertiser*

Almost 2,000 local film-goers, under the instigation of Sharon McCourt, the manageress of Taylor's newsagents opposite the cinema, signed a petition protesting against the closure of the cinema. She presented the petition to the Durham City MP Gerry Steinberg. In receiving it, Mr. Steinberg said that the petition would be presented to the courts. He said it would be a great shame if the cinema closed. The Robins manageress Brenda Ryder said that it was good to know that so many people cared about the cinema. "But," she added, ruefully, "the issue to be put before the County

Court was the application for a drinks licence not the loss of the cinema."

On 8th November, despite representations from the police, local residents and the Durham City Trust, Durham Crown Court granted a liquor licence to Regent Inns plc and spelled the end of the Robins Cinema. The district judge, Beatrice Bolton, sitting with four magistrates said that there were insufficient late drinking venues to meet demand in Durham, and she believed that the presence of the Walkabout facility in North Road would encourage an improvement in surrounding licences premises. She criticized the authorities for failing to tackle problems of late night transport and the shortage of public conveniences in the city centre. She also accused some of the objectors of showing a degree of snobbery in assuming that all late night drinkers in North Road were 'animals'. "These young people are no better and no worse than any others," she said.[50]

The Giant Screen at the Gala Theatre complex *(Durham Environmental services)*

The continuance of cinema entertainment in the City has been left in the hands of the city council. In February 2002, the Gala Theatre complex had been opened with the Giant Screen facility provided within the building. The auditorium could accommodate 116 patrons. Matthew Baker, a former Durham resident, who was now a presenter of the BBC Children's programme 'Blue Peter', performed the official opening. A special edition of the Disney Animated film *Beauty and the Beast* was shown to an invited audience by means of the 8-70 large format projector. In March a city council-commissioned 20-minute film concerning the Life of St. Cuthbert, *The Sacred Journey*, was given its first public viewing. Following the premières, both films were very much neglected by audiences, and there were reports that the 116-seat cinema was sometimes showing its films to one person. On 26th December 2002, the big-screen version of *The Lion King* was presented at the cinema. The management of the cinema, which incidentally was employing former projectionists and staff from the Robins, expressed their hope that they would be able in the future to shows 35mm mainstream films in the auditorium.

An amended plan for the Walkergate site was reported at the end of November 2002. AMEC Development had lodged a plan with the Durham City Council for six restaurants, a bar, a 94-bed hotel, a 506 space multi-storey car park and 35 apartments. Temporary drinks licences for the restaurants had already been obtained. The city council's Environmental Services Director John Jennings had said that there was still a hope that a northern extension of the National Portrait Gallery might feature in the development.[51] This proved to be something of a red herring, however.

THANK YOU AND GOODBYE

The Robins Cinema finally closed on 5 January 2003. During the previous month there had been sell-out audiences for *Harry Potter and The Chamber of Secrets* in Screen One. The fact that some scenes in the film were shot in Durham Cathedral precincts provided an ironic twist to the cinema history of Durham.

By an ingenious arrangement of the 'cake-stand' film supply, the latest James Bond film *Die Another Day* was shown in the adjacent Screens Two and Three from a single print.[52] There was also a special showing for the University James Bond Society. On the final night *The Lord of The Rings, the Two Towers* was shown to a half-full house in Screen One, *Harry Potter* in Screen Two, *Die Another Day* in Screen Three and *Sweet Home Alabama* in Screen Four. The cinema staff distributed soft drinks and confectionary to the audience during the intermission and created a final message on the interior and exterior display boards.

The last-night audience at the Robins Cinema. *Photograph by author.*

In the week of 14th to 22nd April, there was a cancelled booking for the Gala Theatre. The City Council, which was now running the theatre, decided to put on a week of classic films by means of the video projector in the auditorium. The films were grouped into themed days of musicals, dramas and classics and included *South Pacific, West Side Story, Grease, Saturday Night Fever, Little Shop of*

Horrors, Gone With the Wind, Singing in the Rain, and Notting Hill.
Audience figures were encouraging.

During the same week, a 35mm projector was being housed in
the projection box of the Big Screen cinema, and on 1st May, the
film shown was *X Men-2*, a 12a rated first-run adventure film. It
played to packed houses for its three week run.[53] The opening
ceremony was conducted by the Mayor of Durham.

Projectionists Steve Riddle and Neil Robinson shared the
duties on the brand new Cinemechanica machine. Panavision and
full Cinemascope lenses were incorporated, and there was
surround-sound Dolby. The second film *Matrix Re-loaded* was also
very popular with the largely student audience. In August 2003, it
was announced that a second screen would be created out of the
vestibule area known as the St. Cuthbert Sanctuary. This would
only have 70 seats but it would enable a wider range of films to be
shown and, in conjunction with the Durham City Library opposite,
provide an opportunity for art and educational showings.

Gala Theatre projectionist Steve Riddle checks the threading of the machine.

The technical process of moving film through a projector has changed very little since the first pictures flickered onto a Durham screen. Sound, colour, wide-screen, constant-speed motors have all enhanced the process, but there are still sprocket-holes down the film-edge, and the Maltese cross and the sprockets still engage them, though the digital revolution is beginning to make exhibitors look at other methods. Cinemas still need licences to operate and councils still have the right to inspect and approve programme content. But cinema is only one element of nationwide and global visual entertainment. It will survive in one form or another and, despite ever-increasing budgets of major film producers, public access to sophisticated non-professional means of production will enable it to be more than a spectator-only medium.

Durham in recent years has been the location for a number of films. Some scenes of *Get Carter* (1971) were filmed in Belmont; in Michael Winterbottom's BBC-funded film *Jude* (1996) several scenes were shot in the cathedral and the bailey; in 1998, the cathedral nave was cleared for filming Channel Four's *Elizabeth*; other scenes were shot at Raby Castle in the county.

Christopher Eccleston and Kate Winslet in Bow Lane for *Jude*. *(BBC)*
Durham Cathedral laid bare for *Elizabeth*. *(Channel Four Films)*

In 2000 and 2001, some consternation was caused amongst sections of the cathedral community when key scenes in the first two Harry Potter films were shot there, but both the cathedral and some of the choir school members benefited financially from the experience.

For over 100 years then, cinema has played a part in the culture of the city. And this has been the story of those years.

* * * * * * *

Notes to
Chapters

Chapter Notes

One

1. Northern Echo May 4 1896
2. In an advert by R. W. Paul in *The Era* of Dec. 19 1896, both Newcastle-on-Tyne and Sunder-land are listed.
3. The Loise Fuller film referred to is probably one the Edison Kinetoscope bands of Anabelle performing her Serpentine dance. Her dance had been filmed at least three times by the Edison Company, in 1894, 1895 and in May 1897. Her Serpentine Dance film has also been billed in other places as *A Parisian Dance*. Loise Fuller was at this time performing in Paris and there is no record of her making any films for the Kinetoscope or anyone else. Phillips, Ray *Edison's Kinetoscope and Its Films* Flicks Books, 1997 pp. 115-116.
4. Durham Ad. Dec. 24 1897
5. Durham Ad. Feb. 4 1898
6. Barnes, J. *The Beginnings of Cinema in England* vol. 2 1983 pp.67-68/120.
7. Durham Ad. Apr. 30 1899
8. Durham Ad. Dec. 15 1899
9. Durham Ad. Apr. 4 1902
10. Durham Chron. Sept 5,12,19 1902
11. Bird, J. H. *Cinema Parade* 1946 p. 24
12. Durham Chron. Nov28/Dec5 1902
13. Durham Chronicle Feb.13 1903
14. Durham Chronicle 20 Mar 1903
15. Durham Chronicle Mar. 4 1903
16. Barnes, J. *op.cit.* vol 3 (1983) pp. 77-79
17. Durham Chronicle Apr. 17 1903
18. Durham Ad. Apr 17 1903
19. Details of British films in the programmes have been obtained from Gifford, Denis *The British Film Catalogue 1895-1985* (David & Charles 1986) and those of other films from contemporary editions of *The Optical Magic Lantern Journal*, and its successor *The Kinematograph and Lantern Weekly*.
20. *Durham Ad.* July 22nd 1904. The photograph by Mrs Gee appears in Michael Richardson's book *Durham: Cathedral City* 1997
21. Low, R. and Manvell, R. *The History of the British Film* (1950) vol.1 p.69.
22. *Durham Chronicle*, Sept. 2nd 1904.
23. *Durham Chronicle* Nov 4 1904
24. *Durham Chronicle* Jan 6 1905
25. *Durham Chronicle*, Jan.19 1905
26. *The Optical Lantern and Kinematograph Journal* 1906 pp. 135 and 136 lists all 19 episodes and includes four frame enlargements.
27. *Durham Chronicle* Aug.3rd 1906

Two

1. Durham County Adver. Feb 22 1907
2. Durham County Ad. Mar 1st 1907 and Exeter Flying Post Feb 23rd 1907. Pooles were showing the film within 2 days of the disaster.
3. Durham Chronicle Mar 8 1907
4. Durham Chronicle Mar 15 1907
5. World's Fair Jan 1st 1908
6. Brownlow, Kevin Hollywood: The Pioneers p.26
7. *The Movie* (Orbis Publications) volume 9 page 2052. Still
8. Durham County Ad. Mar 6 1908
9. Durham County Ad. Ap 24 1908. *The Attractions of Durham*
10. World's Fair Ap 25 1908
11. World's Fair Jan 8 1908
12. World's Fair May 2nd 1908.
13. World's Fair May 16 1908
14. Durham County Ad. Sept 11 1908
15. Durham County Ad. Nov 27 1908
16. Durham County Ad. Dec 25 1908
17. Durham County Ad. Mar 5 1909
18. *The Music Hall and Theatre Review* Mar 19 1909.

19. *The Music Hall and Theatre Review* Mar 19 1909 and D. C. R. O.

20. Durham County Ad. Aug 6 1909

21. Durham County Ad. Aug 13 1909

22. Durham County Ad. Aug 27 1909

23. Durham County Ad. Oct 1 1909

24. Durham County Ad. Nov 26 1909

25. Durham County Ad. Dec 10 1909

26. Durham County Ad. Jan 7 1910

27. Walton R. *Coxhoe* p82. Durham County Ad. Feb 11 1910

28. Durham County Ad. Feb 18 1910

29. Durham County Ad. Feb 25 1910

30. *Rink World and Picture Theatre News*. Feb 12 1910 page 17

31. World's Fair June 27 1908

32. Durham County Ad. Mar 18 1910

33. Durham County Ad. May 13 1910

34. Durham County Ad. May 27 1910

35. Durham County Ad. July 1st 1910

36. Durham County Ad. Aug 12 1910

37. Durham County Ad. Aug 19 1910

38. Durham County Ad. Aug 12 1910

39. Durham County Ad. Sept 2 1910. Film Notes *The Cloister's Touch* American Biograph dir. D.W. Griffith. Released in U.S. Feb 1910. *Lt. Rose R.N.* G.B. Clarendon Film with P.G. Norgate as Lt. Rose.

40. Durham County Ad. Aug 19 1910

41. Durham County Ad. Sept 9 1910

42. Durham County Ad. Sept 16 1910

43. Durham County Ad. Nov 25 1910

44. The South Durham and Auckland Chronicle July 28 and Aug 4 1910

45. The World's Fair Aug 13 1910 P 10

46. Durham County Ad. Sept 16 1910

47. Durham County Ad. .Sept 30 1910 for perf. on Tues Oct 11 10.

48. Durham County Ad. Oct 21 1910

49. Worlds' Fair Dec 17 1910 and Durham Chronicle Feb 3 1911

50. World's Fair Sept 17 1910

51. Durham Chronicle Feb 10 1911

52. Durham Chronicle Fri 10 Feb 1911

53. Durham Chronicle Mar 3 1911

54. Durham Chronicle Mar 10 1911

55. Durham County Ad. Feb 24 1911

56. Durham Chronicle Mar 24 1911

57. Durham Chronicle Mar 31 1911

58. Durham County Ad. Feb 3rd 1911

59. Durham Chronicle Mar 31st 1911

60. World's Fair. Ap 22nd 1911

61. Durham County Ad. May 12 1911

62. Durham Chronicle May 19 1911

63. Durham County Ad. May 19 1911

64. DCRO Licences June 8 1911

65.   Durham Chronicle May 26 1911

66. Durham Chronicle June 2nd 1911 and 1912 Directory.

67. Bowers, Q. *David Thanhouser Films: An Encyclopaedia and History* (CD-rom 1998)

68. Durham County Ad. June 9 1911

69. Durham Ad. June 30 1911

70. Durham County Ad. Aug 4 1911

71. Based on listings in *The Bioscope Weekly* for June and July 1911.

72. Durham County Ad. Aug 18 1911

73. Durham County Ad. Sept 1 1911

74. Durham County Ad. Dec 29 1911 Jan 5 and 26 1912

75. Durham County Ad. Jan 5 1912.

76. Durham County Ad. Jan 19 1912

77. Durham County Ad. May 17 1912

78. Durham County Ad. Feb 16 1912.

79. Durham County Ad. June 7 1912

80. Durham County Ad. Aug 2 1912

81. Christies (East) *catalogue 100 years of Cinema* Dec 11 1995

82. Durham County Ad. Aug 16 1912

83. Durham County Ad. Sept 13 1912

84. Durham County Ad. Nov 22 1912

85. This is obviously a misprint for Kalee.

86. Durham Chronicle Nov 15 1912

87. Durham County Ad. Dec 13 1912.

88. Durham County Ad. Febr 7 1913

89. The World's Fair Jan 18 1911

90. The World's Fair Jan 11 1913.

91. Low, Rachel *History of the British Film 1906-1914* Allen and Unwin London 1948

92. Durham County Ad. Jan 28 1938

and Jan 31 1913.
93. Durham County Ad. Mar 28 1913
94. Low, Rachel *op. cit.*
95. Durham County Ad. Ap 11 1913
96. Durham County Ad. May 2 1913
97. Durham County Ad. May 9 1913
98. The Durham Chronicle for May 2nd 1913 gives this name as Harkness.
99. Durham County Ad. May 9 1913
100. This June showing must have been the Brightonia version of 'East Lynne', only 2,200ft in length. It was directed by Arthur Chaddington and starred Neil Emerald and H. Agar Lyons. The Brightonia Company was founded in 1912 by W.H. Speer, originally the proprietor of the Queen's Theatre Brighton. In its short life, it specialized in a string of film versions of stage adaptations. (*Low, Rachel: The History of the British Film pp.102, 222*) The Assembly Rooms advertised on 15 Aug that they were showing the 7,000ft Barker version.
101. The 1912 *Quo Vadis* produced by the Cines company in Italy was eight reels long. *The Little Tease* shown at bo the Globe and the Assembly Rooms was a modest 1½ reel film directed by D. W. Griffith and released in America in Ap 1913, starring W. Christie Miller, Henry Walthall, Mae Marsh, Kate Bruce and Robert Harron: another Griffith drama about the Kentucky Hills
102. Durham County Ad. Jun 27 1913
103. Durham County Ad. Aug 1 1913
104. Durham County Ad. Aug 1 & 8 1913.
105. Durham County Ad. Aug 1 1913
106. Durham County Ad. Aug 15 1913
107. Coe, Brian *The History of Movie Photography* Ash and Grant London 1981 p.118
108. Durham Chronicle Aug 23 1913
109. Durham Chronicle Sept 26 1913
110. Durham County Ad. Sept 19 1913
111. Durham Chronicle Sept 26 1913 Report and Editorial
112. Durham Chronicle Oct 10 1913
113. Durham County Ad. Sept 26 1913
114. Durham County Ad. Sept 1913
115. Durham Chronicle Oct 3/Nov 14 1913and DCRO Plans UD/BB 157 no 221 7 Jul 13
116. Durham Chronicle Oct 31 13 and DCRO PS/CE 30 Oct 2 15.
117. Durham Chronicle Oct 24 1913 and DCRO PS/CE30 Oct 18[t] 13.
118. Durham County Ad. Oct 17 1913
119. Durham Chronicle Oct 31 1913
120. Durham County Ad. Nov 7 1913
121. Durham County Ad. Dec 12 1913
122. Durham Chronicle Dec 12 and 19 1913
123. *Tit-bits Magazine* Nov 1 13; Dec 13 13; *et seq.* to Jan 31 14 and Feb 14 14. There was also a nameless film for *Pearson's Weekly* at this time.
124. *The Cinema, News and Property Review* Nov 6 1913
125. Durham Chronicle Dec 12 1913
126. Durham Chronicle Dec 19 1913
127. DCRO PS/CE28 Feb 10 11 and Sunderland Daily Echo Feb 10 13.
128. Sunderland Daily Echo Mar 8 1913
129. Durham Chronicle Jan 16 1914.
130. Durham Chronicle Feb 6 1914.
131. Tit-bits *Cinema Notes and News* Feb 14 1914 Gifford, D. *op.cit.* film 04581 Durham Chronicle Jan 30 1914
132. Durham Chronicle Jan 30 1914
133. Feb 6 1914
134. Low, Rachel *The History of the British Film* vol. 2 p105 / Durham Chronicle 6 3 1914
135. Durham County Ad. Mar 6 1914
136. Durham Chronicle Mar 20 1914
137. Coe, Brian *The History of Movie Photography* p.97 & The Bioscope Oct

7 09

138. Durham County Ad. Mar 6 1914
139. Durham Chronicle Mar 13 1914
140. Durham Chronicle Mar 27 1914
and Gifford, Denis Film 04463
141. Durham Chronicle Ap 17 1914
142. Durham Chronicle Ap 24 1914
143. Durham Chronicle June 26 1914
144. Durham Chronicle July 3 1914
145. Durham Chronicle July 31 1914
146. Durham Chronicle Aug 7 1914
147. Durham Chronicle July 31 1914
148. Durham Chronicle Sept 4 1914
149. Durham Chronicle Aug 14 1914
150. Durham Chronicle Sept 11 1914
151. Durham Chronicle Nov 6 1914
152. Durham Chronicle Nov 13 1914
153. Durham Chronicle Nov 20 1914
154. Gifford, Denis: *The British Film Catalogue 1895 - 1985*
155. Durham Chronicle Dec 18 1914
156. Durham Chronicle Dec 25 1914

Three

1. Durham Chronicle Feb 5 1915
2. Durham Chronicle Febr 19 1915
3. The Bioscope Ap 1st 1915
4. Durham Chronicle Ap 16 1915
5. Durham Chronicle Aug 27 1915
6. Durham Chronicle Aug 27 1915
7. Durham Chronicle Aug 14 1915
8. Durham Chronicle and Durham Ad. Sept 24 1915
9. The Durham County Ad. gave the figure as 950
10. Durham County Ad. and Durham Chronicle Oct 1st 1915
11. Low, Rachel. *The History of The British Film* Volume Three page 85
12. Durham Chronicle Oct 15 1915
13. Durham Chronicle Oct 29 1915
14. Durham Chronicle Nov 12 1915
15. Durham Chronicle Nov 12 1915
16. Durham Chronicle Dec 3 DCRO plan no. 1800 Mar 4 1915
17. *In the Ranks* (Neptune films 1914 (4000ft) *Rupert of Hentzau* London

Films 1915 (5,500ft) *The Middleman* London Films 1915 (4,900ft)
18. Durham Chronicle Dec 24 1915
19. Durham County Ad. Jan 28 1916
20. Durham Chronicle Feb 4 1916
21. Durham Chronicle Feb 25 1916
22. Durham Chronicle Mar 17 1916
23. Durham Chronicle Feb 4 1916
24. Durham Chronicle Feb 25 1916 pages 116-127. 92
25. Durham Chronicle Mar 17 1916
26. The Bioscope 23 Mar 1916
27. Williams, D. R. *Ladies of the Lamp* Film History vol 9 no. 1 1997
28. Durham Chronicle Mar 31st 1916 and Low, Rachel op.cit. Volume Three page
29. Durham Chronicle Ap 7 1916
30. Durham Chronicle Ap 28 1916
31. Durham Chronicle May 12 1916
32. Durham Chron. May 5 & 12 1916
33. Durham Chronicle May 26 1916
34. *Ibid.*
35. Durham Chronicle June 9 1916
36. Durham Chronicle Aug 11 1916
37. Durham Chron. Aug 4 & 11 1916
38. Kinematograph Weekly Aug 4 1916
39. Durham Chronicle Sept 22 1916
40. Durham Chronicle Sept 29 1916
41. Reprinted in Durham Chron. Sept 8 1916
42. Brownlow, K. *The War, The West and The Wilderness* Secker & Warburg 1978 p.62
43. Durham Chronicle. Sept 22 1916
44. Durham Chronicle Oct 13 1916
45. Durham Chronicle Dec 15 1916
46. Durham Chronicle Feb 9 191
47. The Bioscope Jan 18 1917
48. Durham Chron. Feb 9 & Mar 2 1917
49. Durham Chronicle Mar 30 1917
50. Durham Chronicle May 6 1917
51. Durham Chronicle Ap 13 1917
52. Durham Chronicle Ap 20 1917
53. Durham Chronicle Ap 27

54. Durham Chronicle Aug 31st 1917 and Clive Herschhorn *The Universal Story* Octopus Books 1983 page 22
55. Durham Chronicle May 25 1917
56. Kinematograph Weekly Mar 5 1917
57. Durham Chronicle Jun 8 1917 Rachel Low *op. cit.* Pages 294 and 295
58. The Bioscope Oct 6 1917
59. Durham Chronicle Mar 20 1918
60. The Globe advert for Ap 4 1918
61. Durham Chronicle June 14 1918
62. Kevin Brownlow devotes a section of a chapter to the film in his *Behind the Mask of Innocence* pp.50-55
63. Bioscope Nov 16 1916
64. Durham Ad. July 12 1918
65. Durham Ad. July 12 1918
66. Durham Chronicle Aug 16 1918
67. Durham Chronicle Sept 13 1918
68. Durham Chronicle Nov 15 1918

Four

1. Durham Chronicle Jan 24 1919
2. Durham Chronicle Ap 4 1919
3. Durham Chronicle Aug 8 1919
4. Durham Chronicle Sept 26 1919
5. The cards were in full colour and on the reverse gave space for advertising the venue and dates.
6. Durham Ad. Jan 2nd 1920
7. Durham Ad. Jan 6 1920
8. Durham Ad. Oct 15 1920
9. Durham Ad. Feb 20 1920. It is not clear when it re-opened as a cinema. It was licensed from 1924.
10. Durham Ad. Feb 22nd and Mar 19 1920
11. Durham Ad. Ap 9 1920
12. Durham Ad. Ap 9 1920
13. Brownlow, K. *Behind The Mask of Innocence* Jonathan Cape 1990 p. 69.
14. Durham Ad. May 21 1920
15. Durham Ad. Sept 10 1920.
16. Durham Ad. Dec 31 1920
17. Durham Chronicle Jan 28 1921
18. Durham County Ad. Mar 11 1921
19. Durham Ad. Ap 15 1921
20. Durham Ad. May 27 1921 and DCRO PS/DU55
21. Durham Ad. Mar 11 1921
22. Durham Ad. July 15 1921
23. Durham Ad. Aug 26 1921
24. Durham Ad. July 22nd 1921
25. Durham Ad. June 3rd 1921
26. Durham Chronicle Aug 5 1921. A very detailed description is given.
27. Durham Ad. July 29 1921
28. Durham Ad. Aug 5 1921
29. Durham Ad. Jan 2 1922
30. Durham Ad. Dec 23 & 30 1921
31. Durham Ad. Sept 9 1921
32. Durham Ad. Sept 30 1921
33. *The Bioscope* Jan 19 1922
34. Durham Ad. Jan 29 1922
35. Lowe, Rachel *The History of the British Film* Volume Four pp.140, 408
36. Durham Ad. Jan 29 1922
37. Durham Ad. May 19 1922
38. Durham Ad. May 26 1922
39. Durham Ad. Aug 11 1922
40. Durham Ad. Nov 17 1922
41. Durham Ad. Mar 30 1923
42. Durham Ad. *Ibid.*
43. Durham Ad. June 22 1923
44. Durham Chronicle Oct 19 1923
45. Durham County Record Office, PS/Du55. William Turnbull is shown as the licensee until the cinema closed on Feb 4 1929.
46. DCRO PS/Du55 45
47. Rachel Low. Vol 4 *The History of the British Film 1918-1929* p.48
48. Durham Ad. May 23rd May 30 and June 6 1924.
49. Durham Ad. June 20 1924.
50. Durham Ad. July 4 1924
51. Durham Ad. Aug 8 1924
52. Durham Ad. July 11 1924
53. Durham Ad. Sept 19 1924
54. Durham Ad. Aug 22, 29 & Oct 3 1924
55. Durham Ad. Oct 3rd 1924

56. Durham Ad. Nov 7 1924

57. Durham Chronicle Sat Jan 3 1925

58. Coe, Brian *The History of Move Cinematography* page 167

59. Durham Ad. Friday Jan 2 1925

60. Durham Ad. Jan 30 1925

61. Durham Chronicle Sat Feb 7 1925

62. Durham Ad. May 15 1925

63. Durham Ad. June 5 1925

64. Durham Ad. June 26 1925

65. Durham Ad. Dec 11 1925

66. Durham Ad. June 19 1925

67. Durham Ad. May 1st 1925

68. Durham Ad. Oct 2nd. 1925

69. Durham Ad. May 15 1925

70. Gifford, Denis *op.cit.* ref. 9869 and Durham Ad. July 3rd 1925

71. Durham Chronicle Mar 14 1925

72. Durham Ad. Dec 18 1925

73. Durham Ad. Jan 1st 1926

74. Maltin, L. *Of Mice and Magic* New American Library 1987 Page 91

75. Coe, B. *History of Movie Photography* Page 104

76. Maltin, L. *op.cit* page 91

77. Durham Ad. Jan 22nd 1926

78. Kinematograph.Weekly Jan 20 1921

79. Gifford, Denis *British Animated Films 1895-1985.* Page 68

80. Durham Ad. Mar 5 1926

81. Durham Ad. Mar 12 1926

82. Durham Ad. Ap 9 & Ap 16 1926

83. Durham Ad. May 7 1926

84. Durham Ad. May 14 1926 Kinematograph Weekly Sept 25 1925

85. A. Pyle *Cinema in Middlesborough 1900 – 1971* p.99 Unpublished M.A. dissertation, University of Tyneside 1986. The description is given by Mr. C., one of the persons interviewed by the author. Born in 1907, he says that, as an employee of Mr. Thompson, he designed the film poster. Information about the two films comes from Peter Hallinan *The Bug and Flea* p.64 Unpublished M.A. dissertation,

University of East Anglia, 2002.

86. Durham Ad. Sept 17 1926 Palace advertising for Sept 16-18

87. Durham Ad. Dec 10 1926

88. Durham Ad. Feb 4 1927

89. Durham Ad. Mar 3rd 1927

90. Durham Ad. Mar 24 1927

91. Durham Ad. Aug 11 1927

92. Durham Ad. Sept 15 1927

93. DurhamAd. Oct 27 1927

94. Durham Ad. Nov 17 1927

95. Durham Ad. Nov 24 1927

96. Durham Chronicle Dec 30 1927

97. Durham Ad. Jan19 1928

98. Mar Hunnings *op.cit.* page 55

99. Kinematograph Weekly May 28 1928. Sheffield Council approved the showing but Doncaster banned it: the only town in S. Yorkshire to do so.

100. Durham Chronicle Febr 3 1928

101. Durham Ad. Feb 10 1928

102. DCRO PS/Du 55,122, 123

103. DCRO Durham City Plan no 000431

104. Durham Ad. Mar 1st 1928

105. Durham Chronicle June 1st 1928

106. Durham Ad. Feb 23rd 1928

107. Durham Ad. Mar 18 1928

108. Durham Ad. Ap 26 1928

109. Durham Ad. Oct 4 1928

110. Durham Ad. Aug 2nd 1928

Five

1. Durham County Ad. Jan 25 1929

2. Kine Weekly June 14 1928. 3,000ft yields a c.30 minute programme.

3. Coe, Brian *op. cit.* Page 104

4. Durham Chronicle Feb 25 1929

5. Durham County Ad. Mar 7 1929

6. Durham County Ad. Febr 21 1929

7. Durham County Ad. Mar 7 1929

8. Durham County Ad. Mar14 1929

9. Durham County Ad. Mar 21 1929

10. Durham County Ad. Mar 14 1929

11. Hunnings, N. *op. cit.* page 55

12. Durham County Ad. Ap 4 1929

13. Durham County Ad. Mar 21 1929

14. Durham County Ad. Mar 28 1929

15. Durham County Ad. Mar 28 1929

16. Durham County Ad. Ap 11 1929

17. Durham County Ad. Ap 11 1929. Charlotte Greenwood was a vaudeville and radio comedienne. Her subsequent screen career was long though undistinguished. She made cameo appearances in a number of 1940s comedies and at the age of 63 played Aunt Eller in the 1956 Todd-AO film version of *Oklahoma*. She died in 1978.

18. Durham County Ad. Thurs May 16 1929

19. Mellor, G.J. *Picture Pioneers* Frank Graham 1972 page 72

20. Durham County Ad. Aug 1 1929

21. Durham Ad. Aug 22 1929

22. Durham County Record Office OPS/DU 55

23. Durham County Ad. Aug 29 1929

24. Durham County Ad. Sept 9 1929

25. Durham County Ad. Aug 1 1930

26. Durham County Ad. Febr 13 1930

27. Kinematograph Weekly Jan 2 '30. The death toll was eventually 71.

28. Durham County Ad. Jan 9 1930

29. Durham County Ad. Jan 9 1930

30. Durham County Ad. Jan 30 1930 and the event as related by Mr. Kenworthy to Mr. R. Swainton.

31. Durham County Ad. Feb 6 and Feb 27 1930 and Nov. 27 1931; and DCRO RD/DU55 Pal No. 2253.

32. Durham County Ad. .Feb 6 1930

33. Durham County Ad. .Nov 14 1931

34. Durham County Ad. Feb 17 & Ap 3 1930

35. DCRO PS/ Du122

36. Durham County Ad. Jan 23 1931 (The Durham Ad. and the Durham Chron. combined at this time and the issue date changed from Thurs to Fri.)

37. Durham County Ad. Jan 30 1931

38. Durham County Ad. Dec 12 1930

39. Durham Ad. Jan 23 1931

40. Durham County Ad. Jan 30 1931

41. Durham County Ad. Jan 30 1931

42. Durham County Ad. Feb 6 1931

43. Durham County Ad. Feb 6 1931

44. Durham County Ad. Feb 20 1931

45. Durham County Ad. Ap 17 and Leicester Mercury Oct 1 1931

46. Durham County Ad. Mar 27 1931

47. Durham County Ad. Ap 24 1931

48. Durham County Ad. May 8 1931

49. Durham County Ad. May 15 1931

50. Durham County Ad. May 22 1931

51. Durham County Ad. July 17 1931

52. Durham County Ad. Mar 27 1931

53. Durham County Ad. Oct 16 1931

54. Durham County Ad. Oct 30 1931

55. Durham County Ad. Nov 13 1931

56. Durham County Ad. Nov 20 1931

57. A copy of this film has been preserved. The opening scene shows the newly built Palladium behind the carpet factory buildings.

58. Durham County Ad. Jan 22 1932

59. Durham County Ad. Jan 22 1932

60. Herschorn, Clive *The Universal Story* Octopus Books 1983 page 71

61. Eames, John *The Paramount Story* Octopus Books 1985 Page 75

62. Durham County Ad. Feb 5&12 '32

63. Durham County Ad. May 6 1932

64. Hunnings, Neville op.cit. p. 141 and B.B.F.C. Web site (2003)

65. Durham County Ad. Dec 9 1932

66. Durham County Ad. Feb 3 1953

67. Durham County Ad. Feb 10

68. Durham County Ad. Mar 3 1933

69. Durham County Ad. Mar 24 1933

70. Durham County Ad. June 23 1933

71. Durham County Ad. June 23 1933

72. Durham County Ad. July 7 1933

73. Durham County Ad. Sept 13 1933

74. Durham County Ad. Oct 27 1933

75. Durham County Ad. Oct 27 1933

76. Durham County Ad. Nov 24 1933

77. Durham County Ad. Dec 15 1933

78. Durham County Ad. Jan 19 1934

79. Durham County Ad. Feb 9 1934

80. Durham County Ad. Mar 2 1934
81. Durham Ad. Mar 23 & 30 1934
82. Durham County Ad. Ap 6 1934
83. Durham County Ad. Ap 6 1934
84. Durham County Ad. Ap 27 1934
85. Durham County Ad. May 4th1934
86. Durham County Ad. May 11 1934
87. Durham County Ad. June 29th
88. Durham County Ad. Aug 24 1934
89. Durham County Ad. Aug 17 1934
90. Durham County Ad. Sept 14 1934
91. Durham County Ad. Dec 14 1934
92. Durham County Ad. Mar 22 1935
and Manders, Frank *The Cinemas of Newcastle* page 111
93. Durham County Ad. Dec 21st 1934
94. Durham County Ad. Sept 12 1930
95. Durham County Ad. Feb 1st 1935
96. Durham County Ad. Dec 14 1934
97. Durham County Ad. May 24 1935
14 June 1935 and Oct 11 1935
98. Durham County Ad. July 5 1935
99. Durham County Ad. June 14 1935
and Aug 27 1935
100. Manders, Frank *op.cit.* pp.187-189
101. Durham County Ad. Jan 10 1936
102. Durham County Ad. Jan 10 & 17 1936
103. Durham County Ad. Feb 7 1936
104. Durham County Ad. July 10 36
105. Durham County Ad. Feb 26 37
106. Durham County Ad. May 14 37
107. Durham County Ad. May 14 37
108. Durham County Ad. July 2 37
109. Durham County Ad. July 16 37
110. Durham County Ad. Dec 24 1937
111. Durham County Ad. Dec 31 37
112. Durham County Ad. Feb 4 & 11 1938
113. Durham Ad. Mar 18 1938
114. Durham County Ad. Feb 18 & Mar 4 1938
115. Durham County Ad. Oct 14 & 28 1938
116. Durham Co Ad. Oct 7 & 14 1938
117. Durham County Ad. Nov 18 38

118. Durham County Ad. Nov 18 38
119. Durham County Ad. Dec 23 38
120. Durham County Ad. Mar 10 39
121. Durham County Ad. June 9 39

Six

1. Durham County Ad. Sept 8 and Sept 22nd 1939
2. Durham County Ad. Sept 15 1939
3. Durham County Ad. Sept 22nd 1939
4. Durham County Ad. Oct 13 1939
5. Durham County Ad. Nov 10 1939
6. Durham County Ad. Nov 10 and Hunnings, Neville M. *op.cit.* p.142
7. Durham County Ad. Feb 16 1940 and May 17 1940
8. Durham County Ad. Mar 14 1940
9. Today's Cinema July 11 1945 page 3
10. Durham County Ad. Ap 12 1940
11. Durham County Ad. 16 Aug 1940
12. Durham County Ad. Aug 2 1940
13. Durham County Ad. Oct 11 1940
14. Durham County Ad. Nov 1st and Nov 29 1940
15. DCRO PS/Du55, 122,123, and DCRO plan 3330 and 001392
16. Durham County Ad. Feb 7 1941
17. Durham County Ad. Mar 28 and Ap 3rd 1941
18. Durham County Ad. May 2 1941
19. Durham County Ad. May 23 1941
20. Durham County Ad. 20 June 1941
21. Durham County Ad. Nov 7 1941
22. Durham County Ad. Nov 7 1941
23. Durham County Ad. Nov 21st 1941
24. Durham County Ad. June 26 1942
25. .Durham County Ad. July 3rd 1942
26. DCRO PS/Du 122
27. Durham County Ad. Nov 13 1942
28. Durham County Ad. Feb 19 and Mar 12 1943
29. Durham County Ad. Ap 20 1943
30. Durham County Ad. Ap 28 1944
31. Durham County Ad. Mar 2nd 1945
32. Durham County Ad. June 25 1944
33. Durham County Ad. Aug 11 1944

34. Durham County Ad. June 16 1944
35. Durham County Ad. Aug 11 1944
36. Durham County Ad. 28 July 1944
37. Durham County Ad. 28 July 1944
38. Report of the Quarterly meeting Durham County Ad. Jan 12 1945
39. Interview with local residents, Mary Herron and Mary Hutton.
40. *Britain Can Take It* Aldergate and Richards Blackwell 1986 page 3
41. Durham County Ad. July 20 & 27 1945

Seven

1. Durham County Ad. 21st Sept 1945
2. Hornsey, Brian *The Essoldo Circuit* Mercia Cinema Society 1995
3. Durham County Ad. Nov 9 1945
4. Durham County Ad. Jan 11 1946
5. Durham County Ad. Feb 22nd 1946
6. Durham County Ad. Aug 9 1946
7. Durham Ad. Aug 23rd 1946
8. Durham County Ad. Oct 11 1946
9. Durham County Ad. Oct 25 1946
10. Durham County Ad. Nov 29 1946
11. Durham County Ad. Feb 28 1947
12. The Kinematograph Year Book 1947 page 514
13. Daily Film Renter Mar 10 1947 p11
14. Today's Cinema Dec 24 1947 p 3
15. Durham County Ad. Mar 14 1947
16. Durham County Ad. Mar 21st/27 1947 Re photo illustration in 21.3.47
17. Durham County Ad. Ap 18 1947
18. Durham County Ad. 12 Sept 1947
19. Durham County Ad. Jan 2nd 1948
20. Brian Hornsey, *The Essoldo Circuit op. cit.* Appendix II p.20
21. Kinematograph Year Book 1968
22. Durham County Ad. 23 July 1948
23. Durham County Ad. Oct 1 and 9 1948, and interviews with her son Patrick Rawes and with family friend, Grace Hindmarsh.
24. Durham County Ad. 22 Oct 1948
25. Durham County Ad. 29 Oct 1948
26. Durham County Ad. 28 Jan 1949
27. Durham County Ad. 11 Feb 1949
28. Durham County Ad. Sept 13 1946
29. Durham County Ad. Nov 22 1946
30. Interview with Mr. Middlemass, assistant projectionist at the Globe in the 1940s.
31. Durham County Ad. Oct 28 1949
32. Durham County Ad. Dec 16 & 23 1949
33. Durham County Ad. June 30 1950. Has this film survived?
34. Durham County Ad. Aug 25 1950. The film referred to was *State Secret*, which was actually trade shown in Ap 1950. It was a Launder & Gilliatt production for British Lion. It came to the Essoldo the week of Jan 22 1951
35. Durham County Ad. Sept 29 1950
36. Durham County Ad. Oct 6 1950
37. Durham County Ad. Dec 8 1950
38. Durham County Ad. Jan 25 1951
39. Durham County Ad. July 20 1951
40. Durham County Ad. Oct 19 1951
41. Kine Weekly Aug 30 1945
42. Kine Weekly July 4 1946
43. Kine Weekly Jan 18 1951
44. N. Mar-Hunnings, *Film Censors and The Law* page 144
45. Durham County Ad. Feb 29 1952
46. Durham County Ad. June 13 1952.
47. Durham County Ad. June 29 1952
48. Durham County Ad. Dec 26 1952
49. Durham County Ad. Nov 3rd 1952
50. Durham County Ad. Jan 30 1953. The figures have been rounded up to exact pounds.
51. Durham County Ad. Oct 30 1953
52. Durham County Ad. Nov 27 1953
53. Mr. Wallace Langley, former projectionist, confirms this.
54. Durham County Ad. May 28 1954
55. Durham County Ad. July 30 1954
56. Durham County Ad. July 30 1954
57. The Widescreen Museum Website
58. Durham County Ad. Mar 4 1955
59. Durham County Ad. Mar 11 1955

60. Durham County Ad. Jan 27 1956
61. Durham County Ad. Feb 3rd 1956
62. Durham County Ad. Aug 31st 1956
63. Durham County Ad. Nov 30 1956
64. Durham County Ad. Feb 15 1957
65. *Technical note:* The projectors were still using carbon arcs at this time, and the D.C. current was supplied by a mercury bottle rectifier. These normally supplied about 45-55v. at 90+ amps. As the mains voltage fluctuated, so would the output current. The rectifier would also feed the ice-cream spot.
66. Durham County Ad. Feb 22 1957
67. Durham County Ad. Feb 22 & 29 1957
68. Durham County Ad. Mar 1 1957
69. Durham County Ad. Aug 2 1957
70. K.Y.B. 1968

Eight

1. Durham County Ad. Mar 8 1957. The last Sunday show at the Rex was *My Son, My Son* (1940 with Madeleine Carroll and Brian Aherne)
2. Durham County Ad. Jan 24 1958
3. Durham County Ad. Jan 2 1959
4. Durham County Ad. May 24 and June 19 1959
5. Durham County Ad. July 28 1960
6. Durham County Ad. Nov 24 1961
7. Durham County Ad. Jan 12 1962.
8. Durham County Ad. Jan 26 1962 and Feb 2nd 1962
9. Durham County Ad. Ap 27 1962
10. As chance would have it, the film which won the Junior section of the competition that year (by the children of the Caldecote Junior School, Leicester) was supervised by the present author.
11. *Chaplin, His Life and Art* by David Robinson Collins 1985 pages 682-688.
12. Durham County Ad. July 13 1962
13. Durham County Ad., Nov 9 1962

14. Durham Ad. Jan 25 1963
15. Durham County Ad. Feb 15 1963 and Mar 29 1963
16. Durham County Ad. Aug 16 1963
17. Durham County Ad. Oct 9 1964
18. DA Nov 6 1964
19. DA Nov 5 1965
20. DA Jan 10 1965
21. .DCR ORD/Au 92 no2708 D.A. Feb 4 1966
22. DA Nov 17 1967
23. DA Ap 7 1972
24. DA June 23d 1972
25. DA 14 Oct 1972
26. DA Oct 6 1972
27. DA Oct 14 1972
28. DA Oct 31st 1975
29. DA Friday Nov 28 1975
30. DA Dec 5 1975
31. DA Nov 28 1975
32. DA Ap 15 1977
33. DA Jan 9 1976
34. DA Dec 5 1975
35. DA July 6 1979
36. DA Oct 12 1979
37. DA Dec 28 1979
38. DA Jan 4 1980
39. DA May 16 1980
40. DA Jan 4 1980
41. DA June 6 1980
42. DA Nov 4 1983 and Nov.25 198
43. Statistics from pages 17 and 18 of the web site of 'Cultural Trends 1990 to 1996' by the Policy Studies Institute
44. DA June 2lst and June 28 1990
45. Durham Ad. July 20 1991
46. DA Jan 24 1985
47. Durham City Trust Feb 2000
48. Private Eye. Ap 7 2000 page 11.
49. Northern Echo (Mark Summers) Tuesday Mar 6 2001
50. Durham Ad. Nov l6 2002
51. Durham Ad. Nov 23rd 2002
52. Interview with John Lackenby, the last projectionist at the Robins cinema.
53. Durham Ad. 25 Ap 2003

Index

Index
Numbers in *Italics* denote illustrations

* * * * * * *

Publicity Postcard for the Transatlantic serial *Greed* shown at the Empire, Langley Moor in 1916. *From the author's collection.*

WHY NOT JOIN — ?

The

MERCIA

CINEMA

SOCIETY

is a national society (registered educational charity No.1001524) founded to promote and publish research into the history of cinema buildings - whether flea-pit, super-cinema, or converted theatre. We are the largest publisher of cinema building history in the country and run an information network for cinema & theatre building history open to all.

Also we publish our quarterly journal the *Mercia Bioscope* - free to members (fully-indexed triennially). Do join us - membership entitles you to our quarterly *Mercia Bioscope* and book and other discounts, and costs only £10.00 per year.

www.merciacinema.org.uk

Further details, and a free copy of the *Mercia Bioscope,* are available from the administrator:
Mervyn Gould 29 Blackbrook Court Loughborough LE11 5UA
01509 218393 Mervyn.Gould@virgin.net
For a booklist and orders please contact the sales officer:
Stuart Smith 100 Wickfield Road Hackenthorpe Sheffield S12 4TT
0777 155 4605